Development and Dilemmas
in Science Education

CONTEMPORARY ANALYSIS IN EDUCATION SERIES
General Editor: Philip Taylor

Contemporary Analysis in Education Series

Development and Dilemmas in Science Education

Edited by

Peter Fensham

The Falmer Press
(A member of the Taylor & Francis Group)
London · New York · Philadelphia

USA   The Falmer Press, Taylor & Francis Inc., 242 Cherry Street, Philadelphia, PA 19106–1906

UK   The Falmer Press, Falmer House, Barcombe, Lewes, East Sussex, BN8 5DL

First published 1988

British Library Cataloguing in Publication Data

Development and dilemmas in science
  education.
  1. Schools. Curriculum subjects. Science
  I. Fensham, Peter J. (Peter James),   *1927–*
  II. Series
  507'.1

  ISBN 1-85000-350-5
  ISBN 1-85000-351-3 Pbk

Typeset in 10/12 Bembo by
Mathematical Composition Setters Ltd, Salisbury, Wilts.

Printed in Great Britain by Taylor & Francis (Printers) Ltd, Basingstoke.

Contents

Contents

General Editor's Preface

In what has come to be one of the most important tracts in education, *What Knowledge is of Most Worth?*, Herbert Spencer argued and urged that the knowledge of most worth is science. 'Its truths', he said, 'will bear on human conduct ten thousand years hence', and though it is hardly one hundred since he said that, there is little to suggest that he will be proved wrong. He went on to say that 'rational knowledge has an immense superiority over empirical knowledge' and because of its sheer rationality, he claimed, science was *the* knowledge to learn. He also gave other reasons including practical and social ones.

Today there is no need to argue that Science should be seen along with mathematics and one's own language as a key subject of schooling. It has become self-evident.

Even so there is much to be debated and discussed when it comes to *Science Education* which is the subject of this sharply acute, ably constructed and up-to-date reader. It really is a compendium of the best kind: informative, comprehensive and likely to be an important stimulus to thought and action. It leaves little in the teaching of science at all levels unexamined. One might have expected such under Peter Fensham's able editorship. That he has actually achieved it must be a cause for great satisfaction among science educators everywhere and of sincere congratulations to him and the many contributors whose work has made possible a book of great worth.

Philip H. Taylor
University of Birmingham, 1988

To Christine
whose support and tolerance
made possible the encounters that
have created this book

Foreword

In choosing authors for the chapters of this book I had a number of criteria in mind. Firstly, from my knowledge of them as persons or from their work and other writing, I believed that they had important things to say about science education. Secondly, they responded to the framework or description of the reality of science education I suggested for the book and which I have argued for in the first chapter. Thirdly and as a corollary of this sense of reality, they are science educators who, in their own ways, take the content of science seriously, see learners as active constructors of scientific meaning, and/or have recognized the importance of social context and effect as neglected aspects of science education.

Others could also have met these criteria but within the limits of editorial coherence I wanted a range of national contexts from which the chapters would be written. In the end, nine such contexts are included and among these are India and Thailand. In my own numerous contacts with science educators from both industrialized and less industrialized countries I have been increasingly aware in the 1980s that some of the best organization, effective practice, and most original insights and innovations are occurring in some of the latter countries. Even with the substantial efforts that UNESCO has made over many years to provide international communication in science education, the developments in science education in the second group of countries (the world's majority) are much less well known than they should be.

In inviting the authors I asked them to focus their contribution on a particular theme although I knew full well that each of them sees science education more holistically. The selection of these themes for the chapters was, for me (and no doubt for the authors), a fragmenting of an interactive whole. To avoid the themes appearing to be definite discrete components of science education (and for several other reasons) I chose to seek alternative views on themes rather than multiply the themes themselves. In this way, readers will have reinforcement of some aspects and a sense of different emphases and connections about others. They will also more readily be able to discern how the tradition from which an author comes, the context in which they live and work, and the literature on which they draw, shapes the way they address and respond to current issues in science education.

In my opening chapter I juxtapose the sense of importance school science education is now assuming with a realistic appraisal of what we have learnt in the twenty-five years since 1960 when it was also very much front stage as far as the curriculum of schooling was concerned. I suggest that science education is now much more complex and interesting but also that it is much more difficult than we thought in 1960. In the process of this rather too grand scale account of a number of contemporary dilemmas facing science education and of some of the interesting possibilities that seem now to be worth exploring, I touch on the various themes that are taken up in the subsequent chapters.

Douglas Roberts (chapter 2), using a normative perspective, addresses the question, What counts as science education? In doing so, he sets science education firmly in a social context within which at any time there are a diversity of stakeholders so that this context is, in fact, not one but many. Each context has its purpose for science education and this leads to the stakeholders for each one choosing to emphasize a particular set of science learnings. Science curriculum policy, he argues, is always a compromise among these various curriculum emphases, and as such presents dilemmas and even sharp conflicts for the teachers who are required to implement it. One of the emphases Roberts identifies is a science, technology and decisions one that is taken up later in the book by Solomon, and by Eijkelhof and Koortland.

John Baird (chapter 3), on the theme of teachers, argues strongly against the simplistic view that certain behavioural competences in teachers will lead to successful learning in science and for a more complex picture of what and how teaching and learning are determined. Accordingly, he does not see the emphasis on the teacher's overt behaviour in the classroom that has so often been put by researchers and teacher educators (both pre- and in-service) as helping us to understand the teacher's role in science education. Instead he sees some recent developments in metacognitive research and in particular, action research projects in which classroom teachers are active collaborators, as important new directions for science education research which could lead to improvements in science teaching.

Dick Gunstone in chapter 4 on learners in science education has addressed the quite enormous literature that is now available (after only about ten years of research) on learners' views about natural phenomena and the conceptions they hold of the scientific description of these that are usually included in school science. He avoids yet another review of this work (since a number are available) by relating and contrasting this recent work, with its generally constructivist orientation towards science learners, to the much older Piagetian line of research on learners. In two other parts of this chapter he pursues and teases out the images of learners and of science that these constructivist researchers are generating and the ways of bringing about conceptual change in classrooms that are consistent with their theoretical position about teaching and learning.

Bonnie Shapiro, without referring to metacognition, and Rosalind Driver who does, both provide in their chapters (5 and 7 respectively) examples of the sorts of research in science classrooms that Baird is advocating. Shapiro, through her own case study of children in a primary class studying light, provides insights into the thinking of young learners of science in context that goes much further than the alternative frameworks research has been able to do with its concentration on science concepts, albeit methods that have so often involved individual learners.

Driver and Dick White (chapter 6) have both written on 'Theory into Practice'. Driver outlines in some detail her interpretation of the constructivist view of learning that she (and most of the other authors) acknowledges as the theoretical base for the projects and practices her group is undertaking in the Children's Learning in Science Project in Britain. She describes the way they have worked with science teachers to develop approaches to teaching a number of common science topics that take seriously constructivist principles and what this sort of research has shown us are commonly held conceptions about these topics.

White's chapter, also from a constructivist base, moves more freely into a less theoretically defined future, or rather one characterized by chains of theory-practice-revised theory, etc. He uses the series of research projects which he has shared with Baird and a number of science teachers to argue a way forward that could lead to realistic research in science education that would not present teachers (as has been so common in the past) with credibility and applicability gaps, because it has been so largely developed and validated by teachers like themselves.

In chapter 8 Kulkarni presents a Third World perspective as he addresses some of the language problems confronting his country, India, as it seeks in its post-colonial independence to universalize education and in particular science education. He outlines various sociolinguistic problems that are starkly obvious in his context but which do have their counterparts in all societies where such social differentials are often overlooked. A number of studies he and his colleagues have undertaken are described and these are characterized by practical interventions that have made positive contributions in what could have seemed most daunting situations.

Sunee Klainin from Thailand (the discoverer of some remarkable findings about girls and science education) and Avi Hofstein from Israel are the authors of chapters 9 and 10 on the theme of practical work or the role of laboratory in science education. This theme is associated with some of the most fascinating dilemmas of science education. Klainin reminds us of the accepted place the laboratory has had in school science education in some countries for a century at least, and of the central role it was meant to play in the new curricula of the 1960s and 1970s. Nevertheless, as she and Hofstein point out, practical work was ignored by many of the evaluators of these innovations, and when it was considered the findings were discouraging. Both authors, however, argue that the new bases do now exist for teachers to use practical work in their science teaching in ways that promote sorts of learning that are readily understood by teachers and students, and in addition that contribute strongly to the latter's enjoyment of the subject. Klainin, in particular, emphasizes that good assessment procedures are now available (Hofstein was a contributor to these), and that this is a major difference from the earlier period of the so-called activity-based science curricula.

Svein Sjøberg and Gunn Imsen from Norway and Jane Butler Kahle from the USA, in chapters 11 and 12, address the concerns that are now very widespread about gender factors in science education. The former focuses on the male image of science and how that image affects the teaching and learning of science in schools and the aspirations about science that girls and boys have. From the two chapters, enough about current participation patterns, achievement and aspirations emerges to justify the general concern that science education in the schools of many countries is a major factor for, rather than a corrective to, the disadvantages girls and women so regularly face in contemporary technological society. Kahle draws on some recent research literature to suggest ways in which the image of science and science education could be changed. Sjøberg and Imsen combine social and cultural analysis with some very intensive psychometric data from girls and boys in Norway to point to the depth of the problems. They are able, however, also to point to some features that are encouraging as efforts to redress these imbalances occur. Their data on the contributions more girls in science and technology may make to their practice and image are particularly interesting.

Science education and technology education are so often now spoken of together that the Science-Technology-Society theme was obviously an important one to include. In chapter 13 Joan Solomon from Britain traces several of the main influences for the current interest and press to introduce STS courses in schools. In doing so, she points to the tangle of objectives and variety of conceptions of STS that already exist. She goes on to look at what we know of students' reception and learning of such courses. Harrie Eijkelhof and Koos Koortland from the PLON physics project in the Netherlands describe in some detail in chapter 14 the evolution of that project team's thinking about the way science learning can, or should, be related to the impact its science content as technology has on members of a society. This description of an actual example of the development and use of STS science materials (particularly from such a pioneering group as PLON) provides a helpful, practical case to relate to Solomon's more general chapter. This sort of counterpoint occurs several times in the book and is a happy additional outcome of the strategy of asking two authors for most of the themes.

Books like this rarely rest on the shoulders of their authors alone. Behind my own efforts in science education there has been, over many years, the very direct support of numerous colleagues and several secretaries in the Faculty of Education at Monash University. My thanks go to each of them and to their counterparts at the University of Leeds where most of the final editing was done. No doubt each chapter author has had their own support from similar persons and the final manuscript is, in that sense, theirs as well as ours.

Peter J. Fensham
February 1987

1
Familiar but Different: Some Dilemmas and New Directions in Science Education

Peter J. Fensham

Introduction

At a time of general economic restraint and cutbacks in education, a Learning in Science Project was set up in New Zealand in 1979 for three years that has so far been extended to nine, and in 1982 Britain's Department of Education and Science established the complex and expensive Secondary Science Curriculum Review. Almost before the last staff, lingering into the 1980s after a longish period of depression in American science education, had left their posts at the National Science Foundation, this body, and a number of others in the USA, were reviewing and reporting on the state of this field in schools and establishing new projects to remedy its deficiencies.

In 1984 UNESCO's Regional Office for Asia and the Pacific was asked by its member states to make 'Science for All' a top priority area for development over the remaining years of the decade. Australia, one of these member states, has lagged behind the efforts that, for example, Thailand, Malaysia, Indonesia and the Philippines have been recently putting into science curriculum developments. In 1986, it did, however, begin to review its school science education seriously and several projects with strong government backing have now begun. Canada, a country with many similarities to Australia, undertook a very extensive review of its school science education earlier in the 1980s and its provincial governments are now responding with a number of new curriculum initiatives.

This list of renewed national concern and activity about science education in schools could be substantially extended. It will, however, suffice to testify to a widespread political and economic concern, and to a willingness on the part of authorities to provide funds, personnel and other resources for the improvement of science education in schools.

This situation, with its positive climate of support, should at first sight be a very pleasing one for science educators. To many of us it does, however, present one very general dilemma and a great number of more specific ones as the various aspects of what should be done in this field of curriculum development are considered.

The general dilemma relates to the fact that the 1960s and early 1970s are so recent that the very similar rhetoric and enormous effort that went with the science curriculum reforms of that period have not been forgotten. Even today's younger science educators, through their own training, are aware of these similarities because the documentation of that earlier period is so extensive and because its residues in the schools have been their own experience of learning and teaching science at school. Furthermore, for any who are prepared to turn to the histories of science curricula (see, for example, Layton, 1973, and Jenkins, 1979, in Britain; Hurd, 1961, and Bybee, 1977, in the USA; and Fawns, 1987, in Australia) there is ample evidence that the generation of the 1960s (let alone the 1980s) was certainly not the first to expect great things for learners at school from science education. There is a strong sense of déjà vu.

The great burst of activity in curriculum development in science began in Britain and the USA in the late 1950s and continued there till the early 1970s. It did much to give a new meaning to curriculum development and to professionalize its procedures. These new conceptions spread beyond science to many other parts of the programme of schools as curriculum development centres or departments rapidly became established as part of the educational scene. Nor was the notion of 'curriculum development' confined to these two countries for it rapidly spread to many others. Some of them did not, however, embark on truly indigenous curriculum development till the 1970s. In a number of cases this delay was due to the fact that a form of educational imperialism occurred. That is, materials for the school populations of Britain, the USA or France were exported, with or without minor adaptation, to the school systems of other countries where quite different sociopolitical and socioeducational needs and demands prevailed. These differences were very apparent in the countries of the Third World that had only recently gained their political independence. Nevertheless, it was the education systems of some of these (under persuasive advice from now 'foreign' consultants) that, in a number of instances, took up these new materials more extensively than did the schools in their countries of origin. Countries like Australia and Canada, which in some senses were socially similar to the USA, also made extensive use in some of their centralized provincial school systems of materials from the National Science Foundation's projects in the USA. It can now be seen, however, that this period of direct importation of science curricula, even in these countries, distorted the educational scene and inhibited more appropriate local developments.

As I wish in a number of ways to relate the present and future prospects for science education to the situations, events, and products associated with this earlier period of interest and activity in science education I shall refer to it as 'the 1960s' knowing full well, as I have just indicated, that some of its effects on science curriculum reform were more evident, in fact, in the 1970s.

In the various rationales that were provided for the activity in science education in the 1960s and in those for the 1980s two similar targets are addressed. These are a scientifically-based work force and a scientifically literate citizenry.

The stress on the former is quite evident. The National Science Foundation's 1983 report 'Educating Americans for the 21st Century' sees school science education as important to produce the scientific and technological professionals who will enable the USA to compete economically with Japan. This is so reminiscent of the Rickover report in the 1960s although the threat then was the USSR and in a political sense rather than an economic one. Likewise, in their reference to the latter target, the statements for the two periods are also quite similar, generally presenting a picture of more science education, along with more science and technology, as being unquestionably good things for societies to have.

It is surprising to find this recurrence of such an uncritical stance about science in society in the 1980s, but the NSF report referred to above is indeed as devoid of reference to the disastrous state of the environment and the contributions of American industry and technology to it as were its 1960s counterparts. Reading its arguments for 'making American science education the best in the world' (!!) is as if Rachel Carson, Paul Erlich and Barry Commoner were part of science fiction, and there have been no problems with acid rain, species depletion, waste disposal and nuclear accidents in the twenty-five years since the 1960s.

So it is both what the contemporary reports say about science education and what they omit that heighten the sense of déjà vu and contribute to it being a dilemma for the efforts that are being made to improve the teaching and learning of science in schools.

It might be (and it is a possibility that would be quite consistent with the framework I present a little later in this chapter), that this déjà vu simply means that science education is now being challenged to do for the coming generations of school learners what was achieved by the reformers in the 1960s. In other words, the societal conditions have now so changed that what were good solutions for science education in the 1960s are now no longer appropriate.

Alas, the dilemma cannot be so simply dispelled for this interpretation assumes that solutions were found in the 1960s to the problems of science education as they were perceived at that time. Unfortunately the record of achievement from the 1960s does not support such a position. Quite literally, by the late 1970s in some of the countries which first embarked on these reforms to their science curricula in the 1960s their managers had run out of excuses and ideas. Initially it had seemed that all that was needed were first class suggestions for what science education in schools should be like and an adequate supply of carefully prepared supporting materials (texts, films, laboratory exercises, etc). Even when these proved unattractive to the majority of teachers in countries where they were not mandatory, or were distorted almost beyond recognition where they were, the momentum of this approach was so great that most of the available resources continued to go into revisions of these first materials or into other attempts to design 'the package' of science education that could, when developed, be handed over to teachers to use in their schools. Along with this 'package' approach to improving science education a number of countries put considerable resources into upgrading their school science facilities in the form of more and better laboratory provision in schools and/or the introduction of ancillary technical staff. Somewhat belatedly, attention then began to turn to teachers as 'the problem' in relation to the implementation of these improved science courses, and by the early 1970s in-service education courses to induct teachers into the intentions of the new science curricula were being conducted on a large scale in a number of countries. Almost invariably these courses were conducted away from the teachers' schools, in centres like universities and colleges. The perception of the 'teacher as problem' was of the teachers' own interactions with the curriculum package. The contextual features of their particular schools and classrooms were not seen as relevant.

In the latter half of the 1970s a number of major evaluations of these attempts at solutions to the problems of science education were conducted. In Britain, Harding *et al.* (1976) investigated the implementation of the products of the Nuffield science projects, and in the USA, several separate evaluations of the effects of the NSF projects were carried out (Hegelson *et al.*, 1977; CSSE, 1978; and Research Triangle Institute, 1977).

These, and evaluations from many other countries, were shared at an international conference in Israel (Tamir *et al.*, 1979). When the range of problems that were tackled and when the extent of the implementation of the proposed solutions are taken into account, a reasonable summary would be that success was at best patchy.

In Australia, one of the countries were schools throughout the country had been equipped with new laboratories and technical assistants, there was evidence that there was less practical work in senior secondary science than earlier. Only two of the nineteen countries participating in the first IEA study of science education (Comber and Keeves, 1973) chose to include practical tests despite the centrality they were giving to the laboratory in their curriculum rationales.

I am not saying that there were no educational achievements as a result of the 1960s efforts. Clearly there were a number, and it is important to recognize the sorts of changes that were possible since these may be the easiest sort to change again. Equally, however, for the good of what might be achieved in the next decade, we would be foolish not to recognize that we now know that effective science education in many of its aspects is much more difficult to achieve than the reformers of the 1960s ever dreamt.

In an attempt to dispel the déjà vu dilemma, I intend in this chapter to do three things. First I shall provide a framework for discussing what was happening and what was achieved in the efforts of the 1960s. Next I will use it and some of the features of the contemporary scene to argue that the present and the more immediate future are very different from the 1960s. Finally I shall point to some of the more specific challenges and developments that seem to me to be important to heed if real advances are to be achieved on a wide scale in school science education.

A Sociopolitical Framework for Science Education

The curriculum movement of the 1960s has rightly been criticized (for example, Young, 1971, and Waring, 1979, in Britain; Gintis, 1972, and Apple, 1979, in the USA; and Bourdieu and Passeron, 1977, in France) for often behaving as if schooling, and science education in particular, takes place in a social and political vacuum. The export of science curricula to which I referred earlier is an example of this attitude. The fact that science does have some 'universal' aspects was used to justify and make possible the transferability of science curricula across national boundaries. Another example of this 'social vacuum' attitude to science education is the 'desocializing' of science and science education that occurred in many of the projects. References to scientists as persons and citizens contributing to our understanding of nature and its manipulation in their own societies almost disappeared in the first wave of these new curriculum materials, as did any serious reference to industrial and science applications of science. There was accordingly little or no discussion in these new science courses of the social implications and consequences of science (Fensham, 1976). As one further example, I can refer again to the naivety project after project displayed in assuming that implementation in complex social systems like schools was essentially only a function of the science education 'package' or of this package and its interaction with a science teacher, abstracted from the social realities of her/his school and classroom.

Historians and curriculum theorists, like those mentioned above, have helped us to see that schools are established by societies to fulfil a number of educational functions. The curriculum, in its parts and in its totality, is the instrument to serve these functions as well as being the field where the competition between these societal demands on schooling is resolved. In figure 1 I have tried to indicate some of the societal demands that compete for priority in a science curriculum's emphases (see also chapter 2).

The sciences, particularly the physical sciences, in many societies, are gateway subjects that filter the relatively few students who are allowed to

Figure 1: Competing societal demands on schooling and science education

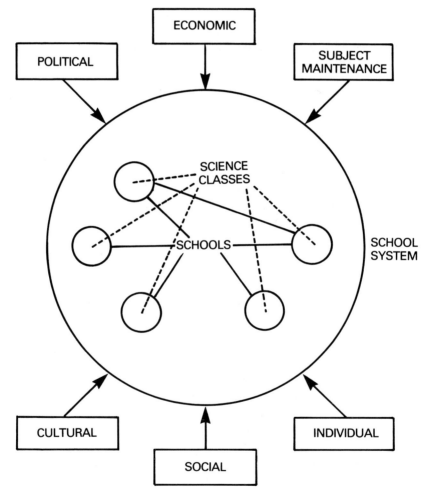

move into certain professions of high status, societal influence and economic security. Because of the societal power associated with these positions, we can call this a *political* demand on schooling. Again, a limited but definite number of persons with scientific skills and expertise are needed in any society to maintain and expand a variety of aspects of its economy. This is an *economic* demand. Scientists, particularly in research institutions and universities, are now a powerful faction in society with a major interest in *maintaining their subject* as an elite and important field. They are thus keenly interested in having the schools begin the process of reproduction of the sciences as those in higher education define them. In addition, there are clearly many ways in which all *cultures* and *social life* are now influenced by knowledge and applications from the sciences. Science education can assist people to have a sense of control rather than of subservience and to take advantage of what science in these ways has to offer them. The fascination of scientific phenomena and the role of human inventiveness in relation to them offer much potential for school science education to meet the demands of its learners for *individual* growth and satisfaction.

If there are, as I suggest (and figure 1 portrays), a number of different societal demands on the science education that schools provide, it is not surprising that not all will be equally well met. Indeed the possibility exists that the curriculum of a science education that meets one or several of these demands may not serve the interests of the others. Recognition of this possibility, unfortunately, is still quite rare in the reports and policies of the 1980s as it was in the 1960s. Without it, some critical implications for science curriculum are likely to be missed in the decision making for the current reforms in science education, just as they so largely were in the development and implementations of the 1960s reforms.

Curriculum Competition in Action

An example of this competition for science education at school is how it relates to the two distinct targets of a scientifically-based work force and a more scientifically literate citizenry (Fensham, 1986a). The former, related to the top three demands in figure 1, is needed so that societies and economies can keep pace in a world where scientific knowledge and technology are being exploited in a rapidly increasing way. The latter, more related to the lower three demands in figure 1, consists of those who should benefit from the personal and social applications of science and who will be prepared to respond appropriately to changes of a scientific or technological kind.

At first sight it can appear that the achievement of either of these two targets will also be a contribution to the other. That is, as the first target is met and exceeded, school science education is on the way to meeting the second.

7

Or, if the second is met to any significant extent, on the way the first will be achieved. Just such a simplistic cooperative view of the interactions of societal demands and the curriculum of schooling operated in the reforms of the 1960s. Under the advice and guidance of well meaning university scientists and encouraged by some slogans about the nature of learning that were current at the time, the 1960s projects aimed at inducting all learners at school into the world of the scientist. Not surprisingly, it was the research scientist they chose as their 'model scientist'. There was, it seems, a genuine belief that both targets would be met if all children, in appropriate ways for their level of schooling, were to learn some of the ideas and some of the ways these sorts of scientists use to describe and explore the world. All (or as many as learnt successfully) would have gained a degree of scientific literacy, and enough of them would be interested to continue on to become the specialist work force of tomorrow.

Right from the start, however, it is now clear that the apparent even-handedness in the statements of intent gave way in practice to the interests the first target represents. The first curricula to be redesigned in the USA, Britain, Australia, Canada, Thailand, Malaysia, etc. were those for the upper secondary school — the very level where only those, from whom the specialist work force will be drawn, are present at school. By giving priority to the curricula for this level, the projects were explicitly rejecting the interests of the target group of scientific literacy since very few countries in the 1960s had a majority of each age cohort still at school at this level or even most of them studying science.

Under their terms of reference which included updating the content of school science education (long overdue as a result of the Second World War) these first projects did suggest radical changes indeed to what should be learned. The changes did not, however, take the form of a massive infusion of recently acquired knowledge from the sciences or even of their contemporary explanations or issues. Rather, these courses and their guiding papers emphasized the structure of the knowledge of the major disciplinary sciences and the ways it can emerge from their empirical studies.

It so happens that part of this intended new content for learning namely, the concepts and the relations between them, was essentially what, by this time, had become firmly entrenched as what university courses in science were about. In general it is only these aspects of the proposed new content that gained emphasis when the new courses were implemented in the schools. The considerable extent of these changes in content can be seen in figure 2 which shows a content analysis of senior chemistry courses over forty years (Fensham, 1984).

We should perhaps not put all the blame for this outcome of the 1960s reforms on the projects or their scientist advisers. It is not their fault directly that the scientific reasoning that leads to these concepts and the way models of

*Figure 2: Changes in the content of school chemistry
1940-1980 and some features of the secondary school age
population*

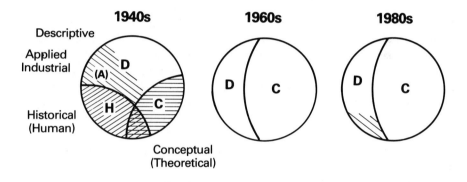

explanation evolve from empirical findings in science, and the processes of scientific enquiry were largely ignored by secondary teachers and secondary science examiners. After all, few undergraduate science courses in which these teachers are trained put much weight on these philosophical, historical or syntactical aspects of the science disciplines.

It is possible, however, in terms of societal demands, to understand what happened once the two choices, of senior secondary courses as the first to be reformed and of the research scientist as model, had been made.

Subject maintenance meant an emphasis on continuity of content for science learning between school and higher education. It meant the choice of content that would ensure that students moving from school to further studies in science in higher education would have a familiarity with the concept words and relations between them that would be used and further developed in the first years of specialist training. If they succeeded in becoming scientific professionals their apprenticeships in research or in technology would, in due course, provide them with the syntax of their science, so that it was not necessary earlier in school or undergraduate science.

The political and economic demands then turned out to mean that a sufficient supply of science students for the nation's needs is important but that an oversupply is not to be encouraged. On a number of occasions since the 1960s school science has, in both more and less industrialized countries, succeeded in oversupplying the number of students who had 'successfully' completed studies in science and mathematics. Rather than being welcomed as a contribution to scientific literacy these oversupplies have been embarrassing to governments since the students involved have themselves seen their success essentially in vocational terms, and have expected places in the expensive technical facilities of higher education and in employment (unlike their counterparts in the humanities) that makes use of their specialized training in ways the economy of the time could not afford.

Accordingly, the science curriculum at these levels was required to be such that they did prepare enough students for future studies but that they also provided a spread of learning achievements among them so that selections can be easily and evidently done.

This selective requirement has been reinforced by other changes in school curricula in this period which have increasingly given the sciences (along with mathematics) the responsibilities for the sieving and sorting processes that employers and the next levels of education impose on all school systems, and that were in the past served by language studies.

We can summarize the outcome of these demands on school science education and of the priority given to the target of the specialist work force by listing the characteristics of learning content that has prevailed since the 1960s reforms in most, if not all, school systems as the science content of 'most worth' for learning.

(a) It involves the rote call of a number of facts, concepts and algorithms that are not obviously socially useful, rather than allowing obvious social usefulness to determine what scientific information should be so learnt.

(b) It involves so little familiarity with many of these concepts that their scientific usefulness is not experienced, rather than concepts being learnt in the process of exploring their usefulness in scientific and common life.

(c) It involves concepts that have been defined at high levels of generality among scientists without their levels of abstraction being adequately acknowledged in the school context so that their consequential limitations in real situations are not adequately indicated.

(d) It involves an essentially abstract system of scientific knowledge, using examples of real objects and events to illustrate this system, rather than using scientific knowledge to elucidate life experiences and social applications of science.

(e) It reduces the role of practical activity in science education to the enhancement of conceptual learning rather than being a source for learning essential skills and gaining confidence in applying scientific knowledge to solve real societal problems.

(f) It gives a high priority (even in biology) to quantitative aspects at the expense of understanding of the concepts involved.

(g) It leaves to the later study of scientific disciplines in higher education or employment the balance, meaning and significance that is lacking in (a) to (f).

(h) It determines its 'knowledge of worth' by selecting those concepts and principles that are logical starting points for learning the increasingly abstracted knowledge that is such a dominant component of what lies ahead in the continued study of the sciences.

It will be obvious from the way I have described these characteristics that other sets with quite different priorities and outcomes for the nature of science curricula are possible and may, prima facie, be more consonant with a science education for scientific literacy.

Before considering what has happened at the other two broad levels of schooling where science education occurs, some of the other outcomes of the senior curricula since the 1960s should be noted.

The quantitative achievements of school science education with respect to the first target are the more remarkable since they occurred during a period of unprecedented expansion of higher education in many countries. The supply of sufficient students from school who have been formally 'successful' in science has, however, turned out to be not wholly satisfying to the subject maintenance demand of science faculties in higher education. Since the 1970s a number of senior university scientists have been expressing dissatisfaction with the quality of the preparation in science of this elite group of school students. Furthermore, using rather different criteria, a number of studies that have involved first year university students have seriously questioned the quality of their preparatory learning in science. Rote recall seems to characterize their conceptual learning rather than depth of understanding or ability to use it to explain (see for example, Champagne, Gunstone and Klopfer, 1985; West, Fensham and Garrard, 1985; Brumby, 1981; and Hewson, 1981).

A number of the new curricula for a senior secondary study of the sciences (particularly those required for further study) have proved to be unattractive to students. Despite the increased numbers of students studying them (and hence meeting the first target as described above) there has been a decline, in a number of countries, in the proportion of the students at school choosing to study physics and chemistry when these subjects (or science more generally) cease to be part of a compulsory curriculum. This lack of attractiveness has been particularly marked in some sectors of the school population such as girls and students from some social groups who are now participating much more in these levels of schooling than they were in the 1960s.

On the other hand, certain other senior science curricula that were developed later in the 1970s along rather different lines and which could have been more attractive to more students have been strongly opposed, when it has been suggested that they become the primary source of the science education of students at these levels. In other words, there has been strong suspicion of the logical possibility that if science curricula at schools were successful for widespread literacy in science they should be an adequate base from which to draw those going on to be science professionals. Accordingly, minor revisions that leave unchanged the essential character of the disciplinary senior science courses have been allowed to occur but the more radical changes that the alternative science courses represented have not been approved. There is, thus, a great deal of evidence, at least in many of the more industrialized countries, that the curriculum of science education for the latter years of secondary education has been shaped to service the top three demands of figure 1 to the exclusion of the interests of the lower three.

Lower Secondary Science Education

The earlier years of secondary education (roughly for students with ages from 12 to 15) were already, for many countries when they embarked on the 1960s reforms, part of compulsory schooling and so involved the student populations for whom the second target is relevant. They may, however, have been differentiated into streams that already had different ends in view. For example, in Britain about 20 per cent of this age group were in schools that had the senior levels of science education that have just been discussed at length, and the other 80 per cent were in schools without such senior levels and where there was an expectation that students would move more directly into the work force after age 15 or so. In contrast, in the USA there was no such streaming by schools but a streaming by choice of subject could occur that affected the science education of many students.

It is thus not surprising that two sorts of science curriculum projects were developed for the lower secondary years in the later 1960s once the priority projects for the senior level were sufficiently far advanced.

In Australia, there was JSSP, a course of study that was made up of sequential modules and in each year there were some for chemistry, physics, biology, earth science and astronomy. There was also ASEP (sequential only in the intended learning demand of some of its units) which drew its content in a more integrated way from a wider range of sciences. In Britain, there were Nuffield Combined Science and Nuffield Secondary Science, a pair paralleling in their emphases the two Australian ones. Likewise in the USA, there were IPS and ISCS in the first category, and ESCP and Environmental Science in the second.

At these levels the interests of the two target groups were more evenly reflected in the development resources. Most of these projects claimed that they were aiming at scientific literacy but the restricted choice of science content and its conceptual emphasis in the first category ones were evidence of their continued subservience to a sense of being preparatory to the courses at the senior level. Wherever streaming of these students has occurred it has also been notable that the curricula of the first type have almost invariably been used with the more 'academic' streams or, in other words, with those most likely to go on to further study in science. From the point of view of scientific literacy for the majority this may have been reasonable although it did mean that the group of more able students (many of whom in the end would not continue with science) would not learn the much broader sense of science that the curricula in the second category contained. In the dynamics of a period when the purpose of these years of schooling changed rapidly as more of each age were retained in increasingly comprehensive secondary education, such a comfortable co-existence could hardly last. The two sorts of science courses have been hierarchically ranked as to worth so that, from the available evidence at the end of the 1970s, it is reasonable to conclude that the mainstream science curricula in these earlier years of the secondary school were char-acterized by learning emphases that are not very different from those listed above for senior secondary science. The content for learning in science had again been shifted from a descriptive and socially practical science to a more conceptual one. The focus for learning had been largely moved, as at the senior levels, from natural phenomena and other objects of scientific study and application to the concepts scientists use to describe them.

Primary School Science Education

When we turn to science education in the primary school we find a very different scene. Here, far removed from the point of schooling where the upper three demands in figure 1 have relevance, the explicit intentions of the projects of the 1960s were to contribute foundations to the scientific literacy of learners. In doing this, primary schooling would also provide a broad base of learners confident in, and ready for, science in the secondary school.

Almost all the projects for this level of schooling were, however, still within the *induction into science* approach referred to above. A range of learning outcomes consistent with this approach was used as the basis for developing materials. Some, like Concepts in Science and the Science Curriculum Improvement Study, continued to try to marry conceptual instruction with the science skills of observing and questioning phenomena and of applying concepts. Others played down specific concept learning in the interests of the acquisition of so-called science processes. Some of the latter followed Nuffield Junior Science in Britain and ESS in the USA and aimed to encourage any processes that enabled general enquiry and exploration of natural phenomena to occur. Others followed the lead of Science — A Process Approach in the USA or Science 5–13 in Britain and set out to develop a set of clearly defined reasoning skills. The phenomena in association with which this learning took place were very much secondary in importance to the skill or 'science processes' themselves. Some of the topics suggested by Science 5–13, for example, as appropriate ones to interest learners of these ages also, as it happened, served to indicate that these skills were not particularly 'scientific'. (They could certainly be applied to social phenomena and they are perhaps better described as being means of rational enquiry or problem solving.)

Both sorts of projects encountered great difficulties of implementation because of the lack of confidence and knowledge of science that teachers at these levels almost universally have. With so little understanding of the science concepts themselves, it is not surprising that teachers found it very difficult to teach how and why they emerge in science. On the other hand, teaching the 'content-free' processes required great logistical skills in classroom management, and did not seem to be science to these teachers (or to their learners' parents) for whom science was a body of information they had failed to master during their own education.

Even on the criterion of 'preparing for the next stage' these approaches to primary science education 'failed'. The concepts, in the rote form in which they were largely taught, were topics that already had established places in secondary curricula, and the process skills were largely ignored by secondary teachers who did not require them in their students for learning the factual and conceptual knowledge of secondary science.

In a few countries a less separate approach was taken to the inclusion of science in primary schooling. Thus in Thailand it is meant to be part of a major segment of the timetable called Life Experiences. This does relate it to more socially relevant phenomena but in practice, in the hands of primary teachers, this has often reduced science to just a few more facts or definitions to add to the social content of these topics with which these teachers feel more comfortable and more familiar.

At a level of schooling where the influence of the political and subject maintenance demands on science curricula might well be expected to be low, they have reappeared through the attitudes primary teachers and the secondary teachers have towards what was proposed as learning of worth in science.

Nevertheless, as a result of the efforts of the 1960s, science has become more clearly established as a formal part of the overall learning that children are expected to have in these primary years. There are, however, few reports from any countries that would suggest that we have yet found in science education the analogue of the situation in mathematics. That is, everybody outside primary schools — secondary mathematics teachers, parents, employers, administrators — identify with and welcome the teaching of the basic mathematical operations on numbers as wholly appropriate for primary schooling. Primary teachers, too, accept this as their responsibility and their only problem is to fulfil it effectively.

Primary teachers seem generally, despite the effort of all the projects of the 1960s and early 1970s, to have been confused and not convinced about the role of science in the education of the primary learner. In their practice of what is now often a formal requirement they rarely seem to identify with the optimistic contention of one of the earliest pioneers in the 1960s who claimed that science education would be the easiest subject to teach in the primary school. He argued that it was the only one that almost all children were prepared for before they start school, namely, they could observe things and orally report with accuracy what they saw!

Different Learners for Science

In most countries there have been quite significant changes since 1960 in the socioeconomic characteristics of the school populations for whom science education is now seen as possible and necessary. This is particularly obvious for secondary schooling which, in so many countries in the intervening years, has moved from an elite to a mass phenomenon. However, for science education the changes have also arisen from quite major shifts in a society's perception of who should participate in, and benefit from science education. Thus, the primary and lower secondary levels of schooling are affected as well as the higher levels of secondary in both more and less industrialized countries. They stem from a push by parents who see more education as a means of societal gain for their children, and a pull from governments which have encouraged students to stay longer at school for more general education, for more relevant skill training, and to reduce the costs and embarrassments of youth unemployment (a widespread phenomenon since the mid-1970s).

The multicultural character of the school population is now recognized in a number of European and North American countries and in Australia, New Zealand and Israel. This population change has arisen as a result of national economic demands that led to employment policies in the 1960s and 1970s that involved the parents of these students. The children of the immigrant families that take these sorts of risks and initiatives often bring attitudes and cultural expectations to learning in general, and to science in particular, that present quite new challenges to teachers most of whom come from more educationally established sectors of the society.

Particularly in the last decade as the feminist movement has gained renewed vitality, there has been a consciousness and a concern that science education has been a gender biased (in favour of boys) feature of schooling. While this concern is most evident in countries that have had a Protestant Christian tradition, a similar gender bias is obvious in many other countries. Indeed, in only a small number do girls and boys participate equally at school in the physical sciences — the gateway subjects to scientific careers — and in even fewer (Thailand is an interesting case) are their achievements comparable.

In 1960, participation of the children of the poorer families in upper or elite secondary education (where science education mainly occurred) was still, in quite a number of countries, essentially restricted to those who gained scholarships. Since then the proportion of students from lower income families has increased dramatically, but this rise is often not yet reflected in science education. This is a matter of serious concern when the changing nature of work and employment prospects are considered. Mass secondary education is itself partly a product of the reduced opportunities for traditional skilled and unskilled youth employment. Unless those, who would in the past have left school to enter the skilled and unskilled trades, participate more equally in science education at school, they will find themselves, despite more schooling, still at a disadvantage later in life as society and its employment opportunities become more and more technically derived.

These great changes in the culture, gender and class of school populations for whom effective science education should now be available mean that the societal realities of the 1980s and beyond are quite different from the ones in which the reform movement of the 1960s occurred. If those, who are now responsible for, and concerned about, the quantity and quality of school science education, can be persuaded that what they seek should be shaped and implemented as a function of these realities then the déjà vu dilemma will be dispelled. Furthermore, there will be some hope that some of the promising new directions that are already being trod (a number of which are outlined in later chapters) will have some chance of gaining mainstream recognition as science education. As a start we shall need to recognize that the two targets need their own forms of science education and that the second, with its concern for all learners, is the key to the first rather than the first being the key to the second as was the way in the 1960s reforms.

More Specific Dilemmas in Science Education

Limited Access to Experience

In 1960 school science education was outdated and static almost everywhere. By the late 1980s a majority of the world's countries have experienced major reforms or revisions of their science curricula.

Despite its extensiveness, the readily available international literature on science education does not reflect the richness of these experiences. The great bulk of the shared literature (curriculum materials, exhortative writing, evaluation reports and research studies) comes from a few countries that have English as their first language. Furthermore, some of these countries, such as the USA, Britain and Australia, have degrees of curricular freedom in their educational systems that render much of their curricular debate irrelevant to the majority of countries where the educational systems and hence curricula are more centralized.

Accordingly science educators face two dilemmas. The first is how to sort out from the available literature the ideas and outcomes that may apply to their own schooling contexts. This is not easy when so much of this literature has assumed that the contexts of origin are transferable or does not even recognize that context is important. All science teachers have some degree of freedom in what and how they teach but there are very significant differences in the way external constraints like national or more local curricula, examinations and available facilities constrain or encourage the exercise of this freedom. Failure to identify these constraints and encouragements in most of the reporting has made the transferability of much useful experience more difficult than it should have been.

The second dilemma is the sheer unavailability of most of the world's experience of science education since 1960. Only small fragments of it are available for sharing, either because only a few of the reports and materials are translated, or because there is little educocultural support for such information

17

to be made mutually available. This dilemma is particularly unfortunate since the time sequence for the reform of science education in a number of less industrialized (and less publicized) countries has turned out to be advantageous. To begin with they have confronted, and hence recognized, more revolutionary societal changes in schooling whereas the changes in industrialized countries have been more evolutionary and hence less obvious. Then they have been in a position to learn not only from the ideas that influenced the well known projects of the 1960s but also from their success and failure in practice. Furthermore, at least in some of these countries, there has been access to a wider range of sources and expertise than was available to the earlier projects. These sources include the internationally available literature on science education (surprisingly unavailable in parts of the USA and Britain to judge by the citations of some authors in these countries), regional and international conferences, international documents and sources such as UNESCO (more widely known in the developing world than in the developed world), study tours, consultancies and staff development. It is not really surprising then, with these advantages, that some excellent developments have taken place.

The two IEA studies of comparative science education bear testimony to the quality of the developments in Japan. Thailand has provided very clear structural support for its efforts in curriculum development and that country's remarkable achievements in relation to the gender dilemma seem to be in large part due to this well planned aspect of their implementation (Fensham, 1986b).

We need more details about what lies behind these and the many other successes that are known to exist but are not yet in an exchangeable form.

Language and Culture

In the 1960s, as will be apparent from a number of things already referred to, the social and cultural context of the learners outside the school was not a factor of concern to the curriculum developers. Perhaps they reasoned that, if science itself had universal or transcultural characteristics, education in it would be equally so. On the other hand, it is more likely that, implicitly, these first developers built into their materials the language and examples that stemmed from the sub-culture they shared with their essentially middle class students.

Gardner's (1971) pioneering work on *Words in Science* in Papua New Guinea and Australia (later repeated in the Philippines, Israel and Britain) began to show the differential advantages that some students have as a result of their facility with the language used in science classrooms. Much of this stemmed from what can be described as the 'middle' words of science discourse. These are not the invented and technical words of science but the many words like 'solution', 'pour', 'energy', 'burn', 'agent', 'volume', 'because', 'so', etc. that have meaning in everyday discourse that is different from, or more varied than it is in science.

The links between language and science education have turned out to be an exciting field for research and a number of studies have now shown that the language of learners' cultures can raise problems for their learning of science. These problems are particularly acute and obvious in societies where the language of learning in school is different from the language used at home and in the wider society. Furthermore, because so much of modern science has been developed in Western countries its thought forms, concepts, and concomitant language are consonant with the languages of these societies. For example, most of these will have words that distinguish 'heat' and 'burn', and 'dissolve' and 'melt', but this is not so in many other societies where it has not been important to have such distinctions in the language. Some of these languages are, on the other hand, much richer than the Western languages in descriptive words for familiar objects, but this too can become a handicap when the scientific description and categorizations of them involve fewer, or even quite other characteristics.

These problems of language are, however, by no means confined to 'bilingual' situations. The many studies of children's conceptions in science have often reported the ambiguity that learners encounter between everyday and scientific usage of words and ideas (Osborne and Freyberg, 1985). Sutton's (1979) work on metaphors in science education, and his and Schaefer's (1979) interest in what they call the 'burr' model of science concepts have also contributed to our understanding of how language and culture can blur the precision of the sciences and hence interact strongly with their learning.

Lemke's (1982) sociolinguistic work on discourse in science classrooms has opened a window on how analogy can be both a powerful aid and a barrier to learning science. A few other reports have hinted that there may be major differences (and hence learning differentials) in the way students from different social class or ethnic backgrounds respond to the language of enquiry and of explanation as they are used in teaching science.

In 1981 Wilson produced a bibliographic guide to more than 600 studies since 1960 that related some aspect of the social and cultural context of learners to their science or mathematics education. There is no doubt that if we are serious about science education at school contributing to scientific literacy or to better understanding of its concepts, much more attention will have to be given to the role of these sorts of social and cultural factors.

The Role of Affect in Science Education

Most of the research on the learning of science has assumed that it is predominantly a cognitive process. Affect has been, however, of considerable interest as an accompanying learning outcome. Gardner (1975) put some order into the study of attitudes to science that students acquire as a result of science studies at school, and the findings of a number of well conducted studies are now available. A disconcerting number of these show that there is not a ready link between cognitive learning in science and a positive attitude to science. Indeed, it seems that often the longer students have studied science at school the more their attitude to it declined. The unpopularity of some of the sciences in secondary school has already been mentioned. Such negative attitudes to science in school are damaging to both targets of science education. Once again, curriculum developers in the 1980s have to face the evidence of a dilemma that was blissfully absent in the 1960s. Then it was generally assumed that learners would respond positively to 'good' curriculum materials and through their learning of science based on them acquire a strong affect for and an appreciation of science.

In 1985, Gardner (and Lehrke and Hoffman) edited the proceedings of a conference at IPN in West Germany that brought up to date the many ways that science as a learning outcome has been explored in the decade since his earlier work. Affect certainly continues to be of considerable interest as a learning outcome since it is likely to be an indicator of these future citizens' responses to science. There is also concern that the relative unpopularity of science in school does lead to social inequities in the outcomes of schooling and to a threat to the supply of the specialist work force.

Apart from the oft-reported positive contribution that active participation in small groups in practical work can make, much less attention has to date been paid to the role of affect in the learning process itself. A number of the leading cognitive researchers, such as Novak (1981), White and Tisher (1986) and West and Pines (1983) have drawn attention to its importance but, as yet, have not undertaken or reported studies that give others a sense of how it should be incorporated into learning.

Some of the reports of gender differences in interest are suggestive for science education. Harding (1983), for instance, draws heavily on Head's (1979) findings in suggesting and designing science education that is likely to be more gender balanced, and others have recently reported projects which change either or both the classroom context and the social examples that are used to teach science.

Minssen and Nentwig (1983) and Snively (1987) have reported two small but intriguing studies of affect in action. They share an unusual emphasis on the affect learners have for the objects they are learning about in science. The former made use of the very different attitudes he found that German students displayed to various chemical materials and to the shapes in which they were presented. The latter sought to build into science lessons about the seashore for primary children a recognition of several sorts of affective dimensions her research suggested different learners used when they thought about this complex object of study. We need many more studies of affect in action in the next few years if we are to harness it as the major factor it undoubtedly is for improving science education.

New Directions for Science Education

In the chapters that follow many of the new directions in contemporary science education that are interesting and promising are described. It will suffice therefore at this stage to mention two that relate to two areas in which quite major changes occurred as a result of the reform movement in the 1960s. As I said earlier, areas where change has occurred before may be areas that hold out more hope for change again.

New Content for Learning

One of the achievements of the 1960s that has been noted earlier is the major redefinition they gave to the content for science learning in schools and hence to what became its 'knowledge of worth'.

The new conceptual emphasis in the content for learning was, however, by the mid-1970s, being criticized from many sides. Reference has already been made to dissatisfactions about the quality of the conceptual learning. Another set of criticisms came from those who were concerned with the impact of science on society and with the social relevance of its learning to learners at school. That is, the a-social nature of the science content of the 1960s curricula was seen to be inappropriate in the face of the internationally recognized *Environmentale Problematique* and the technological realities of society (including the many new biomedical ones that are questioning public views of such fundamental concepts as birth, death and the biology of human relations).

It is both important and pleasing to be able to note that both these and other sorts of criticisms have now progressed beyond the polemical stage. Science educators, out of their own analyses of the outcomes of the 1960s, have recently developed a number of different schemes that define alternatives for the content of school science education. Furthermore, a number of current curriculum projects are promoting these quite new sorts of objectives as learning of worth for science at school

Some of these objectives are based on new analyses of the nature of science and science education (see, for example, Hodson, 1985; Millar, 1988; and Kass and Jenkins, 1986). Others recognize that knowledge in the sciences is a socially powerful way of knowing about natural objects and phenomena but it is nevertheless only one of the ways that various groups in society know about and deal with them (see for example, Fensham, 1983; and Osborne and Freyberg, 1985). Yet another group have given a new prominence to the interfaces between scientific knowledge and society (see Aitkenhead, 1986; Zoller, 1985; Brumby, 1984; and Eijkelhof and Koortland in chapter 14).

It is interesting to note that a number of these redefinitions of possible science content have recognized the discreteness of some of these objectives and hence their need of distinct recognition in the curriculum and its supporting materials. There is no doubt they will need their own recognition in the structure of schooling if most of them are not to be submerged by more traditionally powerful ones.

Each of these redefinitions of the possible content of school science education contributes to the idea that science at school should be recognized as a rich and much more variegated source of human knowledge and endeavour than it usually is at present. They also imply that a wider range of appropriate and recognizably distinct aspects of science need to be selected and converted into a pedagogy that makes up the curricula of school science education if they are to be effective for most learners. The basic steps in this process are epistemological tasks of a major order. They are also, I suspect, such radical ones that they are quite beyond the groups of university professional scientists to whom we have hitherto turned as sources and for legitimation. The intensity of the *induction into research science* of these sorts of scientists has been such that it is almost impossible for most of them to set it aside and give adequate value to other ways of encountering science. Elsewhere I have described my own attempts to step outside the chemistry into which I was inducted and to see anew how my field of science is about people and products and raw materials, rich colours, smells and scents, and other social properties of matter (Fensham, 1984).

I have argued that school science education after the 1960s has been essentially a form of *induction 'into' science*. The suggestions being made for it now in the 1980s are more aptly described as being a learning *'from' science*. These two curriculum processes are fundamentally different. In the first, teachers who have themselves been inducted into an acquaintance with some of the conceptual knowledge of science attempt to repeat the first steps of this process with their students. In the second, science teachers, as persons with some familiarity and confidence with the corpus of science, act as couriers between it and their students. As these students move through school their experiences in society (home, community and school) change and they encounter new situations to which science can contribute. It is these student needs that should determine, in the second process, the messages that the teacher couriers bring as science education to their lessons.

A number of quite new ways of defining science learning are now available that leave the 1960s behind. Some of these have already been translated into new materials and new sorts of ways of teaching. How rapidly and to what extent these will achieve normative status in school science is yet to be determined but it does seem that some of them would serve better the new and different societal imperatives that schools now face. They will, however, need more than their intrinsic merits to survive the competition between the differentially powerful interest groups. Structural supports will be essential. The form in which education in the sciences is made available and is required in schooling is one such critical support. The examinations, in whatever form they exist, are another since they so largely determine, for each school population, what is the 'knowledge of worth' in science.

New Notions of Curriculum Development

Science education in the 1960s led to new conceptions of curriculum development. Although a number of the recent projects seem to be following similar conceptions, that is, they will culminate in a 'package for better science teaching', a number of others are quite different. These, compared to the 1960s, give much more centrality either to the teacher, or to the teacher and the learner in their conceptions of curriculum development. Teacher development is what these projects interpret curriculum development in science as primarily being. It is interesting, however, to compare the rather different views they have of teachers and learners in the process of science education. Some still decontextualize teachers and see them as either deficient in science knowledge or in certain teaching competencies, and set up projects to remedy the deficiency. They pay no attention to the learners who thus are also perceived as essentially without context and effectively as 'tabula rasas' as far as science knowledge is concerned.

Others recognize that teaching science is not divisible into 'teaching' and 'science' in such a simplistic way and are attempting to assist teachers to see that the teaching of a science concept needs to be related to the ways learners (and teachers) conceptualize the phenomena it describes. The new 'didactics' approach in Sweden (Marton, 1985; Andersson, 1987), some of the CLIS projects in Britain (see Driver in chapter 7) and the large project at Stanford (Shulman, 1986) in the USA are different examples within this category.

Some other projects now rest on a still more complex view of the teaching/learning process. Not only is the teacher 'teaching science' but she/he is also teaching learners what it means to be 'learning science'. The work of Novak at Cornell and White at Monash has helped to shape this view and some examples of the sorts of curriculum development that follow from it appear in chapters 3, 4, 5 and 6.

A common feature of some of these approaches is networking of classroom science teachers. This particular reconceptualization of curriculum development is an encouraging development as it does suggest that its proponents are heeding the effects of the divorce, so apparent in the 1960s reforms, between the development of a curriculum and its materials, and its implementation subsequently in classrooms. It is also saying that the contexts of the classroom and the school in which the science teacher works are important features that again were quite discounted in the 1960s. Networking implies that groups of science teachers need to be brought into association with each other and with the curriculum developers for the sharing of ideas, information and experiences. It also leads to a more realistic recognition that teachers need time and support from outside themselves if such sharing is to bring about changes in their behaviour and in the learning of their students.

References

AIKENHEAD, G. (1986) 'Collective decision making in the social context of science'. *Science Education*, 69, 4, pp 453–75.

ANDERSSON, B. (1987) *Chemical Reactions*, EKNA Report No.12, Molndal, Institute for Pedagogy, Goteburgs University.

APPLE, M.W. (1979) *Ideology and the Curriculum*, London, Routledge and Kegan Paul.

BOURDIEU, P. and PASSERON, J-C. (1977) *Reproduction in Education, Society and Culture*, London, Sage.

BRUMBY, M. (1981) 'The use of problem solving in meaningful learning in biology', *Research in Science Education*, 11, pp 103–10.

BRUMBY, M. (1984) *Issues in Biology*, Melbourne, Nelson.

BYBEE, R. (1977) 'The new transformation of science education', *Science Education*, 61, 1, pp 85–97.

CHAMPAGNE, A.B., GUNSTONE, R.F. and KLOPFER, L.E. (1985) 'Effecting change in cognitive structures among physics students' in WEST, L.H.T. and PINES, A.L. (Eds) *Cognitive Structure and Conceptual Change*, New York, Academic Press.

COMBER, L.C. and KEEVES, J.P. (1973) *Science Education in Nineteen Countries*, International Studies in Evaluation I, International Association for the Evaluation of Educational Achievement, New York, Wiley and Son.

CSSE (1978) *Case Studies in Science Education*. Urbana-Champaign, CIRCE and CCC, University of Illinois.

FAWNS, R.A. (1987) *The Maintenance and Transformation of School Science*, PhD thesis, Clayton, Monash University.

FENSHAM, P.J. (1976) 'Social contention in chemistry courses', *Chemistry in Britain*, 12, 5, pp 148–51.

FENSHAM, P.J. (1983) 'A research base for new objectives of science teaching', *Science Education*, 67, 1, pp 3–12.

FENSHAM, P.J. (1984) 'Conceptions, misconceptions, and alternative frameworks in chemical education', *Chemical Society Reviews*, 13, 2, pp 199–217.

FENSHAM, P.J. (1986a) 'Science for all', *Educational Leadership*, 44, 4, pp 18–23.

FENSHAM, P.J. (1986b) 'Lessons from science education in Thailand: A case study of gender and learning in the physical sciences', *Research in Science Education*, 15, pp 92–100.

GARDNER, P.L. (1971) *Words in Science*, Melbourne, Australian Science Education Project.

GARDNER, P.L. (1975) 'Attitudes to science: A review', *Studies in Science Education*, 2, pp 1–41.

GARDNER, P.L., LEHRKE, M. and HOFFMAN, L. (1985) *Interests in Science and Technology Education*, Kiel, IPN.

GINTIS, H. (1972) 'Towards a political economy of education', *Harvard Educational Review*, 42, 2, pp 70–96.

HARDING, J.M. (1983) *Switched Off: The Science Education of Girls*, York, Longmans for the Schools Council.

HARDING, J.M., KELLY, P.J. and NICODEMUS, R.B. (1976) 'The study of curriculum change', *Studies in Science Education*, 3, pp 1–30.

HEAD, J. (1979) 'Personality and the pursuit of science', *Studies in Science Education*, 3.

HEGELSON, S.L., BLOSSER, P.E. and HOWE, R.W. (1977) *The Status of Pre- College Science, Mathematics and Social Science Education: 1955–1975, Vol.1, Science Education*.

HEWSON, P.W. (1981) 'A conceptual change approach to learning science', *European Journal of Science Education*, 3, pp 383–96.

HODSON, D. (1985) 'Philosophy of science, science and science education', *Studies in Science Education*, 12, pp 25–57.

HURD, P. (1961) *Biological Education in American Secondary Schools, 1890–1960*, Colorado, Institute of Biological Science.

JENKINS, E. (1979) *From Armstrong to Nuffield*, London, Murray.

KASS, H. and JENKINS, F. (1986) 'Normative perspectives on the nature of curricular knowledge in chemistry', paper presented at annual meeting of National Association for Research in Science Teaching, San Francisco.

LAYTON, D. (1973) *Science for the People*, London, Allen and Unwin.

LEMKE, J. (1982) *Classroom Communication of Science*, Report to N.S.F./RISE:SED R79–18961, (ERIC:ED222–346).

MARTON, F. (1987) 'Towards a pedagogy of contents', Publication No. 4, Department of Education and Educational Research, Mölndal, University of Gothenburg.

MILLAR, R. (1988) 'What is scientific method and can it be taught? in WELLINGTON, J.J. (Ed) *Skills and Processes in Science Education*, London, Methuen.

MINSSEN, M. and NENTWIG, P. (1983) *Journal of Chemical Education*, 60, pp 476–8.

NATIONAL SCIENCE FOUNDATION (1983) *Educating Americans for the 21st Century*, The National Science Board Commission on Precollege Education in Mathematics, Science and Technology, Washington, DC, National Science Foundation.

NOVAK, J.D. (1981) 'Effective science instruction: The achievement of shared meaning', *Australian Science Teachers Journal*, 27, 1, pp 5–14.

OSBORNE, R. and FREYBERG, P. (1985) *Learning in Science: The Implications of Children's Science*, Auckland, Heinemann.

RESEARCH TRIANGLE INSTITUTE (1977) *National Survey of Science Education Curriculum Usage*, Research Triangle Park, North Carolina.

SCHAEFER, G. (1979) 'Concept formation in biology: the concept "growth"', *European Journal of Science Education*, 1, 1, pp 4–19.

SHULMAN, L.S. (1986) 'Paradigms and research programmes in the study of teaching: A contemporary perspective' in WITTROCK, M.C. (Ed) *Handbook of Research on Teaching*, 3rd edn, New York, Macmillan, pp 3–36.

SNIVELY, G. (1987) 'The use of a metaphor interview in the collection and analysis of interview data' in NOVAK, J. (Ed) *Proceedings of Second International Seminar, Misconceptions and Educational Strategies in Science and Mathematics*, Ithaca, Cornell University.

SUTTON, C.R. (1979) 'Language and curricular innovations, 33–36' in TAMIR, P. *et al.*, (Eds) *Curriculum Implementation and Its Relationship to Curriculum Development in Science*, Jerusalem, Israel Science Teaching Center.

TAMIR, P. *et al.* (1979) *Curriculum Implementation and Its Relationship to Curriculum Development in Science*, Proceedings of Bat-sheva conference, Jerusalem, Israel Science Teaching Centre.

WARING, M. (1979) *Social Pressures on Curriculum Innovations: A Study of the Nuffield Foundation Science Teaching Project*, London, Methuen.

WEST, L.H.T., FENSHAM, P.J. and GARRARD, J.E. (1985) 'Describing the cognitive structure of learners following instruction in chemistry, 29–50' in WEST, L.H.T. and PINES, A.L. (Eds) *Cognitive Structure and Conceptual Change*, New York, Academic Press.

WEST, L.H.T. and PINES, A.L. (1983) 'How "rational" is irrationality?', *Science Education*, 67, 1, pp 37–9.

WHITE, R.T. and TISHER, R.P. (1986) 'Research on natural sciences' in WITTROCK, M.C. (Ed) *Handbook of Research on Teaching*, 3rd edn, New York, Macmillan.

WILSON, B. (1981) *Cultural Contexts of Science and Mathematics Education: A Bibliographic Guide*, Leeds, Centre for Studies in Science Education, University of Leeds.

YOUNG, M.F.D. (1971) 'An approach to the study of curricula as socially organised knowledge' in YOUNG, M.F.D. (Ed) *Knowledge and Control*, London, Collier Macmillan.

ZOLLER, U. (1985) 'Interdisciplinary decision-making in the science curricula in the modern social context', in HARRISON, G. (Ed) *World Trends in Science and Technology Conference, Report on Second International Symposium*, Nottingham, Trent Polytechnic.

2
What Counts as Science Education?

Douglas A. Roberts

Introduction

This chapter develops a way to make sense of events involved in shaping the content for science education. Many people contribute to this shaping. Committees appointed by government departments and ministries of education do so, when they formulate curriculum policy for science education. Writers and publishers of science textbooks and curriculum innovations do so, when they produce materials for student and teacher use. Science teachers' associations do so, when they formulate and promote position statements about science education. Curriculum committees in schools and school systems do so, when they develop science course guides and other resources. University professors do so, when they teach science and science education to beginning and experienced teachers. And science teachers, in their turn, do so, when they teach.

Of these, the first and last mentioned are the two areas of focus in this chapter: the shaping done by legitimated (authorized, warranted) curriculum policy makers for educational jurisdictions, and the shaping done by classroom teachers. It is tempting to search for understanding in two bodies of research: one on educational policy formation and the other on curriculum implementation. My intent, however, is not to draw from that research to any significant extent. Instead, the chapter aims to provide an analytical framework for understanding what is involved for policy makers, and for science teachers, when they shape answers to the question: What counts as science education? To accomplish this task, the chapter proceeds through three major argumentative moves.

1 The question itself — namely, 'What counts as science education?' — is tackled first, to tease apart what sort of question it is and why the answer seems to depend on who is asked.

2   The formulation of official (authorized, warranted) policy for science education is examined next, emphasizing that the most important features of this sociopolitical process consist of satisfying the demands of those with a stake in the outcomes of science teaching — hereafter referred to as 'stakeholders'. Those holding a stake in science education include teachers, students, parents, prospective employers, and universities. Their demands are multiple and often are in conflict, requiring choices and compromises not easy to accommodate in a single policy statement. (Also, the final form of the policy statement will depend on which stakeholders are consulted and on how much weight is given to whose position.) Making sense of what happens in this process provides one way to look at the shaping of what counts as science education.

3   The role of science teachers in shaping what counts as science education is considered from two points of view: teacher interpretations and teacher loyalties. The first develops a way to analyze teacher understanding of what science education means — a conceptual or intellectual component of science teachers' reasoning. The second explores a value-laden component of teacher reasoning, in search of an explanation for the fact of teacher allegiance to some meanings for science education but not others.

In recent years phrases like 'scientific literacy' have emerged as umbrella goals for science education, apparently offering the potential to shape automatically what counts as science education, thus doing away with all the messiness of policy formulation. These phrases have often commanded a remarkable amount of consensus yet they are educational slogans rather than definitions. Hence they defy accurate specification and do not remove the problems policy makers have in adjudicating amongst the conflicting wishes of stakeholders — even though they appear to many to hold out that promise. Such slogans cannot automatically shape what counts as science education.

Such a Sticky Question

What counts as science education? It seems to be such a straightforward question. There should be a definitive answer. Yet consider for a moment that the question can be taken in two ways.

First, the question could be asking for an account of what is done in the name of science education in some setting — an educational jurisdiction, a school, a teacher's classroom. Suppose a researcher observes and interprets what is going on, and reports that 'X counts as science education here'. This can be called an *empirical* thrust or sense of answering the question; the answer can be found by going out and looking. Interestingly, for a given educational jurisdiction the researcher might find that science curriculum policy suggests one answer, while external examinations required of students suggest another, observation in a few classrooms suggests a third, interviews with teachers suggest yet a fourth, and interviews with students suggest another answer still.

Second, the question could be asked in a *normative* sense: 'What (properly) counts as science education?'. It is this second sense that is most appropriate for consideration in the present chapter. Science curriculum policy makers specify what it is proper to count as science education, when they formulate policy. That is their mandate. Likewise, teachers when they teach are doing what they think counts properly as science education. (No teacher deliberately mis-educates.) The normative sense of getting an answer to the question, then, expresses something other than an empirically determined comment about what is going on; it expresses the value positions people honour and believe in. 'What counts as science education', when stated normatively, expresses the point that people are willing to put their weight behind the particular formulation they espouse: *this*, they will say, is what (really) counts as science education.

Still, can there not be a definitive answer to the question — an answer that will be binding on everyone involved, from policy makers through to teachers? One strategy that comes to mind right away is to start listing science topics — cell theory, chemical bonding, Newton's laws of motion, continental drift — and then find out which ones command the agreement of the most people (the so-called Delphi technique). Even if several iterations were used, a strategy based on the Delphi technique would fail, for two reasons.

1   A universal, general answer is being sought. Yet all science teachers know that they make choices in the classroom about the science topics they teach, how much depth is appropriate for which students, and so on, according to the unique requirements of their teaching situations. Chances are, therefore, that it would be impossible to find even two teachers who would either agree upon, or be willing to be bound by, a single list of science topics as a definition of what counts as science education for all of their students.

2   No one teaches a science topic in a vacuum. Science topics are taught in the context of a purpose for learning them — a curricular context such as preparing for university, understanding familiar technological processes and devices, developing 'process skills', or coming to see how

scientific knowledge is generated and changed over time. These curricular contexts (which will later be called *curriculum emphases*) are themselves objects of choice for science education. The shaping of what counts as science education thus involves making choices about contexts, or curriculum emphases, as well as topics.

Would the augmented list-of-science-topics-and-curriculum-emphases approach work if a massive vote were held of all of the stakeholders in science education world-wide? Would it work if a panel of experts were asked to adjudicate the question of which topics and which curriculum emphases to include and which to exclude? Would it work if more research were done — for instance on what topics students can learn best at what ages?

All of these approaches have been either tried or advocated at one time or another in the history of science education, but all of them are wrongheaded. Shaping what counts as science education is not the kind of procedure that has a general universal outcome for 'the world'. Outcomes of the procedure have to suit the requirements of unique situations, ultimately the unique situations of individual teachers' classrooms but intermediately the unique situations of different educational jurisdictions. This is to say that the matter of deciding what to teach is a problem in the realm of human affairs which Aristotle labelled 'the practical' — meaning the kind of problem that must eventuate in a defensible decision tailored to a unique situation. In the pursuit of such a decision, generalized information might be helpful, but it has the status of a consideration rather than an answer.

So the sticky question 'What counts as science education?' has three characteristics. First, the answer to it requires that choices be made — choices among science topics and among curriculum emphases. Second, the answer is a defensible decision rather than a theoretically determined solution to a problem theoretically posed. Third, the answer is not arrived at by research (alone), nor with universal applicability; it is arrived at by the process of deliberation, and the answer is uniquely tailored to individual situations. Hence the answer to the question will be different for every educational jurisdiction, for every duly constituted deliberative group, and very likely for every science teacher.

'Authorized' Shaping of What Counts as Science Education: Making Sense of Curriculum Policy Making

What Is Science Curriculum Policy?

Science curriculum policy making is an area of science education that has begun to receive the attention of researchers only recently. Nonetheless, for purposes of this chapter it must be acknowledged that science curriculum policies are official, legally binding statements of what counts as science education. At least, they are wherever they are issued, for example, by provincial departments or ministries of education in Canada and state departments of education in the United States.

Virtually every educational jurisdiction in the world has its ways of making science curriculum policy known to its schools. The document intended to communicate policy may be a syllabus which specifies science topics. Or it could be a 'curriculum guideline' that lists, in addition to science topics, some intended outcomes for learners (the 'objectives') in terms that *go beyond* understanding of the topics themselves. Consider an example of such a list of objectives, as these were made policy for schools in the Canadian province of Alberta in the late 1970s. (The policy statement is currently being revised.) In addition to specifying required and optional science topics for each science course in grades seven through twelve, the policy includes the following statement.[1]

> The objectives of Secondary School Science are:
> 1 To promote an understanding of the role that science has had in the development of societies:
>   (a) history and philosophy of science as part of human history and philosophy;
>   (b) interaction of science and technology;
>   (c) effect of science on health, population growth and distribution, development of resources, communication and transportation, etc.
> 2 To promote an awareness of the humanistic implications of science:
>   (a) moral and ethical problems in the use and misuse of science;
>   (b) science for leisure-time activities.
> 3 To develop a critical understanding of those current social problems which have a significant scientific component in terms of their cause and/or their solution:
>   (a) depletion of natural resources;
>   (b) pollution of water and air;
>   (c) overpopulation;
>   (d) improper use of chemicals;
>   (e) science for the consumer.
> 4 To promote understanding of and development of skill in the methods used by scientists:
>   (a) processes in scientific enquiry such as observing,

> hypothesizing, classifying, experimenting, and interpret-
> ing data;
>
> (b) intellectual abilities such as intuition, rational thinking,
>   creativity, and critical thinking;
> (c) skills such as manipulation of materials, communication,
>   solving problems in groups, and leadership.
>
> 5 To promote assimilation of scientific knowledge:
>   (a) emphasis on fundamental ideas;
>   (b) relevance of scientific knowledge through inclusion of
>   practical applications;
>   (c) application of mathematics in science;
>   (d) interrelationships between the sciences;
>   (e) open-endedness of science and the tentativeness of sci-
>   entific knowledge.
> 6 To develop attitudes, interests, values, appreciations, and
>   adjustments similar to those exhibited by scientists at work.
> 7 To contribute to the development of vocational knowledge
>   and skill:
>   (a) science as a vocation;
>   (b) science as background to technical, professional, and
>   other vocations.

These seven objectives do not specify science topics; earlier I referred to them as *contexts in which science topics are taught*. In this case they have been mandated as science curriculum policy; therefore, so long as the policy remains in force, they are part of what counts as science education for the province of Alberta. The point is clear, then: what counts as science education is not just science topics. It never has been and, indeed, the content for any school or university course is never 'just the subject'. Implicit (and sometimes explicit) in the way the subject is taught are reasons or purposes for students to learn it — curricular contexts in which they are to understand the subject.

Thus students not only learn a subject, they also learn some fringe-benefit lessons at the same time — including the reason the teacher or professor (or curriculum policy maker) believes students should learn the material. For example, the lesson of the day may focus on the theory of chemical bonding, but the implicit/explicit reason for learning it could be (a) this is an important part of your preparation to learn more chemistry (Alberta objective 5(a)); or (b) the chemical bond is an ingenious conceptual invention allowing us to explain why substances cling to each other with differing degrees of tenacity (Alberta objective 6); or (c) the chemical bond is an abstraction which permits us to account for certain data (Alberta objective 4(a)); or perhaps (d) now we have the scientific background to understand certain technological processes involved in, say, making some types of 'miraculous' household glue (Alberta objective 1(b) or 5(b)). Such fringe benefits to the main lesson will be referred to as *meta-lessons*, following Schwab's usage.[2]

Conceptualizing what counts as science education thus requires that two components be considered (much like one identifies two separate strands in a twisted-pair cable): the topics (or lessons) and the curricular contexts (or meta-lessons). Furthermore, anyone concerned with shaping what counts as science education can *choose* the meta-lessons as well as the topics. When a substantial sequence of science topics (say, five or six weeks' worth) is taught in the context of a selected, consistently related set of meta-lessons (say, about understanding the way scientific knowledge is generated), the instruction develops for the students what I have called a *curriculum emphasis*. Just as one can imagine planning a science course by 'chunking' the lessons (science topics) coherently into extended blocks of instruction, one can imagine also 'chunking' the meta-lessons, in order to give coherence to a similarly extended treatment of the curriculum emphasis. As demonstrated in the next section, the relationship between science topics and curriculum emphases can be seen clearly in science textbooks.

Based on the sample from Alberta and the discussion above, two points need to be reiterated. First, a science curriculum policy can be seen to consist of two components: science topics, and objectives which embody curriculum emphases. (Even a syllabus has an objective and expresses at least one curriculum emphasis.) Second, the matter of which topics are to be taught in the context of which curriculum emphases is not addressed in the Alberta policy used here as a sample. Neither is it specified how much attention is to be given to each of the major categories of objectives. So, even though there has been authorized shaping of what counts as science education, much has been left to teacher interpretation and to other factors (what is stressed in provincial examinations, which textbooks and other materials are approved for classroom use, etc.). Let us turn next to the blending of science topics and curriculum emphases as seen in textbooks.

Science Topics and Curriculum Emphases

'Why are we learning this stuff?'

Formulating a satisfactory answer to that student query frequently causes science teachers a great deal of discomfort. Yet, students do ask the question, and thereby remind us of a point already made: that there is more to science education than science topics alone. To illustrate the point and its significance, let us use that ancient and venerable teaching device, the textbook.

Consider two science textbooks, written for students in grade nine, that deal with the topic of heat. Both deal with basic principles that summarize a scientific understanding and explanation of thermal phenomena — such familiar items as the three means by which heat travels, the basic points of kinetic-molecular theory, and the differences between heat and temperature. Yet the one text embeds the science topics in a series of discussions about ways in which the principles can be seen to apply in the technology of everyday life, explaining, for example, the workings of convection currents in hot water heaters and the differential expansion of bimetallic strips used in thermostats; the other embeds the same topics in a story line showing that the caloric theory of heat has been replaced by kinetic-molecular theory in the development of physics. The first text teaches the student that the purpose of learning the science is to be able to understand familiar everyday gadgets. The second gets across the message that one learns science in order to understand how scientific knowledge develops.[3]

Whenever one finds two textbooks that treat the same topics yet have a distinctly different 'flavour', one can be sure it is the curriculum emphasis, or purpose for learning the material, that is responsible for the difference. The same is true of teaching: a curriculum emphasis, by the very nature of education, is always present. (Science textbooks and teaching which seem to present nothing but 'straight content' also teach the student a message about the purpose of learning: Learn the stuff for its own sake.)

Curriculum emphases in science education

Seven curriculum emphases can be found in the history of science education practice in elementary and secondary schools in North America.[4] In what follows, a brief description and an example are provided for each, in order to clarify what the curriculum emphases are and the manner in which science topics are contextualized within them.

An *Everyday Coping* emphasis directs science teaching towards the student's use of science to comprehend objects and events of fairly obvious importance. Topics in biology, for instance, can be organized and taught so that the student's purpose in learning them is to understand the functioning and intelligent care of the human body. Chemistry topics can be taught in the service of knowing about familiar chemical processes which occur in the home, the automobile, and industry. Physics topics can be oriented to show how various common home devices — such as the telephone, the furnace, or the electric iron — function and can be maintained. The emphasis was common in North America in the 1930s and 1940s. Notice how the science topics in the following passage from a 1939 textbook are contextualized in this curriculum emphasis.

> Chinooks probably give Alberta a greater variety of winter climate than is found anywhere else in the world. These prevailing westerly winds sweep in from the Pacific Ocean. They are warm, moisture-laden winds that hit the mainland of British Columbia. As they ascend the mountains, they become cooler and the water vapour is condensed. Fog forms and is followed by rain and snow. As the air ascends the mountains, the pressure on it is decreased. Hence, it expands. This expansion results in cooling .... Condensation of the vapour to rain, and also the formation of snow raise the temperature of the air .... On the eastern slopes, the pressure on the descending air increases, and the resulting contraction is followed by a higher temperature.[5]

A *Structure of Science* emphasis, common in the American and British science curriculum reforms of the late 1950s and 1960s, orients teaching in such a way that the student comes to understand how science functions as an intellectual enterprise. Attention is given to the relationship between evidence and theory, the adequacy of a model to explain phenomena, the self-correcting features of the growth of science, and similar matters relating to the way in which scientific knowledge is developed. Here is a sample.

> Gases are found to react in simple proportions by volume, and the volume of any gaseous product bears a whole-number ratio to that of any gaseous reactant. Thus, *two* volumes of hydrogen react with exactly *one* volume of oxygen to produce exactly *two* volumes of water vapor (all at the same temperature and pressure). These integer relationships naturally suggest a particle model of matter and, with Avogadro's Hypothesis, are readily explained on the basis of the atomic theory.... All of contemporary chemical thought is based upon the atomic model and, hence, every successful chemical interpretation strengthens our belief in the usefulness of this theory.[6]

A *Science, Technology and Decisions* emphasis brings out the interrelatedness among scientific explanation, technological planning and problem solving, and decision making about practical matters of importance to society. Currently this emphasis is receiving a great deal of attention under such names as 'science in a social context' and 'STS' (science-technology-society). The sample textbook passage below follows after a thorough explanation of how eutrophication occurs in lakes, the effects of that process, and the role played by phosphates.

What can be done about phosphates in laundry and dish-washing detergents? Recall that they are added to control pH and to prevent the formation of precipitates of hard-water ions with the detergent molecules. An extensive search is under way for a non-phosphorus compound that will perform these functions. The leading candidate for a phosphate substitute was sodium nitrilotriacetate, NTA, whose structure is [diagram of molecular structure presented here].... For a while, NTA appeared to be an ideal substitute for phosphates and was beginning to replace them in detergents during 1970. However, during December 1970, the detergent industry halted the use of NTA after it was found that NTA in combination with heavy metals such as mercury and cadmium causes increased infant mortality and terato-genic effects in rats and mice.... That's where things stand today. Phosphates are under attack by many governmental units and environmental groups. Some localities have banned the sale of detergents that contain phosphates, but NTA may cause more serious problems than the phosphates.... Both the detergent manufacturers and the housewives are left in a quandary as to the choice of a washing product that is both safe in the household and unlikely to cause environmental degradation.[7]

The *Scientific Skill Development* emphasis has science topics taught in the service of developing sophisticated conceptual and manipulative skills — collectively labelled as 'scientific processes' — such as observing, measuring, experimenting, hypothesizing, etc. It represents an emphasis on the *means* of scientific inquiry. Here is a sample which deals with the skill of classification.

Linnaeus grouped as a species those organisms which he felt were very similar in structural features. But just how similar must the organisms be in order to be classified as the same species? ... [Here some clusters of similar-looking animals are depicted, but their classification is not what one would expect from their appearance and there are specific comments about that.] ... Appearances can be deceiving. Clearly something more than similar structural features is needed to classify organisms into species. Today a *species* (plural also *species*) is defined as *a group of individuals that are alike in many ways and interbreed under natural conditions to produce fertile offspring. Fertile* means that the animals are capable of producing offspring. This means that members of the same species can, if left alone in their natural environment, mate with one another to produce offspring which, in turn, are also able to produce offspring. Members of different species cannot fulfill all these condi-tions.[8]

The *Correct Explanations* emphasis concentrates on the *ends* of scientific inquiry, rather than the means. The emphasis is familiar to anyone engaged in science teaching as the 'master now, question later' approach. This is one emphasis in which no explicit communication is provided to the student about the purpose for learning science. The message is communicated by default, as it were: 'Learn it because it's correct'. The following passage illustrates the emphasis, which is not bound to any particular time in the history of science education.

> Newton believed, wrongly we now know, that this change in direction of light when moving from air to glass was due to an increase in the speed of light in the denser medium.... Curiously enough, the correct theory which explained the change in direction or *refraction* of light when moving from one medium to another was proposed in 1621, some forty-five years before Newton's corpuscular theory and fifty-seven years before Huygen's wave theory of light.[9]

The *Self as Explainer* emphasis informs the student's understanding of his/her own efforts to explain phenomena by exposing the conceptual underpinnings that influenced scientists when *they* were in the process of developing explanations. More than any other curriculum emphasis, this one provides students with grounds for understanding the process of explanation itself which, incidentally, offers the opportunity for comprehending such other modes of explanation in human history as magic and religion. Accordingly, it is within this curriculum emphasis that the perplexing educational problems arising from the creation/evolution controversy can be explored and dealt with most fruitfully. Notice how the underpinnings of Kepler's thought are revealed, in the following passage.

> The quest of a scientist depends in part upon the scientific framework of his era and the questions he asks. Kepler regarded the search for a planetary model as a cosmic mystery, the solution of which would reveal a design of God. He accepted the Copernican theory and was fascinated by the question, 'Why are there only six planets?' Kepler's answer was based on his belief that this number was by divine plan rather than chance. This answer led to a model of the solar system that had as a basis the five solid figures, or regular polyhedra, used by Plato in his description of the fundamental parts of matter. It had been proved by Euclid that there are only five regular convex solids. He believed that his model provided a geometric perfection which reflected that perfection of deity.[10]

The *Solid Foundation* emphasis answers the student query about the purpose of learning 'this stuff' in a straightforward manner: 'To get ready for the stuff you are going to learn next year'. In some ways this is a reassuring curriculum emphasis, for it indicates to the student that he/she is learning something that fits into a structure that has been thought about and planned. This is the familiar curriculum emphasis which invites secondary school teachers to tell elementary school teachers what they should teach, and in turn invites university professors to tell secondary school teachers what they should teach, graduate schools to tell undergraduate instructors what they should teach, etc. (This is another emphasis whose message is communicated by default.) The following excerpt can be compared with the earlier passage about chinooks.

> Although an air mass may be stationary for several days, eventually it will move. No two things can be in the same place at the same time. If one air mass moves into an area, another must move out. If two or more air masses are headed for the same place at the same time, there is a problem. By now you probably know which air mass will 'win'. The heaviest, coldest, most dense air mass will push underneath all the others. The 'losers' will be forced up and over the outer surface of this cold air mass.[11]

Curriculum emphases in science curriculum policy

Different curriculum emphases have been in fashion at different periods in history. Economic, cultural, and nationalistic factors are among those determining which emphases are present in a science curriculum policy at any given time. The emphases are selected by a sociopolitical process of deliberation, thus it is not the case that there are some correct emphases and other wrong ones. Each is a legitimate candidate for choice.

A further point is worth noting about the making of policy choices concerning curriculum emphases. A single curriculum emphasis does not necessarily have to control the science education orientation for a child's entire school career, or even for a period as long as one year. Technically speaking, a curriculum emphasis can be made to materialize in a learner's experience in the course of teaching about five to six weeks' worth of science subject matter — roughly what is referred to as an instructional unit. That is, there is a minimum of time required for an emphasis to be developed, but a given program for a school year could incorporate several emphases in sequence (though, by definition, not simultaneously).[12]

Stakeholders and Policy Formulation

The deliberative process by which an educational jurisdiction formulates what counts as science education is a complex balancing act, in any democratic society. Different stakeholders typically express strong views about different curriculum emphases, and any governmental body formulating or reformulating science curriculum policy for public education in a democracy has to take those views into account.

One of the reasons why curriculum policy formulation is studied so little is that preliminary stages of the process have to remain confidential, yet the best data are lurking there in the early deliberations of advisory committees. To continue using Alberta as an example (and surely this is typical), current policy remains in force until the Minister of Education formally declares that new policy is in force. What the policy actually *is* at any time is thus a matter having substantial legal implications, and 'leaks' have to be seen as providing misinformation to teachers and school systems. Hence the deliberations conducted by advisory committees set up to formulate and recommend new policy are usually held in camera, out of the researcher's view.

One approach to understanding what happens is, of course, to analyze and seek understanding about a policy change in retrospect, an approach taken by Gaskell and his associates with respect to the physics program authorized for the province of British Columbia in the early 1960s.[13] One is at the mercy of several factors with respect to the data, even if one works retrospectively: whether the committee's records and correspondence were preserved, more or less intact, and whether permission can be obtained to make the data public for research purposes. In what follows I am capitalizing on a rare opportunity to inspect statements prepared by stakeholders for presentation in a public deliberative forum. It will be seen that these four individuals — a university scientist, a representative of organized labour, a grade twelve student, and a science teacher — press the case for revising curriculum policy by stressing, to different degrees, the importance of three different curriculum emphases. The occasion of their presentation merits some explanation.

Between 1981 and 1984 the Science Council of Canada conducted a major study of Canadian science education.[14] Termed 'deliberative inquiry', the research model involved first assembling a substantial national data base on science curriculum documents, textbooks, teachers, and teaching. Then a series of deliberative conferences was held in each of the ten provinces and two territories of the country, to examine the findings and deliberate about future directions for science education in the separate educational jurisdictions. (In Canada, the responsibility and authority for educational matters rest solely with the provinces and territories.) While members of the deliberative conferences could not make *authorized* recommendations about policy, their deliberations nonetheless could not be ignored; each group consisted of influential representative stakeholders. The illustrative position statements reproduced below were presented at the Alberta deliberative conference held in

May 1983.[15] (The statements have been edited substantially for the sake of brevity, but their meaning is intact.) The first is an excerpt from the statement by a university professor in an applied science field.[16]

> We in the universities are at the receiving end of the product of schools. Each year in my faculty [Engineering] we accept 415 school graduates into our first year. We find the majority are almost illiterate both in the literary and in the scientific sense. This majority has no knowledge of calculus, of matrix algebra, of simple laws of mechanics and thermodynamics, and often even no clear understanding of such fundamental and basic things as phase equilibrium, rate processes, or Newton's laws of motion. What is more frightening, however, is that our students' ignorance of sciences is exceeded only by their total inability to speak or to write simple, concise, and precise English. In the Engineering Faculty, more than one-half of our first year students regularly fail in the university's own English proficiency tests, and more than one-third of them fail the first year. I believe the main reason for the inadequacy of our young students is that the schools have moved away from the pursuit of high academic standards.

Clearly, the curriculum emphasis being espoused by this stakeholder is Solid Foundation. The following statement, by a person representing the viewpoint of organized labour for the deliberative group, stresses Science-Technology-Decisions in a highly personal way.

> The dominant ideology in this society presupposes that the things we study, the things we deal with, are asocial, ahistorical, apolitical. The emphasis in schools then will be on hard, objective, testable information. If labour can be said to have any stance on the teaching of science, it can be said that we favour the approach that attempts to understand things in their social, historical context. And probably labor can complain that working people have suffered most from the opposite approach. The vast majority of students will join the labour force. If there is *anything* to be said about the nature of the work world they'll be joining, I suppose that it should be referred to in the teaching of science. Yet the analysis of the curriculum and the textbooks listed problems caused by advances in science such as pollution, illnesses, overpopulation, and a disturbance to the ecosystem. There was no mention of the leaks in health and safety hazards that can also be attributed to advances in science, or the sheer disruption and reorganization of the work place that can also be attributed to the advance of science. Since most students will be joining the labour force, and the working world provides the major aspects of that context, these things have to be recognized.

A viewpoint stressing Everyday Applications was presented by a highly articulate grade twelve student.

> One of the things that I would like to see changed is the lack of relevance between the theory that we're learning in our courses and the practical problems and knowledge that we need. In one of my physics classes we had just had a test about gears and things like that and how they related. Two girls walked in and said, 'I thought he was talking about something like car gears'. And yet they don't realize that the gears that were on the test paper *were* car gears — they didn't make that connection. These weren't students in the 50 to 60 per cent range; they're the ones that get 80s and 90s. I would like to see more practical experimentation within the physics program and maybe even the use of computers and that kind of thing.

The following statement by a science teacher acknowledges the importance of Science-Technology-Decisions but introduces as well a cautionary note about *balancing* curriculum emphases in the science program.

> When heroes of mine, such as David Suzuki, point out that there is such a glut of scientific knowledge now available that we cannot expose students to all of it with any realistic expectation of retention, then it does seem to indicate that there must be a change in what we're doing. Many of my colleagues would argue that the content is not really being taught for content's sake alone, but used as a vehicle to develop a number of extremely important tools including process skills and, believe it or not, to actually develop discussion skills the students have, and to make them aware of the impact of science on our society. There seems to be a real concern that students be able to discuss the interface between science and society, and be able to look at societal problems in a scientific manner. While I think this is good and certainly should be a *part* of courses, to dedicate the entire program to it is, I feel, highly questionable. Where do students get the knowledge base to discuss these at anything other than an emotional or gut level if they don't have some content that they can fall back on? I also think when you get into an area such as the values aspect of science, that you're starting to place teachers, who have been trained in a completely different manner, in a position that's a little suspect. The social studies teachers have already had some of this training. If we're going to produce students who are capable of solving societal problems from a scientific perspective, I think we've got to be able to somehow or other meld the content with the application of that content in an everyday sphere, and that's not an easy task.

To return now to the hypothetical setting of a curriculum policy advisory committee, imagine that these stakeholder positions (and others) are known to committee members (indeed some will be held by various members) who have a mandate to produce an acceptable policy statement. Clearly the statement will be a compromise, and its formulation will be accomplished by an uneasy process of deliberation, which will probably resemble trial and error more than anything else. Deliberation has received considerable attention in the curriculum literature during the past two decades; Schwab comments as follows about it.

> The method of the practical (called 'deliberation' in the loose way we call theoretic methods 'induction') is, then, not at all a linear affair proceeding step-by-step, but rather a complex, fluid transactional discipline aimed at identification of the desirable, and at either, attainment of the desired or at alteration of desires.... Deliberation is complex and arduous. It treats both ends and means and must treat them as mutually determining one another. It must try to identify, with respect to both, what facts may be relevant. It must try to ascertain the relevant facts in the concrete case. It must try to identify the desiderata in the case. It must generate alternative solutions. It must make every effort to trace the branching pathways of consequences which may flow from each alternative and affect desiderata. It must then weigh alternatives and their costs and consequences against one another, and choose, not the *right* alternative, for there is no such thing, but the *best* one.[17]

Despite the complexities of deliberation over science curriculum policy, it simplifies one's view of the process if it can be seen as a matter of arriving at a satisfactory balance among competing curriculum emphases (and, of course, a satisfying array of science topics). The balance must be tailored to the unique requirements of the particular jurisdiction for which the policy is intended, of course — there are no generic solutions to the practical problem of curriculum policy formulation.

Classroom Shaping of What Counts as Science Education: Toward Understanding Teacher Interpretations and Loyalties

Many science teachers of my acquaintance do not take science curriculum policy statements very seriously, especially the 'objectives' section of policy. (The topics tend to receive very serious attention though.) Some claim that objectives are simply 'what you hope the kids will get, sort of by osmosis', others see objectives as window dressing. Many teachers remark that when they receive a new science curriculum policy document they flip through it and then put it on the bookshelf to gather dust.

When a new authorized version of what counts as science education is released by a governmental education authority, it is usually accompanied by the authorization of particular textbooks and other teaching materials designated as supporting the policy. In the heyday of science curriculum innovation in the late 1950s and 1960s, the prestigious names of the National Science Foundation in the US and the Nuffield Foundation in the UK seem to have been enough to gather at least the tacit support of education authorities in many places for innovation of the materials in the classroom. In short, the prestige made the policy decision. So we can see a sameness, in principle, between the authorization and implementation of a new science curriculum policy and the release of new curriculum materials developed 'externally'. Both require the implementation of new policy, yet implementation of the prestigious programs in science has been examined much more than the mundane problems faced by school systems wrestling with new government curriculum policies.[18] 'The science curriculum implementation literature', then, is largely filled with studies of what happened when externally developed materials were implemented in classrooms. Welch's review gives the picture.[19]

In general, the view that shines through in all of the curriculum implementation literature is that educational innovations most frequently falter because teacher actions in the classroom are inconsistent with innovators' intentions. The same point could be made about the intentions of curriculum policy makers. In fact, let us lump innovations and policies together for purposes of discussion, under the single rubric 'curriculum proposals'. The view summarized by one of my colleagues as the 'teacher deficit image'[20] puts a negative cast on what teachers do with (or to) curriculum proposals. A more balanced view is found in an analysis by Connelly which respects the work of curriculum developers and innovators external to the classroom, on one hand, and teachers (referred to as 'user' developers) on the other. The view can readily be extended to include curriculum policy statements, not just curriculum materials developed as innovations. Connelly comments as follows:

> The function of externally based development is to elaborate theoretical conceptions of society, knowledge, teacher, and learner, and to translate these conceptions into coherent curriculum materials, each of which serves as a clear-cut alternative available to teachers.... The function of user-based development is to construct images of particular instructional settings by matching a variety of theoretical conceptions with the exigencies of these particular settings, and to

> translate these images into a curriculum-in-classroom-use.... Interpretations will be, and should be, made.[21]

Connelly notes that 'the teacher's first responsibility is to particular classroom situations, and, provided he knows what he is doing, and why, there is little reason to expect, or want, a teacher's allegiance to the goals of even the best programs'.[22] Much is packed into that statement: acknowledgement of a teacher's autonomy in dealing with the unique requirements of his or her classroom, assumptions about the level of knowledge and competence of teachers in understanding curriculum proposals, and allowance for the possibility that a teacher might understand but *reject* the orientation of a curriculum proposal.

How can we come to understand how teachers think when they interpret curriculum proposals, specifically in science education? A misfiring of the intentions of those external to the classroom can be seen to come about in two different ways. Teacher *interpretation* could be responsible, in that a teacher's image of what is required by materials or policy could be inconsistent with that of the external developer or policy maker. Teacher *loyalties*, though, could be another source of explanation — perhaps the teacher understands clearly enough what is required but actively disagrees with it and rejects it.

Unpacking the Substance of Science Education

Every science teacher has a conceptualization of appropriate science education. If we view that conceptualization as guiding the teacher's shaping of what counts as science education in the classroom, what are we to make of the arrival on the teacher's desk of some new curriculum proposal — either a new policy directive (in educational jurisdications where they are issued by governmental agencies) or some new curriculum materials (sponsored by, say, a high-prestige organization)? I would characterize what happens, perhaps simplistically, by noting that it poses two questions for a teacher.

1 What does this new curriculum proposal mean?
2 Is this new curriculum proposal appropriate for my students?

Elsewhere I have characterized the task of making sense of the demands of the first question as a matter of 'unpacking' the meaning of the new item.[23] This follows Schwab's concept that four curriculum 'commonplaces' constitute the elements of meaning of any curriculum proposal. That is, four matters can be seen to be essential, when a curriculum proposal is formulated: there will be an image (or view) of (i) the subject matter; (ii) the learner; (iii) the teacher; and (iv) the society in which the teaching occurs.[24]

Table 1: Four curriculum commonplaces inherent in seven curriculum emphases for science education

CURRICULUM EMPHASIS	VIEW OF SCIENCE	VIEW OF LEARNER	VIEW OF TEACHER	VIEW OF SOCIETY
Everyday coping	A meaning system necessary for understanding and therefore controlling everyday objects and events.	Needs to master the best explanations available for comfortable, competent explanation of natural events, and control of mechanical objects and personal affairs.	Someone who regularly explains natural and man-made objects and events by appropriate scientific principles.	Autonomous, knowledgeable individuals who can do mechanical things well, who are entrepreneurial, and who look after themselves, are highly valued members of the social order.
Structure of science	A conceptual system for explaining naturally occurring objects and events, which is cumulative and self-correcting.	One who needs an accurate understanding of how this powerful conceptual system works.	Comfortably analyzes the subject matter as a conceptual system, understands it as such, and sees the viewpoint as important.	Society needs elite, philosophically informed scientists who really understand how that conceptual system works.
Science, technology, decisions	An expression of the wish to control the environment and ourselves, intimately related to technology and increasingly related to very significant societal issues.	Needs to become an intelligent, willing decision maker who understands the scientific basis for technology, and the practical basis for defensible decisions.	One who develops both knowledge of and commitment to the complex interrelationships among science, technology, and decisions.	Society needs to keep from destroying itself by developing in the general public (and the scientists as well) a sophisticated, operational view of the way decisions are made about science-based societal problems.
Scientific skill development	Consists of the outcome of correct usage of certain physical and conceptual processes.	An increasingly competent performer with the processes.	One who encourages learners to practise at the processes in many different contexts of science subject matter.	Society needs people who approach problems with a successful arsenal of scientific tool skills.
Correct explanations	The best meaning system ever developed for getting at the truth about natural objects and events.	Someone whose preconceptions need to be replaced and corrected.	One responsible for identifying and correcting the errors in student thinking.	Society needs true believers in the meaning system most appropriate for natural objects and events.
Self as explainer	A conceptual system whose development is influenced by the ideas of the times, the conceptual principles used, and the personal intent to explain.	One who needs the intellectual freedom gained by knowing as many of the influences on scientific thought as possible.	Someone deeply committed to the concept of liberal education as exposing the grounds for what we know.	Society needs members who have had a liberal education — that is, who know where knowledge comes from.
Solid foundation	A vast and complex meaning system which takes many years to master.	An individual who wants and needs the whole of a science, eventually.	One who is responsible to winnow out the most capable potential scientists.	Society needs scientists.

45

One way to conceptualize the task, then, is to compare the teacher's understanding to that of the proposal for each of Schwab's matters in turn. For example, suppose that proponents of the proposal have built in a view of science as subject matter that is in line with the Scientific Skill Development curriculum emphasis. One is then in a position to ask, for an individual teacher: Is that view of science one the teacher understands? If not, it certainly is not going to count as science education, in that teacher's mind, as he/she thinks about carrying out the intent of the proposal.

If we examine the seven curriculum emphases, we see a different view of science inherent in each (some of the differences are greater than others). We find likewise a somewhat different image of the learner, the teacher, and the society in each. To be sure, there is a degree of consistency among these images *within* any given emphasis; that is to be expected. The resulting matrix of categories (table 1) can be used as a guide to analyze the basis for a teacher's thinking about a curriculum proposal in science. More importantly, it shows part of a significant agenda for science teacher education — especially, but not solely, for in-service education.

Teacher Loyalties and Conflict over Science Curriculum Policy

What if the hypothetical teacher mentioned above *understands* the view of science in a curriculum proposal but *actively rejects* it? Suppose that a new science curriculum policy is being proposed, with increased attention to a Science, Technology and Decisions curriculum emphasis. This is actually happening at the present time in many educational jurisdictions, of course. The impetus to incorporate 'STS', or science-technology-society, material (the same as Science-Technology-Decisions, in all important respects) into science programs has increased dramatically in the past few years. Yet consider the following comment, which I overheard from a science teacher at a recent discussion of the matter: 'That stuff isn't science, it's social studies.' His tone of voice suggested 'and I am not about to teach it.' How is one to make sense of that sentiment?

Status, loyalties and politics

One way to interpret the teacher's remark is that *status is at stake*. In the schools' pecking order, high status is associated with teaching science as a subject aligned with what Goodson calls the 'academic tradition' of subjects in the curriculum. The introduction of soft material, such as discussion of social issues, can readily be seen to threaten the academic status of science education, hence the curriculum proposal is rejected. Whether or not that interpretation is correct is determined by checking with an individual science teacher. (It could be that the teacher feels ill-prepared to teach the material, which is a different matter altogether.) Let us return to the matter of status nevertheless. Goodson writes as follows, describing how subjects came to be defined in the history of education in England.

> Since the nineteenth century 'academic subjects' and written examinations have become closely interconnected. This alliance, whether viewed as divine or malign, was formally enshrined in the School Certificate examination defined in 1917. Since that date certain material implications have followed for those sub-groups and school subjects promoting or representing the academic tradition. ... For the groups and associations promoting themselves as school subjects, and irresistibly drawn to claiming 'academic status', a central criterion has been whether the subjects' content could be tested by written examinations for an 'able' clientele. Acceptance of the criterion of examinability affects both the content and form of the knowledge presented but carries with it the guarantee of high status. The academic tradition is content-focussed and typically stresses abstract and theoretical knowledge for examination.[25]

Goodson interprets the development of support for, and loyalty to, an image of a subject in the curriculum according to some significant social and professional processes.

> The years after 1917 saw a range of significant development in the professionalisation of teachers. Increasingly with the establishment of specialised subject training courses, secondary school teachers came to see themselves as part of a 'subject community'. The associated growth of subject associations both derived from and confirmed this trend. This increasing identification of secondary teachers with subject communities tended to separate them from each other, and as schools became larger, departmental forms of organization arose which reinforced the separation.[26]

Such loyalties — the one to an academic tradition and the other to a science subject community (including a science subject professional association) — are important explanatory devices in understanding what counts as science education for teachers. Alternatives to the academic tradition are described thus by Goodson, cast in a way to make them seem definitely less palatable.

> The utilitarian tradition is conversely of low status, dealing with practical knowledge sometimes not amenable to the current 'A' level mode of written examination. Utilitarian knowledge is related to

those non-professional vocations in which the majority of people work for most of their adult life. The low status of utilitarian knowledge also applies to the personal, social and commonsense knowledge stressed by those pursuing the pedagogic tradition. Whilst all school knowledge has at least an implicit pedagogy this tradition places the 'way the child learns' as the central concern in devising subject content.[27]

Two important maxims emerge from this discussion, if one wants to promote science teacher loyalty to a science curriculum proposal: guarantee the status of the content by enshrining it in an acceptable, recognized examination, and secure the support of the subject community. Otherwise the spectre is ever present, for the teachers, that the proposal's academic status will degenerate to utilitarian and pedagogic limbo. Successful curriculum policy makers and educational innovators are well aware of the need to garner the support and loyalty of science teachers, which is quite a different matter from the need for in-service education to ensure that the teachers *understand* a new proposal.

The influence of the subject community is an especially potent force in science education. In general, the 'hero image' (as someone dubbed it) of the science teacher tends to be the scientist rather than the educator. Many school teachers of biology, chemistry, and physics have the irritating habit of referring to themselves as 'biologists', 'chemists', and 'physicists', displaying thereby a blatant disregard for (or at least astonishing insensitivity to) correct use of language, the source of their income, and the mandate of their employers. Still, there is a halfway house between the scientists and the science teachers, and it is the science teachers' professional associations. Fortunately for our understanding of teacher shaping of what counts as science education, the history and workings of at least one subject association in science education have been chronicled in some detail. In his very engaging work on that subject, Layton notes that 'a profession can be interpreted as a means of controlling an occupation, in this case of defining what counts as *teaching science*'. A portion of his history, then, is devoted to the Association for Science Education member associations' 'activities in the curriculum field, their advocacy of particular versions of school science and of the ways they have attempted to ensure adoption of their point of view'.[28] Layton's work is a penetrating and highly valuable account, for understanding teacher loyalties and school science politics.

Science teachers' loyalties and curriculum emphases

It is easy enough to see that the curriculum emphases which have emerged in science education can be categorized according to the three traditions described by Goodson. Solid Foundation, Correct Explanations, Nature of Science and Scientific Skill Development all fit the academic tradition, while Everyday Coping fits the utilitarian tradition, and Self as Explainer and Science-Technology-Decisions (both with a heavier emphasis on the learner than on the subject) fit the pedagogic tradition. Given the intense, almost fierce, affiliation to an academic tradition which school science teaching tends to show, one would hypothesize that science curriculum policies promoting the first four emphases would be more likely to command science teachers' loyalties than would the other three. Layton captures the point nicely when, he thus describes the Nuffield projects in England.

> They round off just over a century of science education in which the emphasis has been placed in varying degrees on the achievement of two broad objectives — first, an understanding of the conceptual structures of science, science as a body of knowledge, and second, an understanding of the procedures of science, science as a process.... The balance between the two objectives has varied from time to time, but the emphasis has been unwaveringly on an understanding of science in its internal disciplinary aspects, its vocabulary, grammar, syntax and literature.... What school science has so far failed to establish as a worthwhile objective is the importance of an understanding of science in its external relations, of the nature of the science-society interface, ... an understanding of science in its external relations with technology and society.[29]

It would be hazardous to try to predict whether an individual science teacher would or would not see as worthwhile the objectives inherent in such curriculum emphases as Everyday Coping or Science-Technology Decisions. The point is that the work of both Layton and Goodson gives one a way to understand the dynamics of how teacher loyalties influence their shaping of what counts as science education in the classroom. Conflict over, or the distortion that occurs in the implementation of science curriculum policy or other curriculum innovations can thus be analyzed from this point of view, as well as from the point of view which considers how teachers actually interpret what a curriculum proposal means.

Concluding Remarks

This chapter began with the question 'What counts as science education?' — not to provide an answer, but rather with a view to making sense of an exceedingly complex professional activity. In any democratic society the expression of preferences about what counts as science education is a right of the people. They are legitimated stakeholders. At the same time science teachers are both stakeholders and final arbitrators by virtue of their interpretations, their loyalties, and their actions in the classroom. If one views the matter of shaping what counts as science education from that perspective, some conclusions emerge from the discussion in this chapter.

First, it should be abundantly clear that no single individual, no matter how 'expert', has the answer to the question 'What counts as science education?' — not because no one is smart enough, but because the question has a socially determined answer rather than one theoretically or academically determined. Hence all attempts to answer such a question by research alone, or by stakeholders who share only one opinion, are futile.

Second, the pessimism expressed so frequently about the fate of innovations in science education might be a bit more understandable. Innovations which have succeeded in crashing through the science classroom door are those which have commanded teacher loyalty, for whatever reason. If what showed up in the classroom did not match the innovators' intentions, that should now be no surprise — given the range of curriculum emphases (and therefore the potentially large number of teacher interpretations) which science education has seen in the past eighty-five years. Among the most promising recent developments in educational research, for understanding teacher interpretation as discussed here, is the work on teacher thought processes, reviewed recently by Clark and Peterson.[30] Most of that research is decontextualized from individual subjects, but the methodologies would be helpful guides for understanding science teacher interpretation were they to be employed specifically in the context of school science.

Finally, of course there are, inevitably, implications for science teacher education. In the light of what has been presented in this chapter, it is appropriate to comment on the difference between educating a science teacher and winning an ideological convert — a 'gun-slinger', as one of my colleagues says. In all likelihood, every science teacher preparation program and in-service education program delivers a message about what counts as science education, and the chief delivery person is the professor of science education. Far too often, in my experience, the message is dogmatic and is presented (perhaps subtly, perhaps overtly) in a doctrinaire fashion: 'science education is the processes of enquiry', or 'science education must foster an understanding of science in a social context', or even 'science education is the promotion of (some brand of) scientific literacy'. These are statements of *individual ideological preference* of professors of science education, and they indoctrinate science teachers into believing that what counts as science education is the ideology of a single curriculum emphasis (or perhaps a few emphases). Whenever this happens, science teachers are not being taught how to do a sophisticated job of shaping what counts as science education. They are being presented with an oversimplified view of the question with which this chapter started, to an extent that makes a mockery out of the science teacher's professional autonomy. At the very least, teachers deserve to be taught that different curriculum emphases are possible, and that a particular view of what counts as science education (whoever holds or presents it) has been selected (by that person, albeit a professor of science education) from an array of alternatives.

One of the most promising recent developments for rethinking the problem of ideological indoctrination is the effort to articulate and legitimate a calculus of practical thought as it occurs in professional work. Schön has called it 'reflection-in-action' and, although his work concentrates on professionals other than teachers, it can be applied readily to science teacher education.[31] Connelly's approach, in the 'Personal, Practical Knowledge Project', has been directly focussed on teaching.[32] What is so valuable about a calculus of practical thought is that it demonstrates clearly for those involved in science teacher education that ideological indoctrination is patently inappropriate. That is, teachers have to think in very complex ways about science teaching and science curriculum proposals. Doctrinaire science teacher education will not do the trick, and it is high time the word got out.

Notes

1 From ALBERTA EDUCATION (1978) *Program of Studies for Senior High Schools*, Edmonton, Government Printer, pp. 191–2.

2 See SCHWAB, J.J. (1962) 'The teaching of science as enquiry' in SCHWAB, J.J. and BRANDWEIN, P.F. (Eds) *The Teaching of Science*, Cambridge, MA, Harvard University Press, p. 45.

3 For elaboration on this analysis, see ORPWOOD, G. and ROBERTS, D. (1980) 'Curriculum emphases in science education III: The analysis of textbooks', *The Crucible*, 11, 3, May, pp. 36–9. (*The Crucible* is the journal of the Science Teachers Association of Ontario.)

4 By saying that seven can be found (not six, nor eight) I realize that I am opening up a debatable question about conceptualizing and categorizing just what constitutes a curriculum emphasis in science education. For purposes of using the concept, however, this really is unimportant. To review the basis for claiming that seven can be found, see ROBERTS, D.A. (1982) 'Developing the concept of "Curriculum emphases" in science education', *Science Education*, 66, 2, pp. 243–60.

5 BOWERS, H. and SHEANE, G.K. (1939) *Experiences in General Science: An Introductory Study of Our Environment*, Toronto, J.M. Dent and Sons (Canada) Ltd., pp. 134–5.

6 PIMENTEL, G.C. (Ed) (1963) *Chemistry: An Experimental Science*, 4th edn, San Francisco, CA, Chemical Education Material Study and W.H. Freeman and Co., p. 236.

7 GORDON, G. and ZOLLER, U. (1975) *Chemistry in Modern Perspective*, Don Mills, Ontario, Addison-Wesley Publishing Co., pp. 253–4. Other examples of this

emphasis include the 'SISCON' materials: see ADDINELL, S. and SOLOMON, J. (Eds) (1963) *Science in a Social Context Teacher's Guide* (and student manuals as well), Hatfield, Hertfordshire, Association for Science Education; and LEWIS, J.L. (Project Director) (1981) *Science in Society Teacher's Guide* (and student manuals as well), London, Heinemann Educational Books Ltd. Information about the emphasis itself is presented eloquently in AIKENHEAD, G.S. (1980) *Science in Social Issues: Implications for Teaching* (A Discussion Paper), Ottawa, Science Council of Canada.

8 ANDREWS, W.A. (Ed) (1980) *Biological Science: An Introductory Study*, Scarborough, Ontario, Prentice-Hall of Canada Inc., p. 36.

9 LANG, H.M. and SPEED, F.M. (1962) *Basic General Science, Book 2*, Toronto, The Macmillan Co. of Canada Ltd., p. 244.

10 PAUL, D. *et al.* (1973) *Motion in the Heavens*, Toronto, Holt, Rinehart and Winston of Canada Ltd., pp. 31–2. This is Unit 2 in the series 'Physics: A Human Endeavour'; adapted for Canadian use from the Harvard Project Physics course. For another example of this curriculum emphasis, see materials published by Connelly and his associates in the Patterns of Enquiry Project, notably PALMER, W. and DIENES, B. (1972) *Honey Bee Communication: An Enquiry into Two Conceptions of Animal Behavior*, Toronto, OISE Press.

11 HELLER, R.L. *et al.* (1979) *Challenges to Science: Earth Science* (Teacher's Edn), Toronto, Webster Division, McGraw-Hill Book Company, p. 67.

12 A curriculum emphasis ought be 'watered down' by inclusion of other curriculum emphases. To illustrate the point and the need for consistency of curriculum emphasis throughout a unit of study, a set of three alternative approaches to teaching the same science topics has been developed to show the topics embedded in three different curriculum emphases. See ROBERTS, D.A. and ORPWOOD, G.W.F (1979) *Properties of Matter: A Teacher's Guide to Alternative Versions*, Toronto, OISE Press.

13 ROWELL, P.M. and GASKELL, P.J. (1987) 'Tensions and realignments: School physics in British Columbia 1955–80' in GOODSON, I. (Ed), *International Perspectives in Curriculum History*, Beckenham, Croom Helm Ltd.

14 For published accounts of the study, see ORPWOOD, G.W.F. (1985) 'Toward the renewal of Canadian science education: I. Deliberative inquiry model', *Science Education*, 69, 4, pp. 477–90; and ORPWOOD, G.W.F. and SOUQUE, J. (1985) 'Toward the renewal of Canadian science education: II. Findings and recommendations', *Science Education*, 69, 5, pp. 625–36. The actual results of the study are found in one volume presenting conclusions and recommendations, namely SCIENCE COUNCIL OF CANADA (1984) *Science for Every Student: Educating Canadians for Tomorrow's World*, Ottawa, Supply and Services Canada; and three background volumes presenting the findings: ORPWOOD, G.W.F. and SOUQUE, J-P. (1984) *Science Education in Canadian Schools I* (Introduction and Curriculum Analyses), Ottawa, Supply and Services Canada; ORPWOOD, G.W.F. and ALAM, I. (1984) *Science Education in Canadian Schools II* (Statistical Database), Ottawa, Supply and Services Canada; and OLSON, J. and RUSSELL, T.L. (1984) *Science Education in Canadian Schools III* (Case Studies), Ottawa, Supply and Services Canada.

15 The public record of the conference is NAY, M.A. and GAY, G. (1984) *Choosing*

Our Future: Proceedings of the Alberta Deliberative Conference on Science Education, May 1983, Edmonton, University of Alberta Department of Secondary Education.

16 Some of these position statements were used as data for a presentation at the Fifty-seventh Annual Meeting of the National Association for Research in Science Teaching, New Orleans, 1984: ROBERTS, D.A. and CHASTKO, A.M. 'Who speaks for what and why? Analyzing curriculum policy debate related to science education'.

17 SCHWAB, J. (1978) 'The practical: A language for curriculum' in WESTBURY, I. and WILKOF, N.J. (Eds) *Joseph J. Schwab: Science, Curriculum, and Liberal Education*, Chicago, University of Chicago Press, pp. 291 and 318–19. (This piece was published in two other places prior to its appearance in this festschrift for Schwab.)

18 For a sensitive and thorough analysis of a school system's work in implementing policy, see CHASTKO, A.M. (1986) *Translating Science Curriculum Policy into School Program*, PhD thesis, Calgary, Alberta, University of Calgary.

19 WELCH, W. (1979) 'Twenty years of science curriculum development: A look back' in BERLINER, D.C (Ed) *Review of Research in Education*, 7, Washington, DC, American Educational Research Association, pp. 282–308.

20 See FRITZ, J.O. (1981) 'The teacher in curriculum reform' in LEITHWOOD, K. and HUGHES, A. (Eds) *Curriculum Canada III*, Vancouver, Centre for the Study of Curriculum and Instruction, University of British Columbia, p. 113.

21 CONNELLY, F.M. (1972) 'The functions of curriculum development', *Interchange*, 3, 2–3, pp. 168–9.

22 *Ibid.*, p. 169.

23 See ROBERTS, D.A. (1980) 'Theory, curriculum development, and the unique events of practice' in MUNBY, H. *et al.*, (Eds) *See Curriculum in a New Light: Essays from Science Education*, Toronto, OISE Press (republished in 1984 by the University Press of America).

24 Schwab has discussed these in several of his published works. One of the most informative treatments is found in his 'The teaching of science as enquiry' (*op. cit.*), pp. 31–41.

25 GOODSON, I.F. (1987) *School Subjects and Curriculum Change*, Lewes, Falmer Press, p. 27.

26 *Ibid.*, pp. 32–3.

27 *Ibid.*, p. 27.

28 LAYTON, D. (1984) *Interpreters of Science: A History of the Association for Science Education*, Hatfield, Hertfordshire, Association for Science Education, p. vii.

29 LAYTON, D. (1972) 'Science as general education', *Trends in Education*, 25, p. 12. Layton's analysis and documentation of the development of science education in England during that period certainly confirms his comment, and also sheds a great deal of light on the way teachers shape what counts as science education: (1973) *Science for the People*, London, George Allen and Unwin Ltd.

30 CLARK, C.M. and PETERSON, P.L. (1986) 'Teachers' thought processes' in WITTROCK, M. (Ed) *Handbook of Research on Teaching*, 3rd edn (American Educational Research Association), New York, Macmillan Co., pp. 255–96.

31 See SCHÖN, D.A. (1983) *The Reflective Practitioner*, New York, Basic Books, Inc.;

and SCHÖN, D.A. (1987) *Educating the Reflective Practitioner*, San Francisco, CA, Jossey-Bass Inc. For application of Schön's work to science teacher education, see MACKINNON, A.M. (1985) *Detecting Reflection-in-Action among Preservice Teachers Enrolled in an Elementary Science Methods Course*, MSc thesis, Calgary, Alberta, University of Calgary (ERIC accession no. ED 274 521); and ROBERTS, D.A. and CHASTKO, A.M. (1986) 'Absorption, refraction, reflection: Beginning education students think about science teaching', paper presented at the annual meeting of the American Educational Research Association, San Francisco, April.

32 Among the many publications of this project, one which might interest science educators the most is CONNELLY, F.M. and CLANDININ, D.J. (1986) 'On narrative method, personal philosophy and narrative unities in the study of teaching', *Journal of Research in Science Teaching*, 23, 4, pp. 293–310.

3
Teachers in Science Education

John R. Baird

Introduction

This chapter is predicated on the belief that research and development efforts in science education over the last few decades have had disappointingly little influence on science teachers and science teaching. While the arguments I shall present below do not provide conclusive evidence for this belief, they do indicate some limitations of previous work. They also highlight a research perspective which I believe has the potential to redress this situation. The boundaries of argument are not limited to science education. While the teaching and learning of science do pose particular problems, these problems in other senses are subsumed within more general considerations concerning the nature and process of teaching and learning. Thus, I shall first allude to these more general considerations and then, in later sections, set them within the science context.

A central consideration is related to our lack of understanding of what teaching is, and how it works. While the nature and process of teaching in a generic sense remains a matter of debate (for example, Fenstermacher, 1986), what constitutes 'good' (whether meaning 'morally defensible' or 'successful') teaching must remain even more problematic and ephemeral. For example, what constitutes 'good' or 'successful' teaching may change with the content of the classroom and context, and with changes in society and its mores. Uncertainty in the meaning of teaching, and of 'good' (in its successful meaning) teaching, will now be considered.

Teaching often assumes its meaning through definition of the tasks involved. For example, Fenstermacher (*ibid.*) lists the tasks of

instructing the learner on the procedures and demands of the student-ing role, selecting the material to be learned, adapting that material so that it is appropriate to the level of the learner, constructing the most appropriate set of opportunities for the learner to gain access to the content ..., monitoring and appraising the student's progress, and serving the learner as one of the primary sources of knowledge and skill. (pp. 39–40)

Even these generally acknowledged tasks of teaching can be interpreted differently by people with different perspectives regarding teaching. However, Fenstermacher argues that, by stating the tasks in these terms, an emphasis is given to the effect of teaching on the learner's behaviours (i.e., a task sense of learning), rather than on the acquisition of content (i.e., an achievement sense of learning). This perspective is useful for defining limits of accountability for teaching. It reminds us that teachers have a primary responsibility to train their learners *how* to learn.

The perspective also relates to recent moves in educational research on teaching and learning towards a greater emphasis on *process* and a greater acknowledgement of the importance of *context*. These moves are associated with what Biddle and Anderson (1986) describe as a shift from the 'confirmatory' to the 'discovery' approach. This dichotomy in approach has been described alternatively as positivistic/interpretive (Erickson, 1986) or, less satisfactorily, as quantitative/qualitative (Fenstermacher, 1986). To contrast these approaches, let us consider 'good' (meaning 'successful') teaching in the context of the traditional (but spurious) axiom 'good teaching results in good learning'. This rule causally links good teaching and good learning across time, content and context. Using a confirmatory perspective, this rule is tested through the study of the relationship between posited exemplars of the independent variable, 'good teaching' and the dependent variable, 'good learning'. For example, the extent of covariation between 'wait-time' (the interval between the teacher's question and a typical student's response) and students' achievement scores may be examined. Or, alternatively, the extent of causality of the relationship may be investigated through a controlled experiment linking achievement to manipulation of the wait-time interval. Thus, researchers with a confirmatory perspective ask such research questions as 'what is the effect of increased wait-time on student achievement?', and ensure that variation due to individual differences, content and context is controlled as much as possible.

On the other hand researchers with a discovery perspective have different interests, and ask different questions. They are more interested in meanings and mechanisms, rather than the lawful nature of relationships. They are concerned to find the meaning of wait-time, and how it operates for the individuals within the particular classroom context. They ask questions such as 'How do these learners interpret an increase in wait-time?' and 'How does increased wait-time influence the learning decisions they make?'. The emphasis on individuals and the meanings they ascribe to a variable such as wait-time bears on the process of learning, which renders some other variables, such as achievement score (divorced in time and context from the studied instances of wait-time) less relevant for study. The emphasis on individuals and the meanings they ascribe also requires that researchers adopt a more holistic approach, where features of the individual and of the classroom, school and societal context are all taken together to seek understanding of decisions made and behaviours exhibited. Indeed, the very nature and meaning of 'good' teaching appears to be dependent on such contextual features. For example, the criteria for 'good' teaching have been shown to differ with the classroom content (for example, Evertson, Anderson, Anderson and Brophy, 1980).

While numerous research questions may be appropriate and productively pursued through a confirmatory perspective, some shortcomings of this type of research have emerged. One shortcoming is that general rules, free of content and context, seem often not to work well for the practitioners — the teachers and students. This is because these rules, by eschewing the particularities of the individuals involved, and of the social mores and dynamics of the classroom context, do little to foster the participants' understanding of how to operate effectively in their classroom. As Easley (1982) says, teachers 'need something else besides predictions; they need to understand what is happening ... so that they can change their role in the social interaction to get better results' (p. 192). Indeed, as Erickson (1986) argues, 'prediction and control, in the tradition of natural science, is not possible in systems of relations where cause is mediated by systems of symbols' (p. 127). By symbols, he means the meanings and interpretations that are placed by the individuals involved on the actions and events they share together.

A related shortcoming stems from uncertainties associated with broad general relationships, that tend to transform behaviours into personal attributes. For example, various teaching behaviours have been classified within two contrasting teaching styles, called Transmission or Interpretation (Barnes, 1976). Where interpretative teaching subsumes behaviours which encourage students' active participation in the lesson through question-asking and discussion, transmissive teaching involves behaviours which limit lesson activities largely to one-way information transfer from teacher to students. Having reduced a complex range of teaching behaviours to such a categorical dichotomy, the danger is that the teacher may be similarly categorized (for example, Gardner, Gray and Taylor, 1981). Thus, 'Mr Watson is an interpretative teacher'. The argument to justify this translation from behaviour to personal attribute is that a teacher holds certain consistent theories, values and beliefs regarding teaching and learning which are exhibited as a predictable predilection towards one style or the other.

As with many categorizations, simplification is accompanied by loss of meaning. We simplify the reality of the mass of seemingly incomprehensible detail (for example, teacher behaviours; teacher-student interactions) by ascribing causes for it (for example, teaching styles; teacher attributes). We then work with our interpretations of the reality as if they are the reality itself. The need to maintain this distinction is emphasized by researchers with a discovery perspective. They view the uniformity in social interaction which precedes such categorization differently — 'the behavioural uniformity from day to day that can be observed for an individual, and among individuals in groups, is seen ... as an illusion — a social construction akin to the illusion of assessed ability as an attribute of the person assessed ... once a child is assessed as having low ability, we assume not only that the entity *low ability* actually exists, but that it is actually an attribute of that child' (Erickson, 1986, p. 126). Again, the abstraction of reality that goes with a confirmatory perspective moves the focus of research or action from the centre to the periphery. For example, it has recently been argued that the appropriate action in the classroom to implement the change in societal mores from the individual expression/social egalitarianism of the 1960s and 1970s to the 'back to the basics' movement of the 1980s is to exhort teachers to change behaviours from those characterizing interpretative teaching to those of transmissive teaching. However, such changes will not work as well as desired, simply because manipulation of categories of effect, without proper understanding of the factors which influence them or their mechanisms of operation, is a mechanistic and reactive response to a complex situation rather than an imaginative and active one.

Successful teaching is a complex activity which requires the teacher to select from the diversity of possible strategies and actions the ones most appropriate for his/her existing classroom conditions. We need to do more to assist the teacher in this decision making process by discovering information from classroom situations which fosters understanding of the nature and meanings of the factors involved. Only when we have achieved sufficient insights into meanings and mechanisms should we attempt to induce either theory (by ascribing relations and laws) or rules-for-action. Perhaps if such a point is reached, it may be appropriate to test such theories through confirmatory research, and cycles of discovery and confirmation can recur.

In this chapter, I shall consider some of what is known about some factors which influence teachers and teaching. These factors will be grouped under the headings *The teacher and teaching*, *The learner and learning*, *Conditions under which teaching and learning occur* and *Teacher education*. In fact, it is to the factors under the first heading that particular emphasis will be given and, where possible, findings from the context of science education will be given. Finally, I shall suggest some implications of the findings for teachers, teaching, and the curriculum, and present some recommendations regarding the type of research required and the management of the process of teacher change.

The Teacher and Teaching

Given that teaching is done by individuals, with their unique collections of thoughts, beliefs, aspirations, values, concerns, perceptions and abilities, it is surprising that so little research has been directed to what teaching means to individual teachers and how they describe how they go about it.

I shall consider below the wide range of personal attributes which can influence teaching performance. In so doing, I shall introduce two terms — *intellectual competence* and *intellectual performance*. Use of these terms emphasizes the interrelatedness in meaning and function of the various attributes involved, and thus supports the need for a holistic approach to research on them.

Teacher Intellectual Competence

I define *intellectual competence* as comprising four major components: Attitudes (including values and concerns); Perceptions (including expectations); Conceptions (including theories and beliefs); and Abilities. As an example, let us consider a teacher's intellectual competence in relation to the issue of negotiated curriculum (i.e., a curriculum in which teachers and their students share together responsibilities for planning and undertaking some significant aspects of the teaching and learning). Our teacher may hold certain *attitudes* to (or assign particular values to, or take a particular stance regarding) a negotiated curriculum. It is likely that these attitudes would be consistent with related attitudes to such things as the appropriate classroom roles of teachers and students, the professional responsibilities of teachers, and the desirable aims of schooling. Whatever these attitudes, they will be closely related to his or her *perceptions* of what a negotiated curriculum would look like in practice, and of the manner in which it would operate. In turn, these attitudes and perceptions both influence and are influenced by the person's *conceptions* of the nature and meaning of such terms as 'negotiation' and 'curriculum'. Finally, each of the three components so far described would interact with the *abilities* our teacher has such as his/her perceptiveness, logical thinking, capacity to determine and reflect on the needs of others, and so on.

It is reasonable to assume that this composite and complex intellectual competence will influence the subsequent *intellectual performance* of our teacher as he/she engages in an attempt to negotiate the curriculum in practice. Intellectual performance, like intellectual competence, is not a simple unitary thing for it also includes a number of components, such as specific attitudinal states, perceptions, decisions and behaviours that are all associated with the tasks of teaching.

Given that a teacher's intellectual performance has an important influence on classroom activities and student behaviours, and thus on the learning that results from teaching, it is unfortunate that so little research has been done on the non-behavioural components of teachers' intellectual performance. Even less research has been directed to the relationships between components of teachers' intellectual competence and their intellectual performance. Much research has, however, been done on the behavioural components. This is the 'process-product' research which blossomed in the later 1960s and early 1970s (Dunkin and Biddle, 1974). Process-product research is firmly grounded in the confirmatory perspective discussed above. It centres on the systematic observation of classroom processes according to predetermined categories of behaviour. Behaviours were initially correlated with, and later experimentally manipulated in terms of, characteristics of the teacher (presage variables), characteristics of the students, school or community (context variables), or evidence of student learning and growth (product variables). A major thrust of process-product research was on 'teacher effectiveness', which linked generalized teacher classroom behaviours to generalized student achievement on standardized assessments (Shulman, 1986). The first sort of wait-time studies described above is an example of research in this tradition. By focusing on behaviours, process-product research ignores the individuality of the teacher decisions which give rise to behaviours, and the influence that teachers' attitudes, perceptions, conceptions and abilities have on these decisions.

I shall now review some research that does relate in a broader way to first the intellectual competence and then the intellectual performance of teachers.

Teacher intellectual competence: attitudes and perceptions

With a few exceptions much of the research on science-related attitudes of teachers has been set within the process-product framework, where various scales, instruments, and inventories, aiming to measure attitudes to science, science pedagogy, and scientists, are completed individually but resultant data are processed in groups. Some of the research has sought to relate such attitudes to teachers' classroom activities and student achievement, but often there have been mixed results (for example, Power and Tisher, 1973).

Some other sorts of studies suggest that teacher's science-related attitudes are vague and confused (for example, Schibeci, 1980), that primary teachers especially lack confidence in science pedagogy (for example, Osborne and Biddulph, 1985), and that teacher attitudes to some particular science topics (for example, energy, Kirkwood, Carr and McChesney, 1986) have been found to be particularly negative.

Research on perceptions of scientists, or of self in the science classroom, has almost never concentrated on the practising teacher as subject. The self-report scales or inventories which have been adapted or designed for the contexts of science have been directed primarily at students, and again, their data have almost always been analyzed according to grouped responses rather than individually.

A line of research which has, however, been directed to teachers, and which preserves the individuality of response, has been that on the notion of teacher concerns. As a result of the work like that of Fuller (1969), such teacher concerns have been used as a focus for structuring both pre-service programmes for teachers and in-service support for innovations they have been expected to implement. Teachers have a wide variety of concerns regarding their teaching. These concerns have been viewed by some researchers as relating to the three levels of self (for example, sense of adequacy as a teacher), task (for example, availability of instructional materials) and impact (for example, the effect of teaching on each student). They argue that teacher change is a process of the individual sequentially addressing and surmounting her/his concerns at each of these three levels.

Teacher intellectual competence: conceptions

Only during the last few years has research begun on practising teachers' conceptions (that is, their theories and pedagogical beliefs) regarding particular content or subject matter. Recent studies, for example, of teachers' conceptions of energy in New Zealand (Kirkwood, Carr and McChesney, 1986) and in Australia (Arzi, White and Fensham, 1987) indicate that this topic is not well understood. Much more research on teachers' conceptions (and particularly on belief aspects) of this sort of content topic needs to be done if we are to understand the ways that teachers' understanding of content can influence their intellectual performance during lesson planning and their subsequent classroom interactions with students.

Similarly, teachers hold a wide range of implicit theories and beliefs about teaching and learning. Clark and Peterson (1986) reviewed some recent research which has studied teachers' theories and beliefs regarding curricula, their role as a teacher, and the principles upon which they seek to explain their classroom behaviours. Perhaps the most promising of the research reviewed was that on teachers' theories and beliefs about the attributions they hold for the causes of student performance. The evidence suggests that these beliefs strongly influence how teachers perceive student behaviour in the classroom, and how they interact with particular students (for example, the number of interactions and the type and pattern of reward and punishment).

Teacher intellectual competence: abilities

It appears increasingly unlikely that there are any simple, general teaching abilities or competencies which apply to all subjects, grade levels, and contexts. However, certain teacher attributes are considered by students to be associated with good teaching (for example, Wittrock, 1986). These attributes relate to the establishment of positive interpersonal relations (for example, friendly, fair, tolerant, supportive) and of respect (for example, orderly, competent, firm).

As discussed above, there has been a tendency to subsume patterns of classroom behaviours within notions of teaching style and then to transform these notions into stable personal attributes or abilities. (There is a similar tendency regarding learning styles and students.) Furthermore, some researchers have sought to distinguish 'types' of teachers using such bases as age, teaching discipline, or level of teaching. For example, Fuller and Brown (1975) distinguished primary teachers from secondary teachers being 'warmer, more hopeful, more supportive, and less critical ... more exhibitionistic, more orderly, more dependent, less bright, and more consistent in their views ... more directive and teacher-centred' (p. 28). On the other hand, recent discovery-type (interpretive) research, by highlighting the complexity of the individual, interpersonal, content, and contextual influences on teaching and learning, has challenged the meaningfulness, significance, and predictive power of such gross categorizations.

Teacher Intellectual Performance

The vast majority of research on teachers' planning and teaching has been directed to overt behaviours. Little research has described the attitudes, perceptions and decisions they associate with these behaviours. Accordingly, I shall consider teacher behaviours first, and then move to teacher thoughts and decisions.

Teacher intellectual performance: behaviours

Much of the research on interaction patterns in science classrooms has been within the process-product model. The data have been obtained according to predetermined scales or categories either directly, through classroom observation, or indirectly, from teachers' perceptions. A wide variety of findings have come from such studies, but it is a variety which seems not to illuminate practice much further than to 'highlight the complexity of science-learning environments' (White and Tisher, 1986, p. 877).

A popular focus for these studies has been teacher questioning, particularly the effects of cognitive level of questions and of wait-time on student learning outcomes. Manipulation of these two variables has had varied effects in different studies, probably because of the wide differences among them in types of participant, context and procedures. A not surprising and consistent result is that increased length, complexity and comprehensiveness of student answer accompanies an increase in teacher wait-time. However, White and Tisher point out that student attitudes, perceptions and achievement do not necessarily show concomitant improvements. The sought-after simple, general, linear relationships remain elusive or do not exist. As I argued above, what is required is research which reveals the significance and meanings that both the teachers and their students ascribe to wait-time.

Teacher intellectual performance: thoughts

Even though it is well recognized that 'teachers' behaviour is guided by their thoughts, judgements and decisions' (Shavelson, 1983, p. 393), research on teacher thoughts is very recent. It also still lacks the complexity and subtlety of method of research that has occurred on student thoughts.

In the process-product tradition, teachers' thought and decisions have often been treated simply as processes that precede their behaviours. The behaviours of interest have been predominantly the classroom-management type, and the thoughts studied are those associated with such behaviours (see Shulman, 1986). Thus, for lesson planning, research has centred on teachers' thoughts and decisions regarding the nature and extent of planning, and the emphasis they give to objectives, content, activities, student characteristics, and so on.

No substantive research has been done to link a teacher's intellectual performance in planning a lesson to her/his intellectual performance during teaching. In fact, little research has been done on teachers' classroom thoughts and decisions beyond the use of such methods as stimulated recall to assign teachers' statements to predetermined response categories in the process-product tradition. The object of most of the research which has been done has been to categorize the content of teachers' thoughts, the nature and frequency of teachers' decisions, and the classroom antecedents of these decisions. In their review of this research, Clark and Peterson (1986) argue that, because the research has been based on the mistaken assumption that the primary determinant of teachers' decisions is student behaviour, it has been too limited in scope. They believe that more descriptive research on teachers' decisions is necessary, in order to understand more about what they mean and how they come to be made. For example, in relation to teachers' attributions for the causes of student performance, mentioned earlier, they make the point that there have been 'no studies that have investigated the relationship between teachers' attributions and teachers' planning, or between teachers' attributions and teachers' interactive thoughts and decisions' (p. 285). This is but one of many areas where research is needed to understand the associations that exist between teacher cognition and action.

The Learner and Learning

The arguments presented above regarding the need for attention to the different components of teachers' intellectual competence and performance hold equally true for learners, and more research has been done on their science attitudes, perceptions, conceptions, decisions and abilities.

As the science learner is considered in detail elsewhere in this book, I will simply underline two aspects of their learning as ones that I regard as in need of urgent research. The idea of context as an influence on the intellectual performance of learners in science needs to be considered in both its school meanings and its various out of school, societal meanings.

The second aspect relates to integrating the process and content of science learning. Much has been learned recently about learners' existing conceptions in the subject matter of the sciences. However, less is known about the process by which conceptual change occurs during learning. A useful focus for relating content and process may be metacognition (Baird, in press). Metacognition refers to the knowledge, awareness and control of one's own learning. It subsumes various aspects of intellectual competence and performance, such as conceptions of the nature of learning and teaching (metacognitive 'knowledge'), perceptions of the nature, purpose and progress of the current learning task ('awareness'), and the decisions made and behaviour exhibited while managing the task ('control').

Conditions under Which Teaching and Learning Occur

The science curriculum is central to the conditions of teaching and learning. The nature of a curriculum can be viewed according to two contrasting stereotypes (White and Tisher, 1986). The first stereotype is the one that was dominant in the 1950s and 1960s. It is a large, discipline-based package designed principally by subject-matter experts (for example, PSSC, Chem Study). The treatment of content is 'academic' and often not closely allied to contemporary societal issues. The teachers' job is mainly to follow the sequence set down in the textbook or printed materials. A contrasting stereotype emerged in the 1970s. It is characterized by a more integrated syllabus, more modular organization, more flexible presentation, and more attention to societal issues. Curricula which exhibit features of this stereotype include Science 5-13, SCIS, and the Australian Science Education Project — ASEP. This stereotype places greater demands on the classroom teacher, particularly in relation to selection of sequence and modes of presentation appropriate to the students' needs, and in classroom organization and management. With few exceptions, however, teacher training and support for implementation of either sort of curriculum has been inadequate. The training is patchy, of short duration, and removed from the teacher's classroom context.

Research has demonstrated that teachers modify or 'domesticate' the intentions of curriculum developers, so that they are brought into line with the teacher's implicit beliefs about effective teaching (for example, Olson, 1981; Tisher and Power, 1975). For many science curricula, it seems that the further in time we get from their conception — still in many instances the early to middle 1970s — the greater the disparity between the rationale and the reality. This is true, for example, of two of the most significant Australian science curricula of the 1970s — the Australian adaptation of BSCS Biology and ASEP. The former package, called the Web of Life, sits more towards the first stereotype above. Both these curricular packages were introduced with high levels of enthusiasm, emanating largely from the writers and developers, many of whom were experienced teachers. Some teacher in-service was provided to raise awareness and facilitate implementation. However, both these science curricula are now suffering from the stagnation which accompanies lack of new content and ideas and of continued adequate teacher support. The crucial issue is not the curricula *per se*, but the lack of a teacher development priority in the current funding of Australia's education system.

Any curriculum can only be as good as the teachers which implement it. This is true whether its intentions are expressed in a package of materials as above, or in new ways of planning and conducting teaching and learning and assessment. Furthermore, a number of recent trends in notions of curriculum in a number of countries, such as school-based curriculum and assessment, and more particularly a *negotiated curriculum* and *goal-based assessment*, place quite new demands on teacher time and expertise. In these situations teachers can only be as good as the training, support and time for development given to them allow them to be.

Teacher Education

Knowledge and techniques considered necessary to 'survive' in the classroom are often an overwhelming component of pre-service training of teachers. In-service programmes likewise often centre simply on exposing teachers to new techniques or the related points of view which are considered important for the implementation of a fashionable curriculum or policy.

Insufficient acknowledgement has been given to the personal intellectual development necessary for teachers to improve their teaching standard or to change their pedagogical direction. Long-term teacher change is a demanding and complex process requiring change in all of the components of intellectual competence (attitudes, perceptions, conceptions, and beliefs) (for example, Baird, 1984 and 1986a; Fullan, 1985). This change requires appropriate experiences, opportunities for the teacher to reflect on practice, and protracted support for the teacher during the uncertain and disequilibrating change process. Short-term programmes which are essentially forums for transmission of information or techniques, which are removed from the school context, and which provide little or no subsequent on-the-job support, run counter to the fundamental personal requirements for the change process. The research on teacher concerns mentioned earlier provides a useful frame for appreciating one aspect of this process. It seems reasonable, for example, that pre-service teacher programmes should accommodate student teachers' concerns at the levels of 'self' and 'task' early in the programme. However, it is insufficient to limit the programme, even relatively early on, to these two levels of concern to the exclusion of the 'impact' level because the levels are interdependent. For example, a student teacher may only surmount task concerns related to inadequate class control after having attended to the impact concerns about the interest and comprehensibility of the material for the students. Attention to these impact concerns may enhance teachers' perceptions of classroom events, and thus their subsequent attitudes, conceptions and behaviours. In the same way, effective adoption of new curricula by practising teachers requires that the in-service support given to them addresses, in a coordinated and continuing fashion, the differing levels of concern and the needs that arise throughout the adoption process.

A recent trend in teacher education is related to the first of Fenstermacher's (1986) tasks of teaching: 'instructing the learner on the procedures and demands of the studenting role' (p. 39). This trend is towards the teaching of learning strategies (for example, Weinstein and Mayer, 1986). For many teachers, the teaching of learning strategies requires them to reconceptualize their role in, and responsibility for students' learning. The focus of teacher education shifts from the common content achievement sense of teaching towards the task sense of helping students acquire strategies and exhibit behaviours which are associated with increased personal responsibility and control over their own learning — in other words, towards enhanced student metacognition (Baird, 1984 and 1986b).

Implications and Recommendations

Some general implications for science education arise from the above findings — implications for teachers and teaching, for teacher education and for educational research. These three aspects of science education are deliberately not considered separately. Each aspect is a part of a whole, and should be considered thus. Indeed, as I shall argue, advances in science education may depend on closer integration of the three aspects.

Implication 1: The Need to Acknowledge Complexity

To acknowledge the nature and complexity of the intellectual and contextual variables which influence an individual's learning is to acknowledge that learning must always be qualified. It is insufficient to say that 'Peter is a poor learner'. Peter may be a poor learner

— of Year 9 mechanics (prescribed content),
— with his current teacher in his school laboratory (prescribed classroom context),
— at this time of his life, when particular personal and contextual factors — physical, physiological, interpersonal, and social — are operating (prescribed extra-classroom context),
— with his present intellectual competence (prescribed intellectual features).

All of the elements prescribed above interrelate to generate a particular intellectual performance which, in turn, generates a particular level of learning achievement. Thus, all are important, and need to be understood before a clear understanding of Peter's learning can be achieved. An analogous situation exists, I have argued, for Peter's teacher, Brenda, in relation to her teaching.

Implication 2: The Need to Explain

A recent development in exposing children to science in a number of countries is the large interactive science museum that stems from the first such venture, the Exploratorium in San Francisco. These can have a powerful positive influence on children, through the often fascinating phenomena and effects exhibited. They can stimulate interest in science, and promote the relevance of science to everyday life.

However, there is an important consideration regarding these displays. School students are surrounded in everyday life by fascinating and wondrous effects of science. The problem for these museums is not with the fascination, but with the wonder — the want to know. It is with the desire and skills to move from observation to explanation, from effect to cause. It is not sufficient for science museums to present more examples of interesting science phenomena, even if they foster involvement and interaction. They must also set out to provide opportunities for the child to bridge interaction and explanation. No matter how intriguing, science museums or science classrooms which do not directly facilitate understanding of cause may have failed the child by reinforcing feelings of being controlled rather than being in control, of intimidation rather than resolve, of meaninglessness rather than incomprehensibility.

Explanation is at the core of science education. Phenomena which are easy to observe are often hard to explain. Understanding of cause requires observational and intellectual skills, reasoning abilities, cognitive strategies and metacognitive proficiencies. Developing these skills and abilities is central to the task of the science teacher and, to a different but still very important extent, the curriculum developer and science museum creator. All three must foster both cognitive and affective development by nurturing a sense of wonder, a need to know and, concurrently, by teaching skills for generating understanding.

The importance of explanation in engendering positive attitudes and productive behaviours extends beyond subject matter to learning and teaching generally. Learning and teaching effectiveness is linked to effective metacognition — to understand and to be able to explain why things happen in the classroom as they do.

Implication 3: The Need to Describe

The processes of teaching and learning are complex and largely about specifics. Thus, it may be that few general laws are of sufficient validity or importance to warrant being pursued as vigorously as before. It may be time to describe as carefully as possible the specifics of teaching and learning, to try to understand more about what happens and why. Such ethnographic *case studies* which have been done (for example, Stake and Easley, 1978; Elliot, 1976–77) show that they provide data which are understandable and salient to teachers and researchers.

Only recently has it been fully recognized that a tremendous source of research potential has been overlooked. This source is the teachers and the students. Previously, almost all research was done by the educational researchers, who had the time and expertise to do it. For example, which teachers could be relied upon to choose the appropriate Campbell and Stanley research design, or to process data by factor analysis or analysis of variance? Demystification of educational research has accompanied the change from the confirmatory to the discovery perspective. With the discovery perspective, a powerful research method is action research, which can be carried out by teachers and students. Here, the participants in the process are those who research the process, by engaging in a cycle of observation, reflection, action, evaluation and documentation (for example, Baird, 1984). This first-person research method generates findings which preserve the richness and complexity of the classroom context. However, in order to do this, the teacher needs help.

Implication 4: The Need to Collaborate

Advancing the quality of science education requires collaboration — informed, knowledgeable interaction — among teachers, students, and educationists. If, for instance, teachers are to be action researchers in their classroom, they must be given appropriate time, training, and support. In a two-year attempt to improve the teaching and learning in a school (Baird and Mitchell, 1986), support for the teachers' action research was provided through regular group collaboration among the teachers, and between them and consultants from tertiary education. Significant improvements in teaching and in learning attitudes and behaviours occurred in the school but the benefits of this secondary/tertiary collaboration were not simply one-way — senior educational researchers reported gaining significant insights from the process (for example, White, 1986).

Improvement in general classroom practice may necessitate change towards more active and informed collaboration between teachers and their students. This increased collaboration may require prior training to enhance the intellectual competence of both the teachers and their students. The essence of this training is to enhance metacognition. The difficulties experienced in attempting to change students' existing science conceptions should diminish if the student collaborates with the teacher in monitoring and managing change. Effective implementation of goal-based assessment and negotiated curriculum is facilitated by both student and teacher attaining an adequate level of metacognition about the tasks in hand. Appropriate in-service support for the teacher's needs and interests similarly requires informed collaboration between the teacher and those responsible for the in-service, whoever has that role, inside or outside the school.

Implication 5: The Need to Generalize

Centring research attention on specifics and research method on the teacher raises the obvious concern: how can the results be generalized to other teachers, other content, other contexts? Generalization is necessary for gain in theory and practice. Case study research does generalize, through the use to which its findings are put rather than by presenting generalized conclusions. As Erickson (1986) argues, 'the search is not for *abstract universals* arrived at by statistical generalization from a sample to a population, but for *concrete universals*, arrived at by studying a specific case in great detail, and then comparing it with other cases studied in great detail' (p. 130, his emphasis). The reader of a case study report generalizes by generating meaning from the findings in terms of his or her experiences. Theory is generated through a search for meaning; the people who can, and should do this for classroom studies are the teachers.

Implication 6 and General Conclusion: The Need to Educate

Science is integral to modern society. Science education is integral to the education of school children. In order to educate effectively, science education must balance the excitement of scientific phenomena with the rigour of their explanation. The content of school science must be made relevant to both student and societal needs. It must be selected to allow for development in individual intellectual competence towards the goal — the educated person, a person who can control one's own learning.

The future of science education does not lie primarily in curricula or in technology. It lies in the teacher of science. Teachers, teacher educators, administrators, politicians, and the public must reconceptualize the role of the teacher in the profession of teaching. Teachers must be recognized both as the executives of students' affective and cognitive development and the researchers of the theory and practice of teaching and learning. Teachers must devise curricula and orchestrate experiences which allow for coordinated development of students' general attitudes, perceptions, conceptions and abilities, and of their particular classroom decisions and behaviours. In order to do this, teachers must undergo a similar affective and cognitive development. They need training and ongoing support from colleagues and consultants. Above all, they need time for reflection on practice.

Linking the future of science education to the education of the teachers highlights the role of understanding in its development. Teacher reflection on practice will increase the knowledge base of science education. By sharing and reflecting upon this increased knowledge base, teachers and others may generate increased understandings of the meanings of the many factors which influence science teaching and learning, and the mechanisms by which these factors interact. This emerging understanding will help teachers in the future to build more effectively on the experiences of those who have come before, rather than the present situation, where precious little understanding is carried forward from one generation of teachers to the next.

References

ARZI, H.J., WHITE, R.T. and FENSHAM, P.J. (1987) 'Teachers' knowledge of science: An account of a longitudinal study in progress', paper presented at the annual meeting of the American Educational Research Association, Washington, D.C, April.

BAIRD, J.R. (1984) 'Improving learning through enhanced metacognition', unpublished PhD dissertation, Monash University.

BAIRD, J.R. (1986a) 'Reflections on the nature of change' in BAIRD, J.R. and MITCHELL, I.J. (Eds) *Improving the Quality of Teaching and Learning: An Australian Case Study — the PEEL project*, Melbourne, Monash University Printery.

BAIRD, J.R. (1986b) 'Improving learning through enhanced metacognition: A classroom study', *European Journal of Science Education*, 8, 3, pp 263–82.

BAIRD, J.R. and MITCHELL, I.J. (Eds) (1986) *Improving the Quality of Teaching and Learning: An Australian Case Study — the PEEL project*, Melbourne, Monash University Printery.

BARNES, D. (1976) *From Communication to Curriculum*, Middlesex, Penguin.

BIDDLE, B.J. and ANDERSON, D.S. (1986) 'Theory, methods, knowledge, and research on teaching' in WITTROCK, M.C. (Ed) *Handbook of Research on Teaching*, 3rd edn, New York, Macmillan.

CLARK, C.M. and PETERSON, P.L. (1986) 'Teachers' thought processes' in WITTROCK, M.C. (Ed) *Handbook of Research on Teaching*, 3rd edn, New York, Macmillan.

DUNKIN, M.J. and BIDDLE, B.J. (1974) *The Study of Teaching*, New York, Holt, Rinehart and Winston.

EASLEY, J.A. (1982) 'Naturalistic case studies exploring social-cognitive mechanisms, and some methodological issues in research on problems of teachers, *Journal of Research in Science Teaching*, 19, 3, pp 191–203.

ELLIOTT, J. (1976–77) 'Developing hypotheses about classrooms from teachers' practical constructs: An account of the work of the Ford Teaching Project', *Interchange*, 7, 2, pp 2–22.

ERICKSON, F. (1986) 'Qualitative methods in research on teaching' in WITTROCK, M.C. (Ed) *Handbook of Research on Teaching*, 3rd edn, New York, Macmillan.

EVERTSON, C.M., ANDERSON, C.W., ANDERSON, L.M. and BROPHY, J.E. (1980) 'Relationships between classroom behaviour and student outcomes in junior high mathematics and English classes', *American Educational Research Journal*, 17, pp 43–60.

FENSTERMACHER, G.D. (1986) 'Philosophy of research on teaching: Three aspects' in WITTROCK, M.C. (Ed) *Handbook of Research on Teaching*, 3rd edn, New York, Macmillan.

FULLAN, M. (1985) 'Integrating theory and practice' in HOPKINS, D. and REID, K. (Eds) *Rethinking Teacher Education*, London, Croom Helm.

FULLER, F.F. (1969) 'Concerns of teachers: A developmental conceptualisation', *American Educational Research Journal*, 6, 2, pp 207–26.

FULLER, F.F. and BROWN, O.H. (1975) 'Becoming a teacher' in RYAN, K. (Ed) *Teacher Education, National Association for the Study of Education, 74th Yearbook, Part II*, Chicago, IL, University of Chicago Press.

GARDNER, P.L., GRAY, E.E. and TAYLOR, S.M. (1981) 'Teacher transmission-interpretation and students' attitudes to science', *Research in Science Education*, 11, pp 171–9.

KIRKWOOD, V., CARR, M. and MCCHESNEY, J. (1986) 'LISP (Energy) — Some preliminary findings', *Research in Science Education*, 16, pp 175–83.

OLSON, J.K. (1981) 'Teacher influence in the classroom', *Instructional Science*, 10, pp 259–75.

OSBORNE, R. and BIDDULPH, F. (1985) *Learning in Science Project (Primary) Final Report*, Hamilton, NZ, Science Education Research Unit, University of Waikato.

POWER, C.N. and TISHER, R.P. (1973) 'Teacher values and their association with teaching strategies in A.S.E.P. classes', *Science Education: Research*, pp 51–60.

SCHIBECI, R.A. (1980) 'Science teachers and science related attitudes, *Research in Science Education*, 10, pp 159–65.

SHAVELSON, R. (1983) 'Review of research on teachers' pedagogical judgements, plans and decisions', *Elementary School Journal*, 83, 4, pp 392–413.

SHULMAN, L.S. (1986) 'Paradigms and research programs in the study of teaching: A contemporary perspective' in WITTROCK, M.C. (Ed) *Handbook of Research on Teaching*, 3rd edn, New York, Macmillan.

STAKE, R.E. and EASLEY, J.A. (1978) *Case Studies in Science Education* (2 vols.), Washington, D.C, US Government Printing Office.

TISHER, R.P. and POWER, C.N. (1975) 'A study of the effects of teaching strategies in A.S.E.P. classrooms', *Australian Journal of Education*, 19, pp 127–45.

WEINSTEIN, C.E. and MAYER, R.E. (1986) 'The teaching of learning strategies' in WITTROCK, M.C. (Ed) *Handbook of Research on Teaching*, 3rd edn, New York, Macmillan.

WHITE, R.T. (1986) 'Observations by a minor participant' in BAIRD, J.R. and MITCHELL, I.J. (Eds) *Improving the Quality of Teaching and Learning: An Australian Case Study — the PEEL project*, Melbourne, Monash University Printery.

WHITE, R.T. and TISHER, R.P. (1986) 'Research on natural sciences' in WITTROCK, M.C. (Ed) *Handbook of Research on Teaching*, 3rd edn, New York, Macmillan.

WITTROCK, M.C. (1986) 'Students' thought processes' in WITTROCK, M.C. (Ed) *Handbook of Research on Teaching*, 3rd edn, New York, Macmillan.

4
Learners in Science Education

Richard F. Gunstone

Introduction

This chapter focuses on a particular aspect of the learner of science: the nature and importance of the ideas and beliefs the learner brings to the science classroom. The growth in interest about students' ideas and beliefs is the most obvious feature of considerations of science learning in the last decade. Research has pointed to the common existence of ideas and beliefs before formal science instruction is experienced. These ideas/beliefs are frequently at odds with the ideas of science and can be held to tenaciously by students. This is shown particularly by the relatively common finding that students successful on standard forms of science achievement tests can fail to use this learned science to interpret everyday phenomena and analyze usual situations. Instead the interpretation and analysis are often undertaken with the ideas and beliefs held before encountering the science of the classroom. Data pointing to this are commonly argued to indicate superficial learning and lack of understanding of the content of the curriculum.

In this chapter research on students' ideas/beliefs about the world around them are initially discussed. Views of learning to which this research lends support are then outlined. In order to place these views of learning in the broader context of existing practices in science education, the views are then briefly considered beside those of Piaget. Comparing and constrasting with Piagetian theory is undertaken because of the major impact on science learning research and curriculum development which Piagetian-based ideas have had in the last twenty years. Attempts to respond to the research on students' ideas/beliefs are then discussed. The chapter concludes with an analysis of the implications for science learning of these perspectives.

Research on Students' Ideas and Beliefs

Interpretations of Natural Phenomena

Thus far, research on students' ideas/beliefs has largely focused on interpretations of natural phenomena. Hence, this is the starting point of the discussion. Initially some specific examples are described.

Example 1 (from Gunstone and Champagne, in press)

A year 7 class was undertaking a laboratory exercise concerned with solubility and suspension. Five substances were provided, with a small quantity of each to be added to water and observed. One substance was in a reagent bottle with the label 'Sodium chloride', quite accidently, clearly visible. Just after adding this substance to water one student was asked by the teacher about his progress. He responded: 'I knew that [sodium chloride] would dissolve'. When asked how he knew, he replied: 'Because its got chlorine in it, and chlorine dissolves in swimming pools'.

Example 2: (from Driver et al., 1985)

A physics graduate in a one-year course of teacher training was in a group shown a bell jar containing a partially inflated balloon. When asked to predict what would happen to the balloon when air was evacuated from the bell jar, he answered 'The balloon will float'. His reason: 'Because gravity will be reduced'. (p. 86)

Example 3: (from Osborne and Freyberg, 1985)

Large samples of science and physics students from each of the ages 13 to 17 years were given questions about a ball thrown in the air. The questions asked whether the force on the ball was up, down or zero for three positions shown on diagrams — ball rising, ball at highest point, ball falling. The most common response at all five age levels was 'up, zero, down'. This response, which embraces the belief that a force is needed in the direction of motion to maintain that motion, was given by about half of the 16 and 17-year-old physics students (pp. 45–6)

These three examples illustrate four of the consistent findings of research which has probed students' ideas/beliefs.

(i) When students come to formal science learning they frequently already hold explanatory views of phenomena (as shown by example

1). These views are apparently personal and idiosyncratic interpretations of experiences, and are often different from the explanatory views taught in science classrooms.

(ii)   These views can be remarkably unaffected by traditional forms of instruction. Example 2 typifies such a circumstance: a tertiary physics graduate who apparently continues to interpret the world around him via a belief that gravity is an atmosphere-related phenomenon (i.e. without air there is no gravity).

(iii)   Particular views can be quite common, as shown by example 3. That is, the finding of these ideas/beliefs is not a function of the sample of students involved and one view can be held by many students (see also Gunstone, 1987, where data from a complete population of over 5000 senior secondary school physics students are reported).

(iv)   Some students can hold the scientists' interpretation given in instruction together with a conflicting view already present before instruction. The science interpretation is often used to answer questions in science tests, and the conflicting view retained to interpret the world. This is illustrated both by example 2 (where the graduate involved could readily answer questions requiring Newton's Law of Gravitation), and by example 3 (where some of the 50 per cent of senior students holding the force-needed-in-direction-of-motion belief could successfully solve standard $F = ma$ problems).

(v)   A further common research finding is not illustrated by the three examples: these ideas/beliefs are often remarkably consistent across groups differing in age and nationality.

A comprehensive review of the research leading to these five conclusions is not attempted here. A number of such reviews already exist, including books (for example, Driver *et al.*, 1985; Osborne and Freyberg, 1985; West and Pines, 1985), articles (for example, Driver and Erickson, 1983; Gilbert and Watts, 1983; McCloskey, 1983; McDermott, 1984) and conference proceedings (for example, Duit *et al.*, 1985; Helm and Novak, 1983; *Research on Physics Education*, 1984).

These publications also give details of the wide variety of probes of students' ideas/beliefs which have been used in this research. A comprehensive review of these probes is not attempted here. That would require a book in its own right. Instead three examples of probes are briefly outlined in order to give some feeling for the origins of the data on which this perspective on learning is based. The references given for each example will allow the reader to gain more detail. The large majority of probes have involved individual interviews. Usually some common stimulus (for example, a particular event or experience) is the starting point, and then the student's interpretation of or explanation for the stimulus is explored without judgment of the validity of the student's interpretation. Often data from these interviews have then been used to generate a written probe of students' views of the event or experience. The first probe example illustrates this.

Interview about instances/interview about events (see Osborne and Freyberg, 1985)

The stimuli in the first of these (instances) are a series of drawings, each illustrating one instance or one non-instance of the science view of a concept, for example, for the concept animal, drawings of a child, a fly, a worm, a tree and so on. In each case the student is asked if, in terms of the way they think about it, the example is an animal. The reasons for this judgment are then explored through neutral questions such as 'Why do you say that?', 'Can you tell me more about that?' From this, a picture of the student's views of animal is derived. For concepts such as force, the diagrams show situations in which science would have that forces are acting (for example, a person sitting on a chair, a golf ball in the air). Students are asked if there are any forces on the person, or the golf ball. For the second form (interviews about events), the stimulus is a specific event, for example, given boiling water in a jug the student is asked what the bubbles are made of and the reasons for the response explored. In these probes, or any similar interviews, it is crucial to interview, not teach. If the student's ideas/beliefs are to be obtained then evaluation of student statements should not be made through the interview. A variety of other forms of interview stimuli are given in Driver *et al.* (1985).

Predict/observe/explain (also termed demonstrate/observe/explain) (see Champagne, Klopfer and Anderson, 1980; Gunstone and White, 1981)

In this probe, the student is told of some demonstration which will be performed (for example, dropping a heavy and a light ball) and asked to predict what will happen (for example, how will the times for the two balls to fall to the floor compare?). Reasons for the predictions are explored. The demonstration is performed, and the observation made by the student is probed. This is crucial, as discussed in a later section. If the observation and prediction are at odds with each other, the student's explanation for this is also explored.

Concept maps (see Novak and Gowin, 1984)

This probe focuses on the relationship students see between ideas, how they structure ideas. It also differs from the other two examples in that the task required involves an approach which needs to be learned. Briefly, the student is either given a number of terms or generates the terms from class notes or a text book, and then arranges the terms so that they indicate how the student sees the terms to be related. A crucial aspect in this is for the student to draw links between ideas which he/she sees as related, and to write down or talk about the form of the link. Examples of groups of ideas we have used for concept maps are heart, circulation, oxygen, blood veins, arteries, lungs; and current electricity, static electricity, atoms, electrons, metal, plastic.

Constructivist Views of Learning

Research which has probed students' ideas is not restricted to the last decade. Examples of earlier work with the focus of that described above, together with conjecture about the failure of the work to stimulate widespread interest, are given by Gunstone, White and Fensham (1988) and White and Tisher (1986, p. 884). Of course the work of Piaget (for example, Piaget, 1929), briefly considered in a later section, is a major antecedent to the present research.

One significant aspect of the dramatic and recent upsurge of interest in the research appears to be the growth of interest in related concerns in other areas of research, such as educational psychology. These include concern for understanding in learning, for the influence of content and prior knowledge on the nature of the meaning individuals construct from experiences, and so on. Shuell (1986) reviews these developments in psychological research and places work on students' ideas/beliefs in this broader context. Champagne and Klopfer (1984) discuss links between this work and recent developments in cognitive psychology. What is being argued in all these cases about the ways in which individuals develop ideas is widely termed a constructivist view of learning.

Driver and Bell (1986) list six issues which are emphasized by a constructivist view of the process of learning. Firstly, learning outcomes depend not only on the learning environment, but also on the knowledge, purposes and motivations the learner brings to the task. That is, the ideas and beliefs we already hold will be of major influence on the interpretation we place on what we are taught. For example, many students come to a study of falling objects with the view that heavier objects fall faster. When presented with the science generalization that acceleration in a gravity field is independent of weight, some of these students conclude that heavy and light objects have the same weight (for example, Gunstone, Champagne and Klopfer, 1981, p. 28).

The remainder of the issues Driver and Bell see as emphasized by a constructivist view are all logically related to the first. The second of the issues is that the process of learning involves the construction of meanings. The meanings constructed by individual learners from what is said or demonstrated or experienced may not be the meanings intended by the teacher. Of course this implies that understanding cannot be directly transmitted from teacher to learner since each learner creates his/her own understanding. Hence the teacher's role is one of facilitating the development of understanding by selecting appropriate experiences. Thirdly, the construction of meaning is a continuous and active process. The converse of this is that inactive learners will not be constructing meaning — where 'inactive' is used in a mental rather than physical sense. Fourthly, having constructed meanings, learners will evaluate them and consequently accept or reject them. There are may reported instances of students who have constructed the science meaning for some concept or phenomenon, but who do not accept this meaning. This was illustrated earlier in the chapter via examples of students holding a science meaning (generally used only on assessment tests) but not accepting that meaning as a way of interpreting the world. Fifth, learners have the final responsibility for their learning. That is, learners themselves decide what attention they give to a learning task, construct their own interpretation of/meaning for the task, and evaluate those meanings. Simplistically, learners make their own sense of their experiences. Again, this points to the teacher's role being one which encourages learners to make sense of experience rather than one which tells students what that sense is. Sixth, and finally, there are communalities in the meanings students construct. That is, there are many situations for which the meanings constructed by one group of students are quite similar to those of another group.

It is clear that the overarching issue in a constructivist view of learning is that individuals generate their own understanding. This proposition is central to the generative learning model advanced by Osborne and Wittrock (1983 and 1985). In these papers, the authors place research on students' ideas in science in the context of their elaboration of generative learning, and the model is used to argue implications for science learning, teaching and curriculum. The model provides a sound theoretical view for many of the ideas advanced in this chapter.

Constructivist Perspectives on Some Other Relevant Aspects of Science Learning

This discussion of students' ideas and beliefs began with a consideration of ideas about natural phenomena. It then sought to put these ideas in a broader context by outlining issues associated with constructivist views of learning. These constructivist issues are clearly applicable to aspects of science learning other than those already addressed. Two examples are considered here as examples of the wider importance of the personal construction of meaning — the skill of observing and student conceptions of teaching and learning.

Investigations have shown two broad ways in which observation can be substantially influenced by existing knowledge and beliefs: the oft-made assumption that all students will see the same thing as a result of looking at the one event is not reasonable (i.e. what the individual sees is influenced by what the individual already believes); the legitimacy of the observation itself may not be accepted (i.e. if what the individual sees is in conflict with what the individual believes, the observation may be denied).

Driver (1983) summarizes the matter well: "Looking at" is not a passive recording of an image like a photograph being produced by a camera, but it is an active process in which the observer is checking his perceptions against his expectations' (pp. 11–12). Alternatively, 'Seeing is believing, if I hadn't believed it I wouldn't have seen it' (Brilliant, 1979, p. 40).

These two ways in which observation is affected by existing knowledge and beliefs are illustrated by brief reference to data described by Gunstone and White (1981). In that study a large number of tertiary physics students were given Predict/Observe/Explain tasks of the form described above. The events involved a large piece of wood and a bucket of sand suspended over a large pulley (which was in fact a bicycle wheel). For each event the sand and wood were initially stationary. In one case, a very small amount of sand was to be added to the bucket. Some predicted the bucket would then move down a little and come to rest again. Of these students, some reported observing a small movement when the sand was added (even though no one else did) and others reported movement so slight it could not be seen. When predicting the effect of adding a larger quantity of sand, again some suggested the bucket would fall some distance and then stop. The observation that the bucket fell until striking the demonstration bench on which the apparatus was mounted (a distance of about one-and-a-half metres) was universally given. However, some who predicted the bucket would fall a short distance and then stop again concluded that the bucket reached the bench before reaching the position at which it would again have been stationary.

In the first of these events (adding a small amount of sand), belief affected the nature of the observation. In the second, belief seemed clearly in conflict with observation and some reconciled this by effectively denying the observation. Many more examples of this, and closely related pedagogical issues of importance to the learning of science via observation, are given in Driver's (1983) insightful analysis.

The second example of the broader influence of existing ideas and beliefs is that of students' conceptions of learning and teaching. As yet, less work has been done in this area than in others discussed. Hence there are fewer data, but those which do exist are in many ways more striking. Again the significant issue is the way in which student beliefs about learning and teaching influence the meaning the students construct from classroom experiences.

One of the early relevant reports is that of Tasker (1981) who outlined a number of issues subsequently elaborated by Osborne and Freyberg (1985). Among these was the observation that students often perceive science lessons as quite separate and unrelated entities even though the teacher perceives links and cumulative sequences to be most obvious. The belief of students is frequently that such links are not expected, that learning does not involve forming these links. Even within a single lesson, the purpose perceived by students often differs from that of the teacher. Tasker noted a tendency in laboratory classes for student purpose to be 'follow the instructions' or 'get the right answer'. Such purposes are rarely congruent with the overall purpose of the teacher. The student purpose of 'right answer' rings true with many science teachers when they reflect on their own approaches to undergraduate laboratory work.

The possible effects on the nature of learning of student beliefs about teaching and learning are illustrated with two extreme cases, one positive and one negative. The positive case is provided by Champagne, Gunstone and Klopfer (1985) in the context of a study of instructional attempts to change tertiary students' cognitive beliefs about the relationship between force and motion. They report that the significant factor in students changing their cognitive beliefs was students changing their beliefs about their own learning to encompass insights such as 'Some people fight hard not to change preconceived ideas' and 'It's comforting to try to keep certain ideas forever even if there is a chance they may be wrong' (p. 176). The researchers argue that it was only when the learners changed their beliefs about learning to include aspects seen by the researchers to be fundamental to the task at hand that the intended cognitive learning was achieved. Before the change, the learners held views about learning and teaching which assumed that an understanding of the cognitive task could be given to them by the teacher. Once they changed to a constructivist view of learning, they were more able to construct (or better reconstruct) their ideas about force and motion. A number of examples of the negative interactions are given in descriptions of the very early stages of a multi-year, school-based project aimed at having secondary students understand and take control of their own learning (Baird and Mitchell, 1986). In one case, after about six weeks of attempts by a science teacher to move students in such directions, the teacher was informed by students that 'We are doing too much thinking and not enough work' (p. 56). At this time the students' beliefs about what constituted appropriate school learning did not include thinking. There was complete dissonance between student and teacher beliefs about learning. This meant, of course, that the teacher could make no progress towards his goal of student understanding and control of their learning until student ideas and beliefs about learning started to change. In a second case, after about three weeks in the same project, a geography teacher reacted to the difficulties of promoting student control of learning by writing a set of notes on the blackboard. The notes deliberately included many outrageous statements, for example, 'Soil will be lost by evaporation', 'daylight hours vary from town to town depending on altitude', 'the plant's visionary cycle and light condensation greatly affect the amount of hygration that can exist' (Baird and Mitchell, 1986, pp. 30–1). Students were asked to copy the notes, which they did, and then to ask any questions they had about the notes. The teacher's recollection is that only one student asked a question, while a student in her account of the project recollects that about five questions were asked (*ibid.*, p. 88). Both teacher and student interpretations of this incident support the view that students' beliefs about learning at that time included that notes are meaningful (and that failure to see meaning must be the fault of the learner not the notes), and that notes necessarily have value. Again, these views were so much at odds with the purposes of the project that a change in the views was necessary before progress could be made towards achieving the learning goals of the project.

More anecdotal examples of the impact of student ideas and beliefs about teaching and learning have been experienced by teachers: students seeing learning as only the reproduction of class notes, students believing that an understanding of some science concepts is not possible, and so on. In some cases some of these can, unfortunately, be appropriate when judged in terms of the ways by which students know their learning will be assessed. This suggests issues of importance about assessment and its impact on beliefs about learning which are considered later in the chapter. The issue of significance here is that students do hold views about what constitutes teaching and learning, and these views affect the nature of student learning.

Summary

A wide variety of terms has been used to describe students' ideas and beliefs about the world around them. These descriptors include *children's science, alternative frameworks, misconceptions, naive conceptions,* and so on. Gauld (1987) has analyzed the descriptors which appear in the literature into what he calls 'basic terms' (for example, ideas, meanings, conceptions, structures) and 'qualifiers' (for example, mis-, alternative, personal, intuitive). His list contains a staggering twenty-five basic terms and sixteen qualifiers. Of course not all qualifiers have been used with all basic terms, but a surprising range of descriptors has been used for what seems to be one broad issue. The language of these different descriptors can imply characteristics of the ideas and beliefs of students (Erickson, 1984). Consideration of the implications of some of the descriptors is one way of reviewing important points raised by this area of research. It should be noted, however, that the descriptor implications argued in this summary are often not intended by the researchers who coined or have used the term. Rather the implications presented are those which might be inferred by readers of the descriptor.

Consider first the descriptor 'misconception'. This implies 'mistake' or 'wrong'. Such an implication devalues the 'correctness' of the idea/belief, as perceived by the individual who has constructed the belief, and hence underestimates the likely tenacity with which the belief will be held. That the ideas/beliefs are personal constructions, seen by the individual to be appropriate interpretations of experience, is argued by many researchers to be central to the frequent retention of the ideas/beliefs when conflicting science conceptions are presented in classrooms. In the extreme, the labelling of a commonly held view such as 'human beings are not animals' as a misconception is clearly unreasonable. The view is quite consistent with the *social* definition of animal, as illustrated by signs proclaiming 'animals not allowed in this shop', or 'animals not allowed on this freeway'. It fits much of the environment of the student, and results from a logical approach to making sense of the world. Rather than being a misconception (mistake), the view reflects the fact that the science definition of animal differs from the social definition. That the social definition can be retained and used in science contexts after the science definition has been presented indicates that the science definition is not seen as more useful by some students.

The descriptor 'children's science' was initially coined for very good reasons — to emphasize that students construct interpretations of their world in terms of their experience, knowledge and language. Scientists construct interpretations in the same way. Hence the term 'children's science' emphasizes both the similarity of the process of construction of meaning by children and scientists and the differences in the outcomes of that construction. Two other possible implications which might be drawn from the term are, however, not reasonable. Firstly, the construction of alternative meanings is not the province of children alone. Adults (including science teachers) can hold to explanations of the world at odds with the explanations of science. This is clear both from research on teachers' conceptions (for example, Ameh and Gunstone, 1986; Arzi, White and Fensham, 1987) and from personal experience. Many teachers of science have found their understanding of some concept has developed in ways different from the science meaning. For example, I realized after many years of school science teaching that my meaning for evolution was much more Lamarckian than Darwinian. My subsequent reflection suggests that this personal meaning arose largely from two aspects of my interpretation of the concepts. Firstly, as a physicist, I had interpreted the term 'adapt' in a way much more consistent with its everyday meaning than with the science meaning (i.e. implying some sort of conscious, causal act on the part of the adapting organism); secondly I interpreted the example of giraffes' necks, so commonly used as an illustrative example of evolution in general science texts, in ways consistent with my personal understanding of adapt. It was not until my meanings for evolution and adaptation were challenged by the probes of understanding used by researchers (in particular, Brumby, 1984) that I came to realize the nature of the meaning I had constructed. In passing, I would now also suggest that the meanings for evolution and adaptation held by some text book writers have strong traces of Lamarckian views.

So, one implication which might be taken from the descriptor 'children's science' — that it is a characteristic peculiar to children — is unreasonable. Another — that it is confined to science — is also unreasonable, as already argued in the discussion of students' ideas about teaching and learning. Or again, the term should not be interpreted as some watered down or different form of science *for* children.

The third descriptor considered here raises an issue about which less is currently known. The descriptor is 'framework', usually prefaced by either 'alternative' or 'conceptual'. The clearly reasonable logic underlying the use of this term is that there are consistencies in the thinking shown by students' interpretations of the world. These consistencies are found both for one phenomenon across students, and for one student across phenomena. The issue about which less is currently known is quite how far we should assume these consistencies. Recent research by Engel Clough and Driver (1986) points to the complexities in this issue. In particular this research raises the possibility that failure to use the same ideas/beliefs across situations seen by science as conceptually similar may result from students categorizing situations differently from scientists rather than from students failing to be consistent in their use of ideas.

Consideration of these three examples of descriptors has been undertaken to emphasize the important aspects of the view of science learning on which this chapter focuses. These aspects, again, are: individual learners construct their own meanings/ideas/beliefs from experience; these ideas are often formed before formal instruction, and are often different from the meanings/ideas/ beliefs taught in science; the personally constructed ideas can be held strongly, be remarkably hard to change, and be used in interpreting the world in preference to science taught in classrooms; the personally constructed ideas show some consistency across populations; these ideas/beliefs have significant impact on the nature of classroom learning, both for conceptual learning and for aspects which might once have been considered to be content free (for example, skills such as observing, views about what constitutes appropriate teaching and learning).

As an addendum to this discussion of descriptors and their appropriateness, the terminology used in this chapter should be justified. The descriptor 'ideas/beliefs' has been consistently used, together with the qualifier 'students'. The qualifier is a reflection of the focus of the chapter being on learners in science classrooms. 'Ideas/beliefs' has been used as I see it carrying fewer implications of the form discussed above. Even so, implications are there: for example 'beliefs' implies commitment and influence on behaviour, 'ideas' may imply small and unconnected bits of personal meaning. Both of these implications are sometimes reasonable (the first more so) and sometimes not. Readers would be wise to bear them in mind as they construct their own meaning from this text.

Before considering the implications of constructivism for science education, this perspective is further elaborated by brief discussion of some related and wider issues. The next section addresses the communalities with and differences between Piaget's theory (and the work of his interpreters) and the constructivist view of learning as described here. This is done both because of the major influence of Piagetian theory on learning research and curriculum development in science, and because this comparison will elaborate the constructivist position in different ways.

Constructivism and Piaget: Communalities and Differences

Driver (cited in Osborne and Wittrock, 1985) suggests that three traditions in educational psychology have impacted on the teaching of science. These are the developmental tradition (which has emphasized age-related stages argued to have major determining impact on what can be learned), the behaviourist tradition (which has emphasized cumulative learning through small steps and reinforcement), and the constructivist position. It is argued here that the work of Piaget has characteristics of both the developmental and constructivist positions. The reader should note that this argument is presented by a constructivist. Some exchanges between constructivists and Piagetians in the literature have been particularly acrimonious. However, I am in full agreement with a well-known Piagetian researcher who, in discussing exchanges between these two schools of thought, asserts 'I contend that little is to be gained by presenting the two schools as irreconcilable adversaries' (Adey, 1987, p. 7). Head (1982) may well be right when he argues that the most helpful perspective may turn out to lie somewhere in the middle.

For the purposes of this discussion, the stages of development aspects of Piagetian theory are considered separately from the processes Piaget argues to be involved in the construction of meaning by the individual. This is a dangerous exercise, as 'in Piagetian theory, much more than in most psychological theories, everything is related to everything else in an extremely complex fashion' (Groen, 1978, p. 43). Nevertheless, the division is a necessary starting point to seeing how Piaget's theory is viewed by many constructivists, and how the research discussed in preceding sections compares and contrasts with the theory.

Firstly, consider the views of Piaget about the active role of the learner in constructing ideas. The view that the child's thinking develops through 'encounters with experience', 'social transmission', 'assimilation and accommodation' is clearly constructivist in the sense used here (Magoon, 1977). Piagetian researchers have used the term 'constructivist' to describe their work, as has Piaget himself (Gruber and Vonèche, 1982, pp. xxxvi–xxxvii). The work of Piaget has been an obvious and major influence on research probing students' ideas/beliefs. White and Tisher (1985, p. 888) have even suggested that this research is more the true inheritor of the Piagetian tradition than is the developmental-stages-oriented work so common in science education in the last twenty years. This conclusion derives from the view that stage-oriented research has neglected the individual by seeing that individual only as member of a group.

The communality of the two views of learning is then the common focus on constructivism — each position holds that the individual actively constructs his/her own meaning for experiences. The issue of developmental stages is the substantial difference between the two.

Developmental stages are seen by Piagetians as clearly distinguishable and successive periods of intellectual development through which the learner passes. Each stage is characterized by the form of reasoning the child is able to undertake. To the constructivist the particular content on which the reasoning is operating is seen to be a much more crucial factor. That is, research on students' ideas/beliefs does not seek to establish the nature of some general schema of reasoning across contexts, but to establish the nature of reasoning about a particular context. Whether or not the same reasoning is used in an apparently related context is a question for investigation (rather than an assumption), and with 'related' being in terms of content rather than form of logical reasoning used.

Which of these two conflicting views is to be accepted is a contentious issue. As a constructivist I necessarily accept that part of the answer lies in the meaning an individual constructs from available data. In other words, the way in which each of us interprets and makes sense of data relevant to this question is heavily influenced by the ideas and beliefs we already hold and thus use in our interpretation. Constructivists then see great importance in interpretations which support the conclusion that the subject matter involved is a crucial factor in determining the nature of the reasoning used by an individual, that stages of development are much more content dependent than is suggested by

Piagetian theory, and hence that these stages are not helpful in considering science education (for example, Linn, 1986 and 1987; Nixon, 1978; Novak, 1978; Vosniadou and Brewer, 1987). Language is a particular aspect of the context of reasoning argued to be significant (for example, Macnamara, 1982; Stenhouse, 1986). Groen (1978) goes as far as to argue that much stage-oriented research has taken the construct of stages of development out of the context of Piaget's theory as a whole, and consequently led to practices inconsistent with the theory. Piagetians in science education have interpreted these data differently in suggesting that there are stages in the sense of developmental patterns of reasoning (for example, Good, 1977; Lawson, 1982 and 1985; Shayer and Adey, 1981). In some of these sources the constructivist argument of content dependency of stages is specifically addressed.

The purpose of the above discussion has not been to resolve the central question of whether or not Piagetian stages are content dependent in a way which makes the construct of stages not helpful for considering the learning of science. It has been to place constructivist-oriented research into students' ideas into the broader context of existing science educational practices in order to assist an understanding of the research. The basic issue of conflict suggested here is also seen by some constructivists as a contributing factor to disappointments in previous interactions between science education research and curriculum development.

Readers who wish to pursue further the question of stages may find value in the brief discussion of stages and their place in Piaget's theory given by Gruber and Vonèche (1982). In this anthology of his work, Piaget includes in a foreword the evaluation that the volume is 'the best and most complete of all of the anthologies of my work' (p. xi).

Attempts to Change Students' Ideas/Beliefs

Findings that students, even those achieving high grades in science, can continue to use ideas at odds with those taught in their science course have produced one obvious response. That is to explore alternative instructional approaches which might better promote conceptual change. These explorations have largely been motivated by the view that failure to accept the science conception and abandon some existing alternative conception necessarily denotes inadequate understanding, even if the science conception has been used to answer test questions. (This notion of 'accepting' and 'abandoning' carries with it important assumptions that are addressed later in the section on implications).

Research which has explored conceptual change has tended to follow a structure of first making students aware of their existing ideas/beliefs by having them explain or hypothesize about a phenomenon, then using carefully selected events to promote conflict between new observations and existing ideas, and finally using interactive approaches to attempt resolution of the conflict (for example, Champagne, Gunstone and Klopfer, 1985; Nussbaum and Novick, 1982).

Some of this research has been influenced by the ideas of Hewson (1981). He argues that for conceptual change there must first be dissatisfaction with the existing conception. This alone is not enough. The new conception must also be, to the learner, intelligible (i.e. be understandable), plausible (i.e. appear reasonable), and fruitful (i.e. offer a more powerful or more appealing way of conceptualizing the phenomenon or issue). Attempts to change student ideas/beliefs have not always been as successful as the researchers had hoped. Hewson's arguments about conceptual change, particularly the notion of fruitfulness, are one way of interpreting this. By way of illustration, work by Champagne, Gunstone and Klopfer (1985) is considered. That study attempted to change ideas/beliefs about force and motion in gifted middle school students and biology graduates training to be science teachers. (The work with graduates was mentioned above as an example of the importance of student views of teaching and learning.) Considerable success in promoting conceptual change was reported for the graduates, less success for the middle school students. In part this differential success can be seen in terms of fruitfulness to the learner. Fruitfulness can be external or internal. By these descriptors I mean fruitfulness either in terms of improved exam results, peer group acclaim, etc. (external), or in terms of a personally more powerful and coherent way of conceptualizing a phenomenon or issue (internal). Internal fruitfulness is hard to achieve. In the Champagne *et al.* study, the graduates strived for internal fruitfulness because of their awareness of the possibility of their having to teach these concepts to children in the following year. With school students it is very much harder, as shown by the many research examples of students not having any personal commitment to science conceptions taught to them.

The notion of fruitfulness is intertwined with the extent to which students understand and control their learning. Understanding and controlling one's learning is usually called metacognition, and is considered further below.

One other way of considering the outcomes of attempts to promote conceptual change is via Rumelhart and Norman's (1978) suggestion that the learning of a complex topic involves three modes, accretion (addition of new information to the learner's ideas/beliefs about the topic), restructuring (the reorganizing of ideas/beliefs) and tuning (refinements resulting from continued use of ideas/beliefs). Restructuring is then somewhat akin to what is described as conceptual change above. Research findings such as those of Champagne *et al.* (1985) may result from accretion having taken place before restructuring was attempted: the graduates who underwent conceptual change had already in their memories from prior science courses the propositional statements needed for a Newtonian view of motion; the instructional experience then focussed on restructuring.

This discussion of attempts to change students' ideas/beliefs has been a second aspect of the broader context of the research considered in this chapter. The first was the relationships of the research to Piagetian theory, a third is very briefly noted in the next section.

Teacher Reactions to this Perspective on Learning

Teacher reactions to this research have often been much more positive than their reactions to other research thrusts. This is well summarized by an Australian science teacher who, on becoming familiar with these perspectives, said: 'Some of the research data and interview transcripts were uncanny reflections of my own experience'. One consequence of such reactions is the existence of groups of teachers who are involved in reacting to the research findings in their own classrooms, and sharing the insights they form. Such groups exist in Melbourne (Australia), Leeds (UK), and Vancouver (Canada). That the research is sufficiently credible to teachers that these groups can exist and grow is important in its own right. It also points to the potential for teachers to investigate the consequences of the research and hence to inform and improve the science education they offer to students.

Implications for Science Education

Implications for science education to be found in research on students' ideas/beliefs are included in a number of the publications previously cited in this chapter (for example, Driver *et al.*, 1985; Linn, 1987; Osborne and Freyberg, 1985). Here some selected implications are considered as issues of particular importance for research and development in science education. For convenience these are in three sections (general issues of curriculum and learning, teaching strategies, assessment), although there is a clear intertwining of the three.

Curriculum and Learning

Fensham (1983) has argued that the objectives of science education should be reconceptualized in the light of this research. Objectives are often currently expressed in terms of science conceptual knowledge, science processes, science investigations and so on. Fensham suggests an emphasis quite different from this present concern with placing scientists' conceptions in students' minds. He suggests objectives such as 'To introduce students to examples of how scientists have defined concepts in ways useful to them but which conflict with common sense, experience, and usage', 'To enable students to recognize that scientists invent general concepts which over–simplify (or idealize) actual situations' (pp. 8–9). He sees existing common objectives as being concerned with moving students in the directions of science. The six new objectives he lists imply a shift to having students see the direction of science. Driver and Bell (1986, pp. 454–5) express a related view when they argue that this research perspective should lead us to question the assumption that all students should acquire the scientists' conceptions of phenomena. Rather, they argue, we should judge students' ideas/beliefs in terms of whether or not the ideas enable students to function effectively in their world. That is, content and purpose of the science curriculum might be considered in terms of what conceptions are of use to students outside the classroom.

Pines and West (1986) analyze constructivist research on the learning of science and arrive at conclusions which complement these new objectives. They consider two sources of student knowledge: the knowledge students acquire 'spontaneously' from their interactions with the environment, and the knowledge students acquire in a formal fashion through the intervention of school. Depending on the concepts and individuals involved, the two sources of knowledge can be in conflict, be congruent, or exist alone. As a result of this analysis, Pines and West suggest that science learning should be considered in terms of three frameworks: conceptual development (where the major learning is the development of formal knowledge), conceptual exchange (where the major learning is resolution of substantial conflict between the two sources of knowledge), and conceptual resolution (a position intermediate between the other two). They argue that both the purposes and practices of science education should reflect these three frameworks. Different concepts and teaching/learning strategies are suggested as appropriate for different frameworks. This leads to the important point that no one learning situation or one curriculum approach will encompass all aspects of students' ideas/beliefs (and hence a qualifying comment was made in a previous section about the common assumption of 'accepting' and 'abandoning' concepts in attempts to change students' ideas/beliefs).

The Pines and West analysis also suggests that it may be that no one set of purposes is always appropriate for science education. For some contexts and learning frameworks more radical purposes will have greater value for students, in other cases this may not be so.

Even if the challenges to existing purposes for science education con-sidered here are not accepted, one significant curriculum implication remains. If genuine conceptual understanding is a serious purpose for our science courses, then it must be noted that the evidence is strong that this is frequently not being achieved. Many writers have described this in ways which contrast quality in and quantity of learning. It seems most unlikely we can achieve both quality and quantity. If quality (genuine understanding) is to be seriously attempted, then we must spend more time developing ideas and hence accept that we will embrace less content in our courses.

Teaching Strategies (Better Described as Learning Strategies)

The qualifier in this sub-heading has an obvious purpose. It is to emphasize that it is learning that is of prime significance in classrooms, and that teaching strategies should be judged in terms of the learning they promote. This is particularly significant when considered in the light of Hewson's (1981) views of conceptual change discussed previously. Most standard teaching strategies concentrate on making content or task 'intelligible' to students. The requirements of 'plausibility' and 'fruitfulness' present quite different problems for the teacher. Rather than the traditional 'How can I explain it better?', the teacher is led to 'How can I make this interpretation/model/generalization, etc. appear believable to students?' and 'How can I show this interpretation, etc. to be more useful (in particular contexts or generally) than the one they currently use?'. These are fundamental and difficult questions with no simple answers. In part, they relate to the next section on assessment. The questions also raise important issues about teaching strategies. Two aspects are briefly considered here.

(i)   The methods used to probe students' ideas/beliefs are also, almost by definition, excellent teaching/learning strategies. In part, these probes of understanding have been used by researchers because of the ways they promote student introspection and hypothesizing about phenomena. These qualities make them excellent teaching approaches, although their use inevitably requires a classroom where genuine discussion and debate are accepted as appropriate learning behaviours by both teacher and students.

For example, consider the Predict/Observe/Explain technique for probing ideas. Examples of this given above have obvious teaching/learning value, but only if students' predictions are not evaluated. If evaluation takes place, students will quickly fall into the pattern so common on tests, and give the science conception whether or not they have any commitment to this. The observation must also be taken seriously. If not all students make the same observation, this needs to be discussed and considered. If the task is intended to promote an understanding of a generalization which is not supported by direct observation, this also has implications which cannot be ignored. This is well illustrated by the example of dropping heavy and light balls mentioned previously. The prediction of heavier falling faster is made by some students on the basis of previous observations they have undertaken. And they are correct. The science generalization of equal acceleration is an idealized one. It is only approximately 'confirmed' by observation for a limited range of objects and a very limited range of distances. Finally the reconciliation of prediction and observation generally requires considerable debate and reflection. Using Predict and Observe and then asserting the explanation will have little impact except, perhaps, to confirm some students' beliefs about the inherently dogmatic and non-understandable nature of school science.

Many references given above as reviews of this research and as containing details of probes of understanding also indicate the teaching potential of the probes. Osborne and Freyberg (1985) and Baird and Mitchell (1986) are particularly valuable.

(ii) Probes of understanding often point to implications for the use of traditional approaches to the learning of science. The discussion of Predict/Observe/Explain above is an example, in that this is essentially an alternative approach to using demonstrations. The discussion of students' ideas/beliefs about teaching and learning in a previous section raised important issues for the consideration of laboratory work, in particular the common failure of students to recognize and respond to the teacher's purpose for the laboratory exercise. Gunstone and Champagne (in press) consider implications for laboratory work.

Assessment

The issue of assessment has also been mentioned in a previous section. The significance of assessment for student learning is best seen in terms of fruitfulness, particularly the distinction between internal and external fruitfulness already described. In ideal classrooms containing ideal students no doubt all would seek internal fruitfulness. However this is never the case. Student assessment is frequently the most obvious and most important influence on what students will see as fruitful. The evidence is strong that traditional forms of assessment do little or nothing to make fruitful the substantial effort required of students to construct an understanding of science concepts. This implies that alternative assessment approaches are a necessary part of encouraging students to seek understanding. A substantial discussion of alternative modes of assessment, their purposes and places is again something which would require a book in its own right. Only two rather obvious points are made here. Firstly, any reconceptualization of the objectives of science courses carries a clear obligation to reconsider assessment practices so that they reflect the new objectives. Secondly, alternative assessment practices are again suggested by probes of student understanding (and, again, the reader is referred to previously cited reviews).

Conclusion

One common thread can be seen in the discussion of implications of research on students' ideas/beliefs just completed. The suggested new objectives, new ways of thinking of learning, new teaching/learning strategies, and thoughts on assessment all point in some way towards the importance of metacognition. Having students understand and control their own learning is a major step towards accommodating many of these issues. This thread can be traced further back through the chapter. It is fundamentally consistent with a constructivist view as well as being a logical consequence of the view.

Attempts to have students develop their metacognitive insights and accept the importance of metacognition for learning have been made (Baird and Mitchell, 1986). Some substantial success has been achieved, but has taken a considerable time, has involved teachers accepting different purposes for their courses, has involved the use of new teaching/learning strategies, and new approaches to assessment. What is of major significance is that the nature of learning outcomes has been clearly changed by the focus on metacognition. The development of this change in the nature of what is to be learnt in science education is, I argue, the most important response to research on students' ideas/beliefs.

One final comment about this research area is needed. As Pines and West (1986) argue, research on students' ideas/beliefs might hinder rather than help science education. Some researchers have a tendency to use their data to ridicule students' and teachers' ideas/beliefs. This interpretation of the research thrust is often associated with 'attempts to "butterfly around the curriculum" in search of new misconceptions and trying to motivate teachers to remove these misconceptions from their students ...' (p. 597). Such approaches devalue the efforts of learners to construct meaning. Hence the issue of real importance in the research — that learning is a constructivist process — is missed and the multitude of positive reactions is ignored. Such researchers and developers are ignoring the fact that their own learning is also constructivist in nature.

References

ADEY, P.S. (1987) 'A response to "Towards a Lakatosian analysis of Piagetian and alternative conceptions research programs"', *Science Education*, 71, pp. 5–7.

AMEH, C.O. and GUNSTONE, R.F. (1986) 'Science teachers' concepts in Nigeria and Australia', *Research in Science Education*, 16, pp. 73–81.

ARZI, H.J., WHITE, R.T. and FENSHAM, P.J. (1987) *'Teachers' knowledge of science: An account of a longitudinal study in progress'*, paper presented at the annual meeting of the American Educational Research Association, Washington, DC, April.

BAIRD, J.R. and MITCHELL I.J. (Eds.) (1986) *Improving the Quality of Teaching and Learning: An Australian Case Study — the PEEL Project.* Melbourne, Monash University Printery.

BRILLIANT, A. (1979) *I May Not Be Totally Perfect, But Parts of Me Are Excellent,* Santa Barbara, CA, Woodbridge Press.

BRUMBY, M.N. (1984) 'Misconceptions about the concept of natural selection by medical biology students', *Science Education*, 68, pp. 493–503.

CHAMPAGNE, A.B., GUNSTONE, R.F. and KLOPFER, L.E. (1985) 'Effecting changes in cognitive structures among physics students' in WEST, L.H.T. and PINES, A.L. (Eds) *Cognitive Structure and Conceptual Change,* Orlando, FLA, Academic Press.

CHAMPAGNE, A.B. and KLOPFER, L.E. (1984) 'Research in science education: The cognitive psychology perspective' in HOLDZKOM, D. and LUTZ, P.B. (Eds) *Research Within Reach: Science Education.* Charlestown, WV, Appalachia Educational Laboratory.

CHAMPAGNE, A.B., KLOPFER, L.E. and ANDERSON, J.H. (1980) 'Factors influencing the learning of classical mechanics', *American Journal of Physics*, 48, pp. 1074–9.

DRIVER, R. (1983) *The Pupil as Scientist?* Milton Keynes, Open University Press.

DRIVER, R. and BELL, B. (1986) 'Students' thinking and the learning of science: A constructivist view', *School Science Review*, 67, 240, pp. 443–56.

DRIVER, R. and ERICKSON, G. (1983) 'Theories-in-action: Some theoretical and empirical issues in the study of students' conceptual frameworks in science', *Studies in Science Education*, 10, pp. 37–60.

DRIVER, R., GUESNE, E. and TIBERGHIEN, A. (Eds) (1985) *Children's Ideas in Science,* Milton Keynes, Open University Press.

DUIT, R., JUNG, W. and VON RHÖNECK, C. (Eds) (1985) *Aspects of Understanding Electricity: Proceedings of an International Workshop,* Keil, West Germany, Vertrieb, Schmidt & Klaunig.

ENGEL CLOUGH, E. and DRIVER, R. (1986) ' A study of consistency in the use of students' conceptual frameworks across different task contexts', *Science Education*, 70, pp. 473–96.

ERICKSON, G.L. (1984) *'Some issues on cognitive structure and cognitive change in science education: One perspective from North America'*, paper presented at the annual meeting of the American Educational Research Association, New Orleans, April.

FENSHAM, P.J. (1983) 'A research base for new objectives of science teaching', *Science Education*, 67, pp. 3–12.

GAULD, C. (1987) 'Student beliefs and cognitive structure', *Research in Science Education*, 17 (in press).

GILBERT, J.K. and WATTS, D.M. (1983) 'Concepts, misconceptions and alternative conceptions: Changing perspectives in science education', *Studies in Science Education*, 10, pp. 61–98.

GOOD, R.G. (1977) *How Children Learn Science*, New York, Macmillan.

GROEN, G.J. (1978) 'The theoretical ideas of Piaget and educational practice' in SUPPES, P. (Ed) *Impact of Research on Education: Some Case Studies (Summaries)*. Washington, National Academy of Education.

GRUBER, H.E. and VONÈCHE, J.J. (Eds) (1982) *The Essential Piaget*, London, Routledge & Kegan Paul.

GUNSTONE, R.F. (1987) 'Student understanding in mechanics: A large population survey', *American Journal of Physics*, 55, pp. 691–6.

GUNSTONE, R.F. and CHAMPAGNE, A.B. (in press) 'Promoting conceptual change in the laboratory' in HEGARTY-HAZEL, E. (Ed) *The Science Curriculum and the Student Laboratory*, London, Croom Helm.

GUNSTONE, R.F., CHAMPAGNE, A.B. and KLOPFER, L.E. (1981) 'Instruction for understanding: A case study', *Australian Science Teachers Journal*, 27, 3, pp. 27–32.

GUNSTONE, R.F. and WHITE, R.T. (1981) 'Understanding of gravity', *Science Education*, 65, pp. 291–9.

GUNSTONE, R.F., WHITE, R.T. and FENSHAM, P.J. (1988) 'Developments in style and purpose of research on the learning of science', *Journal of Research in Science Teaching* (in press).

HEAD, J. (1982) 'What can psychology contribute to science education?', *School Science Review*, 63, pp. 631–42.

HELM, H. and NOVAK, J.D. (Eds) (1983) *Proceedings of the International Seminar on Misconceptions in Science and Mathematics*, Ithaca, NY, Cornell University.

HEWSON, P.W. (1981) 'A conceptual change approach to learning science', *European Journal of Science Education*, 3, pp. 383–96.

LAWSON, A.E. (1982) 'The reality of general cognitive operations', *Science Education*, 66, pp. 229–41.

LAWSON, A.E. (1985) 'A review of research on formal reasoning and science teaching', *Journal of Research in Science Teaching*, 22, pp. 569–617.

LINN, M.C. (1986) 'Science' in DILLON, R. and STERNBERG, R.J. (Eds) *Cognition and Instruction*, Orlando, FLA, Academic Press.

LINN, M.C. (1987) 'Establishing a research base for science education: Challenges, trends, and recommendations', *Journal of Research in Science Teaching*, 24, pp. 191–216.

MACNAMARA, J. (1982) *Names for Things: A Study of Human Learning*, Cambridge, MA, Massachusetts Institute of Technology Press.

McCLOSKEY, M. (1983) 'Intuitive physics', *Scientific American*, 248, pp. 114–22.

McDERMOTT, L.C. (1984) 'Research on conceptual understanding in mechanics', *Physics Today*, July, 37, 7, pp. 24–32.

MAGOON, A.J. (1977) 'Constructivist approaches in educational research', *Review of Educational Research*, 47, pp. 651–93.

NIXON, M. (1978) 'The nature of the learner: A point of view and implications for curricula', *Australian Science Teachers Journal*, 24, 3, pp. 15–22.

NOVAK, J.D. (1978) 'An alternative for Piagetian psychology for science and mathematics education', *Studies in Science Education*, 5, 1–30.

NOVAK, J.D. and GOWIN, D.B. (1984) *Learning How to Learn*, Cambridge, MA, Cambridge University Press.

NUSSBAUMN, J. and NOVICK, S. (1982) 'Alternative frameworks, conceptual conflict and accommodation: Toward a principled teaching strategy', *Instructional Science*, 11, pp. 183–200.

OSBORNE, R. and FREYBERG, P. (Eds) (1985) *Learning in Science: The Implications of Children's Science*, Auckland, Heinemann.

OSBORNE, R.J. and WITTROCK, M.C. (1983) 'Learning science: A generative process', *Science Education*, 67, pp. 489–508.

OSBORNE, R.J. and WITTROCK, M.C. (1985) 'The generative learning model and its implications for science education', *Studies in Science Education*, 12, pp. 59–87.

PIAGET, J. (1929) *The Child's Conception of the World*, London, Routledge & Kegan Paul.

PINES, A.L. and WEST, L.H.T. (1986) 'Conceptual understanding and science learning: An interpretation of research within a sources-of-knowledge framework', *Science Education*, 70, pp. 583–604.

Research on Physics Education: Proceedings of the First International Workshop. (1984) Paris: LaLonde les Maures, Editions du CNRS.

RUMELHART, D.E. and NORMAN, D.A. (1978) 'Accretion, tuning and restructuring: Three modes of learning', in KLATZKY, R.L. and COTTON, J.W. (Eds) *Semantic Factors in Cognition*, Hillsdale, NJ, Lawrence Erlbaum.

SHAYER, M. and ADEY, P. (1981) *Towards a Science of Science Teaching*, London, Heinemann.

SHUELL, T.J. (1986) 'Cognitive conceptions of learning', *Review of Educational Research*, 56, pp. 411–36.

STENHOUSE, D. (1986) 'Conceptual change in science education: Paradigms and language games', *Science Education*, 70, pp. 413–25.

TASKER, R. (1981) 'Children's views and classroom experience', *Australian Science Teachers Journal*, 27, 3, pp. 33–7.

VOSNIADOU, S. and BREWER, W.F. (1987) 'Theories of knowledge restructuring in development', *Review of Educational Research*, 57, pp. 51–67.

WEST, L.H.T and PINES, A.L. (Eds) (1985) *Cognitive Structure and Conceptual Change*. Orlando, FLA, Academic Press.

WHITE, R.T. and TISHER, R.P. (1986) 'Research on natural sciences' in WITTROCK, M.C. (Ed) *Handbook of Research on Teaching*, 3rd edn, New York, Macmillan, pp. 874–905.

5
What Children Bring to Light: Towards Understanding What the Primary School Science Learner Is Trying to Do

Bonnie L. Shapiro

When I heard the learn'd astronomer,
When the proofs, the figures, were ranged in columns before me,
When I sitting heard the astronomer where he lectured with much applause in the lecture room,
How soon unaccountable I became tired and sick,
Till rising and gliding out I wander'd off by myself,
In the mystical moist night-air, and from time to time,
Look'd up in perfect silence at the stars.

Walt Whitman in Leaves of Grass, 1965.

Difficulty in Science Learning: 'Weakness' or Window?

Walt Whitman's poem exemplifies a dilemma and a concern for science educators. Here is the student, attracted to a lecture, interested in and wanting to know about astronomy, yet when confronted with the instructor's systematic presentation, 'the proofs, the figures', he becomes 'unaccountably tired'. Empty. He is sickened and leaves. And in this leaving we feel the learner's profound sense of relief. For some science educators, however, this student's experience is not counted as a 'valid' one.

Issac Asimov, the foremost writer and popularizer of science, argues that in this poem, Walt Whitman is 'talking through his hat, but the poor old soul didn't know any better' (Asimov, 1984). In Asimov's view, Whitman ignores the beauty and sense of wonder which is to be gained through science study, suggesting that those who cannot 'stomach' the presentation are missing out on the *true* splendour and wonder to be gained in a study of the universe. In his view, an accumulation of factual knowledge in science is the best way to attain an appreciation of the amazing patterns and beauty in the universe. According to Asimov, '... the poor old poet never knew what a stultified and limited beauty he observed when he looked up in perfect silence at the stars.'

But perhaps Whitman makes, through this poem, an important comment which cannot be so easily argued away. For if we carefully listen to this person's experience it may become a window, enabling us to become more wide-awake to the learner's experience, understanding how it is that aspects of the very nature of the process of this student's education in science have turned him away. To understand students' difficulties and frustrations in learning science, we must understand what our own assumptions about learning science are, how they affect students, and we must listen more to students describing their experience themselves.

Educators' Assumptions about Learning in Classrooms

Most educators have ideas about how their students learn best, and strive to build this thinking into the instruction which they offer. Many educational programs are also rooted in ideas which curriculum writers hold about the nature of students and how they learn. Naturally, the proponents of an educational program believe that their way of viewing school learning is the best approach for learners, but it is also often the case that the actual participants may not be aware of the proponents' basic assumptions about learning. Research in science education is also built upon the assumptions about learning. Curriculum programs which claim to be based on research findings, then, must also be based upon the assumptions which are the basis of the research.

In the effort to understand science learning in the primary (elementary) school it is useful to reconsider some of the fundamental assumptions about students and learning which guide curriculum writers, researchers, and the teacher's direction of classroom events.

> *The Student's Mind as 'Blank Slate' — The Impact of Curriculum upon the Student*

Throughout the 1960s and 1970s research on teaching and learning and its subsequent application to the development of science curriculum materials was based upon a model of school learning rooted in the familiar 'tabula rasa' metaphor. In this view the learner's mind is seen as a 'blank slate' to be filled by the teacher. The learner comes to school to be 'learning outcomed', that is, to eventually emerge from school with all or most of the predetermined objectives of the curriculum, or of the teacher, securely fastened in mind. The 'blank slate' metaphor is further maintained by evaluating the learner at the end of each 'learning sequence'. Here the learner is deemed to have either succeeded or to have failed to accomplish the stated objectives. Success in such a learning system means to exist with the correct answers to the questions posed by the curriculum or the teacher. This is usually the only outcome which is valued in an extreme application of this approach to learning. The learner who fails is easily and systematically 'recycled' back through the experience until success is achieved or until the learner drops out, whichever comes first. It is not the experience of the learner that is paramount here — it is the effect of curriculum upon the student that matters.

This approach to school learning with its assembly line view of student progress was in wide use in the 1960s, changed very little into the 1970s and even now is widely in use in the late 1980s. In recent years, some practitioners and a number of educational researchers have insisted that new or alternative sets of assumptions should replace the 'blank slate' metaphor. It is argued that a complete explanation of how learning occurs in the classroom must include a consideration of the experiences of the learner, the key participant in learning. As Brophy noted in 1982, 'For the most part, educational researchers have considered students only as objects of teacher activity', but now, '... a complete account of classroom events will have to include, besides information about teacher behaviour and its long-term effects, information about what students are doing in their classrooms and how these activities affect their perceptions, knowledge and beliefs.' Little research in education, however, has actually been undertaken to document and convey such insights. 'Emphasis upon the person-as-meaning maker is a dominant theme in educational theorizing, but in practice, the phenomenological world of the learner is often neglected' (Pope and Gilbert, 1983).

Studies in Science Education Which Focus on the Learner

Some efforts from the late 1970s have attempted to shift the focus of research attention to the learner. In science education this attention to the learner has produced studies primarily concerned with learners' preconceptions about natural phenomena. The major effort has been to clarify the ideas learners hold about a particular phenomenon before they experience classroom instruction. Hence, we know that children's pre-instructional ideas about natural phenomena can be very different from those which they are asked to accept in school, the *scientists'* ideas about the nature of phenomena. Learners' deviations from scientists' views were labelled 'misconceptions' in a number of these studies which set out to identify these wrong ideas, which learners hold and often cling to tenaciously in the face of science teaching. It has been suggested by many researchers that the main thrust in the next steps in work in this area should be upon efforts to bring about conceptual change in learners. Posner, Strike, Hewson, and Gertzog (1982) present as their central argument, that learning is a wholly rational activity in which learners must make judgments, based on their interpretation of the available evidence, about the rationality and intelligibility of arguments presented to them.

Several concerns make this view problematic. First, implicit in it is a conception of the human mind as an entity which is separate from the person. This is an old assumption which, as Nyberg (1971) wrote, sees the mind 'as a special isolated datum that functions discretely and is to be approached directly, as one would aim at a target'. In holding this view, we may ignore the importance of the impact of factors like the individual's feelings on the learning process, and the learner's image of science, of science knowledge, and of his/her social interactions in the classroom with other learners and the teacher. Any of these may positively affect the learner's persistence and delight in learning, or may serve to enhance the learner's feelings of inadequacy, frustration, or alienation from the experience.

Freyberg and Osborne (1985) noted that it is likely that the attempt to generate and use any model of learning unavoidably causes some gross oversimplification of what actually happens in practice. No model is likely to be completely useful in helping us to understand all of the complexities of the learning process, so it is all the more important that we are aware that the use of our models might cause us to overlook some important complexities of the learning process.

The Need for Studies Which Focus on the Learner as an Active Participant in Science Learning

The studies to determine students' ideas about natural phenomena have revealed a great deal. The ideas learners hold prior to instruction have been found to greatly influence learning. Learners more readily acquire new knowledge when they are able to relate it to already existing ideas or to language which they already possess. In this way, it is argued, new ideas 'make sense' in terms which are already familiar to students. Yet the experiences of the learner in many of these studies have still been stated in terms of factors and situations that are external to the person. The implications of these studies are then also stated in terms of yet other, albeit different external impacts upon the learner, seeming to ignore the value of the enthusiasm and willingness of the child to learn, or of the frustration and alienation which the learner might hold for those experiences.

As I reviewed the now abundant literature available, there seemed to be a need for studies which take the contribution of the learner into account. Extensive experience with young learners of science and in the development of curriculum materials has made me a frequent observer of science learners. I envisaged a different type of study to be based upon the assumption of the learner as an active participant in science learning. A number, among the conceptions researchers, also view the learner as a maker of meaning, an active participant in the process of learning, and one who can take a major responsibility for his or her own learning behaviour. With this 'constructivist perspective' (Pope and Gilbert, 1983; Driver and Oldham, 1985; Magoon, 1977; and Watzlawick, 1984) such researchers are interested in understanding the processes by which children contribute to their own school learning experiences. The child's experience of school learning is, then, viewed not only in terms of ultimate effects of *curriculum upon the learner* but in terms of *the learner's active involvement with the curriculum*. This body of research is gaining increasing credibility, comment, and audience in the science education community. It certainly has moved conceptions research much more towards the learner's experience than some of the earlier studies did. My concern with the learner's interest in that experience or in a topic to be learned at schools is perhaps another step in this direction that research studies need to take.

My own research into the process of children's learning in science (Shapiro, 1987) grew and developed through an interest in understanding the complexities of children's interaction with a science curriculum. From my preliminary studies a number of observations seemed very significant. Within the same classroom, several children had held nearly identical ideas about the nature of light *before* instruction, but, even though the entire class received the same instruction, only some of these children changed their ideas. This occurred even when the children's incorrect notions about the topic were explicitly addressed by the teacher. I wondered how this difference in individuals might be explained. And why was it that one child delighted in the advent of the science period while another viewed its approach with dread and loathing? What were the children's beliefs about what they were accomplishing as they learned science? Was there a relationship between these beliefs and the ways that they thought and behaved during science study? It seemed that there were factors other than children's previous ideas about the nature of light which interacted with and affected their thinking about it, and in some instances influenced whether or not a change in ideas occurred. It seemed that these other 'sets' or 'constellations' of factors were interwoven with the children's pre-instructional ideas and the experience of classroom learning, and could possibly hold even greater persistence over time, in a learner's ongoing experience of learning science in school, than his or her changing ideas about the nature of phenomena. I was convinced that these factors should also be explored in an account of science learning and conceptual change.

Since these factors seemed to be *highly individual*, an exploration of them would be unlikely to result in a set of general, normed statements, disembodied from real people. Although general statements of learner understandings or trends in learner ideas are clearly very useful to educators and curriculum developers who are interested in the concepts most likely to cause difficulty, it is also clear that not all learners do encounter difficulty, nor do they approach their studies in the same ways. Accordingly, my study should provide an account and an understanding of how individual children's ideas, feelings, *and* their approaches to science learning interweave and interact.

It also became clear from the interviews, which I conducted across grade levels in these preliminary studies, that negative feelings about science study can begin when learners are very young. It seemed all the more important to conduct an intensive study of *individual* children learning science which documented for teachers, student teachers, researchers, curriculum developers, parents and for the learners themselves, not only children's ideas in science, but how they felt about what they were doing and what they, in fact, were attempting to accomplish in their science learning.

Integrating the Two Research Perspectives to Inform Our Understanding of Young Children Learning Science

Two research perspectives that have been described have contributed to my study as it attempted to convey some of the complexities of children's experiences as they learn about a specific topic in science class. The first perspective saw them being asked to accept ideas in science class which may be completely new or are even nonsensical to them. The 'blank slate' metaphor could be appropriate, as these children or some of them may be completely 'blank' about a new idea which they are asked to accept.

The second research perspective would see the children in my study building ideas in the classroom largely through their own actions and efforts to understand and relate to their previous ideas and experience. When a child is asked to consider a new idea about natural phenomena, whether or not the idea will be considered plausible or convincing will depend on how and from what background he or she approaches the idea. Some children approach new ideas in a rational–logical manner, considering all of the evidence available, then making a decision. Some learners will simply memorize the idea. The visitor to any primary classroom cannot ignore the variety of approaches which children take when involved in the process of making a new idea their own.

Both these research perspectives were also useful to me in documenting the interaction of children and new ideas in science. Children's ideas about light are described along with portrayals of each individual's unique approach to study of the topic content. Individuals in the study held very different images from one another about the trustworthiness of science knowledge. During a science class some children focused upon and showed an interest in one type of learning activity, such as class discussion, while others appeared to be bored and uninterested. By their actions, these learners lived out the different images which they held about what was important and interesting in the experience of the study of light.

One of the chief methods of the study was to engage in conversation with each child over an extended period of time. In this way I was able to become thoroughly acquainted through the language they used with the various approaches each took in the structured study of science, and hence I was able to document the interaction of each child's approach to science, along with his/her interpretation of new ideas and the elements of the science story presented in the classroom.

Themes for each child emerged from the records of interviews, the analysis of survey information, from a research technique called repertory grid elicitation of personal constructs, and from reflection on my impressions of comments and behaviour, as I observed and interacted with these learners. These themes were portrayals of pattern in the child's approach to science study, and *personal orientation* to science study was a construct I found useful in describing the patterns of themes of each child's approach to science study. These themes were repeatedly seen in learning incidents, interactions, and conversations with each child. Examples or 'paradigmatic instances' of each child's thought and action were selected from my records. Personal Construct Theory was the theoretical foundation of this aspect of the study and it guided the collection of information and the organization of the examples presented in the case study reports. Because this theory attempts to explain how different *individuals* create meaning in the circumstances in which they find themselves, it proved to be a particularly appropriate research approach in my attempt to understand the interweaving of each child's dialogue with the external presentation of information.

The Metaphors of Personal Construct Theory: 'The Person as Scientist: The Person as a Form of Motion'

Personal Construct Theory was invented by George Kelly (1955) as an attempt to integrate a theory of personality with a theory of knowledge. Kelly considered each person to be an 'intuitive scientist', in that the individual is formulating hypotheses about the world, collecting data that confirm or disconfirm these hypotheses, then altering his or her conception to include any new information. Thus, Kelly asserted, every person operates in a manner *similar* to the scientist who clearly and deliberately attributes meaning to the topic under study. This analogy to the 'person–as–scientist' does not preclude the possibility, for example, that an individual could possess an entirely *aesthetic* set of anticipations, expectations or orientations to science learning. Human beings are thought to behave 'like scientists' in that their actions in the world are affected by the anticipations, expectations, theories or assumptions about the particular circumstances in which they find themselves.

Kelly also considered the person to be a 'form of motion'. He saw the person always 'moving', always interacting with the environment and therefore always changing. This analogy to movement emphasizes his rejection of the view that knowledge possession means acquiring an ever-growing collection of substantiated 'facts'. It is the unique exploration and interpretation of the environment which Kelly considered to be the key to understanding the person. The person's construction of reality is not *only* a rational activity, but is an active, changing, creative, emotional, rational and pragmatic activity. This constructivist view goes considerably beyond that of Posner *et al.*

As each child's actions and personal orientation to science learning were documented throughout the study, the ongoing changes in the children's ideas about the nature of light were also presented, thereby interweaving once again the perspective of the first research approach.

A Study of Six Young Children Learning Science in School

Mark, Donnie, Melody, Martin, Amy and Pierre were three boys and three girls in a grade 5 class whom I observed and spoke with over a six-month period, before, during, and after their class study of the topic, light. The children selected for the study had experienced varying degrees of success in their overall school program. Two students experienced a great deal of difficulty and attended special daily classes in mathematics and reading. Another two students were considered to be relatively average students. The other two were considered to be making high quality progress in their studies.

I interviewed each one to determine his or her ideas about the nature of light prior to instruction in this topic. I also used surveys, group discussion, samples of students' written work, observation, informal conversation, and a reflective journal in my attempt to understand each learner's experience of learning about light in the classroom. During the study, I videotaped all of the lessons presented in the unit. After the lessons, each learner in the study group discussed with me his or her ongoing ideas about light, and thoughts and feelings about the experience of science learning. Analyses from all these sources were developed into an individual case report for each of the six learners. I also explored the interplay of the external presentation of content information by the teacher, Mr Don, with some of the personal, internal and interpersonal factors which affected their processes of learning about the topic, light.

It was not surprising that there were many similarities among the ideas which the children held about the nature of light prior to the study as they have been well documented by other researchers (Guesne, 1988; Andersson and Karrqvist, 1982; Anderson and Smith, 1983; Stead and Osborne, 1980; and Jung, 1981). But the children's approaches to learning about light in class, were strikingly different from one to another. They appeared to be guided by such diverse factors in the individual learner as the image held of self as science learner, by the learner's interest in one type of experience over another during the class sessions, by the image he or she held about science and science knowledge, or the ways that interaction in large and small group settings were viewed and valued. During the study, each learner was guided by a different set of these factors as he or she approached science learning.

The following selections from one learner's case report and some summary findings from others' reports are presented to show the kinds of ideas about light and the images of science and science learning which interweave in some of the children's experiences in the classroom.

Mark: Excerpts from a Case Report

Some of Mark's ideas about the nature of light

Before the unit began, I interviewed each child to determine their ideas about the nature of light and any evidence of previous experiences or attitudes which

Figure 1: How does light allow the child to see the house?

had been developed concerning study of the topic. In one question they were shown a diagram (Figure 1) and were then to use arrows to show how light allows the girl to see the house. I discussed the example and the drawing provided by each child to attempt to get an in depth grasp of each individual's thinking about the question.

Mark drew in the following lines:

Figure 2: Mark's response to the question posed by figure 1

He told me that 'light lets the boy see the house because light falls from the sun onto the house'. Mark said that 'the boy sees the house because there is enough light so that his eyes can see, and then the signal goes to his brain. That's why I have these light rays coming from the sun, and then hitting the house. The lines from the boy mean that he is seeing the sun and the house.' I asked if any light was being reflected from the house to the boy. He said 'no'. In this discussion Mark was not making reference to the scientifically accepted idea that light rays reflect from objects into our eyes, thereby allowing us to see objects.

Mark — The appreciator of science knowledge

At age 10, Mark was the youngest child in Mr Don's grade 5 class. Mr Don regarded him as 'a good student, a reasonably well-behaved boy, though a bit young in some of his ways of relating to others'. To indicate his level of enjoyment of science, Mark checked the highest rating possible, 'I really like it!', on a survey which I asked the children to fill in early in my visit. In fact, Mark embellished his check mark and added an exclamation mark for emphasis. Mark's view of himself as a learner of science became clear to me immediately, and it was summed up in this comment during our first interview:

> I find science pretty easy most of the time. I get things mostly that the other kids don't, or, er, um, that they sort of have trouble with.

Not only did similar comments reappear later in the study, but I observed how on several occasions Mark did indeed grasp difficult concepts and put ideas together more accurately and effectively than his classmates. His self-confidence was apparent. This representation of himself *to* himself as a self-assured and successful learner of science, became the first theme in Mark's case report.

> Theme I: *Self characterization*: 'I'm really getting all of it and I feel sure of myself and what I'm learning. And I'm really enjoying myself.'
>
> *Researcher image/impression*: A regularly successful science learner. Assured and self-confident.

Part of the evidence for each theme is the comparative statements Mark (and the others) produced in response to my use of the Kelly repertory grid technique.

One learning incident, some time into the study of the topic, was particularly helpful in revealing the extent of Mark's ability to connect ideas about the nature of light. In it he came to some conclusions which were extremely difficult for many other members of the class to grasp. It was interesting that Mark came to understand these new ideas even though his pre-instructional ideas were not at all like scientists' ideas about the nature of light. In fact, his ideas were very similar to those of the majority of the other children in his class.

Mark's revolutionary thinking

On 13 March, after six light lessons, Mr Don, the classroom teacher, said he expected that I would find that the children would enjoy the next lesson entitled 'So Deceiving'.

Two mystery problems were presented in this lesson. First, the learners were instructed to place a coin in an ordinary saucer. They then were to move away from the saucer, crouching down, to the point where the coin disappeared from view, yet still keeping the saucer edges in view. Water was then to be slowly poured into the saucer. As the water was slowly poured in, the learners were to remain in the crouched position, watching the saucer closely, and as the water level rose, the 'invisible' coin appeared! The problem for them to explain was how it could be that they were not able to see the coin at one point, but then, with only the slow addition of water, they were suddenly able to see the coin reappear! The second activity instructed them to place a pencil in a beaker half full of water (see later in this chapter).

In the first example, Mark watched with the others in his group as the coin in the saucer slowly appeared. Mark then suddenly jumped up. He pointed to the coin and said excitedly to the others:

> I know! I know what's making it do that! It's the light rays. The water's bending them! The water's bending the light rays!

The other three looked at the saucer, at Mark, and at one another, and appeared perplexed by his comments. They seemed to ignore Mark and continued looking at the saucer from different angles, making statements of observation to themselves. Mark repeated his idea. They listened, but, again with shrugging shoulders and quizzical looks, appeared not to understand. They continued to look at the saucer and proposed explanations about what might be making the coin seem to 'float' to the surface of the water.

Seeming undaunted, Mark walked over to Donnie and Carey's table. I was told Carey and Mark had a very special friendship, a 'crush on each other'. This seemed to serve as a very effective opportunity for both Mark and Carey to verbalize their ideas and findings in various subjects to one another on a regular basis. Mark pointed to Carey's saucer and proclaimed, 'I know why it's doing that!'

The importance of social and collaborative factors in the development of students' ideas was much in evidence in this study, even though in this example Mark was having great difficulty sharing his ideas. Mark often had a strong effect upon Carey, less so with the other students, but on this occasion, Mark's insight was beyond Carey's grasp. She looked up at Mark and said, 'Oh yeah, really?' She did not possess Mark's new insight at this point nor did she ask for his explanation; she continued watching the saucer. Mark chose not to push forward his wonderful idea at this point, and I wondered if he might be slightly discouraged by the lack of enthusiasm of his classmates, but he emptied his saucer, then literally hopped and skipped back around the classroom to his desk. He did not try again to convince his own group of the correctness of his idea, but carefully wrote his explanation on his worksheet. Jason, who sat next to Mark in the science group, watched him put down his answer, then conscientiously copied Mark's answer word for word into his own notebook. It was only much later that several other learners in the class did finally realize what Mark had been trying to tell them.

Mark had been able to explain changes in the appearance of objects which seemed magical and beyond the comprehension of nearly everyone else in his class. I spoke with him after the lesson.

Ms Shapiro: I'm very interested in your telling me more about the activities which you have been involved with today. I heard you say, all of a sudden, as you were looking at the coin, 'It's the reflected light!' I wondered if that idea came to you all of a sudden, or what it was like at that time, what happened for you there?

Mark:	Well, hummm. I guess it's that I just like science a whole lot, and I just think that it was because of being, um, of remembering from *before*.
Ms Shapiro:	I see. You know, it looked like the ideas came together for you all of a sudden. But you say you remembered from *before*.
Mark:	Well, yes, it was sort of all of a sudden. Well, I knew the, um, pretty much the ideas, what were going on *before*.
Ms Shapiro:	Oh, I see. Can you tell me what you remembered and which experiments you found helpful?
Mark:	Well, um I guess mostly when he told us about the light, how people used to see things, like they thought they saw things by something coming from your eye, or thought it was coming from your eye. But we know it doesn't now. And the one, well I guess, with the beaker and the light beams bending through the water, that one was the one that helped me the most. That showed me how the light bends and all when it goes through the beaker and water, you know, from the light source?
Ms Shapiro:	Yes, I remember that. When you started to tell the others in your group today that it was the light that was reflecting off of the coin, how did they react?
Mark:	Oh, yeah. They acted sort of surprised and stuff. At first they didn't understand it and so then I told them again. They thought that the penny floated up to the top or something. (Laughs) I told them that the light was doing it. It was the reflected light.
Ms Shapiro:	Yes, but when the whole class discussion took place later, and when Mr D. was asking, 'What was happening, why do we see the penny, why do you see the coin there?' everyone gave different answers. I wondered why, in the class discussion, that you waited until the end of the discussion to give your answer.
Mark:	Well, I was, sort of trying to figure out what, um, if I was right.
Ms Shapiro:	So, you weren't quite certain whether or not you were right.
Mark:	No. Well, I guess. But I just waited.
Ms Shapiro:	But then when you finally did give your answer, were you sure you were right then?
Mark:	No. (Laughs) Not really at all. But see, I was going a way back in the beginning and putting things I learned together, and I didn't um, I *thought* I was right, but, I could have been wrong, too. I guess, um, it just seemed to fit all together.
Ms Shapiro:	Was there a particular part of this activity that you found that made it most clear to you?
Mark:	Well, like I said, when I was little, and even now, really, um, I

used to always have a really good memory and stuff, so that helps me a lot to remember things.

Ms Shapiro: Were there parts of this lesson itself that seemed to help you to make the connection to this important idea that explained things for you?

Mark: Well, not here, because we were just putting together here all the things we learned from before.

Mark was aware of the 'pieces' of information which he recalled and used to connect ideas from the beginning of the unit with more recently presented ideas to explain the entirely new, mysterious phenomenon the learners were observing in this lesson. His clarity on his own learning processes was quite remarkable, and even though he waited to give what he wanted to be sure was *the correct* answer, he seemed never really to doubt it nor his ability in science. The failure of his fellows to grasp his idea did not discourage him in the slightest.

Mark did not mention explicitly the original idea he recalled and used as the basic fact in building his explanation. This idea (given by Mr Don in the first lesson) was that 'non-visible' light rays reflect from all objects. Mark had no difficulty accepting this idea, but the other five in the study group had commented at the time, that it did not make sense. In fact, two of them claimed that Mr Don was wrong in thinking this way about light.

A second theme which emerged for Mark was also a similar theme for several other students. This theme emphasized *the enjoyment of doing the activities* of the lessons, or what Mark called 'the experiments'. Mark also emphasized the value of 'coming up with something different than the answer that you're supposed to have'. He told me a story about how he and one of his classmates tried to finish the activities of a *Batteries and Bulbs* study early so that they could then try to answer some questions of their own by experimenting. Mark enjoyed the discovery of unique and new ideas, and the physical doing or involvement in the activities for himself.

> Theme II: *Self characterization*: 'I really like to do the experimenting and things, things that I'm doing for myself. I really enjoy doing things myself and coming up with ideas that are different than just what's on the overhead projector.' *Researcher image/impression*: Enjoyment of physical involvement in science activities. Self-motivated, autonomous. Enjoys finding things out for himself.

For another student, Martin, physical involvement with the materials was central to his enjoyment theme. Martin was often unable to read the worksheets well enough to understand the task, but, as a result of his intense interest in frequent manipulation of the equipment to follow his own lines of enquiry, he discovered a great deal about the nature of light and light beam reflection. His tinkering provided him and members of his group with many unique insights. Martin was not able to report these findings, as he was not answering the worksheet questions but his own. He was, however, able to communicate his special insights verbally to the others in his activity group.

The tasks prescribed by the curriculum materials were useful in providing the learners with clear statements of tasks. It was also clear that students like Mark and Martin need the opportunity to exercise their strong interest in and ability to work autonomously, to pose questions of their own, and to communicate their own special findings to others. Although these curriculum materials did suggest some 'optional' class activities, there was no provision to allow individual learners to pursue and value their own questions and findings. A science fair project might have served part of this need, but the science fair was cancelled in the school due to the great demands of the regular school program!

The third theme which emerged for Mark was entirely unique to him:

Theme III: *Self characterization*: 'I like to hear what *science* has to tell us.'
Researcher image/impression: Valuing the *story* of science.
Valuing science knowledge as tentative explanation.

Only Mark made specific reference to his lessons and activities as experiences by which we 'find out what *science* tells us'. In the repertory grid, he contrasted his own phrase, 'Hearing what *science* has to tell us', with 'Telling what *we* think'. He did not equate the two, but spoke of a connection between his own experience of science in the classroom and his experience of hearing *the story of science*, the story told by scientists. Mark was willing to accept an idea even though he would not be able to 'see it with his own eyes'. He considered himself a participant, a contributor to the experience as he was able to verify the science story through his experiments and activities. This link became clearer during a video recall session, when he referred to doing science as, 'It's like you're putting together the pieces of a mystery'. In fact, for his personally selected books to read during the year, Mark chose a mystery selection — twenty-three mysteries, fourteen adventure stories, six other fiction titles, and three humorous pieces.

As in the solving of a mystery, Mark referred to doing science as an effort to find out 'about the way things really are'. He also likened science study to 'a puzzle to be put together to discover an answer', and he told me that 'most things in science are right'. But, despite his apparent valuing of science as 'the search for truth', he simultaneously held the view that science knowledge is tentative and changing. In one of our conversations, I again probed to find out if Mark had some insight how he was able to grasp ideas that other students seemed to have so much trouble with.

Mark: Well, like, most science things are right.
Ms Shapiro: Most science things are right?
Mark: Yeah.
Ms Shapiro: Can you tell me what you mean by *right*?
Mark: Ummm. Well, when you say, like, people used to say that the earth was flat, and it's really round. So science is the right ideas about things. Some of the ideas in the future might change though.
Ms Shapiro: I see —
Mark: And like Mr Don said, people used to think there was something that came from your eye to the object and that let you see the object. But the right idea is that the light reflects on the object and then goes into your eye, like I said before. So that helps.
Ms Shapiro: but ... how do you know that is true?
Mark: Because Mr Don said so. (Laughs)
Ms Shapiro: How do you know that Mr Don's answer is the correct one?
Mark: Well, he's taken 'Light' in college and all and he tells us what he knows from that.

Valuing the tentative nature of science knowledge also implied for Mark a special relationship with Mr Don, who he saw as a person well-educated in science and therefore a valid conveyor of scientific insights. However, acceptance of this authority did not keep Mark from questioning a viewpoint, when, for example, he was given information by Mr Don in an activity involving the colour spectrum which challenged his own sense perception.

Mark: Well, I didn't see white, either. *You* didn't either did you?
Ms Shapiro: No.
Mark: So, I thought maybe Mr Don made a mistake at first. But he said he saw white and that, that's what it's supposed to be. So I thought, maybe that's what it's supposed to be even though it doesn't *look* that way, that's what it should be, because maybe the light here in the classroom isn't the best. But I don't know, because it, if you looked at it a certain way, I could see how somebody might say it was white!

Here, however, Mark realized that he had not seen what he was told he *should* have seen. Revisiting this incident with other aspects of Mark's personal orientation to science learning, we can see that his very positive feelings about himself as a science learner are firmly rooted in his past successful experiences. He values his own perception of colour in the mixed light, yet he is not adamant that his sensory perception should replace what he was told he should have seen. Mark was open to believe that what he was told *could* be true, partly perhaps because of the high esteem which he has for Mr Don's authority, and in part because of the credibility which he places in the story provided by scientists.

Mark's interest in the ways that we learn from science itself showed a fundamental difference between his approach to science learning and that of all of the other children in the study group. Mark did not take complete responsibility for working out the answers to the problems posed. He was willing to accept certain ideas without experiencing them, was *open* to changing his ideas and was interested in knowing what had been the trials and errors of past research. Mark had, then, a sense of the *history* of science, which was often seen in his comments on Mr Don's discussions, in which, for example, he frequently recalled how 'people used to think ...' when referring to the nature of light and colour. In this way, Mark placed himself in intellectual partnership with the past, learning from the work of others while at the same time seeking autonomy, testing things out for himself, confirming for himself. He was able to listen, believe and comment on the story of science, and thus better understand the experience which he was having with the materials. His awareness of the nature of knowledge growth in science was coupled with a delight in active participation in the ideas and materials that were presented to him in science lessons. He attempted to integrate his own experience with the story of science.

Students of all ages have been found to have a great deal of difficulty in grasping this idea that light rays, constantly reflecting from the objects around us, permit the visibility of objects. Not only was Mark able to grasp this idea during the presentation of the unit, but he was also able to *use* this fact to explain other types of light phenomena and to develop an understanding of the concept, refraction.

I saw several other areas of significant contrast between Mark and the others in the group. He asked questions about light phenomena which seemed very different. When I asked him if he ever thought about science or light outside the classroom, he shared with me the fact that he often looked up at the sky at night and thought about such questions 'What makes the stars twinkle?' and 'Is there an end to the universe?' He told me that he wondered what scientists had to say about these questions because he *really* wanted to know. Also he would like to do experiments which would answer some of his own questions, and he would like to see if scientists had possibly asked the same ones. Mark was trying to do something quite different during science than the others in my study, and his teacher's understanding of Mark's orientation to science learning, and the curriculum materials being used were not allowing him to pursue such questions and activities in his classroom.

Another difference seemed to relate to the specific conditions that learners need to consider ideas presented to them as valid. While learning about light, Mark, for example, did not necessarily have to 'see' the light rays reflecting from objects in order to believe that they do. For him, the fact that the teacher had said so was sufficient. Mark saw the teacher as a credible authority, who conveyed to the class the 'true story of science'. But Pierre, another child in the class, found it essential to 'see for himself' whatever he was asked to believe. Even at the end of the unit, Pierre did not grasp the basic concept that light rays reflect off all objects. His situation seemed particularly urgent to me, as I had known him through his intense interest in, and detailed knowledge of, bits and pieces of information on such topics as dinosaurs, rockets, outer space and volcanoes. His great delight in possessing 'natural history' type of knowledge about these topics, and his great joy at the thought of those science classes was a pleasure to observe. But it was sadly evident that a subtle erosion in this joy was occurring, as Pierre found that grasping many ideas about science topics like light was based on acceptance of ideas which were not real or meaningful to him. Pierre was left after almost every class session with the feeling that something was wrong with *him* because he was having difficulty learning about the topic, light, but he did not know precisely what the difficulty was.

Another student in the study, Melody, also could not believe what she could not see for herself, at least, *at first*. In Melody's view, 'We don't really do science like scientists do. They create new ideas. Like, we just study what *they* found out.' Melody's personal orientation to science learning was dominated by a strong social interest in the other children in the classroom. Melody was frequently missing from her activity group when I went to observe her. To the dismay of Mr Don, she constantly roamed the classroom to find out what other students were doing, and to find out what they were thinking. It was apparently because of, not despite, this approach to science learning that Melody was one of the learners who actually did grasp some of the more difficult concepts of the units on light by the end of the study. In my last interview with her, she was able to tell me which activity groups in the classroom had considered ideas about light carefully, and from which individuals she had learned the most in her 'travels' around the classroom.

Amy, who was regarded by her teacher as the top student in the class, could be relied upon by him and her classmates to know precisely what was to be accomplished during each activity working period. Amy was also a person who did not 'believe until she saw'. She told me that Mr Don's idea that light came from objects was 'crazy'. In Amy's words, 'Light doesn't come from objects like people! Light comes from light bulbs and television sets!' Despite such insistence, Amy always had the correct answers on her worksheets. Her science notebook was close to perfection. It seemed sad and surprising to me that Amy spoke in our conversations of really having very little interest in the topic being studied, yet, by appearances, she was the person whose assigned work was the most complete and accurate. Amy's approach to science learning was guided by a strong orientation to achievement, not for the purpose of understanding, but for the sake of achievement itself. Science content was secondary, and wasn't really very interesting to her. The important thing for Amy was to figure out what was to be done in the task assigned, and to complete the worksheet with the correct answers. Though she had the correct answers on all of her worksheets at the end of the unit, Amy never grasped the idea of reflection of 'non-visible' light rays, nor did she understand refraction, colour vision, or how a prism and light created a rainbow.

Implications of the Study for Classroom Practice

Very few studies of individual children are available in the science education literature. Navarra (1951) documented the development of his 2-year-old son's ideas about natural phenomena over a period of several years. Fynn (1974) presents a charming fictional account of a young girl's natural development of ideas about the natural world and the cultural world. Apelman *et al.* (1983) looked at the difficulties experienced by teachers of young children as they attempted to broaden their learning in science. But extended classroom studies of young children have been long overdue.

My attempt at such a study of children learning about light in their primary science lessons suggests a number of implications. These are best stated in terms of how teachers and curriculum makers might help to guide learners' understandings, (i) by becoming aware of, making explicit, building upon, and enhancing the already naturally developing directions of their interest; and (ii) by encouraging learners to reflect on their own learning processes, so that they might take an even more active role in, and responsibility for, their own learning.

In 1973 Frank Smith described twelve easy 'rules' for teaching reading which he believes that teachers follow regularly with the result that learning to read is actually made difficult. He then proposed one difficult rule for teachers to follow which he believed will make learning to read easy. His difficult rule is this: 'Respond to what the child is trying to do.'

Embodied in Smith's rule is the recognition that the motivation for learning to read must come from within the child. He sees learning to read as a problem for the child to solve, and recommends that the teacher of reading change from a focus on imposing reading skills and rules on the child from without, to providing guidance to help the child take a genuinely active part in solving this, her or his problem.

Seeing learners as having an active role in their own individual learning is not a new idea in education. Advocates of 'hands-on' learning have long recognized the value of the physical participation of the learner in learning activities. But understanding and responding to what *the child is attempting to do* implies much more. It requires a greater recognition of the extent of the active involvement of the child. To understand how the child is attempting to do this, we need to assume first that the children are already attempting to make sense of the experiences which we provide for them.

In the study of six children learning science which has been described above, this assumption underlaid my attempt to understand how they solved the problem of learning scientifically accepted ideas about the nature of light. What emerged were snapshot portrayals of Mark and the other five children moving, albeit in very different ways, towards making this sort of knowledge their own.

If we can take this view of the child as a learner who attempts to solve the problem of making meaning in science, he or she becomes a co-architect in the teaching and learning process. We see not only what the curriculum does to the child, but we look to determine what the child is doing with the curriculum. Further, the methods of our research efforts and our teaching and curricular efforts become very similar as we listen to what the child is saying and showing us about his or her ideas and feelings while engaged in studying a topic. We become more receptive to understand what the child is contributing in her or his study of the topic. Putting this view of the child as active learner fully into our teaching practice is, however, quite a new and challenging idea. In the contemporary educational climate, it demands (even more than in 1973 when Smith wrote)

> ... a rejection of formulae, less reliance on tests, and more receptivity to the child. Its main demand is a total rejection of the ethos of our day — that the answer to all of our problems lies in improved method and technology and of the emphasis on method that pervades almost all teacher training. (p. 22)

Personal Construct Theory also emphasizes the great effect of the person's anticipations and expectations of experience upon thought and action. This idea helps to explain why change in children's behaviour and thought is often so difficult to accomplish (as my own and so many other recent studies in science education have found). It also suggests that, to bring about such change, consideration (and acceptance of what is found) will need to be given by teachers (and their learners) to new expectations and anticipations concerning the experience of science learning. This understanding would include a grasp of the images which learners hold in their ongoing school experience of science learning, such as their ideas about the nature of the phenomena being studied, the nature of science knowledge, of themselves as science learners, but also the ways by which these learners (as co-architects in their own science learning) construct meaning and make sense of what is presented to them.

It is relatively easy for teachers to coerce learners into coming forth with the correct answers for a test or worksheet, but for teachers to change the ways that the children in their classes think about their science learning and the manner in which they consider what scientists are conveying to them about natural phenomena is much more difficult (Posner *et al.*, 1982).

Nevertheless, the implications of a study of science learning based upon Kelly's theory lie in our helping the learners themselves to gain insight into the processes of their own minds and learning processes. For teachers, the fruits of this insight would be in the ways that they become conscious of, and recognize the effect and impact of, their children's own approaches to science study. The hoped-for result would be that these learners are then more able to take responsibility for their own learning.

If, as has been implied, an understanding of the nature of science knowledge is far more beneficial to a learner than knowledge of disconnected facts, primary teachers, in their turn, will need help and support to gain a similar understanding of the processes by which science knowledge is created. There is now a rich literature about the ways children think about natural phenomena and this needs to be shared with teachers. Furthermore, teachers will gain greater insights into the significance of these thoughts of children if they are encouraged to explore them for themselves and, in so doing, realize that children's efforts to learn science are guided by what they perceive as important to solve the problem of learning science.

In the view of Personal Construct Theory, self-understanding can expand the realm of choices and possibilities which we see available to us to help cope in the life situation in which we find ourselves. The first step in self-understanding is awareness and hence, the second set of implications from the study of children's approaches to science teaching that all the participants of the teaching/learning activity should be assisted to become aware of and to value the learners' personal approaches as they attempt to understand in science.

The teacher, once the architect but now in this view the other principal co-architect of learning, is essential in helping the learners in a class to become more conscious and aware of their own approaches to learning as it takes place in the classroom. The curriculum can, if appropriately designed, also provide effective guidance to help the learners to understand not only the ideas of science, but to reflect on their own experiences as learners. Once again, there is a continuity in both our research and our teaching efforts, so that there are now many practical possibilities for providing guidance and help to learners to enhance their awareness of their own learning approaches in the science classroom. Videotapes of children who are using learning strategies which they have found effective in the science classroom would be interesting and valuable to other children. Interviews with the learners depicted on the videotapes could encourage other learners to talk about and reflect on their approaches and rationale. Stories written for children describing how learners similar to themselves have effectively approached learning would be another good starting point to generate awareness.

Teachers can also help children become more conscious of the effect of their approaches when they are working together in class by making suggestions for small group interaction behaviours which might enhance the success of everyone in the group. Discussion might emphasize how group members can help one another to organize to accomplish tasks, how group members might help someone who is having difficulty, or how a new idea presented by a group member might most effectively be considered by all members of the group. While the intention of our efforts is to improve the effectiveness of the individual child as learner, it is very important to stress the value and impact of these sorts of social and collaborative features of the activity of learning science in school.

Teachers can also introduce a variety of strategies which a class of learners could experiment with to help them to record, organize and review content information which is presented in class discussions and activities. A class of learners can be guided to consider the validity of others' viewpoints by sharing with them the ideas of all its members and then later those put forward by scientists. This would highlight and emphasize concepts which have been found to be difficult for science learners to grasp. *The Classroom Profile* has been a very useful tool which I devised to help learners and teachers become more aware of the ideas which are held by members of an entire class concerning a particular natural phenomenon. An example of a *Classroom Profile* is given in table 1.

Each child was asked to provide an explanation telling why the pencil in a beaker of water looked as if it was broken. I collected all the answers and found that they could be placed into several categories. These categories were placed on the class profile chart and the names of the children providing the same explanation were listed next to the category. The names could be either used for teacher reference or could be shared with the class, depending on the teacher's preference. The number of learners in each category in the chart in table 1 allows a popularity rank ordering of the responses, and makes it very clear to the class that the most popular response is not always the response which most closely resembles the scientist's. *The Classroom Profile* helps the teacher to understand how individual children are thinking about the ideas presented to them and shows how groups of them are thinking along similar lines. Other information is also available. In this particular profile, three of the learners made descriptive statements when they had actually been asked to

Table 1:   The Classroom Profile — Students' Ideas about 'The Broken Pencil Phenomenon'

Explanation (popularity ranked)	Name (for teacher reference only?)				Number of students
1 'The water makes it look broken.'	Phyllis Donald	Jessica Carlo	Lorene Monty	Di Ching	8
2 'Water bends the light rays.'	Stella	*Mark	Sally	James .	4
3 ·'The shape of the beaker makes it look broken.'	*Pierre	Leslie	Rose		3
4 'The water and the beaker make it look bigger.'	Kim	*Melody	*Amy		3
5 'The water and the beaker act as a magnifier.'	Raini	Hyon Sin			2
6 'The water acts as a magnifier.'	*Martin	Arnie			2
7 'Because we tilted the pencil.'	Arcala				1
8 'The light rays and the glass make it look broken.'	*Donnie				1
9 'The light rays do it.'	Denise				1
10 Descriptive statements only	Susan	Karin	Annie		3
11 Unusual water ideas	Rochelle Lewis	Danny Michael	Trellis		5
				Total	33

* Students in the study group

provide an explanation. The distinction between an explanation and a description could thus be made a matter to clarify with the class.

I have found the sharing of the profiles to be interesting, enjoyable and of great value to the classes. *The Classroom Profile* helps learners (i) to reflect on their own ideas about the nature of phenomena; (ii) become aware of how fellow classmates are thinking about the same phenomena; (iii) to compare (and perhaps reconsider) their own ideas about phenomena with those of their classmates; and (iv) eventually to consider the plausibility of the explanation put forward by scientists.

Some educators put forward the view that the *only* important outcome of science learning is that learners move from their blank, wrong or 'misconceived' views about the nature of phenomena to the adoption of scientifically accepted explanations. Such a view fails to take the child as person into account. It disembodies the child's ideas from the child, who, for reasons which are unique to that person, is fascinated by, is disinterested in, or may even be frightened by the experience of science learning. The experience of learning science as well as the knowledge involved brings about powerful representations of the enterprise of science which will have an impact on the learner, and which may indeed also have deep and long-term consequences for the learner's continuing involvement with science.

The image of science which is grasped by children in their science study in primary school is likely to affect their attitudes towards matters requiring scientific understandings needed to make decisions in daily life. It may also affect their interest in pursuing science studies in the future. The image which children portray to themselves as successful or unsuccessful learners of science must also concern teachers or curriculum designers who have an interest in the learner's experience of joy and personal meaningfulness in pursuing the study of natural phenomena.

I found through observing and conversing with the children in the study described here, that as I became a better listener, the children became more responsive, sharing more and more of their thoughts and feelings about their experience with me. As I became a better listener, the expectation seemed to be developing in the children that what they had to say was important. Because the children knew the purposes of my study, they were aware that what they had to say was not only for me to hear, but that I wanted to share their ideas (anonymously, of course) with teachers, curriculum developers, researchers, and student teachers. I found also that the children became very interested in me, the listener. They would often ask what I thought about an idea or an insight, and several asked if I might help them with their work. Possibly the most important impact of this approach to research and teaching is in the way that our sincere interest in what children have to say creates the expectation in them that their ideas, thoughts and feelings are valued by us. With this expectation they may become more receptive to, and place greater value on, the learning that we attempt to guide them towards accomplishing.

References

ANDERSSON, B. and KARRQVIST, C. (1982) *Ljuset och dess engenskaper*, EKNA-projecektet, Institutionen for praktisk pedagogik, Molndal, Sverige, 1981. *Light and Its Properties*, translated into English by Gillian Thylander.

ANDERSON, C. and SMITH, E. (1983) 'Children's preconceptions and content area in textbooks' in DUFFY, G., ROEHLER, L. and MASON, J. (Eds) *Comprehension Instruction: Perspectives and Suggestions*, New York, Longman, Inc.

APELMAN, M., COLTON, R., FLEXER, A. and HAWKINS, D. (1983) *A Report on Critical Barriers to the Learning and Understanding of Elementary Science*, Boulder, CO, National Science Foundation Contract # SED 80–08581, Mountain View Center.

ASIMOV, I. (1984) 'Science and beauty' in GARDNER, M. (Ed) *The Sacred Beetle and Other Great Essays in Science*, Oxford, Oxford University Press.

BROPHY, J. (1982) 'Schooling as students experience it', *The Elementary School Journal*, 82, 5, pp. 519–29.

DRIVER, R. and OLDHAM, V. (1985) 'A constructivist approach to curriculum development in science', paper presented to the symposium, 'Personal Construction of Meaning in Educational Settings', at the annual meeting of the British Educational Research Association, Sheffield, August.

FREYBERG, P. and OSBORNE, R. (1985) 'Assumptions about teaching and learning' in OSBORNE, R. and FREYBERG, P. (Eds) *Learning in Science: The Implications of Children's Science*, Portsmouth, NH, Heinemann.

FYNN, (1974) *Mr. God This Is Anna*, London, William Collins and Sons, Ltd.

GUESNE, E. (1988) 'Childrens' Ideas about Light', to be published in *New Trends Physics Teaching*, IV, Paris, Unesco Publications.

JUNG, W. (1981) 'Conceptual frameworks in elementary optics', working paper presented at the Conference in Ludwigsburg, Johann Wolfgang Goethe-Universitat Institut für Didaktik der Physik, Grafstrasse 39, 6000 Frankfurt a.M. 90, 14–16 September.

KELLY, G. (1955) *The Psychology of Personal Constructs* (Vols. 1 and 2), New York, W.W. Norton and Company.

MAGOON, A. (1977) 'Constructivist approaches in educational research', *Review of Research in Education*, 47, 4, pp. 651–93.

NAVARRA, J. (1955) *The Development of Scientific Concepts in a Young Child: A Case Study*, Westport, CT, Greenwood Press.

NYBERG, D. (1971) *Tough and Tender Learning*, Palo Alto, CA, National Press Books.

POPE, M. and GILBERT, J. (1983) 'Personal experience and the construction of knowledge in science', *Science Education*, 67, 2, pp. 193–203.

POSNER, G., STRIKE, K., HEWSON, P. and GERTZOG, W. (1982) 'Accommodation of a scientific conception: Toward a theory of conceptual change', *Science Education*, 66, 2, pp. 211–27.

SHAPIRO, B. (1987) 'What children bring to light: Conversations with grade 5 children during their study of the topic light', unpublished doctoral dissertation, University of Alberta, Edmonton.

SMITH, F. (1973) 'Twelve easy ways to make learning to read difficult and one difficult way to make it easy' in SMITH, F. (Ed), *Psycholinguistics and Reading*, Toronto, Holt, Rinehart and Winston.

STEAD, B. and OSBORNE, R. (1980) 'Exploring students' concepts of light', *The Australian Science Teachers Journal*, 26, 3, pp. 84–90.

WATZLAWICK, P. (1984) *Invented Reality*, New York, Norton.

WHITMAN, W. (1965) *Leaves of Grass*, New York, New York University Press.

6
Theory into Practice I

Richard T. White

I imagine that most people can recall knowing at least one outstanding teacher. One with whom I worked had remarkable influence on her students, yet I find it hard to pinpoint just what it was that made her so effective. Was it because she was well-organized and confident? Or her obvious interest in her students and their knowledge that she wanted them to do well? Were they unwilling to disappoint her? Whatever the reasons, they appear to have been bound up with her personality, and that, unfortunately, retired with her. Her skills were not handed on to her colleagues, and the general level of teaching is neither better nor worse through her career.

If personality is not transferable, and there are not enough 'born' teachers to run a mass education system, in order to improve the practice of teaching and the consequent quality of learning we have to know what, apart from displaying their personalities, great teachers do, what principles they follow. Unless we can specify those principles and train other teachers to apply them, the skills of the great teachers will continue to retire or die with them.

Every now and again someone tries to solve the problem by identifying some great teachers and watching what they do. Usually, however, this approach founders on two or three difficulties. One is the effect of context. Teaching is a subtle and complex task, in which slight variations of context can change what is needed to be effective. Even my great colleague became less effective in later years, not because her personality or methods changed but because the context did — the mix of students shifted, and so did their expectations and goals. Because the number of variations in context is infinite, it is hard, or even impossible, to generalize useful principles from watching teachers. One effective teacher might lead you to conclude that the way questions are spread round the class is a crucial act, but then the next one you see does not do that and anyway you have seen ineffective teachers who question in the same way.

The second difficulty is that, though one might think that we could cut through the problem by asking the great teachers the secret of their success, teachers mostly are not able to articulate what they do. From my own experience as a secondary school teacher I can certify the truth of the observation that 'Theorizing about education is not very common among those who teach. The teacher in the classroom has so many other things to do' (Castle, 1961, p. 77).

The third difficulty in trying to learn from watching great teachers is that you have to know what you are looking for before you find it; that is, the observer must have some notion beforehand of what are the principles of good teaching. In other words, observation has to be guided by theory. Unfortunately, a theory is what we are looking for, in the form of a set of principles, so the notion of finding a theory by observing great teachers ends in a circle. Though observation may help us to sort out some useful practices, it is hardly likely to be sufficient on its own to develop a coherent theory.

Another approach to determining principles that can be transmitted and that will improve practice is reflection and logical analysis. Plenty of theories have been formed in this way, often emphasizing similar points. Sometimes these theories are tried in practice, but by-and-large the innovations derived from them have not had major impacts. Though each innovation may leave a trace of its passing, we want something better than a trace. We want something that works and is seen to work, that leads to a substantial lift in the quality of teaching and learning.

Why Theories Fail

Why haven't theories had more effect? Perhaps we should consider one of the best, that had more effect than most yet really had only a negligible influence on the mass of schooling: Bloom's (1968) mastery learning notion that was based on Carroll's (1963) formula for the quality of learning:

$$\text{Degree of school learning} = f\left(\frac{\text{time spent}}{\text{time needed}}\right)$$

where *time spent* is limited by perseverance and time allowed for learning, and *time needed* depends on general aptitude, the quality of instruction, and the ability to understand the instruction.

Bloom's theory plus its practical package had a lot going for it, and should have been widely influential: it was backed by Carroll's and Bloom's high prestige and abilities; its aim of getting at least 95 per cent of students to reach an 'A' grade was admirable and acceptable to all; the package set out readily transmitted techniques; numerous research studies demonstrated its power; widely-sold books described what to do; and Bloom was supported by an enthusiastic group of able followers, who for years ran workshops for teachers and administrators. However, if we draw at random a classroom from North America, Europe, or Australasia the odds are much against finding that mastery learning techniques are practised in it, and indeed it is likely that the teacher will not have heard of Bloom. Despite its strengths and scattered achievements the mastery learning movement failed to change the mass of schools.

One reason why Carroll's theory and Bloom's technique did not sweep the schools and bring about marked permanent changes in practice may have been the isolation of teachers. In the main, teachers inhabit unconnected classrooms; they work away with little professional interchange with colleagues, and few return for further training after obtaining their initial qualification. Few read much about theory or innovations in education. Therefore it is difficult to reach them with a new idea. Even when Bloom did reach them, in-service workshops on mastery learning may have been ineffective for several reasons. Workshops tend to be brief, and change in engrained practice needs long attention and continual support. Mastery learning was developed and promoted by academics, who are seen ambivalently by school teachers. While professors have prestige, their ideas are often rejected because the teachers believe that they do not understand the complexity of teaching. The teachers are right about that, in many cases. Mastery learning ignored context. The practical problems that busy teachers face in running a mastery program, dealing with individual students' problems and keeping track of their progress, were not fully appreciated. The demands on equipment, the restrictions of fixed lesson times, the timetabling of a class in different rooms at different periods through a week, were minor difficulties that added together to form a barrier against easy adoption of Bloom's package. Tertiary level teachers faced fewer of those difficulties, and so mastery learning, in fact, was practised more widely (albeit still rather rarely) in colleges and universities than in high schools.

Mastery learning was resisted because it was laid on schools from outside; it did not grow from within. It was snatched at by some as a simple solution to a complex problem, and when effort was needed to make it work it was abandoned. These summary points need to be kept in mind when we consider what might be done about putting theory into practice.

The tragedy of education lies in two forms of failure: on the one hand teachers do not pass on their skills, through lack of theory; on the other hand, theorists are unable to communicate their principles effectively. To break this impasse we need a theory that teachers will accept and a means of disseminating it. How can these two requirements be met? As yet no-one can guarantee success, but there is hope in, and lessons to be learned from, the Project to Enhance Effective Learning (PEEL) (Baird and Mitchell, 1986).

PEEL is a deliberate attempt to put a theory into practice. Although in an early stage, it can serve as an exemplar of how theory might become effective. Its differences from mastery learning may reveal conditions that aid or hinder the success of an innovation.

Possibly the most significant difference between PEEL and mastery learning is in personnel. Where the mastery learning movement (and other innovations) tended to have two distinct groups of people, psychologists and teachers, at least four merging groups can be identified in PEEL. Again there are psychologists at one end and high school teachers at the other, but in between are a group of former teachers and subject matter specialists who have become psychologists or other specialists in education, and a group of teacher-researchers. These two groups provide a crucial bridge between the first group of psychologists and the fourth group, classroom teachers.

Another Approach to Theory into Practice

In PEEL the first group of psychologists are distant in place and time, and have no direct involvement in the project. The theories of Ausubel and Gagné, of information-processing and metacognition, of curriculum innovation and dissemination, were absorbed and developed further by members of the second group, clustered at Monash University in Australia. This group specialized in science teaching and learning, which may have been fortunate; for their common interest in science encouraged them to bring together theories that initially were not coordinated. Thus White explored Gagné's (1962) notion of learning hierarchies and reached the position that hierarchies are an accurate description of prerequisities for achievement of algorithms but are not essential to the learning of propositions nor the development of understanding (White, 1973 and 1974). Gagné and White (1978) suggested that understanding of algorithms required them to be embedded in a body of inter-linked propositions, which moved them towards Ausubel's (1968) theory of meaningful verbal learning. West and Fensham (1976), during much the same period as their colleague White had been working on hierarchies, had been researching Ausubel's theory in relation to learning of chemistry, so it was relatively easy for these people, who were meeting frequently and discussing their work, to merge the ideas of Gagné and Ausubel into a composite theory, and later, after Wittrock had visited Monash in 1979, to incorporate principles of generative learning (Wittrock, 1974) and information-processing. Their subject matter base in science meant that the theory was always related to specific examples of content and was never abstract or general. That contrasts with writing about mastery learning, which usually is in general terms.

The group's interest in understanding of science made its members receptive to the research that began to appear in the late 1970s on students' conceptions of scientific principles and phenomena. Leaders in this movement, Champagne, Hewson, Driver, Novak and Osborne, who, like members of the group, were former science teachers who had turned to the psychology of learning, were invited to Monash where they stimulated new research (for example, Brumby, 1984; Gunstone and White, 1981) and theoretical statements (for example, Fensham, 1984).

The chief concern of the group at this time was to develop methods of probing students' understanding and to see how alternative conceptions of phenomena could be brought into accord with scientists' conceptions. Both lines of research were carried out in out-of-class settings, though usually in schools or colleges rather than in psychological laboratories. Changing a student's conception proved to be much more difficult than expected (Gunstone, Champagne and Klopfer, 1981). Students would accept new statements about a phenomenon, but on further probing would reveal that this acceptance did no more than place a veneer of new knowledge over their previous, contradictory views that were still retained. Reflection on this remarkable result shifted the group's attention to the strategies that students apply in learning. Psychologists' work on metacognition, especially that of Flavell (1976) and Brown (1978), was absorbed into the group's thinking through studies by Baird (1984) (see also Baird and White, 1982a, 1982b and 1984). This was a crucial step in moving learning theory into the everyday practice of teaching in a school.

Baird's Studies — Crucial Steps

Baird should be considered a further member of the second group, a biology subject matter specialist whose concern for the quality of learning had moved his interests into psychology. His first investigation (Baird and White, 1982a) was a case study of the learning styles in genetics exhibited by three adults. This involved a shift in research method that may be another significant difference between the mastery learning experience and PEEL. Studies of the effectiveness of mastery learning employed the standard experimental designs that had been described so compellingly by Campbell and Stanley (1963), which, though useful in laying foundations for later developments, had a serious weakness in being concerned with differences between mean scores of blocks of students while treating variations between individuals in each block as a nuisance that merely made it harder to demonstrate that one group differed from another. Attention to individuals and an understanding of why they learn or do not learn may well be a vital step in putting theory into practice, and so the turn to case studies at this stage was fortunate.

Baird's second investigation (Baird and White, 1982b) was another case study, an attempt to change the learning styles of three college students. Although it was easy to show the students that there were deficiencies in their styles, six weeks of intense effort produced only slight changes. With hindsight, it was clear that procedures that the students had built up over a dozen years of schooling and that had served them sufficiently well to bring them as far as they had, were not going to be discarded lightly. This result made the group appreciate that putting theory into practice would involve more than a simple demonstration of its advantages. The perceptions, values, and aims of the people who were to use the innovation would have to be understood. Teachers and students would have their existing beliefs (amounting to a theory) and practices, which an innovation would be asking them to discard. Something akin to attitude change would have to be encouraged. Therefore, to put theory into practice would be a lengthy process, involving close collaboration with the teachers who were to take it on and an unusual attention to the beliefs and customs of their students. A presentation at a short in-service workshop would be useless.

These appreciations were put into effect in Baird's third study (Baird, 1986), in which he worked for six months with one experienced teacher and three of his biology classes. Many procedures were used by Baird to bring the students to take on responsibility for their own learning, with some success. The teacher, however, found it difficult to change his ways despite being in sympathy with the aim of the project. Although part of getting students to control their learning involved encouraging them to ask questions instead of merely responding to initiatives of the teacher, most lessons saw the teacher still firmly in control not just of social behaviour but also of intellectual behaviour. He asked the questions and selected who would respond, he chose the topic and the details that would be covered within it, he determined the pace of the lesson and when activities would shift; yet he had declared his willingness to encourage the students to do these things. When this contradiction was discussed with him, it emerged that his problems occurred because he saw his classroom was part of a larger system. The students had only a few lessons a week with him, and in their other subjects they were being trained, as they had been for years, in opposed procedures of speaking up only when invited, of asking few if any questions, and of taking notes when directed; in short, of being controlled in detail. Each gain that was made in the experimental class was wiped out by the next time it met, so bringing about change was a frustrating struggle for the teacher, who did not always feel up to making the effort. Also, he felt he had a responsibility to cover the pre-determined content for the year. When asked why he felt this, when all tests for the class were under his control, he said that although he was free to do what he wished, whoever taught the students the next year would expect them to have covered (not necessarily learned or understood) the specified content, and this new style of teaching meant that he could not be sure that the class would get through it all. Further, he was worried that although the new style of learning was excellent it could handicap the students in a later year when they had to pass an external examination that would require recall of specified content.

An important conclusion from the teacher's reactions in Baird's third study is that forces act against the introduction of an innovation to a single classroom. The social context of the classroom and the perceptions of the people in it have to be considered. Putting theory into practice requires judgment of an appropriate scale for the attempt. If the scale is too small, as it seems to have been in the single classrooms of Baird's third study, the conservatism of the general context is too strong for the innovation. If too large, then resources will be stretched and there will not be close cooperation between theorist and practitioner. Some appreciation of this point about scale determined the nature of PEEL.

Some Critical Features

It was fortunate for PEEL that circumstances allowed an easy link between the second group, of learning theorists who formerly were teachers, and the third, of teachers who would be researchers. The classroom experience of the theorists gave them a credibility with the teachers that psychologists in the first group, without school-teaching backgrounds, would have lacked. The group 2 theorists have better perception of the complexity of teaching and the concerns of teachers than group 1 psychologists have, for they have lived as school teachers. Therefore group 2 theorists and group 3 teachers can communicate easily. It only remained to bring them together.

As a result of the previous studies and the conclusions drawn from them, the group 2 people, led by Baird, wanted to change the learning strategies used by students in a functioning high school by increasing their metacognition, especially their control over their learning. The students were to become more purposeful learners. Though research, this was also to be real practice — it was not a laboratory study in which the students' future was of no real concern. It was to be part of their normal school experience, and any change needed to be seen as long-lasting and beneficial. Therefore the project had to find a school that wanted to be its host.

The link between the group 2 theorists and a school that had teachers who would be researchers was found in Ian Mitchell, who had a joint appointment at Monash University and Laverton High School, an average-sized secondary school in an outer suburb of Melbourne. Mitchell's role in putting PEEL into practice was so crucial that one conclusion is that his counterpart is necessary in any attempt to put theory into practice. He had two main functions, of communicator and of maintainer of the project.

Communication is important in both directions between group 2 and group 3. The theory that group 2 people develop is not worked out as a blueprint for action; rather it sets out principles that still have to be translated into classroom acts. For instance, at the commencement of PEEL the teachers could be told little more than that the aim was *to improve the quality of school learning* through increasing students' knowledge of what learning is and how it happens, their awareness of their own learning processes, and their control of learning through purposeful decision-making. Good and bad learning styles were described, and some procedures that might be followed in classrooms to bring about beneficial changes were outlined, but a lot of detail remained to be filled in. As time passed and each teacher suggested and explored ways of attaining the aim, Mitchell was at hand in the school, available to discuss the procedures and suggest variations. Perhaps a group 2 person could have done that. Baird put in a lot of time in the school, in something of that role. However, it made a difference that Mitchell actually shared the teachers' experiences. Communication is a sensitive and subtle matter, easily broken by perceptions such as thinking that the other person does not fully appreciate factors that affect one's acts. Thus a teacher would not hesitate to tell Mitchell that a procedure failed to work, and would find it easy to tell him why, since it would not be necessary to spell out the complexities of the situation — the nature of the students and their history in the school, the styles of the other teachers they had, the physical conditions of the classroom, the influence of specific customs of the school. It would take too much time (which is always in short supply in schools) to explain all this to group 2 people, even with their former experience as teachers.

Mitchell guided translation of theoretical principles into action. He also provided details of progress to the theorists, who found in consequence that they had to amend their theory from time to time, making it richer and more in accord with events. While the title of this chapter implies that the flow is from theory to practice, PEEL experience demonstrates that contact is two-way, with practice affecting theory as well. It is worth noting that this does not seem to have happened in the case of mastery learning.

Some Lessons from PEEL

A major lesson from PEEL is that an innovation needs commitment from the participants to see it through the early stage, when errors are frequent and new skills have to be acquired, and consequently there can be discouragement. While outsiders can help, it is much more effective when encouragement comes from within, from a colleague. Mitchell's status as a teacher prevented his colleagues from seeing the project as a task laid on them from outside, and gave them a sense of ownership, a direct interest in its success. They were reassured when they saw that Mitchell struck the same difficulties as themselves, was making mistakes and was ready to say so, yet was persevering. Mitchell joined Baird in organizing weekly meetings of the teachers, so these meetings were not seen as imposed by outsiders but something of their own. In their report on the first year of PEEL (Baird and Mitchell, 1986) the teachers emphasize how important the weekly meetings were in keeping the project going. It is probable that PEEL would have collapsed in its first three or four months without the meetings, which initially relied on the combination of leadership provided by Baird, from group 2, and Mitchell, from group 3 with links to group 2.

PEEL experience indicates that it takes a long time to put a relatively untried theory into practice in a school. The project began in February 1985 and it was not until about half-way through that year that there was any assurance that it was getting anywhere. Neither the group 2 nor the group 3 people had appreciated the scale of the costs and risks involved in innovation. The costs were that when teachers replaced the working procedures that they had evolved in the past with the new experimental ones they put themselves back to the state of beginning teachers, a stressful time in which people learn by making mistakes. The risks were that the teachers would have to live with the consequences of any mistakes, consequences that might be unbearable. Outside experimenters can walk away from a disaster, but teacher-researchers are stuck with it. It took time for the teachers to work through the initial period of loss of former effectiveness and to learn to cope with the costs and risks. During that time they needed support and encouragement. As it is likely that similar costs and risks attend any innovation, it follows that theory cannot be put into practice as a result of a brief interaction.

The PEEL teachers met, reflected on their experiences, discussed them with group 2 people, developed techniques as they went, and pointed out places where the theory needed attention. For instance, the teachers discovered that certain techniques worked with certain content. The theorists had not considered that at all. The teachers pointed out the importance of social context as a factor in determining whether individual students would, or could, behave in ways consistent with the aims of the project. Although that had been recognized by the theorists (for example, White, 1985; White and Tisher, 1986) they were not as sensitive to it as the teachers' observations brought them to be. It is worth noting that the teachers did not articulate the importance of social context until well into the second year of the project.

The lesson from the interaction between the group 2 and group 3 people in the first two years of PEEL is that theory cannot be launched as practice like a missile; rather it has to be cultured and nurtured like a plant. The same image should apply to the remaining stage, of disseminating PEEL to group 4 teachers who did not take part in the experimental development. That dissemination may be as difficult as the experimental stage, but there should be more chance of success than in the mastery learning attempt to go direct from group 1 to group 4.

Next Steps

At present it is not clear how best to manage the dissemination of PEEL. The temptation might be to collect together the principles established in PEEL and to broadcast them in in-service programs. While that might do no harm, it probably would not do much good either. It would be quick, apparently efficient, but ineffective. Just as the shift of responsibility from group 2 to group 3 took time and effort and required consideration and sensitivity on both sides, so will the shift from group 3 to group 4. The successful form of putting theory into practice is devolution and growth, not instant change.

Of course one must expect to see mistakes made when the procedures for enhancing effective learning are disseminated to other schools, just as mistakes were made in the initial experimental phase at Laverton High School. Mistakes are an essential as well as inevitable part of the process, for people learn by them. They need not be fatal to the project provided people are willing to recognize them and are flexible in recovering from them. The following recommendations for disseminating the theory and experiences from PEEL may be mistakes themselves, but are worth starting out with.

The project has to be publicized, otherwise it cannot spread. Both group 2 and group 3 people should take initiatives in doing this, through speaking and writing. The only thing that they should lay down dogmatically is the aim of the project: the story of experiences, including accounts of successes and failures in the context of the experimental school, should be told without preaching that this is the way to do it. Preaching would be contrary to the lessons of devolution and growth that were won by such hard experience. Indeed the story should emphasize the devolutionary nature of change, of growth and learning rather than instant success, and the consequent need for patience and commitment. The inevitability of initial difficulties should not be glossed over, for it brings out the importance of feeling that one owns the innovation in maintaining people through the early months. The difficulty for a teacher trying to bring in an innovation alone should not be hidden, for one of the lessons from PEEL is the value of support from colleagues and from people outside the school.

Group 3 people should invite anyone interested in promoting effective learning to visit their school and classrooms, or to correspond with them. Both they and group 2 people should respond to requests for information without prescribing courses of action — they should merely describe what happened at Laverton without presuming that events would follow the same course in another context. It is up to the group 4 people to decide what procedures will work for themselves. For the same reasons, groups 2 and 3 people should be available as consultants but not as directors when the innovation is tried by other people. Direction would prevent the new group from owning the innovation, and would increase the incidence of profitless errors through lack of understanding of the context. If there is to be a director or leader, that person should be a member of the school.

As the innovation is taken up by other schools, a newsletter would provide useful support. At first it would help to keep the various groups in touch, but it must be expected that as the innovation evolves different contexts will encourage it to take different forms. Eventually what happens in different schools will no longer be recognizable as instances of the same principles, but by then the theory itself will have grown into something new. The theory will have been put into practice in diverse ways, and the diverse practices will have changed the theory.

References

AUSUBEL, D.P. (1968) *Educational Psychology: A Cognitive View*, New York, Holt, Rinehart & Winston.

BAIRD, J.R. (1984) *Improving Learning Through Enhanced Metacognition*, PhD thesis, Monash University Printery.

BAIRD, J.R. (1986) 'Improving learning through enhanced metacognition: A classroom study', *European Journal of Science Education*, 8, pp. 263–82.

BAIRD, J.R. and MITCHELL, I.J. (Eds) (1986) *Improving the Quality of Teaching and Learning: An Australian Case Study — The PEEL project*, Melbourne, Monash University Printery.

BAIRD, J.R. and WHITE, R.T. (1982a) 'A case study of learning styles in biology', *European Journal of Science Education*, 4, pp. 325–37.

BAIRD, J.R. and WHITE, R.T. (1982b) 'Promoting self-control of learning', *Instructional Science*, 11, pp. 227–47.

BAIRD, J.R and WHITE, R.T. (1984) 'Improving learning through enhanced metacognition: A classroom study', paper presented at the annual meeting of the American Educational Research Association, New Orleans, April.

BLOOM, B.S. (1968) 'Learning for mastery', *Evaluation Comment*, Los Angeles, Center for the Study of Evaluation of Instructional Programs, UCLA.

BROWN, A.L. (1978) 'Knowing when, where, and how to remember: A problem of metacognition' in GLASER, R. (Ed) *Advances in Instructional Psychology: Vol. 1*, Hillsdale, NJ, Erlbaum.

BRUMBY, M.N. (1984) 'Misconceptions about the concept of natural selection', *Science Education*, 68, pp. 493–502.

CAMPBELL, D.T. and STANLEY, J.C. (1963) 'Experimental and quasi-experimental designs for research on teaching' in GAGE, N.L. (Ed) *Handbook of Research on Teaching*, Chicago, IL, Rand McNally.

CARROLL, J.B. (1963) 'A model of school learning', *Teachers College Record*, 64, pp. 723–33.

CASTLE, E.B. (1961) *Ancient Education and Today*, Harmondsworth, Penguin.

FENSHAM, P.J. (1984) 'Conceptions, misconceptions, and alternative frameworks in chemical education', *Chemical Society Reviews*, 13, 2, pp. 199–217.

FLAVELL, J.H. (1976) 'Metacognitive aspects of problem solving' in RESNICK, L.B. (Ed) *The Nature of Intelligence*, Hillsdale, NJ, Erlbaum.

GAGNÉ, R.M. (1962) 'The acquisition of knowledge', *Psychological Review*, 69, pp. 355–65.

GAGNÉ, R.M. and WHITE, R.T. (1978) 'Memory structures and learning outcomes', *Review of Educational Research*, 48, pp. 187–222.

GUNSTONE, R.F., CHAMPAGNE, A.B., and KLOPFER, L.E. (1981) 'Instruction for understanding: A case study', *Australian Science Teachers Journal*, 27, 3, pp. 27–32.

GUNSTONE, R.F. and WHITE, R.T. (1981) 'Understanding of gravity', *Science Education*, 65, pp. 291–9.

WEST, L.H.T. and FENSHAM, P.J. (1976) 'Prior knowledge or advance organizers as effective variables in chemical learning', *Journal of Research in Science Teaching*, 13, pp. 297–306.

WHITE, R.T. (1973) 'A limit to the application of learning hierarchies'. *Australian Journal of Education*, 17, pp. 153–6.

WHITE, R.T. (1974) 'The validation of a learning hierarchy', *American Educational Research Journal*, 11, pp. 121–36.

WHITE, R.T. (1985) 'The importance of context in educational research', *Research in Science Education*, 15, pp. 92–102.

WHITE, R.T. and TISHER, R.P. (1986) 'Research on natural sciences', in WITTROCK, M.C. (Ed) *Handbook of Research on Teaching*, 3rd ed, New York, Macmillan.

WITTROCK, M.C. (1974) 'Learning as a generative process', *Educational Psychologist*, 11, pp. 87–95.

7
Theory into Practice II:
A Constructivist Approach to Curriculum Development

Rosalind Driver

One important way of describing the teaching of science in schools is as a process whereby students reconstruct their understandings in undergoing conceptual change. How to help teachers to promote conceptual change in an effective way in their classrooms is now a central concern of research groups in a number of countries and reflects the way curriculum development is being understood and approached. It is in contrast with the forms of curriculum development that took place in the 1960s and 1970s in which project teams outside schools developed and promoted a course and a package of related materials.

An Epistemological Basis

The Children's Learning in Science Project at Leeds is one of several contemporary projects working within the general perspective of constructivist epistemology, the central premise of which is that knowledge, whether public or private, is a human construction.

A key feature in this perspective is that human beings construct mental models of their environment and new experiences are interpreted and understood in relation to existing mental models or schemes.

> Human beings ... do not apprehend the world directly; they possess only internal representation of it, because perception is the construction of a model of the world. They are unable to compare this perceptual representation directly with the world — it *is* their world. (Johnson-Laird, 1983, p. 156)

Personal Construction of Knowledge

Research in a number of areas of human cognitive functioning supports this claim. Reading theorists suggest that the process of reading involves the active use by the reader of mental constructions or schemata in interpreting what is on the page (Anderson, 1984; Schank and Abelson, 1977). Research on problem solving, particularly in complex and highly organized domains of knowledge such as mathematics or physics, indicates that the problem solver first constructs a representation of the 'problem space' which governs the way encoding of information is carried out (Newell and Simon, 1972; Greeno, 1978; Larkin, 1983). Research on human reasoning suggests that, rather than being based on generalized principles of formal logic, humans make inferences by constructing a mental representation of the problem as a basis for making deductions (Johnson-Laird, 1983). Indeed as Rumelhart and Norman (1981) argue:

> Our ability to reason and use our knowledge appears to depend strongly on the context in which the knowledge is required. Most of the reasoning we do apparently does not involve the application of general purpose reasoning skills. Rather it seems that most of our reasoning ability is tied to particular bodies of knowledge. (p. 338)

Students' conceptions of natural phenomena are also examples of particular types of mental representations; in this case representations of aspects of the natural world which influence the way future interactions with phenomena are construed.

The view of the learner as architect of his/her own knowledge is a broadly held assumption. There are, however, differences between perspectives on the types of constraints which act to shape the process. Both internal constraints in terms of limitations in processing capacity of the human mind, and external constraints, in terms of influences from both the physical environment and the cultural milieu through language and other forms of communication, are variously recognized as playing a part.

Strauss (1981) argues that much of our common-sense knowledge is spontaneous and universal. He explains this by arguing that:

> the common-sense representation of qualitative empirical regularities is tied to complex interactions between the sensory system, the environment that supplies the information ... and the mental structures through which we organize the sensory information which guides our behaviours. I argue that individuals' common-sense knowledge about qualitative physical concepts is no different today than in the times of, say, Aristotle. (p. 297)

There is some dispute about the last point made here by Strauss; it is argued that some mental models which are used to organize experience are culturally transmitted and that the conceptual environment of humans living in the twentieth century differs significantly from that, say, of the time of Aristotle (consider the extent to which heliocentric models of the solar system or notions of evolution through natural selection permeate our language and culture).

It is likely that individuals' prior conceptions derive from experience with the environment, their existing ideas which are used to model new situations and from cultural transmission through language (Head, 1985).

The process by which knowledge is constructed by the learner is broadly surmised to involve a process of hypothesis testing, a process whereby schemes are brought into play (either tacitly or explicitly), their fit with new stimuli is assessed and, as a result, the schemes may be modified.

> What determines the value of the conceptual structures is their experimental adequacy, their goodness of *fit* with experience, their *viability* as means for solving problems, among which is, of course, the never-ending problem of consistent organisation that we call *understanding....* Facts are made by us and our way of experiencing. (von Glaserfeld, 1983, p. 51)

There is an epistemological implication of this view of knowledge as constructed which has yet to be taken seriously by educators, and that is that to know something does not involve the correspondence between our conceptual schemes and what they represent 'out there'; we have no direct access to the 'real world'. The emphasis in learning is not on the correspondence with an external authority but the construction by the learner of schemes which are coherent and useful to them. This view of knowledge 'has serious consequences for our conceptualization of teaching and learning ... it will shift the emphasis from the student's "correct" replication of what the teacher does, to the student's successful organisation of his or her *own* experiences' (*ibid*).

It is recognized that an individual's purposes play a very significant role in influencing cognition and behaviour; they act to prioritize attention, to select and order activities in complex situations. In educational settings the importance of the varied purposes of the participants, both teachers and pupils, is clearly relevant to shaping what is attended to by whom and to what end.

The Construction of Meanings in Social Situations

The extent to which a scheme 'fits' with an individual's experience may be only part of the story. The way we see the world can be shaped by those we communicate with. Social factors are important in understanding the processes of conceptual change. The important role that communication plays in cognition is becoming more widely appreciated. Learning is not being seen so much as an individual but as a social activity where meanings are shaped through discussion and negotiation between peers and between pupils and teachers (Edwards and Mercer, 1987). Moreover, science classrooms are complex social systems within a wider system of schooling. Teaching children in such environments requires careful considerations of these social and cultural influences on their learning.

Such a perspective suggests that learning depends on the contexts in which it occurs. It follows that studies of learning, which are going to be useful to educators, need to pay attention to educational settings and matters of ecological validity.

Science as Constructed Knowledge

The constructivist perspective outlined in the previous sections applies not only to the development of personal knowledge but also to science as public knowledge.

Although there is considerable agreement among psychologists and educators about the constructive nature of the learning process, the constructivist analysis frequently stops short of addressing the nature of the status of the knowledge to be learned, in this case the nature of scientific knowledge. (Indeed cognitive science, which tends to focus on modelling the knowledge systems of individuals, runs the risk of seriously misrepresenting human learning if it fails to take account of this social dimension in knowledge construction.)

Here a constructivist perspective draws on sociology of knowledge and philosophy of science in considering not only personal knowledge but public knowledge to be a human construction (Collins, 1985).

In science education in particular we have a dominant perspective of a view of knowledge as objective and unproblematic. Textbook presentations and teaching methods in school and higher education reinforce this view. Even discovery approaches in science teaching give implicit support to this perspective in that they tend to assume that the empirical method (observing, classifying, interpreting, etc.) can be undertaken objectively without reference to an observer's way of seeing the world.

Current perspectives on the philosophy of science, on the other hand, tend to reject the idea of an 'objective' base of observations against which theories of the world can be checked. Instead a dominant view is that science as public knowledge is not so much a 'discovery' as a carefully checked 'construction'. In attempting to represent the world scientists construct theoretical entities (magnetic fields, genes, electron orbitals ...) which in turn take on a 'reality'. Rather than viewing observations as the base on which knowledge is built, there is a sense in which it is these constructions of the world which are 'real'. It is through them that we observe, interpret and reinterpret our experience.

Developing a curriculum in science which reflects this perspective needs to acknowledge that science is about more than experiences of the natural world. It encompasses the theories and models which have been constructed and the ways in which these are checked and evaluated as coherent and useful. Perhaps most significantly, from a constructivist perspective, these theories are not seen as absolute but as provisional and fallible. Moreover, theory making and testing is a dynamic human enterprise which takes place within the socially defined community and institutions of science.

Implications for Reconstruction of the Science Curriculum

Viewing the curriculum as a body of knowledge or skills to be transmitted is clearly naive. If we recognize that individuals construct their own knowledge as a result of interaction between their current conceptions and ongoing experiences, then it is perhaps more helpful to view the curriculum as a series of learning tasks and strategies.

In an article in which he relates new developments in cognitive science to curriculum studies in general, Posner (1982) considers the central conception which underlies the view of curriculum to be that of 'tasks'. However, he points out that 'if we want to understand a student's experience, the process of learning, and the reasons why some learning outcomes are occurring and not others, we must understand the tasks in which students are engaging and not just the tasks the teachers think they are "giving" to students' (p. 343).

Adopting such a view necessarily means seeing the classroom learning environment as enormously complex. In describing the implications of a constructivist view for mathematics classes Bishop (1985) points out that:

> ... each individual person in the classroom group creates her own unique construction of the rest of the participants, of their goals, of the interaction between herself and others and of all the events which occur in the classroom. Such 'objects' as children's abilities, mathematical meaning, teacher's knowledge, rules of behaviour, do not exist as objective facts but are the individual products of each person's construction. (p. 26)

The aim in curriculum development is then to create a classroom environment

which 'provides the social setting for mutual support of knowledge construction' (Bereiter, 1985). Such an environment encompasses not only the learning
tasks as set, but the learning tasks as interpreted by the learners. It also includes
the social organization and modes of interaction between pupils themselves
and between teacher and pupils. Viewed in this way curriculum development
is inseparable from teacher development.

There are various features which may be seen to be characteristic of such a
perspective:

(a) Learners are not viewed as passive but are seen as purposive and
ultimately responsible for their own learning. They bring their prior
conceptions to learning situations.

(b) Learning is considered to involve an active process on the part of the
learner. It involves the construction of meaning and often takes place
through interpersonal negotiation.

(c) Knowledge is not 'out there' but is personally and socially constructed, its status is problematic. It may be evaluated by the
individual in terms of the extent to which it 'fits' with their
experience and is coherent with other aspects of their knowledge.

(d) Teachers also bring their prior conceptions to learning situations not
only in terms of their subject knowledge but also their views of
teaching and learning. These can influence their way of interacting in
classrooms.

(e) Teaching is not the transmission of knowledge but involves the
organization of the situations in the classroom and the design of tasks
in a way which promotes scientific learning.

(f) The curriculum is not that which is to be learned, but a programme
of learning tasks, materials and resources from which students
construct their knowledge.

This view of the curriculum also has implications for curriculum development.
A linear means–ends model of curriculum development is clearly inappropriate
as it fails to take account of the purposes and meanings constructed by the
various participants. Instead, the progressive development of curriculum
requires a reflexive process in which feedback from all the participants,
including researchers, teachers and students, provides information on how
each are interpreting a series of tasks which can then be adapted to improve the
extent to which learning is promoted. This implies not only learning by
students but also learning by teachers about the ways students construe
presented tasks.

The next section describes how this process is being implemented in
practice.

Curriculum Development as Action Research

How might the features outlined in the previous section be embodied in actual science classrooms? What might schemes of work which reflect these features be like and how might they be implemented? What might be the outcomes of such a way of working? How might teachers and pupils respond? These were the questions the Children's Learning in Science Project set out to explore over the last three years; the aim of this phase of the project's work being to devise, trial and evaluate constructivist teaching sequences in selected science topic areas.

Before giving an account of the schemes of work and the factors involved in their design it may be useful to outline the organization and work programme of the project.

Since teachers are involved in such a fundamental way in the successful implementation of a curriculum, it was decided by this project that the research and development of constructivist approaches to science teaching should be a collaborative exercise between teachers and researchers. Malcolm Skilbeck puts the point very succinctly when he says 'the best place for designing the curriculum is where learners and teachers meet'.

Secondary science teachers from schools within travelling distance of the University of Leeds were invited to take part in an initial two-year project and over thirty teachers undertook the commitment. The purpose of the project was outlined as involving the development of teaching approaches in three topic areas: (i) energy; (ii) the structure of matter; and (iii) plant nutrition — all ones in which the project had already undertaken research on children's thinking and had found conceptual problems.

The teaching approaches were to take account of students' prior ideas and to promote conceptual change. Although the premises on which the project is based were outlined to the participating teachers (Driver and Bell, 1986; Driver and Oldham, 1986) these were initially construed in various ways by those involved. It is not only the students' prior knowledge which is of concern, teacher's conceptions about knowledge and learning also influence what happens in classrooms. This has meant that the project has in effect had two parallel agendas (a) the development of teaching schemes which promote conceptual change in secondary school students; and (b) the implementation of a way of working as a project which promotes the conceptual development of participating science educators.

In working with teachers in these two agenda tasks, it was most important to recognize that there are constraints in operating in classrooms and schools which need to be taken into account in planning. In addition to the obvious physical constraints of teaching time available, the limitations on teaching space and equipment, there are also more subtle constraints due to teachers' and learners' expectations about knowledge, science, schools and classrooms and their roles in them.

Three working groups of about ten teachers, each with a researcher, were set up, one for each topic area. The programme of work for the two years for each group is represented in figure 1. The first task the teachers in each group undertook was to study the learning of the topic in question by students in their own classes (in age range 12–15 years). All participants taught the selected topic in their normal way (this 'current practice' involved a sequence of lessons over six to eight weeks). Students' learning was studied using a number of approaches. Teachers gave their class a diagnostic test before and after teaching the topic and kept a diary over the period in which the lessons were being taught. The researcher from the group visited some teachers and kept a more detailed account of the lessons involving field notes, audiotapes and interviews with students and the teacher.

The documents which were produced (Bell and Brook, 1985; Brook and Driver, 1986; and Wightman *et al.*, 1986) were used as a basis for reflection on current practice by the group. Students' particular conceptual problems were documented and pedagogical concerns were also identified. At this stage, the groups were attempting to make explicit their views on the scientific ideas to be taught and to share their developing perspectives on the teaching and learning processes.

The outcome of this stage of work included (a) a specification of the ideas to be taught; (b) an analysis of some of the conceptual problems students encounter; and (c) a critique of current pedagogical strategies.

Towards the end of the first year each group worked together for a week

Figure 1: The programme of working groups

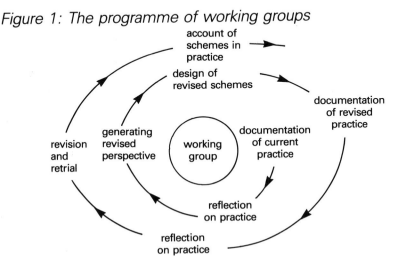

to devise a revised teaching scheme for their topic, drawing on the insights gained over the year and further reading of the research literature. All the schemes were designed to take account of students' prior ideas in the topic and to provide learning activities and a learning environment aimed at promoting conceptual change.

Throughout the development of these schemes we were conscious that their structure should quite explicitly make students aware that learning may involve change in their way of thinking. The teaching schemes themselves followed the general sequence shown in figure 2.

Figure 2: General structure to teaching sequence

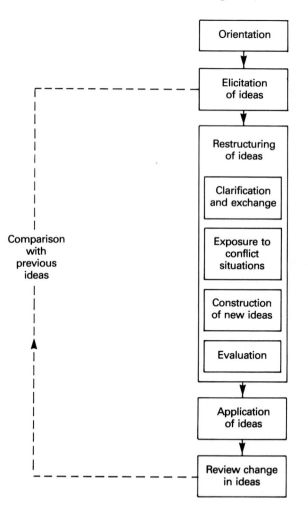

After a scene-setting *orientation* activity in which students' attention and interest in the topic is aroused, the class spends time discussing and reviewing their own ideas or models. This *elicitation* phase is usually conducted in small groups first. Each group is asked to represent their ideas on a poster or by other means and then present these to the class as a whole. Similarities and differences in students' prior ideas are identified and issues for further consideration are noted. The posters remain displayed as a record during the rest of the unit of work and may later be amended or commented on. It is not only teachers who need to be aware of students' prior conceptions, it is important that students themselves make them explicit and clarify them.

The *restructuring* phase, the heart of the scheme, has involved the use of a wide range of strategies which are reviewed in the next section. The lesson sequence then gives students opportunities to try out and *apply* their revised conceptions in a range of ways. This may involve practical construction tasks, imaginative writing tasks or more conventional text book problems to solve. At the end of the lesson sequence classes are given the opportunity to review the extent and ways in which their thinking has changed. The earlier posters may be modified or new ones constructed and compared with the earlier ones.

A learning environment which requires students to make their ideas explicit and to test out new ways of thinking could be very threatening. If students' efforts are evaluated too early by the teacher or by other students then they will tend not to experiment in their thinking but want to be told, thus possibly short-circuiting the knowledge construction process. Techniques were developed to set up such an environment in classes. Students were encouraged to express their ideas in an organized way through small group activities and through their involvement in the preparation and presentation of posters. The group activities have included discussing and representing theories or ideas on a topic, devising experiments to test ideas, developing more complex models to represent experiences, undertaking practical construction tasks in which conceptions are applied. It has also required teachers in many cases to change their class discussion management routines quite radically, avoiding closed questions, accepting a range of suggestions from a class without requiring premature resolution of a point.

The revised schemes were implemented in the second year of work and the learning taking place in the classrooms was monitored again in the same way. The groups met for an extended period to review the findings from the first trial of the schemes. Undoubtedly these first trials led to a greater understanding of some of the students' conceptual problems. It also gave insight into reactions by teachers to implementing a much more open approach in their classrooms. Revisions were made to the schemes which were then retrialled. The resulting published schemes (Children's Learning in Science 1987) include not only an outline of suggested activities but provide a map of the main trends found by the working groups in the kinds of ideas used by students in their classes and the routes they took in their thinking.

Models of Conceptual Change and Science Teaching

What theories can inform the design of teaching sequences and the selection of suitable learning tasks? This is very much an open question but one which is being actively explored by educators and developmental psychologists.

There are various different hypotheses concerning the way conceptual change comes about and it is probably premature and unwise to adopt any single model. Like the fable of the blind men and the elephant, it seems likely that they may be addressing different aspects of a complex process. This is not to say that the development of teaching strategies needs to occur in a totally atheoretical or ad hoc way. There are a number of theoretical developments and experimental studies which can inform instructional design.

Within the teaching schemes developed by this project, a number of different teaching strategies have been used to encourage the construction of new concepts. The choice of the strategy has depended on the nature of the students' prior conceptions and the learning goals. The following are among those that have been used:

(a) *Broadening the range of application of a conception*
Students' prior conceptions may be a resource which can be extended. For example, for younger children energy is attributed to human energeticness and motion. By inviting children to consider what happens to their energy the notion can be generalized to encompass the motion of inanimate objects leading on to an appreciation of energy being 'stored' in springs, etc.

(b) *Differentiation of a conception*
In many areas students' conceptions can be global and ill-defined and particular experiences are necessary to help them differentiate their notions (for example, heat and temperature, force and energy, weight and moment).

In the area of energy, we found that students did not differentiate between the weight of an object and the energy transferred when the object is lifted up (within normal experience, the force of the Earth's gravitational field on the object is constant with changes in height above the Earth's surface). Due to this confusion, students would assert that an object gained weight on being lifted up yet this was not supported by the evidence of spring balance readings. There was a need for a 'something' that changed while 'something else' remained constant (Brook, 1987).

143

(c) *Building experiential bridges to a new conception*

Research by Brown and Clement (1987) with college students has indicated the importance of thought experiments in constructing conceptual bridges for the 'book on the table problem'. Our work has been with younger students and perhaps not surprisingly we find it can be important for such bridges to be constructed through practical experiences.

A prior conception about energy which is widely held is that energy can disappear. In the case of a hot cup of tea in a room, students assert that the tea cools down and the heat energy disappears. To encourage the construction of the notion that energy does not disappear but that it goes somewhere, possibly 'spreading out' so it is less detectable, classes conducted a series of experiments in which a hot cup of water was allowed to cool in outer containers of cold water of progressively larger volumes. The temperature of the water in the inner and outer containers was recorded and plotted at regular intervals of time. After inspecting the resulting graphs, students were then asked to think about what happens when the outer container is the room itself. Having done the activity and plotted the graphs, students were able to construct in their imagination the notion of heat being 'spread out' in the room.

(d) *Unpacking a conceptual problem*

In some cases a conceptual problem occurs which cannot be solved directly but which requires a deeper problem to be addressed. A clear example of this occurs in the teaching of the kinetic-molecular theory of gases where children will accept the existence of particles but have difficulty with the concept of intrinsic motion. The prior conception to be dealt with here is the well known conception of 'motion requiring a force'. An analysis of learning problems of this kind could give some guidance to the sequencing of topics in curriculum as a whole.

(e) *The importing of a different model or analogy*

In the lessons on the structure of matter, students were asked to examine the properties of a range of substances and to describe and explain them. The observation that a gas is 'squashy' elicited ideas among many students that gases are not continuous stuff but made of particles with spaces between them. (An alternative model involving 'squashy molecules' has also been proposed and defended.) Simple experiences with objects in one domain are being drawn on to account for behaviour in another domain.

It is probable that early experiences provide children with a series of schemes which are important for them to draw on in later science teaching. Such basic schemes could include flow in both open and closed systems, spreading out and packing together of objects, and oscillating systems.

(f)   *The progressive shaping of a conception*

In the teaching of the particle theory of matter we find the initial idea that matter is particulate rather than continuous is rapidly adopted by 12-year-old students. The properties of those particles and the way their behaviour accounts for various macroscopic properties have to be treated progressively as students come to explore the range and limitations of their theories. Experiences which focus attention on intrinsic motion of particles and the forces between particles have been found to be important. In adopting a model, students need opportunities to test it out, see where it fails in order to adapt it. Some bits will be constructed which conform to scientific ideas, others will not (for example, the notions that particles are 'squashy', expand on heating or that there is air between particles are commonly used (Scott, 1987)).

(g)   *The construction of an alternative conception*

In some cases students' prior ideas are incommensurate with the scientific conceptions, and attempting to shape their notions into the scientific ideas only leads to problems. In a case of this kind we have acknowledged students' prior ideas and discussed them. We have then indicated that scientists have a different view and an alternative model is built. Students have the opportunity later to evaluate the scientific model in relation to their prior ideas.

This was the approach we took to teaching plant nutrition. Students' prior ideas about plant nutrition focussed on the notion of food as something taken in from outside the plant. Within this conception water, 'goodness from the soil' and even light, are seen as food for plants. The scientific notion, however, hinges on an alternative conception for food — that of providing energy for maintaining the processes of a living system. In the case of green plants, the chemicals which are involved are synthesized. The discontinuity in the students' basic conception and that of scientists was recognized in the teaching and an alternative conceptual scheme for plant nutrition was presented together with practical experiences supporting it.

In this task of designing, trialling and evaluating teaching sequences which are better tuned to learners' understanding it has been necessary to consider the nature of learners' conceptions and how they differ from the learning goals in order to identify appropriate pedagogical strategies. This leads to the suggestion that strategies for promoting conceptual change need to be investigated in the context of particular domains of knowledge. General prescriptions of the conceptual change process by itself are not enough; information about the nature of the conceptual change to be promoted is necessary in designing instructional sequences.

Teacher Reflections

How do teachers feel about putting theory into practice in this way? Most have found it personally satisfying though demanding.

> I found this a particularly useful and interesting exercise ... there was the discipline of the diary and the discussion with the researcher immediately afterwards at a time when everything was still fresh. (John Davidson in Brook and Driver, 1986)

The involvement caused many to reflect on the nature of understanding, both their students' and their own:

> In some ways the constructivist approach seemed to throw up more doubts for the pupils than would a traditional approach. As one pupil stated, 'What we 'ave 'ere is millions of ideas bashing after each other — kicking each other in.' Not for him the measured statements, neat diagrams and superficial understanding of the traditional approach. Until we have inspected some of the shady areas of a subject and have fully examined our own thoughts upon it — can we hope for understanding? (Scott and Wightman, 1985)

Ongoing Issues

In implementing a constructivist approach to teaching and learning science there are a number of features which need to be addressed in the long term.

Experimental Studies on Conceptual Change

Analyses are needed to indicate the nature of the conceptual change required in different areas of concern — then appropriate strategies need to be devised and evaluated. In the evaluations attention needs to be paid to longer-term effectiveness of strategies and to the contexts in which the learning is useful to the learner.

Longitudinal Studies of Conceptual Development

Not only do we need to know how to intervene effectively in students' learning, we also need a better understanding of *when* to intervene. Here longitudinal studies of the development of children's conceptions, such as those reported in the topic of light by Guesne (1985), in biological topics by Carey (1985) and in heat and temperature by Strauss and Stavy (1982) provide important information as to how ideas build on one another from the child's point of view.

Metacognitive Learning

Studies of how students can be encouraged to take responsibility for their learning both personally and within the social settings of classrooms and schools play an important part in a constructivist agenda (Baird and Mitchell, 1986).

Teacher Education

However effective and empirically well-established certain teaching approaches may be, unless the research findings are implemented they are of little value to the educational world. This raises questions not only about how well researchers communicate their findings to practitioners but also who 'owns' and is committed to the enquiry in the first place.

Acknowledgements

The project has been supported with grants from the Department of Education and Science, The School Curriculum Development Committee through the Secondary Science Curriculum Review and the Manpower Services Commission.

References

ANDERSON, R.C. (1984) 'Some reflections on the acquisition of knowledge', *Educational Researcher*, 13, 9, pp 5–10.

BAIRD, J.R. and MITCHELL, I.J. (Eds) (1986) *Improving the Quality of Teaching and Learning: An Australian Case Study — the PEEL project*, Melbourne, Monash University Printery.

BELL, B.F. and BROOK, A. (1985) *The Construction of Meaning and Conceptual Change in Classroom Settings: Case Studies in Plant Nutrition*, Leeds, Children's Learning in Science Project, Centre for Studies in Science and Mathematics Education, University of Leeds.

BEREITER, C. (1985) 'Toward a solution of the learning paradox', *Review of Educational Research*, 55, 2, pp 201–26.

BISHOP, A. (1985) 'The social construction of meaning — a significant development for mathematics education', *For the Learning of Mathematics*, 5, 1, pp 24–8.

BROOK, A. (1987) 'Designing experiences to take account of the development of children's ideas: An example from the teaching and learning of energy', paper presented at the Second International Seminar: Misconceptions and Educational Strategies in Science and Mathematics, Cornell University, July.

BROOK, A. and DRIVER, R. (1986) *The Construction of Meaning and Conceptual Change in Classroom Settings: Case Studies in the Learning of Energy*, Leeds, Children's Learning in Science Project, Centre for Studies in Science and Mathematics Education, University of Leeds.

BROWN, D.E. and CLEMENT, J. (1987) 'Overcoming misconceptions in mechanics: A comparison of two example-based teaching strategies', paper presented at the annual meeting of the American Educational Research Association, Washington, DC, April.

CAREY, S. (1985) *Conceptual Change in Childhood*, Cambridge, Mass., MIT Press.

CHILDREN'S LEARNING IN SCIENCE (1987) *CLIS in the Classroom: Approaches to Teaching*, Leeds, Centre for Studies in Science and Mathematics Education, University of Leeds.

COLLINS, H.M. (1985) *Changing Order*, New York, Sage Publications.

DRIVER, R. and BELL, B. (1986) 'Students' thinking and the learning of science: A constructivist view', *School Science Review*, 67, pp 443–56.

DRIVER, R. and OLDHAM, V. (1986) 'A constructivist approach to curriculum development in science', *Studies in Science Education*, 13, pp 105–22.

EDWARDS, D. and MERCER, N. (1987) *Common Knowledge*, London, Methuen.

GLASERFELD, VON E. (1983) 'Learning as a constructive activity' in BERGERON, J.C. and HERSCOVICS, N. (Eds) *Proceedings of the Fifth Annual Meeting PME-NA*, Montreal, PME-NA.

GREENO, J.G. (1978) 'A study of problem solving' in GLASER, R. (Ed) *Advances in Instructional Psychology*, Hillsdale, NJ, Lawrence Erlbaum Associates.

GUESNE, E. (1985) 'Light' in DRIVER, R., GUESNE, E. and TIBERGHIEN, A. (Eds) *Children's Ideas in Science*, Milton Keynes, Open University Press.

HEAD, J. (1985) *The Personal Response to Science*, Cambridge, Cambridge University Press.

JOHNSON-LAIRD, P.N. (1983) *Mental Models*, Cambridge, Cambridge University Press.

LARKIN, J.H. (1983) 'The role of problem representation in physics' in GENTNER, D. and STEVENS, A. (Eds) *Mental Models*, Hillsdale, NJ, Lawrence Erlbaum Associates.

NEWELL, A. and SIMON, H.A. (1972) *Human Problem Solving*, Englewood Cliffs, NJ, Prentice Hall.

POSNER, G. (1982) 'A cognitive science conception of curriculum and instruction', *Journal of Curriculum Studies*, 14, 4, pp 343–51.

RUMELHART, D.E. and NORMAN, D.A. (1981) 'Accretion, tuning and restructuring: Three modes of learning' in KLATZKY, R.L. and COTTON, J.W. (Eds) *Semantic Factors in Cognition*, Hillsdale, NJ, Lawrence Erlbaum Associates.

SCHANK, R.C. and ABELSON, R.P. (1977) *Scripts, Plans, Goals and Understanding. An Inquiry into Human Knowledge Structures*, Hillsdale, NJ, Lawrence Erlbaum Associates.

SCOTT, P. (1987) 'The process of conceptual change in science: A case study of the development of a secondary pupil's ideas relating to matter', paper presented at the Second International Seminar: Misconceptions and Educational Strategies in Science and Mathematics, Cornell University, July.

SCOTT, P. and WIGHTMAN, T. (1985) 'Teaching the particulate theory of matter — a constructivist approach', paper presented at the annual meeting of the British Educational Research Association Meeting, Sheffield, August.

STRAUSS, S. (1981) 'Cognitive development in school and out', *Cognition,* 10, 295–300.

STRAUSS, S. (Ed) with STAVY, R. (1982) *U-shaped Behavioural Growth*, New York, Academic Press.

WIGHTMAN, T. *et al.* (1986) *The Construction of Meaning and Conceptual Change in Classroom Settings: Case Studies in the Particulate Theory of Matter*, Leeds, Children's Learning in Science Project, Centre for Studies in Science and Mathematics Education, University of Leeds.

8
Role of Language in Science Education

V.G. Kulkarni

Introduction

The problems of education in the Third World are qualitatively different from those in the industrially developed Western world. Historically, the Third World remained colonized in the nineteenth century and in the first half of the twentieth century, a period which saw rapid development of science and technology. Several countries in the Third World acquired political independence soon after the Second World War, and began programmes for development. These countries faced, and continue to face, several problems (apart from poverty) such as huge populations with large growth rates, very high percentage of illiteracy, underdeveloped communication systems, and a poor infrastructure for education. Attempts for development are thwarted by lack of educated and trained manpower, while efforts for universalization of even elementary education are ineffective because of lack of development. The severe nature of this disparity is illustrated vividly by the fact the percentage of students remaining in the educational stream after the age of 20 is less than 5 for the bulk of the Third World, as against 38 for the developed world (see World Development Report, 1987).

The current method of educating people is based on literacy as a prerequisite, and the literacy/knowledge/competence for a job cycle implies that entrants have to stay in the system for over a decade in order to profit from education. Several factors, of which poverty is certainly the most important one, affect the staying power of first generation learners. It can be seen from figure 1, that even in a relatively advanced country like India, the drop-out rate in the first seven years of schooling during the past seven decades is decreasing only slowly.

The main focus of this chapter is to discuss the role played by *language*,

*Figure 1: National retention profiles of pupils in India, grades
I to VII, 1911-1982*

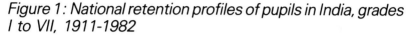

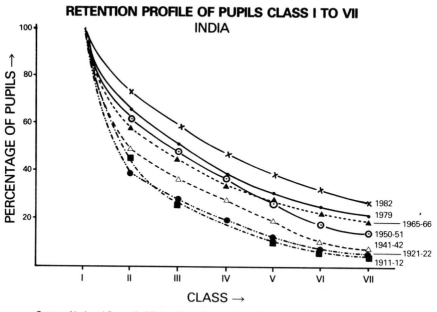

Source: National Council of Educational Research and Training, *All India Educational Survey,* New Delhi.

particularly in science education, in formal and non-formal schools in typically Third World countries, with some reference to similar problems faced by socioculturally deprived communities in the developed countries.

Scope of the Review

It is generally known that language is an important factor in cognition and that the process of language acquisition is strongly culture dependent. However, there are several aspects of the terms *language* and *language acquisition*. The scope of this chapter is restricted to the role language plays in school learning, especially learning of science. It will not be relevant to consider, therefore, the rich literature on how children acquire language in the initial stages, or the literature relating structure of the English language with the process of its language acquisition by children. More relevant is the role played by language in classroom instruction at the school level and a comparison of the language environments in and out of school. It must be pointed out, however, that while the literature on how children acquire language is considerably rich (see, for example, Bloom, 1978), appreciation of the role played by the difference in the language environments in and out of school is relatively recent (for example, Barnes, 1986). Even more importantly, intervention types of studies to design and evaluate programmes to overcome learning hurdles arising from this difference in environments are rather few.

There is yet another aspect of language which will not be considered here. Some linguists, for example, Wharf (1956), have commented upon the underdeveloped nature of some of the primitive languages spoken by some African tribes, claiming that in view of the primitive nature of these languages, science could not be communicated through them. While this issue is open and debatable, it would be more fruitful to assume that most of the languages spoken by large groups of people in the Third World, and which have scripts and literature, are intrinsically capable of communicating modern science. The problem of coining technical words is relatively trivial and can be solved in a variety of ways.

Language Environment

In the Locality

Any modern metropolitan area is rich in the variety of written messages displayed by signboards, advertisements, flashing neon signs, etc. These displays are important inputs to a growing child who even before entering the school learns to associate a variety of signs with their contents. Later, these displays help consolidate the literacy acquired in school. In developed countries the basic difference between the urban metropolitan and the rural areas is in the density of these messages. In the Third World, rural areas are often totally deprived of any such signs.

One of our recent surveys, conducted in rural India in a region not far from the metropolitan city of Bombay, brings out the paucity of such inputs in a striking fashion (Kulkarni et al., 1988). Several small villages did not have any written message, not even the name of the village, displayed anywhere. Bigger villages with populations ranging from 1000 to (say) 5000, had a few displays essentially restricted to signboards on buildings carrying names of institutions housed. Even these were restricted to few institutions like the primary school, primary health centre, office of the local municipality and the name of the village. Tradesmen in the village like the grocer, the carpenter or the tailor, did not have a signboard. There were no advertisements either. Only large villages with populations exceeding 5000 had a variety of signboards and displays. Obviously, even school-going children growing in such a deprived environment cannot hope to receive any reinforcement to language lessons imparted by the school.

Even within the metropolitan towns there is considerable difference in the language environments of the rich and the poor localities. However, city slum dwellers can hope to get some exposure to publicly displayed messages and advertisements. Literature dealing with problems of inner cities and slum areas in the United States describes this difference in environment quite eloquently and attempts to trace differences in scholastic achievements to these environmental factors (see Ward, 1974; and Harrison, 1983). One can imagine the intensity of hurdles involved in universalizing literacy in the Third World where these differences are far more pronounced, and where a vast majority of the population lives in rural areas.

The language environment in rural areas in terms of spoken language is also poor due to the primitive nature of life-styles. Children are seldom exposed to a logical argument, while multiparameter arguments involving quantitative thinking are simply unknown. Any effort to universalize elementary science-based education has to take these factors into account. Acquiring literacy in such adverse conditions is not easy. Even more importantly, sustaining the acquired literacy is difficult since the environment offers so little on which to practise one's literacy skills.

In the School System

In most of the Third World countries the school system, as we perceive it today, has evolved during colonial periods. The primary function of such a school is 'selection'; filtering out the bulk of the population and selecting a few who could help the rulers maintain law and order and carry out simple routine tasks. Under this system children were expected to enter school at the age of about 6. It was also assumed that the population of children entering school would be more or less homogeneous (if not the drop-out would ensure this), except of course, for the differences arising out of a statistical distribution of natural endowment. This also implied that those involved in the development and running of the school system were also its principal users and beneficiaries. In the absence of a political will to democratize and universalize education, these factors resulted in dividing societies into the traditional learning class and the illiterates outside the system.

Independence led to the emergence of a strong political will to universalize education. The school systems were expanded and the doors were thrown open to all, with incentives offered to first generation learners. However, even though the profile of students entering school has changed radically, the practices in the school have hardly been revised to take this change into account. The teacher training programmes continue to be traditional, concentrating on elementary communication skills. What is needed is a strong emphasis on making the teachers aware of the problems of first generation learners and on giving them operational instructions to help these learners overcome their problems.

The Role of Language

The human mind is endowed with an ability (not shared by any other species) of abstracting from natural experience an essence in an abstract form, and articulating it in a manner that permits its transmission and manipulation. It is this facility to manipulate knowledge in a symbolic framework that enables humans to derive deeper meaning from their experiences and to generate new knowledge which natural experiences in their raw form could never reveal. It is this unique ability that distinguishes humans and makes possible an accelerating rate of knowledge acquisition. The emergence of language, the invention of the script, and the application of mathematics (symbolic language) to natural sciences are important milestones in human history. While speech has been internalized, other language skills such as writing, using mathematics, dealing with multiparameter arguments have to be learnt specifically. Thus, in the context of science education, these higher forms of language skills assume considerable importance. It is important to realize that the bulk of the student population in the Third World enter school with only a restricted *speech ability*. The task before the school is to raise their language competence and to teach them science simultaneously. The future of the Third World depends on its ability to solve this problem.

Some Interesting Experiments

This section describes a few innovative and intervention type of experiments. While the author has drawn largely from experiments conducted in his institution which is primarily devoted to studying problems in science education of deprived sections of the community, references have been made to similar studies conducted elsewhere. It is felt that experiments reported in this section are more or less representative of situations prevailing in the Third World.

First Steps in Literacy

A project was undertaken in collaboration with the Indian Institute of

Education, Pune, to design a science-based, non-formal curriculum for the school drop-outs in a rural area located about 250 km south-east of Bombay (see Kulkarni *et al.*, 1988; and Kulkarni, 1985). In this experiment an attempt was made to develop a science curriculum based on about 100 learning situations commonly encountered in that area. A four-page pictorial folder was prepared for every learning situation. Literacy was not assumed to be a prerequisite for understanding the message in a folder. In fact, teachers were advised to use these folders to motivate students to acquire literacy, for which lessons were given concurrently.

The progress made by students in acquiring literacy was measured longitudinally. Since Marathi (the language spoken by these children) is written in the Devanagari script, it made sense to introduce children to simple letters to begin with. After they acquired the skills to read words composed of simple letters (stage 1), sentences composed of such simple words (stage 2), and short paragraphs of such sentences (stage 3), they were introduced to the higher skills of recognizing compound letters. A compound letter is a single symbol standing for several sounds like (say) 'PRO'. Stages 4, 5, and 6 represented abilities to read words, sentences and paragraphs respectively, containing

Figure 2: Percentages of rural 'drop-out' pupils achieving reading stages in science-based, non-formal curriculum

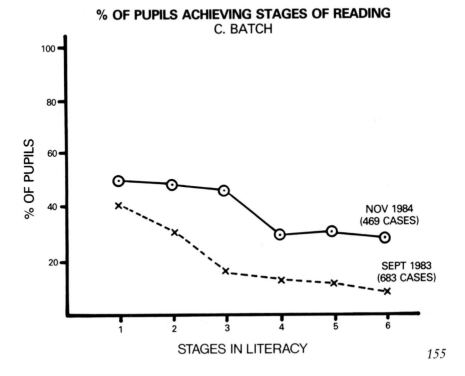

% OF PUPILS ACHIEVING STAGES OF READING
C. BATCH

NOV 1984
(469 CASES)

SEPT 1983
(683 CASES)

STAGES IN LITERACY

Figure 3: Distribution of reading performances of rural, 'drop-out' pupils as a function of training for literacy stages.
(a) Stage 1 (WORD); (b) Stage 2 (SENTENCE); (c) Stage 3 (PARAGRAPH)

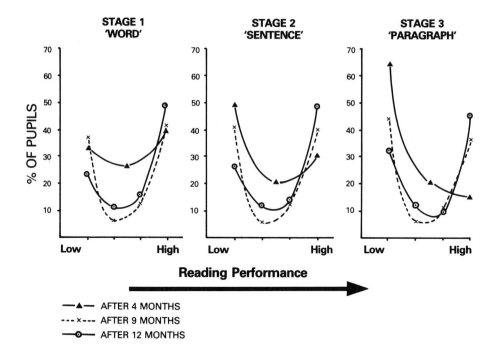

compound letters. It was found that skills for recognizing compound letters were difficult to acquire, but once these skills were acquired, the literacy became truly functional. Figure 2 illustrates this trend clearly.

It is even more interesting to study the distribution of the reading performance of students in the different stages of literacy as a function of time. Such a study was conducted for another batch of students involved in this project, and distributions were obtained after they were exposed to the programme for four months, nine months and one year respectively. Figure 3 shows the distributions of students for the first three stages of literacy, 'WORD', 'SENTENCE' and 'PARAGRAPH' after the three lengths of learning exposure.

These distributions of reading performance are all seen to be 'U' shaped curves which, not surprisingly, rotate counter-clockwise from the first to the third length of learning exposure. The 'U' shaped nature of the curves might demonstrate a limitation of the rating scale used in these measurements, where the intermediate reading performances were not well discerned. However, one might also interpret this shape and the counter-clockwise rotation of the curves as evidence that intermediate performance level between not knowing and knowing how to read either are rare or are very shortlived, and that the transition between illiteracy and literacy is sharp. It is interesting to conjecture whether there exists a typical gestation period in the acquisition of reading skills. Such a study would have important implications for the timing and approach or strategy to be adopted in evaluating literacy programmes.

It would also be interesting to repeat such studies in other areas using a variety of scripts. If one has some experimental evidence for gestation periods involved for acquiring literacy in a given script, the dangers involved in reaching premature conclusions, or in abandoning programmes when success is about to be achieved, could be minimized. Such findings would be of relevance since they would mean that the process of acquiring reading skills would depend upon the nature of the script.

The Concept of Pictorial Literacy

Science literature for children, and also literature for literates, is often illustrated liberally with pictures and diagrams. It is hoped that readers will find illustrated material attractive and easier to comprehend. Evaluation of the non-formal project described in the earlier section shows that this assumption is not quite valid and that it needs to be tested (Kulkarni, 1987). It is not correct to assume that illustrations based on conventions are interpreted uniquely. In fact, conventions like the use of an arrow to show direction or a sequence of steps, or the use of a cross to indicate prohibition, or the use of insets to show

Figure 4: Illustrations used to teach elements of pictorial language common in science education

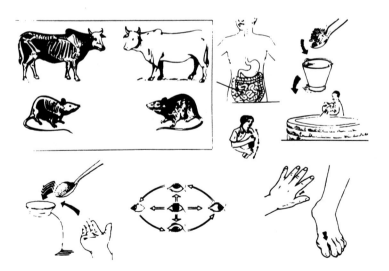

details of a part of an illustration, constitute elements of pictorial literacy which have to be taught. Figure 4 shows some of the illustrations used in pictorial folders. These illustrations were interpreted in many different ways by non-formal students.

The difficulties involved in understanding these illustrations have important implications. Developing countries undertake programmes to educate their people on vital aspects, like family planning and preventive medicine. These programmes often use posters containing written and pictorial messages. The Third World countries have undertaken extensive programmes for providing health services with messages (see Werner, 1978) that are based on complex illustrations. It would be useful to ensure that pictorial literacy is imparted deliberately if these programmes are to succeed.

Can Literacy Be Universalized?

Universalization of literacy has been given priority, and programmes to achieve this goal have been launched with considerable zest and support from international agencies. Is it correct to assume that commitment of resources does ensure success of these projects? Mathematical models of literacy dynamics raise doubts about the validity of this assumption. A model based on the interplay of two contradictory factors, a progressive literacy trend implying that offspring are at least as literate as their parents, if not better, and a fertility rate inversely proportional to literacy implying a higher growth rate for the illiterate sections, shows analytically that 100 per cent literacy cannot be reached regardless of the initial distribution (Kulkarni and Kumar, 1986). A more realistic model taking into account the motivation of the illiterate to ape the literates, and leading to a non-linear Markovian model, also shows that unless this motivation is strong and sustained long enough to include efforts to acquire higher education the society gets locked into oscillations of short-term progress followed by setbacks (Kulkarni and Kumar, 1988). The implications of these findings are that education being a social institution depends for its progress upon the existence of a strong sociopolitical will in the society. Failure of programmes like 'Operation Headstart' in the United States, and the inability of most developing countries to attain the goals of universalization of education need to be examined in the light of these findings.

Concepts in Sociolinguistics

Language plays so important a role in human development that the quality of language acquired by human groups more or less decides the roles and professions available to them. The level of language serves as a predictor of relative positions of groups in various social strata (see Fowler *et al.*, 1979). What are the distinctive features of language behaviour of various social groups? Can the education system hope to bridge these gaps? Before one can attempt to discuss these questions it is relevant to enumerate four stages in the development of language.

In its initial stage a language is restricted to names of objects and actions, and to adjectives and adverbs to qualify them. Such a language is essentially descriptive and is not equipped to express causal relationships and hence to present an argument. The second stage of development includes causal relationships and an ability to join sentences using conjunctive forms, like *because, hence, even if, therefore*, etc. However, even at this stage its capability is restricted to single parameter arguments.

Ability to handle several parameters simultaneously marks a very important development in language. It is interesting to note that the works of Malthus, Darwin and several other social scientists emerged within a narrow span of time soon after the European languages developed to handle multiparameter arguments. The forth stage of development includes the use of mathematics which greatly enhanced the scope, accuracy and manipulabiliy of human thought. Newton's work provides an excellent example of this stage of language development.

The majority of people in any country exhibit a language behaviour limited to the first two stages. Only highly educated people can operate in the third and the fourth stages. While children of educated parents can express, even at their school-going age, concepts like, 'A cow is useful *because* she gives milk', the first generation learners are not even equipped to speak in full sentences. Rural children growing in poor language environments which offer few opportunities for meaningful linguistic interactions with educated adults do not automatically improve their language behaviour. Programmes have to be undertaken to make teachers aware of these difficulties and to give them operational instructions for improving their pupils' language skills.

The language used in schools also contains several social markers with which the rural learners are not familiar. For example, the question, 'Why do we eat food?' is not aimed at seeking personal information but is designed to introduce human physiological needs. Similarly the question, 'Where do you buy medicines?' is designed to test whether students know that shops selling medicines are called 'chemists' shops'. In the absence of adequate awareness of the linguistic difficulties faced by deprived students, teachers are bewildered by strange and unexpected responses, while the pupils are baffled by a language that looks artificial and crazy. The gap between home and school has to be bridged by the school.

Experiments in Sociolinguistics

Improving Language Capability

In the spring of 1970 the City University of New York guaranteed admission to any high school diploma holder residing in that locality. This decision resulted in much larger enrolment and also in a big change in student profile. Language tests administered to these students showed that the students could be divided into three categories: (i) those who met the traditional requirements, (ii) those who had just survived the system and who showed no flair for comprehension, (iii) those who were so far behind the others that they appeared to have no chance of catching up. Serious attempts were made to analyze linguistic problems faced by the backward students so that proper remedial measures could be designed (Shaughnessy, 1977). The single most important finding of this experiment is that language incompetencies can be analyzed and traced to lacunas in environment and that remedial measures can be expected to work. It is more rewarding to pursue such studies than to adopt a passive stand based on IQ.

Effect of Language Development on Scholastic Performance

In yet another experiment undertaken by the Homi Bhabha Centre for Science Education (HBCSE), an attempt was made to boost the scholastic achievement of socioeconomically deprived students. In this experiment a batch of forty students belonging to the scheduled castes (former untouchables — untouch- ability was abolished by law soon after independence), and studying in class VIII in one of the municipal schools was selected in 1980, on the basis of vicinity of their school to HBCSE laboratories and on the basis of the students' motivation as seen by their performance and willingness to take a two-hour test. Fresh batches were added in subsequent years. Care was taken to ensure that at the time of selection the performance profile of the selected students matched that of the student population from these schools. The selected students were given remedial measures in science, mathematics and language for three hours per week during academic sessions for three years until they appeared for a public Secondary School Certificate (SSC) examination in class X.

The experiment showed that scholastic performance of deprived students could be boosted substantially as seen from figure 5, contradicting the view expressed by Jensen (1969) that scholastic achievement cannot be boosted. Detailed reports of this experiment have been published (Kulkarni and Agarkar, 1985) and reported in international seminars (Kulkarni, 1984). It is,

Figure 5: Comparison of learning achievement of socio-economically deprived pupils (BATCH F) given remedial curricula with Bombay Municipal Corporation pupils: (a) science performance, (b) mathematics performance

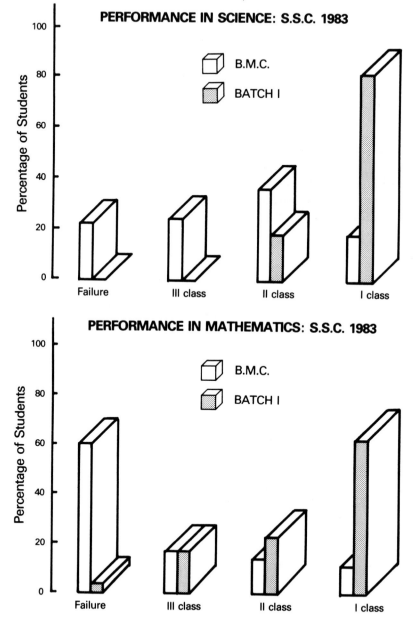

however, relevant to present here yet another finding of this experiment; that improving linguistic capabilities was a prerequisite for remedial measures to work.

All the project students were literate in the conventional sense. However, they were poor in reading comprehension. They lacked the ability to abstract from a paragraph the essential central theme, and were, therefore, forced to remember everything they read. This important lacuna had to be remedied by introducing the system of asking students to read simple booklets and encouraging them to present their summaries orally and later in writing. The students were also encouraged to describe their reading material to members of their families. Their reading comprehension improved over a period of two years which affected positively their motivation to read. Improved linguistic ability was an important factor in boosting performance in other subjects.

The project students had to offer English as a compulsory subject for the SSC examination. It was found that their vocabulary in English was poor as compared to that of typical students from better schools. There was no obvious reason for this disparity since most students learn English as a second (and foreign) language mainly in schools. At the same time, when an attempt

Figure 6: Comparison of learning achievement in English of socio-economically deprived pupils (BATCH I) given remedial curricula with Bombay Municipal Corporation pupils

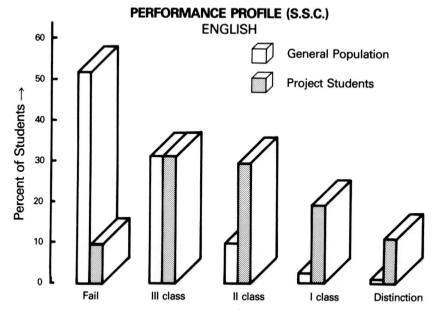

was made to teach words, the students were bored. It was important to realize the significance of active and dormant vocabularies. Games like making words using letters from a given word like (say), TABLE or STATIONERY, served to convert part of their dormant vocabulary into an active one and also to draw upon the active vocabulary of their peers. Once equipped with a larger vocabulary the project students had little difficulty in understanding structures in English. A comparison of the performance of project students in English with that of students from the Corporation schools, presented in figure 6, brings out this point.

These experiments have significant implications. Students from deprived sections of the society are demanding access to higher education. They can no longer be denied this access on the basis that they do not 'qualify'. It has, however, been a common experience that remedial measures have often not been successful. The contents of these remedial programmes need to be re-examined on the basis of the results described above. Perhaps the relative weightings given to science, mathematics, and language (including pictorial literacy and schematic diagrams) need bold changes.

Matching Textbooks to Students' Language Skills

While programmes to improve linguistic abilities of students to enable them to read science texts may be appropriate at the secondary level, it is relevant to examine whether instructional material in science prescribed for lower levels is unnecessarily difficult and clumsy. It was found that the language level in science textbooks prescribed in the state of Maharashtra (India) for grades V, VI and VII was higher than that of the corresponding language texts. A project was, therefore, undertaken to test the effect of simplifying the language of exposition of these texts (Kulkarni and Gambhir, 1981). Linguistically simplified versions were prepared and tried over a large sample (involving 10,000 students). The experiment did not involve any other parameter, like teacher training, better laboratory facilities, or availability of supplementary reading material. Only the language of exposition of the texts was simplified, removing double negatives, constructions in passive voice, and clumsy sentences.

As expected, the scholastic performance of students reading simplified texts improved significantly. The teacher–pupil interaction also improved since the teachers talked in simpler language. However, the most significant finding was the removal of disparity in the performance of students coming from different socioeconomic backgrounds. Since the sample of students in this experiment was fairly large, it was possible to divide it into three categories, slum areas, labour class area, and low middle class area. Students from these three areas normally perform at different levels. However, with the introduc-

Figure 7: Comparative achievements in science in different socio-economic school districts for the experiment of simplifying science text books

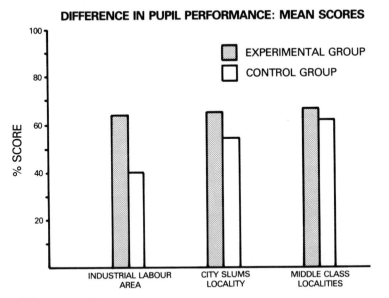

DIFFERENCE IN PUPIL PERFORMANCE: MEAN SCORES

tion of linguistically simplified versions, this difference in performance is eliminated as seen from figure 7. This finding is significant since it shows that the school system can overcome some of the barriers arising out of differences in home background.

It is important to ensure that school students are not put off by unnecessarily complex language in their science textbooks. Even if it is argued that poverty is the main cause for drop-out at this stage, it would be relevant and useful to ensure that other causes such as 'complex' language are eliminated. It would also be important to examine why texts continue to be written in such complicated language. It is not unlikely that part of the complexity arises from the fact that the material is translated into local languages from an English version.

Oral and Literate Modes of Language Behaviour

Linguists have recognized at least two aspects of language which are relevant in science education. Firstly, it is now realized that there is a difference between what is observed or seen, and what is interpreted (see, for example, Scribner and Cole, 1973 and 1981; and Olson, 1986). When one extends the concept of literacy from an ability to encode and decode symbols in the script, to include comprehension, one is dealing with the higher skills of interpreting texts. It is significant to note that traditional curricula do not contain any deliberate programmes to impart these higher skills, for which a learner seems to depend essentially on-out-of school inputs, enhancing the importance of home background.

The other aspect deals with oral and literate modes of language behaviour. These terms are not to be confused with literacy. People operating in an oral mode of language behaviour may be literate in a conventional sense, but are not equipped to make a multiparameter argument, or to present a logically connected sequence of events, or to plan a strategy where the choice of each subsequent move depends upon the outcome of the previous move. In other words, their language is restricted to the first two stages of development covering description and single parameter arguments. It is typical for a student in the oral mode to fumble in narrating an episode like,

> I wanted to see the movie. *So* I went to the city. *But* I could not get tickets. *Therefore*, I was disappointed. *Even so*, I am going to try again this Sunday.

Inability of students in an oral mode to join sentences using the right conjunction seems to be a widespread phenomenon (Gardner, 1980). Moreover, the need to pay attention to non-technical parts of the language in science texts is also a common problem (Gardner, 1974).

Role of Science in Improving Language

While the importance of improving language skills for better science education is being appreciated, the role science can play in improving language skills is not yet fully realized. Science is ideally suited to present the correct usage of various conjunctions. Science, even elementary science, that can be linked easily with daily life, can be used to construct simple multiparameter arguments. Obviously, it is possible to draw students' attention to the fact that simple statements like, 'water boils at $100°C$' are valid only conditionally. Curriculum designers should use this aspect of science sensitively. In the old days the focus was on classics. Modern trends highlight science even at the expense of language. What is needed is a boot-strap approach using science to introduce pupils to higher language skills which in turn could be used for better science education.

Acknowledgements

Thanks are due to all my colleagues at the Homi Bhabha Centre for Science Education on whose work I have drawn heavily.

References

BARNES, D. (1986) 'Language in the secondary classroom' in BARNES, D., BRITTON, J. and TORBE, M. (Eds) *Language the Learner and the School*, 3rd edn, Harmondsworth, Penguin, pp 11–87.

BLOOM, L. (Ed) (1978) *Readings in Language Development*, New York, John Wiley and Sons.

FOWLER, R., HODGE, B., KRESS, G. and TREW, T. (1979) *Language and Control*, London, Routledge & Kegan Paul.

GARDNER, P.L. (1974) 'Language difficulties of science students', *The Australian Science Teachers' Journal*, 20, 1, pp 63–76.

GARDNER, P.L. (1980) 'Difficulties with non-technical scientific vocabulary amongst secondary school students in the Philippines', *The Australian Science Teachers' Journal*, 26, 2, pp 82–90.

HARRISON, P. (1983) *Inside the Inner City*, Harmondsworth, Penguin, pp 277–98.

JENSEN, A.R. (1969) 'How much can we boost IQ and scholastic achievement?', *Harvard Educational Review*, 39, 1, pp 1–123.

KULKARNI, M.S. and KUMAR, A. (1986) 'A mathematical model of progressive literacy', *Journal of Mathematical Society*, 12, 3, pp 275–98.

KULKARNI, M.S. and KUMAR, A. (1988) 'Interactive Markovian models of progressive trends', *Journal of Mathematical Sociology*.

KULKARNI, V.G. (1984) 'Designing and testing the effectiveness of remedial measures to improve the scholastic achievement of students coming from socio-economically deprived class', *3rd International Symposium on World Trends in Science and Technology Education*, pp 144–8.

KULKARNI, V.G. (1985) 'Alternatives in education', *Man and Development*, March, pp 35–58.

KULKARNI, V.G. (1987) 'Role of language in science education', *Journal of Education and Social Change*, 1, June, pp 113–31.

KULKARNI, V.G. and AGARKAR, S.C. (1985) *Talent Search and Nurture among the Underpriviledged*, Bombay, Homi Bhabha Centre for Science Education.

KULKARNI, V.G. and GAMBHIR, V.G. (1981) 'The effect of language barrier on science education', *Indian Educational Review*, 16, pp 48–58.

KULKARNI, V.G., RAMADAS, J., OZARKAR, S.P., BHAT, N.R. and GAMBHIR, V.G. (1988) *Non-formal Science-Based Education*, Bombay, Homi Bhabha Centre for Science Education.

OLSON, D.R. (1986) 'The cognitive consequences of literacy', *Canadian Psychology*, 27, 2, pp 109–21.

SCRIBNER, S. and COLE, M. (1973) 'Cognitive consequences of formal and informal education', *Science*, 182, pp 553–9.

SCRIBNER, S. and COLE, M. (1981) *The Psychology of Literacy*, Cambridge, MA, Harvard University Press.

SHAUGHNESSY, M.P. (1977) *Errors and Expectations*, New York, Oxford University Press.

WARD, C. (1974) *The Child in the City*, Harmondsworth, Penguin.

WERNER, D. (1978) *Where There Is No Doctor*, New York, Macmillan.

WHORF, B.L. (1956) *Language Thought and Reality*, Cambridge, MA, MIT Press.

WORLD DEVELOPMENT REPORT (1987) Oxford, Oxford University Press (for the World Bank), pp 262–3.

ZIGLER, E. and VALENTINE, J. (Eds) (1979) *Operation Head Start*, New York, The Free Press, pp 399–514.

9
Practical Work and Science Education I

Sunee Klainin

Introduction

Ever since experimental science was advocated in the sixteenth century, it has been well accepted that practical or empirical work is the major task of scientists. Thus, in order to educate each new generation in science, there is a widespread belief that students should learn science by doing what scientists do. This sort of learning in science, furthermore, is seen by most science educators as likely to be more effective because the child is involved in practical activities and takes an active part in the learning procedure. Practical work has been a prominent feature of school science teaching from the late nineteenth century when science was established as part of the curriculum of schooling in a number of countries. Once it was introduced it became a part of science instruction and though its practice has varied considerably it has never been wholly neglected. Jenkins and Whitfield (1974) in the United Kingdom could, accordingly, write with confidence that:

> Whatever teaching methods are employed, considerable importance is likely to be attached to laboratory work carried out by pupils themselves. Practical work is a characteristically strong feature of school science teaching in the United Kingdom. (p. 83)

In the United States, laboratory work was recognized as an essential part of science teaching in the 1880s when Harvard University required laboratory chemistry as a prerequisite for admission. This decision led to a drastic change in American school science education, and laboratory work has been an accepted part of it ever since.

Although the new science curricula in many countries in the 1960s and 1970s put such a lot of emphasis on practical activities, surprisingly little research was done in these years on this aspect of the intended learning processes. Jenkins and Whitfield (*ibid.*) asked rather rhetorically of the British system of education,

> ... an enormous amount of time and money is still invested in pupil practical work. On what grounds might such an investment be justified? (p. 85)

The Role of Practical Work in Science Instruction

Although practical work has, for so long, been part of science education in many countries, its role has changed back and forth between elucidation and verification, and investigation to find facts and arrive at principles. In most science curricula prior to the 1960s, practical work had been used primarily as demonstration or confirmation of the factual and theoretical aspects of the science course. The new science curricula of the 1960s and the 1970s set out to shift the laboratory exercise from simply demonstrating or verifying known information to raising problems, developing enquiry skills, and providing opportunities for 'discovery'. While practical work had long been used to provide students with direct experiences of objects, concepts and experimental procedure, in the new curricula the laboratory was assigned the roles of being an instrument for the learning of scientific enquiry and for developing cognitive abilities in the learner.

These were not entirely new roles for practical work. They had been introduced in the late nineteenth century when H.E. Armstrong initiated enquiry into the teaching of chemistry which became known as 'heuristic method' or the art of making children discover things for themselves. In fact, discovery learning was advocated long before Armstrong's time. The first recorded advocate of discovery learning was probably Socrates. For the education of children it was made very clear in Rousseau's *Emile*.

> Let him know nothing because you have taught him, but because he has learnt it for himself. (p. 131)

Rousseau's ideas were passed on and were formally taken into the teaching and learning of science in the late nineteenth century by persons like Armstrong.

In Armstrong's heuristic method, the learning process was to become more attractive and challenging because it aroused curiosity, interest and experimentation. The desire to solve the difficulties that present themselves in the process of experimentation was to be derived from the enthusiasm and the drive of the learner discoverer. The exercises to be included in practical work thus must be ones for which the answers are not known to the learners in advance. Despite its goods intentions, Armstrong's heuristic method gained acceptance only slowly. It was costly in time and did not fit the existing system of examinations and their syllabuses. Further, it was too novel for many teachers to accept its challenge. Nevertheless, his work did lead to some changes in the mode of science education, in examination syllabuses, and in science instruction with greater emphasis being placed on individual practical work. Many schools were equipped with laboratories for practical science and laboratory classes were almost universal in British secondary schools by the early years of the twentieth century.

Prior to the 1960s the role of practical work in the United Kingdom had moved far away from the heuristic purposes that Armstrong urged for so long. Practical work was almost entirely elucidation and verification. It was helped in its swing back to heuristic purposes when Kerr (1963), in his well popularized study, suggested that practical work should be closely integrated with theoretical work and should be used for the important contribution it can make to finding facts by investigation, and hence to arriving at principles that related these facts. This modified form, sometimes called 'neo-heuristic' and known by words such as 'discovery', 'enquiry' or 'guided-discovery', became a major feature of the several Nuffield science projects.

In the United States, Rousseau's ideas were carried by Dewey into twentieth-century American education. 'Learning by doing' is the keystone of Dewey's theory of learning (1951). In Dewey's ideal, experience was the only source of knowledge. This clearly has a very strong implication for science education. Indeed, in some places it was translated to mean that the practical work performed by students was the keystone of science instruction.

However, science has also been seen by many scientists primarily as a body of knowledge. These scientists saw science only as a matter of seeking the facts of nature and of reporting what was found out. The teaching of science they thus confined to the presentation of the known scientific facts, laws and principles with some applications. They, and science educators like them, argued that a substantial amount of this knowledge of science is needed before the learning of other aspects of science can begin, and science education in schools has often reflected these views, as students were expected to absorb the knowledge of science and it was assumed that in itself this would be worthwhile to them.

By 1960, for many concerned with science for learning in school, science was no longer considered simply as a body of knowledge. Instead it was regarded as a dynamic process of enquiry. Many scientists and philosophers of science education regarded science as a process of thought and action, as a means of acquiring new knowledge and a means of understanding the natural world (Schwab, 1962; Rutherford and Gardner, 1970; Jenkins and Whitfield, 1974; Tunnicliffe, 1981). For Schwab, for example, the nature of science itself is a process of enquiry. Science is a search for cause and effect.

These ideas were strongly supported by Michels (1962) and Ramsay (1975) who suggested that the processes of science should be adopted as the methods of learning science. A consequence of this change is that the nature of science education becomes not only the acquisition of scientific knowledge but also it is learning the process of scientific enquiry. Indeed, the changes give both aspects high priority but the second gains a sequential preference, since the teaching of science is now based on the belief that the learners learn the processes of science first, and through this learning, the facts, the principles, the theories and models of science follow.

These ideas, were, of course, not suddenly invented as the science education profiles of the 1960s began. The Sputnik satellite coincided with, and contributed a spur to, a growing recognition that something was wrong with science education in the Western world. An opportunity had come to reform the purpose and method of science teaching and hence for an enquiry method to be strongly recommended.

In order to teach science as enquiry Schwab (a key contributor in general and to the BSCS project in biology in particular) suggested that the laboratory is easily converted to enquiry by making two changes. Firstly, a substantial part of the laboratory work 'is made to lead rather than lag the classroom phase of science teaching'. Secondly, the demonstration function of the laboratory is subordinated to the two other functions, namely, to provide a tangible experience of some of the problems dealt with in science and of the difficulty of acquiring data, and to provide occasions for an invitation to conduct miniature but exemplary programs of enquiry.

With suggestions like this as their basis, a series of science curriculum development projects was established from 1957 onwards in the United States, the United Kingdom and a number of other countries. These projects set out to change the methods of teaching science and the role of practical work. Practical work became an essential part and, in fact, acquired a central role in the intentions of these curricula. Laboratories, as in the traditional sense, were still important but they were to be used in new ways. These curriculum projects, that provided quite new sorts of materials in the 1960s, have had a worldwide influence. Some English speaking countries or those countries with English as the instructional medium (like the Philippines), adopted some of the USA projects, while others (like Malaysia and the West Indies) adopted science curricula from the United Kingdom.

In a number of non-English speaking countries like Israel, Brazil, Iran, etc., some of the American or British project materials were translated for use, but in the case of some other non-English speaking countries in the Third World, like Thailand and some countries in Africa, these materials were not adopted directly or in adapted forms. In Thailand, for example, a large-scale science curriculum project and a new Institute for the Promotion of Teaching

Science and Technology (IPST) was established to develop new science courses for use at all levels of schooling. The project teams in carrying out these tasks did, however, borrow ideas and adapt some of the approaches from these well-known and already tried projects. Accordingly, the science curricula in Thailand, that were developed in the 1970s and revised late in that decade to their present forms do have many similar characteristics to these other curricula. In the intentions of these new science curriculum projects, the values of practical work are often stated as lying in the students' involvement in discovery about science and in learning about scientific method.

Several other values have also been assigned to practical work. For example, Gagné and White (1978) developed a model of the way in which memory can aid or inhibit learning. The model describes the relations between instructional variables and learning outcomes with the learner's memory structure as the intermediate. They distinguished several sorts of memory structure among which are 'images' and 'episodes'. White (1979) then suggested that these two are particularly relevant to the problem of making the laboratory a more effective context for science learning. Images are described as figural representations in memory of diagrams, pictures or scenes, and practical work and science laboratories should provide many of these. Episodes are the representations in memory of past events in which the individual was very personally involved and again, practical work, if it is actively engaging the student with science, should be a source of these.

Johnstone and Wham (1982) used a similar model involving a memory hypothesis in their designs for science instruction. In practical work in chemistry, they identified various kinds of information pouring into the working memory such as (i) written instruction; (ii) verbal instruction; (iii) new manipulative skills; and (iv) unfamiliar labelling of reagents. There is also input from the long-term memory such as (v) recall of manipulative skills; (vi) associations of names and apparatus; and (vii) recall of background theory. There are also inputs from the experiment itself such as various changes that are observed, etc. All these pieces of information about the practical situation need to be processed. This can be quite confusing, but if, by design, they can be 'chunked' and formed into images and episodes they may thus be built into long-term memory. In these ways practical work is assigned another role, namely, that of assisting what Ausubel (1965) described as meaningful learning.

A number of other authors have emphasized priorities for practical work that are independent of its link with the learning of scientific knowledge. Beaty and Woolnough (1982) use it to foster attitudes and interests. Denny and Chennell (1986) and Hodson (1985) gave similar lists of four principal objectives — (i) to stimulate interest and enjoyment; (ii) to teach laboratory skills; (iii) to teach processes of science; and (iv) to assist in learning scientific knowledge.

Fensham (1984b) argued that the laboratory should be the place where teachers assist students to put 'flesh on the bone' of theoretical work, and where a sense of mastery of new and useful skills is achieved. Earlier he had advocated an alternative science curriculum which emphasized the systematic development and mastery of practical skills that are based on scientific knowledge but which did not place a priority on learning this knowledge since it has been such a barrier to extending science education to a wide spectrum of learners (Fensham, 1981). His argument is that practical skills in science education should be recognized as important in their own right. Practical work is not only useful and essential for the teaching of science in schools that aim to train students to become scientists or technicians. Nor is it simply a helpful context to assist concept learning or to develop attitudes and interests. It should be seen as the means whereby practical skills that are useful in the real world of an increasingly technical society are learnt. Students, whether they go on to further study of science or whether they do not, should get from the practical experiences of their science education, skills and hands-on confidence that will be useful in their future lives as citizens.

Dilemmas of Practical Work

The research findings on laboratory learning in science education, even in situations where it is commonplace, are surprisingly disappointing. As a medium for learning cognitive knowledge, or even for mastering psychomotor skills, the evidence for the effectiveness of the time in the laboratory is not very good. Schools in many countries do, however, sustain a belief in practical work in science and continue to allocate time and considerable resources to it. A number of problems seem to be commonplace and these, no doubt, contribute to its ineffectiveness. They fall under two broad headings, problems of implementation and of incentive.

Problems of Implementation

Practical work for school science classes is very expensive in money, and time and human resources. To introduce such expensive experiences into school curricula is not simple and there are many problems. This discussion of these problems will focus particularly on the Third World countries although some of them are also evident in a number of more developed countries.

Lack of equipment

Third World countries have not been reluctant in designing their science curricula to accept the challenge of using practical-based approaches to science learning. However, many problems then arise. How can equipment be obtained? Can the teachers make use of it? How can it be maintained? How can it be stored? How can a large class experience activity when only one set of equipment (or a few sets) are available? These are just some of the problems which can turn the intentions of practical-based learning and teaching into frustrating dilemmas for the science teachers in schools. The result may be worse than a course which had not assumed practical-based learning as a central feature.

In a number of Third World countries, attempts have been made to introduce so-called 'low-cost equipment' for use in schools and two main ways have been used. One is equipment made and distributed by a national centre, like the equipment made by IPST in Thailand. The second way ought perhaps to be called 'no-cost' equipment since it does assume costs or supply from a central source. The equipment is to be made by teachers in their own schools or with the aid of local craftsmen and women. The UNESCO *Source Book for Science Teaching* is designed for this second way and includes suggestions and plans for producing simple equipment from locally available materials.

In spite of these two approaches, the problems are not solved in many situations and, indeed, low-cost equipment has presented its own problems. There are differential problems of transportation for equipment made by a centre. Teacher-made equipment does not overcome these locational effects because some of the suggested raw materials do not exist in some places. Teachers also often have such heavy teaching loads that they cannot spare time for making such equipment even when they have the skills or local contacts.

Some of the centrally designed low-cost equipment has not been robust enough for use by teachers in the range of teaching contexts they face. Some of it functions so crudely that the data it gives have serious limitations for developing the concepts and skills for which it is intended. In these cases, low-cost equipment may indeed mean 'low learning'! Most low-cost equipment does not stay in use for very long because there are no mechanisms for its maintenance.

There are also other problems in getting teachers to use this sort of equipment. Most of the teachers who graduated from college and university are familiar with standard equipment. Accordingly their attitudes and expectations about practical work in science are associated with such equipment and these are a barrier to their use of the low-cost alternatives. Even with enthusiasm for these alternatives, they need new skills to make use of them. IPST has conducted extensive in-service training courses that aim to train teachers for these specific skills. However, this does not seem to have happened in many countries so that teachers are unable to use even the low-cost equipment with which they may be supplied or to handle in class the sorts of experimental results that arise from its use (Ratnaike, 1987).

Time consuming

Practical work requires time. Schools in general often have a fixed timetable for each subject which does not recognize this particular feature of science education. (This problem is common in the USA also.) Teachers feel committed to use the time available in effective ways that enable them 'to finish the course'. For many teachers in Third World countries the emphasis of the examinations is on the factual and theoretical knowledge of science and to spare time on practical work seems to be a luxury. As Ausubel (1965) was able to say about the very different context of North American schools:

> They (students) wasted many valuable hours collecting empirical data ... or to exemplify principles which the teacher could have presented visually in matter of minutes. (p. 262)

When there is a sense of pressure from what seems like more topics to be covered than there is class time, and when many students do not have access to textbooks as sources for extra learning of the science knowledge required, teachers find the time aspect of practical work does pose a very real dilemma. Accordingly, to cover the course and to keep faith with a belief in practical work in science, the teacher may do a demonstration or even lecture about practical results instead of attempting to engage the students in practical activities themselves.

Safety

Laboratories to accommodate practical work for large classes need to be orderly and safe. Most of the classes in Third World countries are large. In Thailand, for example, the average number of students is forty to forty-five. Nevertheless, teachers in that country have been trying to do their best to have practical work done by students in small groups in class. This has, of course, presented a lot of problems for the teachers, and they can easily end up stopping the practical work simply because the class is out of control.

Degree of pupil participation

Even in developed countries, practical work in schools is usually conducted with the students in small groups of two or three. There are many logistical reasons for this such as the amount of equipment available, the number of service points in a school laboratory, and the relative economy of materials consumed. This arrangement of practical classes is also argued for on pedagogical grounds, since students can help each other, and the small groups can provide the teacher with a manageable number of interactive exchanges for advice and discussion during a practical session.

Relatively little research has been directed to the learning effectiveness of the small group arrangement for practical work, but there is evidence that the arrangement is one of the features of practical work in science that contributes to students' positive attitudes. Although undoubtedly there is a degree of positive peer-peer instruction about the immediate practical procedures that are involved in handling equipment, more systematic studies of the cognitive interchanges between members of small groups are not encouraging about the extent and the equality of peer-peer learning. There is often a dominant or confident member who tends to be the regular handler of equipment while the others act as passive note takers or mere attendants, intermittently observing. The outcome of these uneven patterns of participation is very differential learning (Suan, 1976).

Klainin (1984) in a recent study in Thailand, where senior secondary students work in groups of three in the laboratory, obtained striking evidence of a phenomenon all too familiar to those who have been insecure in laboratories at school or at university. When she tested the groups on their ability to carry out a practical task they had learnt earlier in the year, about 80 per cent of the groups were successful, but a little later, as individuals, only about 20 per cent were able to carry out the task correctly! Achievement in a group does not ensure internalization of this learning by all its members.

These sorts of findings again pose dilemmas about practical work and especially if science education is to be extended to more of each age cohort of learners. More practical learning is needed yet small group organization which provides realistic cost savings does not seem to lead to effective learning for all. One alternative that seems to be worthy of exploration is the large group practical project. With only one or a few groups, the teacher can, over time, ensure that all the learners do take turns at critical tasks and his/her more extended presence with the larger group may provide cooperative learning that is more effective than present small group approaches.

Change of emphasis in school curriculum

Science subjects were given an important priority in many Third World countries during the 1970s. From 1980 onwards priority and emphasis have been moving to language and mathematics, especially in primary education. This trend can be seen in Vietnam, Burma, Indonesia, Malaysia, Philippines,

Nepal and also in Thailand as a sense of national identity becomes more important and the role of language and the school in this identity is recognized. In the case of Thailand, science in primary schooling is a part of the so-called 'Life Experience course' which includes social science, humanities, etc. Thus, the nature of science in this subject is dominated by the nature of other subjects which are non-practically-based.

Problems of Incentive

Incentive is another important factor that causes dilemmas about practical work. Different groups in schools and the education system hold very different values for it, and consequently there is conflict over the rewards for it, especially between different levels of the education system.

Value of practical work held by students and by teachers and curriculum developers.

The values of practical work described earlier are in general recognized but not with equal weight by curriculum developers, science educators and teachers. It is, however, important to consider how students recognize the value of practical work and how they perceive practical work affecting their learning.

Reports of the agreement between students and teachers on the value of practical work are inconsistent. For example, the study by Denny and Chennell (1986) found that the curriculum developers and science teachers suggested that the value of science practical work lies in 'discovery, in learning about scientific method, and in acquiring strategies for problem solving etc.,' but the students saw it as providing concrete experience and empirical testing of ideas for themselves as 'students' not as scientists. Klainin (1984) reported that students and teachers in Thailand agreed that practical work in chemistry was 'assisting concept learning', but the former also associated time in laboratory with their enjoyment, 'a chance to relax', and 'a welcome break from the heavily loaded chemistry class'.

Many studies have reported that students see time in laboratory as contributing positively to their enjoyment of science, but they do not associate it with more academic learning. Johnstone and Wham (1982) in Scotland noted that 'pupils enjoy practical work, pick up hand skills with varying degree of proficiency, but learn little of the theoretical information which practical work is alleged to illustrate or to initiate'.

Tan (1980) in Malaysian schools (where the British Nuffield science courses were adopted for use in the 1970s), found that practical work always ended by students writing reports that did not include a discussion of the empirical aspects of their findings or suggestions about the practical investigation. Presumably, such aspects were not valued or rewarded by their teachers and hence would not be seen as important by students.

Klainin, Fensham and West (1988), in their study of physics learning in Thailand, were also able to differentiate features of what was learnt by the students when solving practical problems in physics. They found that the students in general had acquired considerable degrees of proficiency in planning to solve the problem, in executing these plans and in making and recording their observations. They scored, however, very low in the ability to 'draw conclusions from the experimental data.' This study suggests that students can learn in practical work those aspects that they perceive as important and which may have been stressed and rewarded by their teachers. Other aspects which are seen as important by the science educators or curriculum developers are not learnt.

Lack of reward for the learners

The lack of rewards gained by students for practical work is a major deterrent to learning in it and from it. The immediate interest of students is the good results in the examination that publicly (within the school or more widely in the education system) acknowledges the extent of their learning. Teachers also have a commitment to prepare students for the requirements of these examinations.

Although the dictum 'Exams are powerful agents for good and evil in teaching' was quoted by Mathews (1984) in relation to science education, in the field of practical work it is well documented that the role of the examination has very often been neglected. Despite the fact that curriculum evaluators often claim to base their work on the objectives of a course and design instruments that reflect these objectives, it appears that the objectives about the practical work in science courses have usually been overlooked. Many science educators have urged for years for practical examinations. For example, Klopfer (1971) suggested that any evaluation of a science course should include the practical skills it embodies. A decade later a group of Third World science educators at the South East Asian Regional Workshop of UNESCO (1982) were still recommending that practical work should be assessed.

Unfortunately, the practical examination proves to be most difficult in operation at both its macro and micro levels. Thus, it has usually been left out of the test battery. For example, the IEA first science study tried to include a practical test in its Science Achievement Battery (Comber and Keeves, 1973), but the test was hardly used in the participating countries except Japan

(Kojima, 1974) and Israel. A decade later, Tamir (1984) expressed regret that although a range of practical tests was developed and offered for the second IEA study most countries again chose not to use them.

Conflict between two systems of education

It is not only in the normal processes of teaching and learning but also in the critical processes of educational selection that practical work has been ignored. Particularly critical in this regard are the upper secondary courses which, at the end of schooling, become the selection interface for continued study in university and other institutions of higher education. Science subjects have particular importance at this interface because science-based faculties of universities in most countries do make assumptions that students will have acquired quite detailed knowledge from these subjects in school. Almost invariably, however, it is the students' abilities in answering only certain sorts of cognitive questions from the total range of knowledge, skills, and attitudes these science curricula set out to foster that determine whether or not they will be selected into university to continue their ambitions as learners.

There is thus a potential for conflict between the learning intentions of school science curricula and those that are rewarded by universities through their selection procedures. Fensham (1980) found that the effects of this conflict on the curricula for physics and chemistry in Australian schools were quite different from what they were for biology and that the universities do not make the same sorts of prior knowledge assumptions (as evidenced by the written examinations used for selection) about school learning of biology that they do for the other two sciences. Fensham (1984a) has analyzed the content of chemistry examinations in the UK and in Australia to provide more evidence of the limited range of learning objectives that these powerful systems reward and hence, declare to students and teachers as being of worth.

The lack of congruence about the values of various sorts of learning between the two systems of education can result in a change in the emphasis of practical work, both in terms of its role and its practice. Denny and Chennell (1986) demonstrated that in the early years of secondary schooling students regard practical work as 'investigatory-discovery oriented' whereas the students of the later years who are on the examination track regard it as 'confirmatory of the theory'. A teacher in their study stated,

> From year IV onwards, with examination syllabuses dominating the work, practicals are used to a great extent to verify and consolidate in a much more formal and overt way ideas already presented by the teacher. (p. 331)

Lynch and Ndyetabura (1984) reported similar shifts whereby students'

Figure 1: *The plots student's scores on problem solving test and its subscales*

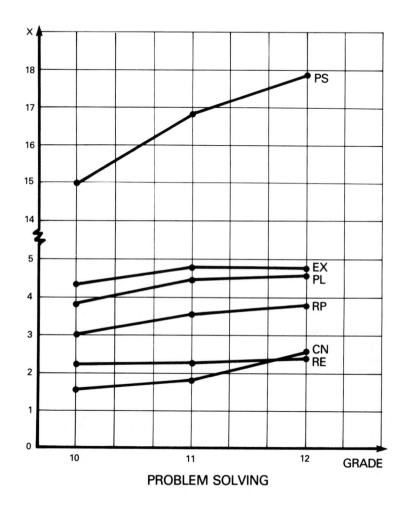

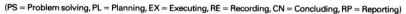

(PS = Problem solving, PL = Planning, EX = Executing, RE = Recording, CN = Concluding, RP = Reporting)

positive response to affective components of practical work was high at year 9 but low at year 12 while their response to cognitive components was in the reverse direction.

In Thailand, where a practical examination is non-existent in both the schools' examination syllabus and in the university selection system, it was found that chemistry teachers in the 10th and 11th grades included a substantial amount of practical experience (about 40 per cent of total class time). This was, however, reduced in grade 12 which is the final year of upper secondary schooling in Thailand although the intended curriculum is just as practically based (Klainin, 1984).

Klainin and Fensham (1987) and Klainin, Fensham and West (1988) in two studies that looked at students' learning in chemistry and physics included measures of the following aspects of practical work — manipulative skills (with sub-scales for planning, executing, observing and recording, concluding and report writing), scientific attitudes, and preference for laboratory experiments as the source of evidence in science. The results revealed that the students' learning in these practical outcomes, in general, do develop in the first two years of upper secondary schooling, but that as the pupils move up to grade 12, these outcomes either remain constant or show a considerable decrease. These findings are illustrated in figure 1.

The students in the first two years seem to be more responsive to the value the curriculum intends for the school system, but in the third year they become responsive to the university values that are evident in the public examinations used to select students to enter the universities and which usually are based only on more theoretical aspects of science learning.

As a result, students and their teachers come to devalue science practical work. At best, they see it as confirmation or elucidation of the important factual and theoretical parts of the course.

Resolution — A Way Forward

In science education, or any other explicitly purposeful education, the objectives can be important in guiding and organizing the learning activities and they should be the grounds for an evaluation of its effectiveness. Furthermore, it is quite widely accepted that evidence should be made available to the learners to indicate whether or not they are achieving the objectives or goals of a course. Direct assessment is a powerful tool that can provide such evidence and that can guide the direction of the teaching and learning process. The assessment of practical work in many of the new science curricula of the 1960s and 1970s was not sustained and it became a neglected area within science education (Hofstein and Lunetta, 1982). There is, thus, little from sound research into those curricula with which to encourage school systems and science teachers who would like to introduce this essential aspect of practical work as learning into their science classrooms. Few ready means were developed for teachers to feed back information to provide an incentive for students to take their time in practical classes seriously.

A major contribution to the resolution of the dilemmas that practical work raises for science education would thus be better understanding and widespread use of practical assessment as a regular part of science teaching and learning.

What to Assess

If it is agreed that practical assessment should be done, there is still a problem about what should be assessed and the criteria that should apply. The lack of widespread agreement on the definition of the skills components of practical work is, of course, one of the reasons for the failure of practical assessment to occur in classrooms or for that matter as part of the final examinations system in many countries, although the overt reasons given may be more mundane and logistical.

Only in the last decade or so has some light been cast on these aspects of the assessment of practical work. Hofstein *et al.* (1976) suggested three domains of practical work — (i) skill in the performance of routine laboratory tasks; (ii) ability to make observations; and (iii) problem solving ability. The first two domains were familiar in the science curriculum projects but the third domain of problem solving ability via practical work was a new emphasis. Ben-Zvi *et al.* (1977) saw successful practical work as involving four phases: — (i) planning and designing of investigations; (ii) performance of experiment; (iii) observation of particular phenomena; and (iv) analysis, application and explanation. In their view these four phases (components of Hofstein *et al.'s* third domain) are not only sequential but also hierarchical. In practice not all the phases are involved in every piece of practical work, but specification of the phase involved and its subcomponents can make its purpose clear to the students, and its assessment possible with reliability and validity.

At IPST (1977) the process of problem solving was similarly described in four phases — (i) seeing problems and planning to tackle them; (ii) collecting data; (iii) observing phenomena to find regularities; and (iv) processing data, interpreting them and drawing conclusions to answer the problem. Klainin (1984), in her evaluation of the Thai chemistry curriculum, accordingly identified the major tasks of problem solving as planning and designing of the investigation, manipulating equipment and executing the experiment, observing and recording the experimental outcomes, analyzing and interpreting data and drawing conclusions from them and writing up a report.

How to Assess

In the area of manipulative skills, Eglen and Kempa (1974) developed a practical test to use with students in the sixth-form chemistry course in England. Its operations covered the four categories of experimental techniques, sequence of procedure, manual dexterity and orderliness.

Kempa and Ward (1975) pointed out that observing chemical phenomena is an important part of the process of chemical enquiry conducted in the laboratory, but its direct teaching and assessment of its skills are often neglected. They suggested several simple test tube experiments to test these skills. These include changes in colour, in the formation or disappearance of solids, in the liberation of gases, and in temperature resulting from evolution or absorption of heat during reaction.

This pioneering work of Kempa and his associates provided science educators, curriculum developers and teachers with detailed information of what practical work and thus, practical assessment could or should be. It offers a basis whereby teachers and evaluators in developing science teaching and courses can have definite strategies to encourage learning and to assess it (see Kempa, 1986).

More recently, other criteria for the assessment of practical work have been suggested and put to use. For example, in Scotland eight categories of skill — observational, recording, measurement, manipulative, procedure, following instructions, inference and selection of procedures are used (Bryce *et al.*, 1985).

In Britain, a national monitoring programme, the Assessment of Performance Unit (APU), was set up in 1974 (Department of Education and Science, 1982). The science part of this programme is responsible for the development and administration of tests that are used in the survey of children's scientific development. In this monitoring framework, science is seen as a mode of thought and activity and the tests thus cover using symbolic representation, using apparatus and/or measuring instruments, using observations, interpretation and application, design of investigations, and performing investigations. In practice, for the second, third and last of these broad categories there are now well-developed practical tests while for the other three the tests are written. The skills that APU include in 'using apparatus and measuring instruments' are basic manipulative skills, the use of a careful and orderly method of observing and recording events, and an understanding of measurement concepts. The ability and willingness to follow instructions with an appropriate degree of initiative and caution is also required.

The assessment of practical work is, in fact, not new in science classes, but a very commonly-used procedure was based on written evidence, namely, written reports or items about practical work on paper and pencil tests.

Hanson (1982) argued that grades based on student laboratory reports penalize delinquent students but do not differentiate among good students. The paper and pencil test can only assess the practical work not the actual perform-ance outcomes. Many research studies have found that this type of test has low correlation to practical skills (for example, Ben-Zvi *et al.*, 1977; Kreiger, 1982). Kruglak (1955) and his associates concluded from their attempts to develop paper and pencil tests that were equivalent to performance tests, that the paper and pencil tests were at best only crude approximations to the evalu-ation of the unique abilities to deal with laboratory material and apparatus. Similar more recent studies by Hearle (1974) and Kreiger (1982) reached the same conclusion about the limitation of the written test as a test of know-ledge about the laboratory work, but these authors also reported that some high performing students actually did badly on the written tests. The assessment of practical work must, if it is to have validity, be done by practical tests.

Hofstein and Giddings (1980) have suggested that practical tests can be done occasionally or continuously by teachers (throughout a course of study) and the latter procedure was recommended by UNESCO (1982). Teachers' continuous assessment is the more common practice in the United Kingdom where it was introduced because a practical examination on perhaps only one occasion was not seen as sufficient to assess practical work. Furthermore, continuous assessment overcomes the design and logistical problems of ensuring a common and fair single testing event. Three schemes for scoring a practical test by an observer in the laboratory were suggested by Eglen and Kempa (1974) as alternative ways to put continuous assessment into operation — (i) an open-ended schedule in which assessment is done subjectively; (ii) an intermediate schedule which is similar to the open-ended except that it does provide separate assessments for each four categories of skills that have been defined as part of the task; and (iii) a check-list schedule which requires the assessment of students' performances to be made according to a checklist of detailed performance points and achievement criteria (expressed in the form of asking for 'yes' or 'no' answers).

Conclusion

One of the distinctive features of science is the diversity of its range of practical activities. In science education practical work has also been assigned a multitude of roles, not always clearly defined and certainly not supported in practice. Nevertheless, curriculum movements in most countries, both developed and developing, have acknowledged the importance of practical work in school science learning. Effective use of the opportunity this acknowledgement of practical work presents is itself fraught with many problems. However, a key issue is the lack of clear rewards from the school and wider educational system for students to take practical work in science seriously. This has created conflict for students and dilemmas for teachers.

Assessment of the practical work of learners is seen as a means of reducing this conflict and resolving these dilemmas. Ways and means for doing this are now available and their implementation as a regular part of science education is a very worthwhile direction for it to take.

References

AUSUBEL, D.P. (1965) 'An evaluation of conceptual scheme approach to science curriculum development', *Journal of Research in Science Teaching*, 2, pp 255–64.

BEATY, T.W. and WOOLNOUGH, B.E. (1982) 'Why do practical work in 11–13 science?' *School Science Review*, 63, 225, pp 768–70.

BEN-ZVI, R., HOFSTEIN, A., and KEMPA, R.F. (1977) 'Mode of instruction in high school chemistry', *Journal of Research in Science Teaching*, 14, 5, pp 433–9.

COMBER, L.C. and KEEVES, T.P. (1973) *Science Education in Nineteen Countries: IEA International Study in Evaluation I*, Upsala, Almquist and Wiksel Informationindustri.

DENNY, M. and CHENNELL, F. (1986) 'Science practicals: What do pupils think', *European Journal of Science Education*. 8, 3, pp 325–6.

DEPARTMENT OF EDUCATION AND SCIENCE (1982) *Assessment of Performance Unit (APU)*, Report No. 1, London, HMSO.

DEWEY, J. (1951) *Experience and Education*, New York, Macmillan.

EGLEN, J.R. and KEMPA, R.F. (1974) 'Assessing manipulative skills in practical chemistry', *School Science Review*, 56, 195, p 261.

FENSHAM, P.J. (1980) 'Constraint and autonomy in Australian secondary science education', *Journal of Curriculum Studies*, 12, 3, pp 189–206.

FENSHAM, P.J. (1981) 'Heads, hearts and hands — Future alternatives for science education', *Australian Science Teachers Journal*, 27, 1, pp 53–60.

FENSHAM, P.J., (1984a) 'Nyholm lecture: Conception misconception and alternative framework in chemical education', *Chemical Society Review*, 13, 2, p 199–217.

FENSHAM, P.J., (1984b) 'Current research in chemical education' in WADDINGTON, D.J. (Ed). *Teaching School Chemistry*, UNESCO, Paris.

GAGNÉ, R.M. and WHITE, R.T. (1978) 'Memory structure and learning outcomes', *Educational Research*, 48, 2, pp 187–222.

HEARLE, R. (1974) paper presented at the National Association for Research in Science Teaching (NARST), Chicago.

HODSON, D. (1985) 'Philosophy of science, science and science education', *Studies in Science Education*, 12, pp 25–51.

HOFSTEIN, A., BEN–ZVI, R. SAMU, L.D. and KEMPA, R.F. (1976) 'The effectiveness of film experiment in high school chemical education', *Journal of Chemical Education*, 53, pp 518–20.

HOFSTEIN, A. and GIDDINGS, G. (1980) *Trends in Assessment of Laboratory Performance in High School Science Instruction, Technical Report 20*, Iowa, University of Iowa.

HOFSTEIN, A. and LUNETTA, V.N. (1982) 'The role of laboratory in science teaching: Neglected aspects of research', *Review of Educational Research*, 52, 2, pp 201–17.

IPST (1977) *The Institute for the Promotion of Teaching Science and Technology of Thailand*, Bangkok, UNESCO.

JENKINS, E.W. and WHITFIELD, R. (1974) *Readings in Science Education: A Source Book, Science Teacher Education Project*, Maidenhead, McGraw-Hill Books.

JOHNSTONE, A.H. and WHAM, A.J.B. (1982) 'The demand of practical work', *Education in Chemistry*, 19, 3, pp 71–3.

KEMPA, R.F. (1986) *Assessment in Science*, Cambridge, Cambridge University Press.

KEMPA, R.F. and WARD, J.E. (1975) 'The effects of different modes of task orientation on observational attainment in practical chemistry', *Journal of Research in Science Teaching*, 12, pp 69–76.

KERR, J.F. (1963) *Practical Work in School Science*, Leicester, Leicester University Press.

KLAININ, S. (1984) 'Activity-based learning in chemistry', PhD thesis, Melborne, Monash University.

KLAININ, S. and FENSHAM P.J. (1987) *International Journal of Science Education*, 9, 2, pp 217–27.

KLAININ, S., FENSHAM, P.J., and WEST, L.H.T., (1988) 'The superior achievement of girls in physics and chemistry in upper secondary schools in Thailand', *Research in Science and Technological Education*, in press.

KLOPFER, L.E. (1971) 'Evaluation for learning is science' in BLOOM, B.S., HASTING, J.T. and MADAUS, G.F. *Handbook of Formative and Summative Evaluation of Student Learning*, New York, McGraw-Hill.

KOJIMA, S. (1974) 'IEA science study in Japan with reference to practical work', *Comparative Education Review*, 18, pp 26–276.

KREIGER, A.G. (1982) *Journal of Chemical Education*, 59, 3, pp 230–1.

KRUGLAK, H. (1955) *American Journal of Physics*, 23, pp 82–7.

LYNCH, P. and NDYETABURA, V. (1984) 'Students' attitudes to school practical work in Tasmanian schools', *Australian Science Teachers Journal*, 29, 2, pp 25–9.

MATHEWS, J.C. (1984) 'Assessment of students' in WADDINGTON, D.J. (Ed) *Teaching School Chemistry*, Paris, UNESCO, pp 223–74.

MICHELS, W.C. (1962) 'The role of experimental work', *American Journal of Physics*, 30, pp 172–8.

RAMSEY, G.A. (1975) 'Science as an instructional system', in GARDNER, P.L. (Ed) *The Structure of Science Education*, Hawthorn, Longman.

RATNAIKE, (1987) personal communication.

ROUSSEAU, J.J. (1950) *Emile*, Everyman Library, London, Dent.

RUTHERFORD, J. and GARDNER, M.H. (1970) 'Integrated Science Teaching', in UNESCO *New Trends in Integrated Science Teaching, Vol. 1*, Paris, UNESCO, pp 47–56.

SCHWAB, J.J. (1962) *The Teaching of Science as Enquiry*, Cambridge, MA, Harvard University Press.

SUAN, M.Z. (1976) 'An evaluation of A.S.E.P. — A case study approach', MEd thesis, Melbourne, Monash University.

Sunee Klainin

TAMIR, P. (1984) 'Teaching and learning in high school biology classes in Israel', paper presented at the Australian Science Education Research Conference, Melbourne, Australia.

TAN, Y.L. (1980) 'Toward achieving the central objective of school practical work', *Journal of the Association of Science and Mathematics Education (Penang)*, 2, 1.

TUNNICLIFFE, S.D. (1981) 'What is science?' *School Science Review*, 62, 220, pp 548–50.

UNESCO (1982) *A Report of Regional Design Workshop on Chemistry Curriculum and Teaching Materials in Asia*, Bangkok, UNESCO.

WHITE, R.T. (1979) 'Relevance of practical work to comprehension of physics', *Physics Education*, 14, pp 384–7.

10
Practical Work and Science Education II

Avi Hofstein

While reading a textbook of chemistry, I came upon the statement, 'nitric acid acts upon copper' ... and I determined to see what this meant. Having located some nitric acid, ... I had only to learn what the words 'act upon' meant. ... In the interest of knowledge I was even willing to sacrifice one of the few copper cents then in my possession. I put one of them on the table; opened the bottle marked 'nitric acid', poured some of the liquid on the copper; and prepared to make an observation. But what was this wonderful thing which I beheld? The cent was already changed, and it was no small change either. A greenish blue liquid foamed and fumed over the cent and the table. The air ... became colored dark red. ... How could I stop this? I tried ... by picking up the cent and throwing it out the window ... I learned another fact; nitric acid ... acts upon fingers. The pain led to another unpremeditated experiment. I drew my fingers across my trousers and discovered nitric acid acts upon trousers. ... That was the most impressive experiment I have ever performed. I tell of it even now with interest. It was a revelation to me. Plainly the only way to learn about such remarkable kinds of action is to see the results, to experiment, to work in a laboratory. (Ira Remsen, 1846–1927, in Gutman, 1940)

Introduction

The laboratory has long been given a central and distinctive role in science education. It has been used to involve students with concrete experiences with concepts and objects. Since the end of the nineteenth century, when schools began to teach science systematically, the laboratory became a distinctive feature of science education. After the First World War, with the rapid increase of scientific knowledge, the laboratory was used as a means for confirmation and illustration of information learned previously in a lecture or from a textbook.

The role of the laboratory according to Romey (1968) in the years 1918–1960 is illustrated in figure 1. With the reform in science education in the 1960s practical work in science education was used in order to engage students with investigations, discoveries, inquiry and problem solving activities. In other words, the laboratory became the center of science instruction (figure 2). In 1969 Ramsey and Howe wrote:

> That the experience possible for students in the laboratory situation should be an integral part of any science course has come to have a wide acceptance in science teaching. What the best kinds of experiences are, however, and how these may be blended with more conventional classwork; has not been objectively evaluated to the extent that clear direction based on research is available for teachers. (p. 75).

Unfortunately, the question posed by Ramsey and Howe in 1969 are still in existence in the 1980s.

In 1978 in the GIREP conference that was devoted to *the role of the laboratory in physics education*, Ogborn (1978) claimed that, 'Two of the most central questions concerning laboratory work are quite simply, why? and how? What should it be for and how can those aims be brought about in reality?' (p. 3).

In a comprehensive review of the role of the laboratory in science teaching, Hofstein and Lunetta (1982) claimed that 'to date the case for the laboratory in science instruction is not self evident as it once seemed'. One of the reasons for this skepticism is the failure of research studies to provide clear evidence and support for laboratory work as an effective medium for science learning.

The main objectives of this chapter are:

(i)   to review and redefine the goals for teaching and learning in the science laboratory;
(ii) to review the teaching practices used in the science laboratories and to suggest new practices to be tried in the future;
(iii) to suggest learning experiences in the science laboratory that will be meaningful and effective to different student populations.

For the purpose of this chapter, laboratory activities are defined as contrived learning experiences, in which students interact with materials to observe phenomena. The contrived experiences may have different levels of

Figure 1: Role of laboratory: 1918-1960

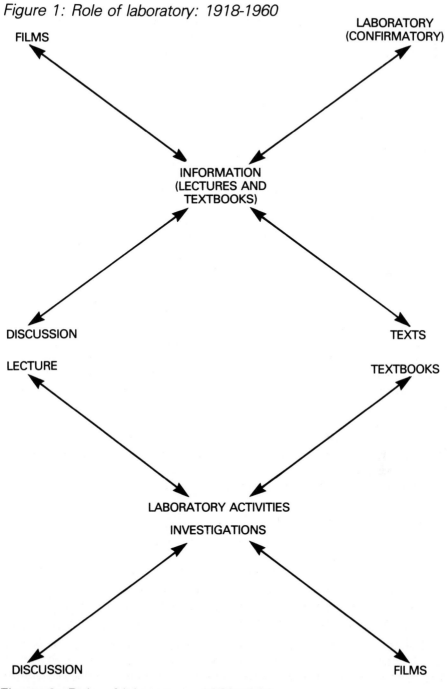

FILMS

LABORATORY
(CONFIRMATORY)

INFORMATION
(LECTURES AND
TEXTBOOKS)

DISCUSSION

TEXTS

LECTURE

TEXTBOOKS

LABORATORY ACTIVITIES
INVESTIGATIONS

DISCUSSION

FILMS

Figure 2: Role of laboratory: 1960-1980

structure specified by the teacher or laboratory handbook, and they may include phases of planning and design, analysis and interpretation and application as well as the central performance phase. Laboratory activities usually are performed by students individually or in small groups, and the definition does not include large-group demonstrations, science museum visits or field trips.

Goals of Laboratory Work

Review of Goals

The history of laboratory work as an integral part of school science learning has roots in the nineteenth century. In 1892 Griffin wrote:

> The laboratory has won its place in school; its introduction has proved successful. It is designed to revolutionize education. Pupils will go out from our laboratories able to see and do (cited by Rosen, 1954). In the years following 1910, the progressive education movement had a major impact on the nature of science teaching in general, and on the role of laboratory work in particular. John Dewey, leader of the progressive education movement, advocated an investigative approach and 'learning by doing'. (Rosen, 1954)

During this period, textbooks and laboratory manuals began to acquire a more applied, utilitarian orientation. Nevertheless, even while the progressive education was gaining momentum, debate about the proper role of laboratory work also was developing. The arguments raised against extensive student laboratory activities included:

(i)   few teachers in secondary schools are competent to use the laboratory effectively;
(ii) too much emphasis on laboratory activity leads to a narrow conception of science;
(iii) too many experiments performed in secondary schools are trivial; and
(iv) laboratory work in schools is often remote from, and unrelated to, the capabilities and interests of the children.

Following the First World War, laboratory activities came to be used largely for confirming and illustrating information learned from the teacher or the textbook. This orientation remained relatively unchanged until the 'new' science curricula of the 1960s, which resulted in several new intentions for the role of laboratory work. In 'the new curricula which stress the processes of science and emphasize the development of higher cognitive skills, the laboratory acquired a central role, not just as a place for demonstration and confirmation, but as the core of the science learning process' (Shulman and Tamir, 1973, p. 1119). Contemporary science educators (for example, Schwab, 1962; Hurd, 1969; Lunetta and Tamir, 1979) have expressed the view that the uniqueness of the laboratory lies principally in providing students with opportunities to engage in processes of investigation and inquiry. According to Ausubel (1968), 'the laboratory gives the students appreciation of the spirit and method of science, ... promotes problem-solving, analytic and generalization ability, ... provides students with some understanding of the nature of science' (p. 345).

In a review of the literature on the place of practical work, Shulman and Tamir (1973) proposed a classification of goals for laboratory instruction in science education:

(i) to arouse and maintain interest, attitude, satisfaction, openminded-ness and curiosity in science;
(ii) to develop creative thinking and problem solving ability;
(iii) to promote aspects of scientific thinking and the scientific method (e.g., formulating hypotheses and making assumptions);
(iv) to develop conceptual understanding and intellectual ability; and
(v) to develop practical abilities (for example, designing and executing investigations, observations, recording data, and analyzing and interpreting results).

Lunetta and Hofstein (1980) suggested a way of organizing the goals for science teaching that have been used over the years to justify the importance of laboratory teaching. These goals are grouped in cognitive, practical, and affective domains (table 1).

Table 1:   Goals of laboratory activity

Domain	Goal
Cognitive	Promote intellectual development
	Enhance the learning of scientific concepts
	Develop problem-solving skills
	Develop creative thinking
	Increase understanding of science and scientific method
Practical	Develop skills in performing science investigations
	Develop skills in analyzing investigative data
	Develop skills in communication
	Develop skills in working with others
Affective	Enhance attitudes toward science
	Promote positive perceptions of one's ability to understand and to affect one's environment

Are These Goals Attained?

Many research studies have been conducted to investigate the educational effectiveness of laboratory work in science education in facilitating the attainment of these sorts of goals. These studies were extensively reviewed and analyzed by Bates (1978) and by Blosser (1981).

A number of these studies compared the effects of different methods of practical work in the laboratory with other instructional methods. It is beyond the scope of this chapter to describe again all these studies but it is worthwhile to mention a few. For example, Coulter (1966) compared inductive laboratory experiments with inductive demonstrations in high school biology; Yager *et al.* (1969) compared three groups, namely, a 'laboratory group', a 'demonstration group' and a 'discussion group' in biology; Lunetta (1974) compared a control group to a computer-simulation group in physics; and Ben-Zvi *et al.* (1976a) compared a laboratory group to a group viewing filmed experiments in chemistry. These research studies have shown no significant differences between the instructional methods as measured by standard paper-and-pencil tests in student achievement, attitude, critical thinking, understanding of the nature of science and in knowledge of the processes of science. Not surprisingly, the one area in which the laboratory approach showed measurable advantage over other modes of instruction was in the development of laboratory manipulative skills.

Bates (1978) wrote that by reviewing the literature he came to the following tentative conclusions:

1 Lecture, demonstration, and laboratory teaching methods appear equally effective in transmitting science content.
2 Laboratory experiences are superior for providing students with skills in working with equipment.
3 Although most research has failed to assess outcomes that might be specific to the laboratory, meaningful laboratory measures can be developed; and the laboratory does appear to represent a significantly different area of science learning from content acquisition.
4 Some kinds of inquiry-oriented laboratory activities appear better than lecture/demonstration or verification labs for teaching the process of inquiry. However, teachers need to be skilled in inquiry teaching methods. Specific inquiry training should be provided for students over extended periods, since students need both time and guidance to become comfortable with the new methods and expectations.
5 Laboratories appear to have potential for nurturing positive student attitudes and for providing a wider variety of students with opportunities to be successful in science.

6 Recent and continuing research on the role of science teaching for nurturing cognitive development may, in the relatively near future, provide important new science teaching strategies in which properly designed laboratory activities will have a central role.

On the bases of these conclusions he claimed that: 'Teachers who believe that the laboratory accomplishes something special for their students would do well to consider carefully what those outcomes might be, and then to find ways to measure them.' He calls for a 'systematic inquiry (of the laboratory issue). For the answer has not yet been conclusively found: What does the laboratory accomplish that could not be accomplished as well by less expensive and less time-consuming alternatives?'

Critical Review of Past Research

The reviews by Bates (1978) and Blosser (1981) should be considered with great care especially in times in which the case for the laboratory in science instruction is not as self-evident as it once seemed. In some countries (for example, the USA) science laboratory requirements have been of special concern to some science educators because of a trend to retreat from student-centred science activities resulting in less time and therefore experience in the science laboratory (Gardner, 1979; and Beasley, 1978).

Hofstein and Lunetta (1982) claim that one of the reasons for this retreat is the failure of educational research to support the educational effectiveness of laboratory instruction. They wrote: 'Past research studies generally examined a relatively narrow band of laboratory skills and the conclusions that were drawn may apply to a narrow range of teaching techniques, teacher and students characteristics and learning outcomes' (p. 204).

More specifically, they argued that many research studies suffered from a number of particular weaknesses:

1 *Selection and control of variables*: Researchers failed to examine or report important variables descriptive of student abilities and attitudes. Generally, they failed to note the kind of prior laboratory experience that most students involved in the studies almost certainly had had. Not enough attention was given to control over extraneous factors, such as instruction outside the laboratory while the research study was conducted.

2 *Group size*: Researchers used comparatively small groups. Furthermore, student samples were of limited diversity and most of the research studies did not examine the effect of different subsets of the population (for example, less able or more able students, see the review by Belanger, 1971).

3 *Instrumentation*: Researchers in science education were often more

concerned with the nature of the treatment than with the validity of the instruments used to measure outcomes in their studies.

Welch (1971) noted that in thirty research reports concerning instructional procedures (including laboratory instruction), no connection between instructional procedure and the test chosen to measure the effect was made.

Another criticism concerning the instrumentation relates to the idea that if the laboratory is a unique mode of instruction in science education, it needs a unique mode of assessment (Tamir, 1972). Therefore it is desirable to develop more sensitive evaluation instruments that will provide reliable and valid information about what the student does in the laboratory and about his/her ability in laboratory-related skills.

Dilemma I: Why Laboratory Work in School Science? Goals That Could Be Attained by Laboratory Work

The main question posed in this section is:

What are some of the special contributions of laboratory work in the context of science learning?

Woolnough and Allsop (1985) in the UK have recently argued that one reason for the failure of many science courses is the attempt to use practical laboratory work for goals such as teaching theoretical concepts to which it is ill suited, instead of focussing on those like the development of basic process skills, a feel for natural phenomena and problem solving skills.

Cognitive Goals

Intellectual development

Instructional programs in science have over the past decade been influenced by the developmental theory of Jean Piaget. Many students in introductory science courses, it is argued, have not developed the capacity for 'formal' thinking that the abstract content of these courses requires in its learning. Providing them with opportunities to manipulate relevant materials ought to enhance their capacity for logical thought. Active involvement with materials in science laboratory activity has thus served as a basis for science learning and logical development in a number of contemporary curriculum projects such as ASEP in Australia, Science 5–13 in Great Britain, and the Science Curriculum Improvement Study in the United States. Research studies have indicated that many activities developed by these curriculum projects are effective with younger children who are described, in terms of this theory, as at a concrete operational stage of development.

Solid, data-based evidence for this sort of Piagetian assertion with older students is more difficult to acquire. Few comprehensive studies have been conducted on strategies for facilitating the logical development of such students. One study by Fix and Renner (1979) showed that student scores on ACT tests were significantly improved as a result of lab-centred science experiences, that were based on Piaget's learning model and on the related learning cycle developed by Karplus (1977). There is reason to assert that laboratory experiences may promote formal reasoning abilities but far more information is needed before definitive statements of this relationship can be made.

Creative thinking and problem solving

If one agrees that promoting creative thinking and problem solving skills are important goals of science teaching, then the student must engage in activities that will enhance the development of these skills. Research studies with students as diverse as 5th grade (Penick, 1976) and first-year college (Hill, 1976) have shown that for some students, involvement in open-ended, process-oriented activities has enhanced creative thinking. Laboratory activities can be designed so that a problem is presented or developed, but for which no standard method for solving the problem is immediately shown, thus necessitating creative, problem solving responses.

A study reported by Reif and St John (1979) showed that students in a specially designed college level physics laboratory course developed higher level skills more successfully than did students in a conventional physics laboratory course. These studies examined the students' ability to:

(i)   apply the underlying theory of an experiment to solve a similar problem involving a different physical situation; or
(ii) modify the experiment to find a different quantity, or to find the same quantity by using different methods; or
(iii) predict the effect of an error in an experimental procedure or measurement. According to the authors, the students in this specially designed lab course used instructional materials that presented 'information in a carefully organized way and incorporated specific features stimulating students to think independently' (p. 952).

The APU (1985) (Assessment of Performance Unit) in Britain has promoted a model of a chain of problem solving processes (adopted from Kempa, 1986) for use as the basis of pupils' performance in practical investigations.

Figure 3: Schematic problem – solving model for practical investigation (APU)

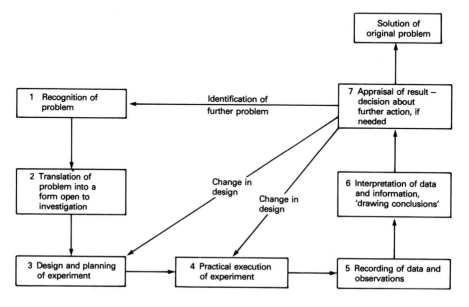

In summary, if we want the students to acquire skills that are used by practising scientists, and if we are concerned with the teaching of the process skills of science, practical work seems to be vital (Woolnough and Allsop, 1985).

Practical Goals

Laboratory activities can enable students to integrate their experiences with materials and with phenomena of science to conceptual aspects of these activities, and also to more formal schemes and models for practical investigations. Laboratory activities can and should involve both manual and intellectual abilities. These abilities are in some ways distinct from those used in work that is exclusively verbal (Kelly and Lister, 1969). In the Reif and St John (1979) study over 80 per cent of the students in the specially designed lab course were able to master basic skills including: estimating lengths and masses, using elementary statistics and making rough calculations, while most students in the conventional lab course did not seem to acquire these skills. The students in the specially designed course could list approximately 80 per cent of the essential ideas of an experiment after doing it while only about 25 per cent of the students in the conventional course could do so.

Laboratory practical skills in this sense have been classified in the following ways:

Jeffrey (1967) suggested six abilities associated with laboratory work in chemistry: communication, observation, investigation, reporting, manipulation and discipline. Kempa and Ward (1975) suggested a four-phase taxonomy to describe the overall process of practical work in science education:

(i)   planning and design of an investigation in which the student predicts results, formulates hypotheses, and designs procedures;

(ii)   carrying out the experiment, in which the student makes decisions about investigative techniques and manipulates materials and equipment;

(iii) observation of particular phenomena; and

(iv)   analysis, application, and explanation, in which the student processes data, discusses results, explores relationships, and formulates new questions and problems.

Tamir (1978), Doran (1978) and Ganiel and Hofstein (1982) have also used a very similar classification.

On the whole, most of the research studies conducted on the educational effectiveness of laboratory work have neglected the range of these abilities, and hence have not addressed the important questions, namely, what is the student really doing in the laboratory? and, what are appropriate ways to measure the effect of his/her activity?

Grobman (1970), for example, observed that in the 'new' science teaching projects:

With few exceptions evaluation has depended on written testing ... there has been little testing which requires actual performance in a real situation, or in a simulated situation which approaches reality ... to determine not whether the student can verbalize a correct response but whether he can perform an operation, for example, a laboratory experiment or an analysis of a complex problem. ... This is an area where testing is difficult and expensive yet since in the long run primary aims of projects generally involve doing something rather than writing about something this is an area which should not be neglected in evaluation of science curricula. (pp 192–3)

Robinson (1969), Tamir (1972), and Ben-Zvi *et al.* (1977) found that a low correlation exists between laboratory-based practical examinations and written paper-and-pencil-type tests. Although some attempts have been made to incorporate practical examinations within evaluation projects (Ben-Zvi *et al.*, 1976a; Eglen and Kempa, 1974; Golmon, 1975), these are rare even in research projects.

In summary, it is reasonable to suggest with Olson (1973) that 'the laboratory provides conditions for the acquisition of both intellectual and motor skills — namely an occasion for performance as well as feedback' (p. 34). Thus, the assessment of these laboratory skills certainly should not be overlooked in teaching, and in evaluation projects.

Affective Goals

Attitude and interest

Developing favourable attitudes toward science has often been listed as one of the important goals of science teaching. Generally, researchers (for example, Kolesnick, 1978) have assumed that the availability of a wide variety of instructional materials will enable teachers to vary classroom procedures, to avoid monotony, and to arouse interest and attention. Smith *et al.* (1968), Ben-Zvi *et al.* (1976b), Hofstein *et al.* (1976) and Raghubir (1979) found, for example, that students enjoy laboratory work in some courses and that it generally results in positive and improved attitudes toward, and interest in, the sciences.

In a research study conducted by Ben-Zvi *et al.* (1976a), chemistry students were asked to rate the relative effectiveness of instructional methods. Students reported that personal laboratory work was the most effective instructional method for promoting their interest and learning when contrasted with teacher demonstrations, group discussions, filmed experiments and teacher lectures. Similar results were obtained in research studies conducted by Charen (1966), Smith *et al.* (1968) and Bybee (1970). Johnson *et al.* (1974) compared three groups of sixth grade science students: (i) a group who learned science from a textbook; (ii) a group that used a textbook and lab materials; and (iii) an activity-centred group that worked comparatively with materials. They found that students who interacted with concrete materials developed significantly more positive attitudes toward learning science than those who studied from books alone. Thus, it seems that the laboratory can strongly affect attitude. More recently, Okebukola (1986a and 1986b) in Nigeria summarized his study with the cautious claim that 'a greater degree of participation in laboratory work may produce a more positive attitude toward the laboratory'. He found this to be specially true when students were involved in laboratory projects that were conducted cooperatively.

Newman (undated) in Australia in his summary of a study (conducted in Scotland) wrote:

> We observed classes who studied chemistry, and found that with few exceptions pupils enjoyed what they are doing (in the lab) even if difficulties arose in the procedure or even if students became aware that they didn't understand what was happening, it didn't seem to matter.

In summary, if there is still an argument with Shulman and Tamir (1973) who wrote that 'we are entering an era when we will be asked to acknowledge the importance of affect, imagination, intuition and attitude as outcomes of science instruction as at least as important as their cognitive counterparts' (p. 1139), affective outcomes of laboratory instruction should certainly be given more emphasis in research studies.

This argument is true especially since a recent research study conducted in Israel (Milner *et al.*, 1987) has clearly shown that the predominant factor concerning students' decision to enrol in science courses in the post-compulsory phase of education is the interest in science in general and in scientific activities (laboratory work and investigations) in particular.

Dilemma II. How Are Laboratories Used?: Bases for Better Use of Practical Work

Woolnough and Allsop (1985) wrote that:

> Many science teachers recognized the importance of practical work. They believed that pupils should have first-hand practical experience in laboratories in order to acquire skills in handling apparatus, to measure and to illustrate concepts and principles. Unfortunately practical work often did not go further than this and few opportunities were provided for pupils to conduct challenging investigations. (p. 2)

Although this is a comment on the schools in England and Wales, the authors suggest it could well apply to practice in many other countries. Indeed, a recent analysis of science education in Canadian schools reports that

> work in the lab is geared towards illustrating facts and theories presented in the classroom, confirming what is discussed in class, obtaining precise facts and getting the right answers to problems ..., teachers emphasize routines, standards of accuracy and thoroughness .... This emphasis on approved explanations and the right answer is at odds with the process of inquiry and the conceptual and tentative status of knowledge in science. Yet, such predictable activities as note-taking, copying activity sheets and lab procedures are valued because the accumulated information provides a base for work in the next grade, and because they control and channel energies by keeping students busy with routine and unambiguous work. (Orpwood and Souque, 1984)

In order to find common practices and what is really happening in the science laboratory, there is a need to take into consideration three distinct factors.

— the teacher's behavior
— the student's behavior and
— type of activity or laboratory exercise (the investigation on which the student is engaged).

These factors play an important role in controlling the student's learning in science education. Hofstein and Lunetta (1982) in their critical review of the goals of laboratory work in science education wrote that most of the research studies had failed to look at these important variables.

Teacher's Behavior in the Science Laboratory

One of the lessons learned during the years of massive curriculum development (in the 1960s) was that the teacher plays an extremely important role in what students learn. The best curriculum materials can result in limited student growth if a teacher is insensitive to the intended goals, to student needs and to appropriate teaching strategies. The teacher provides organizers and an environment that affect whether or not students reach certain instructional goals. For example, if a teacher's goal is to teach observational skills and not just facts that can be observed, this goal should be apparent in the things that the teacher says and does. Shymansky and Penick (1978) wrote that:

> Teachers are often confused about their role in instruction when students are engaged in hands on activity. Many teachers are con-

cerned about an adjustment they may have to make in their teaching style to facilitate hands on programs as well as how students will react to increased responsibility and freedom. An activity oriented classroom in which hands on materials are made available to students is often a very new experience for teachers as well as for his students.

Eggleston *et al.* (1976) found that science teaching style tends to be consistent no matter what form of activity takes place; deductive-oriented teachers teach practical work authoritatively, while more inquiry-oriented teachers teach investigative methods of learning. There is a need for obtaining more objective information about the interactions between teachers, curriculum resources, and students, and about teacher and student behaviors during a laboratory-based learning sequence.

Two examples from the USA of attempts to obtain information about these interactions are available.

A systematic classroom interaction analysis to obtain more information on what actually happens in the science laboratory was made by Penick *et al.* (1976), who developed the Science Laboratory Interaction Category (SLIC-Student), and by Shymansky *et al.* (1976), who developed the SLIC-Teacher. By using these two instruments one can obtain information about the kind of teaching and learning that takes place in the science laboratory. The authors of these instruments found that different subject laboratories (chemistry, biology, geology and physics) demonstrated different instructor behaviors concerning management, and control over different laboratory goals. These instruments were also used to provide teachers with feedback on the work in the laboratory.

The second example is the work conducted by Barnes (1967) who developed an instrument (paper-and-pencil) called the Biology Laboratory Activity Checklist (BLAC). This instrument measures the nature and extent of laboratory work in the context of high school biology instruction as perceived by the students. The laboratory activities and information that were evaluated included: pre-laboratory activities, laboratory activities, post-laboratory activities, and general student reaction to the laboratory. This practical instrument enables one to find out the extent to which high school biology laboratory activities conducted by a certain teacher are in agreement with the activities advocated by the curriculum developers.

The Student's Behavior

Students' behaviors in the science laboratory are significantly controlled by the type of laboratory activities provided by the laboratory handbook.

Different exercises will differ in the relative amounts of responsibility assumed by the learner and the teacher. Lunetta and Tamir (1979) analyzed laboratory handbooks and found great gaps between the stated goals for laboratory teaching and the kinds of activities students are generally asked to perform in the laboratory. In spite of the curriculum reform of the last twenty-five years, students still commonly work as technicians in 'cookbook' lab activities concentrating on the development of lower level skills. 'They are given few opportunities to discuss experimental error, to hypothesize and propose tests, or to design and then actually perform an experiment.' These large discrepancies between goals and practice have been important factors in the mixed research findings on the effects of laboratory activity.

Several methods have been suggested to analyze the types of laboratory activities used in science education. Pella (1961) suggested the idea of 'degrees of freedom' being available to the teacher when using the laboratory (see table 2). Herron (1971) considered, rather similarly, the degree of guidance given in the laboratory which he saw as having three components: problems, way and means of discovery, and answers. Each of these can be analyzed as for their openness and discovery in the science laboratory (see table 3) and were used by him to analyze the various laboratory activities in the PSSC and BSCS programs. Fuhrman *et al.* (1978) designed a task analysis inventory, the Laboratory Analysis Inventory (LAI) consisting of 1 planning and design; 2 performance; 3 analysis and interpretation; 4 application.

Table 2: Degrees of freedom available to the teacher using the laboratory (T = teacher; P = pupil).

Degree of Freedom	I	II	III	IV	V
Steps in procedure:	Performed by:				
1 Statement of problem	T	T	T	T	P
2 Hypothesis	T	T	T	P	P
3 Working plan	T	T	P	P	P
4 Performance	P	P	P	P	P
5 Data gathering	P	P	P	P	P
6 Conclusion	T	P	P	P	P

Table 3: Levels of openness and discovery in the learning laboratory

Level of Discovery	Problems	Ways and Means	Answers
Level 0	Given	Given	Given
Level 1	Given	Given	Open
Level 2	Given	Open	Open
Level 3	Open	Open	Open

Lunetta and Tamir (1979) used this instrument to analyze two laboratory handbooks, Harvard Project Physics and the BSCS yellow version, and to obtain more precise information on the nature of the activities that are likely to occur in a laboratory investigation in such courses.

Type of Activity

Bryce and Robertson (1985) reviewed the use of practical work in science education in different countries. They found that in many countries teachers spent (or claimed that they spent) considerable amounts of time in supervising laboratory work. However, they found that: 'The bulk of science assessment is traditionally non practical.' In other words, the assessment of students' performance in the science laboratory is by and large neglected in most countries and by most teachers. Kempa (1986), concerned about these paradoxial findings, sought a resolution when he stated, 'The view has long been established, that the development of practical skills and abilities must form an integral part of the set of educational goals that is to be associated with science

Table 4: Qualities for consideration in the development of schemes for the assessment of practical abilities

Ability/skill to be assessed	General qualities for assessment
(a) Recognition and formulation of problem	Tenability of hypotheses and postulates; identification of variables to be studied; identification of variables to be controlled.
(b) Design and planning of experimental procedure	Choice of experimental conditions, including choice of apparatus and measuring techniques and procedures; arrangements for varying and controlling variables; sequencing of operations, etc.
(c) Setting-up and execution of experimental work (manipulation)	Methodical working; correctness and safety of experimental technique, manual dexterity in the execution of practical work; orderliness and organization.
(d) Observational and measuring skills (including the recording of data and observations)	Accuracy and precision in the conduct of measurements; reliability of observations. Care and reliability in the collection and recording of data and observations.
(e) Interpretation and evaluation of experimental data and observations	Tenability of conclusions and inferences drawn from experimental data, and their relevance to the problem under investigation. Evaluation of limitations and potential error sources associated with experimental procedure.

education' and went on to suggest the use of the following phases of laboratory work as an organizer for the evaluation of students' performance (table 4). Precisely which of these phases should be evaluated depends, of course, on the teacher's pedagogical objectives and on the nature of the experiment. Kempa claims that these five phases of experimental work are a valid and satisfactory framework for the development and assessment of practical skills. These phases refer both to psychomotor skills (manipulation and observation) and to cognitive abilities, i.e. investigation, processing of a problem and its solution by practical means.

Systems for evaluating student activity in these phases can be classified in three broad categories: (i) written evidence — either traditional laboratory reports or paper-and-pencil tests; (ii) one or more practical examinations; (iii) continuous assessments by the science teacher.

Written evidence

Traditionally, science teachers have assessed their students' performance in the laboratory on the basis of their written reports, during or subsequent to the laboratory exercise. Assessments based on the written reports are only suitable for recognition and formulation of problems and interpretation, and for the evaluation of experimental data and observations.

The second form of written evidence is a paper-and-pencil test, designed to assess students' knowledge and understanding of the use of experimental techniques and of the principles underlying laboratory work and procedures. Such a test can assess two of the components, namely, design and planning of experimental procedure and the interpretation of experimental data and observations.

Practical examinations

Practical examinations are used in some countries as part of the external and terminal assessment of students' learning.

In such external practical examinations the teacher usually has little involvement during the examination although she or he may be required to assess with the marking scheme the end products of the presented investigation (see Bryce and Robertson, 1985). In general, teachers are not attracted to this type of practical examination as a means of collecting information on their students due to problems of implementation and validity of the test.

Ganiel and Hofstein (1982) summarized a number of drawbacks that are associated with these sorts of practical examination.

(a) In many cases different examiners use different criteria to assess student performance.

(b) Examinations are limited to those experiments that can be readily administered to students during a limited time period. This obviously restricts both the scope and validity of the assessment.

(c) Since such examinations are difficult to implement, they cannot be conducted very often. Consequently the element of chance is rather dominant, and this increases the anxiety of the students.

(d) Because of administrative constraints, practical examinations will often be administered to a large group of students simultaneously. Consequently, the examiner will not be able to concentrate on observing each student systematically, and will have to rely in his assessment on the results of the experiment and on the written reports.

In order to overcome some of these drawbacks and to get more precise information on students' manipulative skills, Eglen and Kempa (1974) and Ben Zvi *et al.* (1976a and 1976b) have proposed the breakdown of practical tasks that is presented in table 5. They claim that these can be readily applied for assessment purposes by selecting particular practical tasks.

Tamir (1974) devised a new kind of practical test for the comprehensive assessment of the skills associated with the inquiry-oriented laboratory work that was developed in Israel during the implementation of the BSCS yellow version. In this practical test the students are presented with a novel problems/situation (which requires problem identification) and are required to formulate a relevant hypothesis, design a plan to test the hypothesis, actually perform the experiment and collect data, communicate the findings in a way that draws conclusions and suggests new relevant questions. A detailed

Table 5: A breakdown analysis of manipulative skills

Skill Components	Generalized Assessment Criteria/Performance Features
Experimental technique	Correct handling of apparatus and chemicals; safe execution of an experimental procedure; taking of adequate precautions to ensure reliable observations and results.
Procedure	Correct sequencing of tasks forming part of an overall operation; effective and purposeful utilization of equipment; efficient use of working time; ability to develop an acceptable working procedure on the basis of limited instructions.
Manual dexterity	Swift and confident manner of execution of practical tasks; successful completion of an operation or its constituent parts.
Orderliness	Tidiness of the working area; good utilization of available bench space; purposeful placing of apparatus equipment.

assessment scheme was developed and called the Practical Assessment Test Inventory (PATI).

It contains twenty-one categories beginning with problem formulation and concluding with application of knowledge discovered in the investigation. Tamir *et al.* (1982) found that PATI may be used in the following ways:

(i)   it helps in obtaining standardized and more objective assessment;

(ii)   it facilitates making assessment and increases its reliability;

(iii)   it provides description of skills measured by a particular test;

(iv)   it provides feedback to both teachers and students;

(v)   it may help in the design of inquiry-oriented laboratory examinations.

Continuous assessment

In an attempt to overcome the drawbacks of the terminal practical examination, there has been a movement towards the implementation of continuous assessment by the teacher in normal laboratory sessions. This has been formalized to some degree in the United Kingdom (University of London, 1977; JMB, 1979) and in Israel by Ganiel and Hofstein (1982). In these systems of assessment, the teacher unobtrusively observes each student during normal lab activities and rates him or her on specific criteria. The assessments can be recorded for each student over an extended period of time. Normally only a few students will be carefully observed and rated during each activity.

Continuous assessment on several occasions throughout the year is necessary adequately to cover the variety of tasks and skills which comprise a total program of practical work.

With this involvement in the continuous assessment of practical skills, the teacher is likely to develop a greater awareness of the scope and objectives of the laboratory work, as well as identifying student strengths that otherwise may not have been reflected in more conventional assessments.

In summary, it is suggested that in order to assess the range of laboratory skills both observational methods and written methods should be used.

The Organization and Dynamics of Laboratory Work

Social Setting

Hofstein and Lunetta (1982) have suggested that the laboratory as a unique social setting has (when its activities are organized effectively) great potential in enhancing social interactions that can contribute positively to attitude development and cognitive growth.

A number of studies have been conducted in order to find out the relationship between the science classroom as a learning environment and cognitive and affective outcomes, but little is known specifically about the influence of the organization and dynamics of the science laboratory on learning outcomes (for example, Frazer, 1981).

In most laboratory classes, work is in pairs or in small groups. Work in such small groups can have advantages if the interactions encourage critical discussion between members about results and comparison of results and their interpretation within and among groups. Mutual help can also be provided, so that each member achieves the intended goals.

Unfortunately, little seems to have been done in the past to verify the advantage of the cooperative method in the laboratory. Two recent studies, one in Israel (Cohen, 1987) and one in Nigeria (Okebukola, 1986b) do, however, clearly demonstrate that working in the science laboratory cooperatively (in small teams) results in improvement of students' attitudes towards the topic studied in general and towards laboratory work in particular. A problem in the small group approach is the role of the teacher. The teacher needs to provide direction without offering excessive guidance that interferes with the normal interactions amongst the team members. At the same time, the teacher needs to handle and control the dynamics of social relations which can in the laboratory situation be rather complex.

Diversification of the Level of Difficulty of Laboratory Activities

Johnstone and Wham (1982) claimed that 'When it comes to measuring the amount of learning taking place during practical work the picture is rather pessimistic.' They explain this phenomenon by using the idea that in the laboratory the student has to handle a vast amount of information which causes 'overload on his working memory'. They illustrated this hypothesis as shown in figure 4. They suggest a reorganization of laboratory activities to reduce this sort of overload.

1   The teacher should give clear statements of the points and goals of the experiment.
2   The teacher should state clearly what is 'preliminary', 'peripheral' and 'preparatory'.
3   The teacher should avoid possible overload by trying to teach manipulative skills at the same time as data are sought.

These suggestions are not a revolution in practical work but are ones that could be adapted by teachers in their classrooms. Another problem that teachers

Figure 4: Unstable overload in practical work

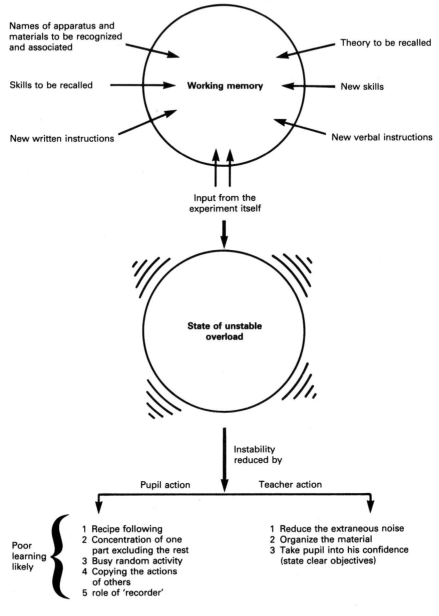

Source: Johnstone and Wham (1982).

sometimes face is how to conduct a laboratory exercise with mixed ability classes. Should he/she tailor the laboratory exercise to the needs and range of ability of the students. One negative solution noted on the other hand by Tobin (1986) is that 'for a variety of reasons most teachers appear to avoid laboratory investigation, particularly in classes of low ability students. When laboratory investigations are implemented, they rarely compose an integral part of the science program.'

Dreyfus (1986) provided guidelines for using the science laboratory with mixed ability classes, by showing how the difficulty level of a given laboratory exercise can be identified by referring to five indicators:

(i) prerequisites — the nature and level of cognitive development and general knowledge needed to enable the pupil to begin the activity and to understand the implications of its results;

(ii) subject matter — concepts and principles as well as the context related to the activity;

(iii) the nature of the activity — number of variables, quantitative or qualitative, complexity of design, expected results, feasibility of statistical analysis;

(iv) type and complexity of equipment, materials and their manipulation;

(v) time needed.

Different versions of the same laboratory exercise may be created by specifying the activities according to their difficulty levels. For example, in reporting an analysis of the results the following requirements can be made:

Lowest level: pupils report the results of one simple experiment using units of measurement specified by the teacher.

Medium level: pupils report the results of several replications of the experiment, choosing themselves the units of measurement and justifying their choice.

Highest level: pupils report the results of several treatments and replications, determine not only the units of measurement but also the most efficient and visually expressive organization and presentation of the complex results.

Similarly different difficulty levels can be worked out for other phases of the investigation (problem and hypothesis formulation, experimental design, etc.).

In situations in which the class consists of students who are highly motivated to study science and able to handle adequately the various components of scientific thinking, the laboratory should be used to teach some general intellectual skills. In fact, Hofstein *et al.* (1976) found that 12th grade students' attitudes to and interest in laboratory work were significantly lower than those of their 11th and 10th grade counterparts. This contra-finding led them to suggest that 12th grade students need more scientifically challenging laboratory experiences. The project approach in the final year of schooling in Scotland may be the answer to this sort of bored familiarity with the simpler laboratory experiments that continue in many science courses regardless of student ability or age.

Summary: A Look at the Future

In the 1960s the laboratory was established as central to learning science in the intended form of most science curricula. By the mid–1970s science educators and researchers were questioning the value and the educational effectiveness of the science laboratory at least as it was practised in many schools and in many places in the world. This has led to a trend in which there is a retreat from student-centred science activities in the laboratory.

This is of great concern to those who believe that the laboratory provides a unique medium for teaching and learning science. Woolnough and Allsop (1985), for example, wrote that:

> Fundamentally, we must recognize that science teaching is concerned with both the content of science and the process of science. ... Both are vital for a full scientific education. If we are concerned to teach the process of science, practical work is vital.

Similarly, Yager (1981) claimed that:

> Laboratories help correct the erroneous idea that scientific information exists only to be learned. Scientific information is valuable only if it is learned and used. A laboratory is a place where knowledge can be used; hence knowledge is exemplified as a means for action, not as an end in itself.

It is true that research has failed to show simplistic relationships between experiences in the laboratory and student learning in science. Furthermore, it is unreasonable to assert that the laboratory is an effective and efficient teaching medium for achieving all goals in science education. On the other hand, sufficient data do exist to suggest that laboratory instruction can play an important part in the achievement of some of these goals. Appropriate laboratory activities can be effective in promoting logical development and the development of some inquiry and problem solving skills. They can assist in the development of manipulative and observational skills and in understanding scientific concepts. They can also promote positive attitudes, and they provide opportunities for student success and foster the development of skills in cooperation and communication.

Science laboratories should enable students to use information, to develop a general concept, to determine a new problem, to explain an observation and to make decisions.

There is a need to search for teaching strategies in the laboratory that will promote instructional goals. Some goals may well be achieved efficiently without the necessity of manipulating materials in the laboratory; on the other hand, to do away with laboratory activities and the manipulation of materials in general, may well distort student understanding of the nature of science and inhibit logical, conceptual and affective development.

In an article titled *Are lab courses a waste of time?* Pickering (1980) wrote:

> The job of lab courses is to provide the experience of doing science. While that potential is rarely achieved, the obstacles are organizational and not inherent in laboratory teaching itself. That is fortunate because reform is possible and reform is cheap. Massive amounts of money are not required to improve most programs; what is needed is more careful planning and precise thinking about educational objectives.
>
> By offering a genuine, unvarnished scientific experience, a lab course can make a student into a better observer, a more careful and precise thinker, and a more deliberative problem solver. And that is what education is all about.

While researchers continue to search for better data and evidence of appropriate procedures, science teachers must do the best they can to base curriculum and teaching decisions upon evidence that is available and upon logical inferences about goals, the nature of science, and the way people learn.

References

AUSUBEL, D.P. (1968) *Educational Psychology*, New York, Holt, Rinehart and Winston.

BARNES, L.W. (1967) 'The development of a student checklist to determine laboratory practices in his high school biology' in LEE, A.E. (Ed) *Research and Curriculum Development in Science Education*, Vol. 1. Austin, TX, University of Texas.

BATES, G.R. (1978) 'The role of the laboratory in secondary school science programs' in ROWE, M.B. (Ed) *What Research Says to the Science Teacher*, 1, pp 55–82.

BELANGER, M. (1971) 'Learning studies in science education', *Review of Educational Research*, 39, pp 371–95.

BEASLEY, W.F. (1978) 'Laboratory psychomotor skill development using physical and mental practice strategies', *Research in Science Education*, 8, pp 135–44.

BEN-ZVI, R. *et al.* (1976a) 'The effectiveness of filmed experiments in high school chemical education', *Journal of Chemical Education*, 53, pp 575–7.

BEN-ZVI, R. *et al.* (1976b) 'The attitude of high school students to the use of filmed experiments in laboratory instruction', *Journal of Chemical Education*, 14, pp 575–7.

BEN-ZVI, R. *et al.* (1977) 'Modes of instruction in high school chemistry', *Journal of Research in Science Teaching*, 14, pp 433–9.

BLOSSER, P.E. (1981) *A Critical Review of the Role of the Laboratory in Science Teaching*, Science Education Information Report. Columbus, OH Center for Science and Mathematics Education, Ohio State University.

BRYCE, T.G.K. and ROBERTSON, I.J. (1985) 'What can they do? A review of practical assessment in science', *Studies in Science Education*, 12, pp 1–24.

BYBEE, R.W. (1970) 'The effectiveness of an individualized approach to general education earth science laboratory', *Science Education*, 54, pp 157–61.

CHAREN, G. (1966) 'Laboratory method build attitudes', *Science Education*, 50, pp 54–7.

COHEN, I. (1987) 'Various strategies for the teaching of the topics chemical energy and chemical equilibrium: Development, implementation and evaluation', unpublished PhD dissertation. Rehovot, The Weizmann Institute of Science.

COULTER, J.C. (1966) 'The effectiveness of inductive laboratory demonstration and deductive laboratory in biology', *Journal of Research in Science Teaching*, 4, pp 185–6.

DORAN, R. (1978) 'Assessing the outcomes of science laboratory activities', *Science Education*, 62, 3, pp 401–9.

DREYFUS, A. (1986) 'Manipulating and diversifying the levels of difficulty and task sophistication of one and the same laboratory exercise', *European Journal of Science Education*, 8, 1, pp 17–26.

EGGLESTON, J.F. *et al.* (1976) *Process and Product of Science Teaching*, London, Macmillan Education.

EGLEN, J.R. and KEMPA, R.F. (1974) 'Assessing manipulative skills in practical chemistry', *School Science Review*, 56, pp 737–40.

FIX, W.T. and RENNER, J.W. (1979) 'Chemistry and experiments in the secondary school', *Journal of Chemical Education*, 56, pp 737–40.

FRAZER, B.J. (1981) 'Learning environment in curriculum education', *Evaluation in Education: An International Review Series*, 5, pp 3–93.

FUHRMAN, M. *et al.* (1978) *The Laboratory Structure and Task Analysis Inventory (L.A.I.): A User Handbook*, Iowa City, IO, University of Iowa, Technical Report No. 14.

GANIEL, U. and HOFSTEIN, A. (1982) 'Objective and continuous assessment of student performance in the physics laboratory', *Science Education*, 66, 4, pp 581–91.

GARDNER, M. (1979) 'Trends in the development and implementation of science curriculum in the U.S.A.' in TAMIR, P. *et al.* (Eds) *Curriculum Implementation and Its Relationship to Curriculum Development*, Jerusalem, Israel Science Teaching Center, pp 271–6.

GOLMAN, M. (1975) 'Assessing laboratory instruction in biology', *Iowa Science Teacher Journal*, 19, pp 4–10.

GROBMAN, H. (1970) *Developmental Curriculum Projects: Decision, Points and Process*, Itasca, IL, Peacock Publishers.

GUTMAN, H.F. (1940) 'The life of Ira Remsen', *Journal of Chemical Education*, 17.

HERRON, M.D. (1971) 'The nature of scientific inquiry', *School Review*, 79, pp 171–212.

HILL, B.W. (1976) 'Using college chemistry to influence creativity', *Journal of Research in Science Teaching*, 13, pp 71–7.

HINEKSMAN, N.O. (1973) 'The function of the school laboratory', *The Australian Science Teacher Journal*, 19, pp 81–6.

HOFSTEIN, A. *et al.* (1976) 'The measurement of interest in and attitude to laboratory work amongst Israeli high school students', *Science Education*, 60, pp 401–11.

HOFSTEIN, A. and LUNETTA, V.N. (1982) 'The role of the laboratory in science teaching', *Review of Educational Research*, 52, 2, pp 201–17.

HURD, P.D. (1969) *New Directions in Teaching Secondary School Science*. Chicago, IL, Rand McNally.

JEFFREY, J. (1967) 'Identification of objectives of the chemistry laboratory and development of means for measuring students achievement of some of these objectives', unpublished PhD dissertation, Texas, University of Texas.

JOINT MATRICULATION BOARD (1979) 'The internal assessment of practical skills in chemistry (advanced) — Suggestions for practical work and advice on sources of information', Universities of Manchester, Liverpool, Leeds, Sheffield and Birmingham, January.

JOHNSON, R.T. *et al.* (1974) 'Inquiry and the development of positive attitudes', *Science Education*, 58, pp 51–6.

JOHNSTONE, A.H. and WHAM, A.J.B. (1982) 'The demands of practical work', *Education in Chemistry*, May, pp 71–3.

KARPLUS, R. (1977) 'Science teaching and the development of reasoning', *Journal of Research in Science Teaching*, 14, pp 169–75.

KELLY, P.J. and LISTER, R.F. (1969) 'Assessing practical ability in Nuffield 'A' level biology' in EGGLESTON, J.F. *et al.* (Eds) *Studies in Assessment*, London, English University Press, pp 121–52.

KEMPA, R.F. (1986) *Assessment in Science*, Cambridge, Cambridge Science Education Series, Cambridge University.

KEMPA, R.F. and WARD, J.E. (1975) 'The effect of different modes of task orientation on observational attainment in practical chemistry', *Journal of Research in Science Teaching*, 12, pp 69–76.

KOLESNICK, W.B. (1978) 'Motivation', *Understanding and Influencing Human Behaviour*, Boston, MA, Allyn and Beacon.

LUNETTA, V.N. (1974) 'Computer-based dialogues: A supplement to the physics curriculum', *The Physics Teacher*, 12, pp 355–6.

LUNETTA, V.N. and HOFSTEIN, A (1980) 'The science lab: A new look at goals and practice', unpublished manuscript, Iowa City, University of Iowa.

LUNETTA, V.N. and TAMIR, P. (1979) 'Matching lab. activities with teaching goals', *The Science Teacher*, 46, pp 22–4.

MILNER, N. *et al.* (1987) 'Variables that affect students' enrolment in science courses', *Research in Science and Technological Education*.

NEWMAN, B.E. (n.d.) 'Practical work in secondary school chemistry', unpublished report, University of New South Wales, School of Education, pp 1–7.

OGBORN, J. (1978) 'Aims and organization of laboratory work' in JONES, J.G. and LEWIS, J.L. (Eds) *The Role of the Laboratory in Physics Education*, Birmingham, John Goodman and Sons (printers) Limited, pp 1–64.

OKEBUKOLA, P.A. (1986a) 'An investigation of some factors affecting students' attitude towards chemistry laboratory', *Journal of Chemical Education*, 63, 6, pp 531–2.

OKEBUKOLA, P.A. (1986b) 'Cooperative learning and students' attitude to laboratory work', *School Science and Mathematics*, 86, 7, pp 582–90.

OLSON, D.R. (1973) 'What is worth knowing and what can be taught', *School Review*, 82, pp 27–43.

ORPWOOD, G.W.F. and SOUQUE, J-P. (1984) *Science Education in Canadian Schools, Vol. 1: Introduction and Curriculum Analysis*, Ottawa, Science Council of Canada.

PELLA, M.O. (1961) 'The laboratory and science teaching', *The Science Teacher*, 28, pp 20–31.

PENICK, J.E. (1976) 'Creativity of fifth grade science students: The effect of two patterns of instruction', *Journal of Research in Science Teaching*, 13, pp 307–14.

PENICK, J.E. *et al.* (1976) *Science Laboratory Interaction Category (SLIC) — Students*, Iowa City, University of Iowa.

PICKERING, M. (1980) 'Are lab courses a waste of time?', *The Chronicle of Higher Education*, 19 February, p 80.

RAGHUBIR, K.P. (1979) 'The laboratory investigation approach to science instruction', *Journal of Research in Science Teaching*, 16, pp 13–18.

RAMSEY, G.A. and HOWE, R.W. (1969) 'An analysis of research in instructional procedure in secondary school science, part II', *The Science Teacher*, 36, 4, pp 72–81.

REIF, F. and ST JOHN, M. (1979) 'Teaching physicists thinking skills in the laboratory', *American Journal of Physics*, 47, 11, pp 273–6.

REMSEN, I. (1978) 'Quoted in the American Chemical Society Publication: guidelines and recommendations for the preparation and continuing education of secondary school teachers of chemistry', *American Journal of Physics*, 46, p 734.

ROBINSON, T.J. (1969) 'Evaluating laboratory work in high school biology', *The American Biology Teacher*, 34, pp 226–9.

ROMEY, W.D. (1968) *Inquiry Techniques for Teaching Science*, Englewood Cliffs, NJ, Prentice Hall.

ROSEN, S.A. (1954) 'History of the physics laboratory in the American public schools (to 1910)', *American Journal of Physics*, 22, pp 194–204.

SCHWAB, J.J. (1962) 'The teaching of science as inquiry' in SCHWAB, J.J. and BRANDWINE, P.F. (Eds) *The Teaching of Science*, Cambridge, MA, Harvard University Press.

SHULMAN, L.D. and TAMIR, P. (1973) 'Research on teaching in the natural sciences' in TRAVERS, R.M.W. (Ed) *Second Handbook of Research on Teaching*, Chicago, IL, Rand McNally, pp 1098–148.

SHYMANSKY, J.A. *et al.* (1976) *Science Laboratory Interaction Category (SLIC) — Teacher*, Iowa City, University of Iowa.

SHYMANSKY, J.A. and PENICK, J.E. (1978) 'Teachers' behavior does make a difference in hands-on science classroom', the 1978 AETS meeting.

SMITH, D.M. *et al.* (1968) 'Affective response to different media in a multimedia system', *Science Education*, 52, pp 16–22.

TAMIR, P. (1972) 'The practical mode: A distinct mode of performance', *Journal of Biological Education*, 6, pp 175–82.

TAMIR, P. (1974) 'An inquiry oriented laboratory examination', *Journal of Educational Measurement*, 11, pp 23–35.

TAMIR, P. (1978) 'Inquiry and curiosity in biology', *Journal of Biological Education*, 12, pp 215–23.

TAMIR, P. *et al.* (1982) 'The design and use of a practical test inventory', *Journal of Biological Education*, 16, pp 42–50.

TAMIR, P. (1987) 'Training teachers to teach effectively in the laboratory', the AETS meeting, Washington D.C.

TOBIN, K. (1986) 'Secondary science laboratory activities', *European Journal of Science Education*, 8, 2, pp 199–211.

WELCH, W.W. (1971) 'A summary of research in science education for the years 1968–69, secondary school level', *Science Education Information Report*, Columbus, OH, ERIC.

WHEATLEY, J.H. (1975) 'Evaluating cognitive learning in the college science laboratory', *Journal of Research in Science Teaching*, 12, pp 101–9.

WOOLNOUGH, B. and ALLSOP, T. (1985) *Practical Work in Science*, Cambridge, Cambridge Science Education Series, Cambridge University Press.

YAGER, R.E. *et al.* (1969) 'Effects of the laboratory and demonstration method upon the outcomes of instruction in secondary biology', *Journal of Research in Science Teaching*, 5, pp 76–86.

YAGER, R.E. (1981) 'The laboratory in science teaching — main course or dessert?' in TROWBRIDGE, L.W. *et al.* (Eds) *Becoming a Secondary School Science Teacher*, Columbus, OH, Charles E. Merryl Publishing Co.

11
Gender and Science Education: I

Svein Sjøberg and Gunn Imsen

Introduction

In this chapter the problem of gender and science education is considered. First, we will discuss how the problem is perceived from different stances, our own perspective and our own 'scene' in Norway. Second, we will discuss possible theoretical frameworks for an analysis of the issues. We will emphasize the need for a theory that goes beyond simple thinking in terms of cause and effect, and will elaborate the concept of gender culture as a tool for understanding the complexity of the issues. Next, we refer to and discuss empirical evidence that throws some light on the same issues and how this relates to our theoretical base. Finally, we discuss possible practical consequences that may be drawn from what has been said earlier.

The Problem

Low Participation — An International Concern

The problem is well-known: compared with boys, a low percentage of girls choose science in schools and few women are found in careers in science and technology. This is a worldwide phenomenon, although educational and employment statistics show great and interesting variations between different parts of the world (for a survey, see Harding, 1985).

The low participation of women in science-related professions has led to an international movement that tries to describe, analyze and understand the situation. Although the perspectives vary greatly, people involved in this movement by and large share the common aim of getting more women into science and technology. A comprehensive survey of the movement cannot even be attempted in an article like this. Suffice it to say that four international conferences on Girls and Science and Technology have been arranged, and the reports from these show the great variety of perspectives and approaches (GASAT I, 1981; GASAT II, 1983; GASAT III, 1986; and GASAT IV, 1987).

Three Conceptions of the Problem

The conceptualization of the problem, and hence the kind of solutions put forward, vary according to the interests of people who conceive the problem. We simplify the problem by describing three different stances:

(i)   For industry and 'society' the problem of low female participation is one of possible recruitment of a hitherto untapped pool of intellectual reserve. It is high time that we start being concerned about the gifted girls. From this perspective, the practices and underlying values of science and technology are unproblematic and given. The focus of interest lies in finding the most efficient intervention program or support system that will channel the gifted girls into these careers.

(ii) Another point of argument is that women have different interests, perspectives, values and priorities than men. Science and technology are seen as important factors in the shaping of a new future. Access to science and technology means good career opportunities for the individual as well as access to political and economic power for women as a group. This position is critical to the uses and practices of established science and technology. The aim is to join the scientific community in order to get access to economic and political power, and to use these positions to change decisions and priorities.

(iii) Some feminist critique goes much further in claiming that contemporary science is a male activity at a very basic level: science is concerned with controlling, dominating and mastering (sic!) nature. Science is conceived as a man-made activity in a literal sense: hierarchical and based on a conception of nature where man stands outside nature instead of being part of it. This view involves a questioning of science in its present form, not only of its use, but also of the basic epistemological assumptions (see Keller, 1985; Harding and Hintikka, 1983).

The above description is crudely simplified in order to make explicit the wide range of perspectives. Part II of *Perspectives on Gender and Science Education* edited by Harding (1986) provides an elaboration of different views.

As indicated above, there are many different conceptions of the problem.

In spite of this, the different groups engaged in this area agree on the necessity to increase the number of women in science and hence the number of girls choosing science in schools. The reasons for wanting this may vary, and the long-term political aims also vary strongly.

So, although the perspectives and motives are different, at least the short-term aims are similar. Hence, one may cooperate to find the most suitable means to achieve these aims.

Two Strategies for Change

When looking at enrolment statistics from obligatory school up to top level, one can clearly see the general pattern: the higher one gets, the lower is the proportion of women. This pattern is essentially the same from one field of study to another, in the humanities as well as in science. This means that the mechanisms that operate against women in their professional careers are much the same from one area to the other.

If the aim is to increase the proportion of women in careers of different fields, two obvious strategies are available: general and subject-specific.

The first strategy involves concentrating on *general* issues of importance for women's careers. The measures are partly political at state or community level: finance, child-care, etc., partly 'private' matters of the particular family, like sharing of household duties.

The second strategy calls for *subject-specific* measures. For the sciences, this involves discussions of all aspects of the science curriculum and out-of-school influences related to science.

The two approaches are of course complementary and do not compete with each other. But as science educators, our focus will necessarily be on the subject-specific measures. The following discussion and presentation of empirical results will therefore have this as the main perspective.

The Norwegian Scene

Equality between the sexes has come relatively far in Norway. A considerable fraction (40–45 per cent) of the adult labour force is female. Most *formal* obstacles to sex equality have been removed; we have legislation against sex discrimination, and textbooks have to pass a test on sex discrimination before being officially approved. Equality between the sexes is considered a central issue for the educational system. In many ways, results are encouraging.

In 1987 women comprised the majority of the total number of freshers at Norwegian universities. Even in the Norwegian Government at present, the Prime Minister and eight out of eighteen members are women. In spite of all this, the percentage of women in science and engineering is extremely low. The high proportion of women in higher education does not seem to affect the numbers of women in science. This paradox requires an explanation.

With this background, a Norwegian perspective may be of some interest. The empirical investigations that will be referred to are mainly published in Scandinavian languages, and are therefore not well-known to many readers. A few words need to be said about the educational system and the role played by science in it. The compulsory school in Norway is nine years (age 7–16 years) and is fully comprehensive, with no streaming and only minor curricular choices. The next three years of upper secondary school involve curricular choices, mainly in the last two years, but there is a substantial common core.

Science is part of the curriculum through the whole compulsory school plus the first year of the upper secondary school. Until that, this level science is taught as an integrated subject including biology, chemistry and physics. The last two years of upper secondary school science are split into separate sciences and are only taken by those who want to specialize in those directions.

The *teachers* have rather different backgrounds for the different levels. At the elementary level (grades 1–6) the students in general have one class teacher, covering all subjects, and following the class through all grades. More than 80 per cent of these teachers are women, and very few have any background in science. At the lower secondary school (grades 7–9) the situation is different. Most of the science teachers are men (81 per cent), and in general they have studied at university level in one or more of the sciences. The situation varies, however, quite a lot across the country. The science teachers in upper secondary school are in general very well qualified through 5–7 years of university studies in science. Some 84 per cent of these are men.

Of the three sciences, *physics* holds the strongest position. Examination in physics is used also as entry qualification for several university studies of high prestige. Physics is therefore the key to careers in science and technology (including medicine, veterinary medicine, odontology, agricultural science, etc.). The enrolment figures for girls are especially low in school physics, and this is, therefore, also an obstacle to the recruitment of girls in the higher parts of the educational system. Hence, the problem of girls' relationship to the sciences can in our context be rephrased to be a problem connected with physics.

In the next section we will develop our theoretical framework. We then go on to present some research from Norway to make our points. Although we could have drawn on a large amount of internationally available research, there are good reasons for limiting coverage.

Modes of Explanation

Nature versus Nurture

There are two approaches to the problem that differ on a fundamental level: the first seeks explanations in biology, the other looks for explanations in the social system. In the following, we will develop a view based on a conception that we have to deal with a problem which by nature is social. This does *not* mean that we reject the existence of biological differences! There may even be differences of biological origin that may shed some light on 'our problem', but we will not attempt any discussion of these possibilities. We do, however, find good reasons to warn against an approach that focuses on biological differences as *the* explanatory factor.

The discussion of nature versus nurture is old, and it is found in different areas of social life. The function of the biological explanation for observed differences between groups of people has historically been to explain observed differences as 'natural'. The argument is used to explain differences between races, between social classes and in our case between women and men. The biological argument often takes the form of biological determinism. Biology is interpreted not as potentiality but as restriction, and provides justification to sexual determinism (Lambert, 1978).

Looking back at the history of these debates provides a perspective for the present situation. The function of the biological argument has always been a defence of status quo. The opponents, those who argue for changes, have always been accused of wanting the impossible, the 'unnatural'. They are accused of the great sin of wanting to 'change nature'.

The function of the argument has always been the same, but the actual form has changed through history. When one form of argument is falsified by the development of science, new arguments are developed, always tailored to the present stage of our biological understanding and always tailored to the particular social institution that needs to be legitimized, in our case, the division of labour and social responsibilities between the sexes and the differences in intellectual capacities and predispositions. The argument used to be based on measurement of the form and volume of the skull (the science of 'craniometry'). Present versions of the old story refer to neuro-physiology, brain asymmetry, visual-spatial abilities, etc. We are not saying that these approaches a priori are unfruitful, but we are warning against any kind of determinism that often emerges from these approaches. For discussion of the misuses of biology for ideological purposes see Gould (1981).

A Comprehensive View

Much research connected with sex differences takes the form of studying *sex differences* in achievement, experiences, interests and attitudes, and correlations between such variables. On the basis of those correlations, one often deduces causal relationships. Although much of this research may give valuable information, we will warn against this empiricist approach that often lacks a clear guiding theoretical framework.

'Our problem' is essentially a problem belonging to the social sciences, not the natural sciences. Social relationships are often of a more complex nature than the problems of natural science. It is very seldom that one can describe social phenomena in terms of simple linear chains of cause and effect. One has to take the totality of influences into account, and one has to treat the people involved as *subjects* with their own personal beliefs, values, aspirations, etc.

Consequently, our stance is that research and discourse on girls and science should aim at *understanding* the problem, that is, how girls themselves conceive the situation, and getting knowledge about what factors seem to influence girls' preferences.

Children as Theory Builders

During their development, children actively construct their own meanings in a complex interaction with other individuals. They are also influenced by material circumstances that may restrict or enhance their possibilities. Both the social and material surroundings contribute to the development of the personality.

Children as well as adults are 'theory builders'. They continuously try to make sense out of the many conflicting influences they are subjected to. They actively construct theories of the external world. These theories may or may not be good tools for coping with reality, and they may or may not correspond to ideas developed by science. Research into this area of 'children's science' or 'alternative paradigms' is currently in rapid growth and is likely to shed light on many of the problems facing science education.

Children also actively construct their own personal identity. They also construct their 'self', a 'theory' about their own personality. This theory may or may not constitute a suitable tool for coping with external reality.

This perspective involves treating girls as vigorous personalities, actively constructing their own identity or self-concept, attitudes and personal expectations. Girls as well as boys actively construct their own reality. External influences play important roles as raw material in the process of construction. But the point is that girls as well as boys are active agents in their own process of socialization. As a consequence, girls are not individually responsible for their lack of interest in science. Rather, we must look for societal and other factors for explanation.

Gender as Part of the Culture

As in many other countries, Norwegian girls and boys have access to the same education, literature, television programmes, music and other cultural institutions. Social inequalities are small in Norway. Children attend mixed–sex classes in a comprehensive school with no streaming and are encouraged to cooperate in out–of–school activities as well. Why do girls and boys apparently acquire different parts of what is offered to them?

A key to this question lies in understanding what gender identity means in an egalitarian society. Gender is a fundamental attribute in most cultures. To be a genderless person, or to have a genderless identity, is inconceivable (Kessler and McKenna, 1978). Gender is generally woven into the social rules that regulate social relationships between people; both same–sex relationships and relationships between boys and girls.

What young girls do know is that they want to be *girls*. To the girl it is crucial to be reassured that she is feminine. Accordingly, she is cautious not to offend the invisible rules of the feminine culture. The 'gender code' has a variety of implications. It means seeking social approval to confirm personal identity as well as getting the assurance of really belonging to the female peer group. This may be more important for her than being attractive to the opposite sex.

The underrepresentation of girls in natural science has to be interpreted in terms of culture. Science in most cultures is socially defined as a masculine domain. Boys engage in science and technology to reinforce their masculinity — while this is not a way for girls to become feminine. For a girl, a choice of science may lead to sanctions from her female peer group — and from the boys! Empirical evidence shows that boys don't like girls to be clever in areas considered as male. They think 'there is something strange about girls who want to be scientists' (Kelly *et al.*, 1984). Boys also expect girls to be afraid of electricity (Lie and Sjøberg, 1984).

While girls' cultural codes may divert them away from science in spite of talents and interests, the opposite problem exists for the boys: many boys are more or less forced to choose subjects and careers 'suited' for men in spite of aptitudes and interests going in other directions. Although this is not the subject for this chapter, we will indicate that codes of 'boys' cultures' may be even harder to change than the codes of 'girls' cultures'. For both sexes the aim should be to help them shape cultures that have less oppressive consequences for themselves. In any case, gender can be removed. It is the social expressions of gender that cannot be changed.

The gender cultures have developed historically, and the social expressions of gender vary between cultures. Historical, ideological, and material conditions have interfered in the moulding of male and female ideals. Division of labour between the sexes has undoubtedly played a major role in this process. During the process of industrialization and urbanization in the nineteenth and twentieth centuries, the division of labour between men and women has partly been redefined in the countries that have undergone those processes. The sexual division of work is still clear-cut. If a particular division of labour becomes obsolete for material reasons, it does not automatically follow that sex inequalities will vanish. For example, the new possibilities for women to work outside home during the 1960s and 1970s do not seem to have changed the ideals of femininity and masculinity. The ideological impact of old patriarchal systems continues to operate in modern society, providing invisible rules for what is feminine or masculine. An important aspect of the cultural system of gender is the way of defining hierarchical relations between the sexes. Masculinity is perceived as a way of expressing superiority and dominance, while femininity is a way of expressing subordination. In a society like Norway, where all kinds of sex discrimination in principle are forbidden by law, this superordinate/subordinate relationship is disguised. It is best traced in the relationship between couples. The male partner is usually considered by society a little superior to the female. She might well be clever and intelligent, but she is frequently not 'allowed' to challenge his position of intellectual superiority in the family. In many important situations, she had better stand a step or two behind her husband. If not, she will break the invisible rules of femininity.

This perspective throws some light at the problem of girls and science. Approaching a typical 'male' discipline increases the risk of breaking important social rules with all its costs. Girls perceive the invisible warning attached to the possibility of becoming more clever than boys on their own territory.

A coherent and all-embracing theoretical framework for understanding girls' underrepresentation in science does not exist. The problem is not likely to be grasped with simple models of cause and effect. The concept of gender culture is more comprehensive and is, in our opinion, likely to generate a deeper understanding of the many aspects of the problem.

Science as Part of the Gender Culture: Empirical Evidence

There is a growing amount of research documenting that girls and boys are treated differently in the classroom (and of course elsewhere!). In general, teachers hold lower academic expectations of the girls, especially in science and mathematics. Classroom research on teacher–pupil interactions also gives evidence that boys are favoured both with respect to the amount of time and of quality of the interactions. Although exceptions as well as significant international variations exist in this respect, the above seems to be a general pattern that is well documented. (For further references see GASAT I, II, III and IV; and Harding, 1986.)

In this section, we will bring empirical evidence from national studies in Norway that throw light on different aspects of the differences between the cultures of girls and boys. We will look at differences in experiences, differences in attitudes and differences in the way they see their future jobs. Finally, we will look at how the two sexes perceive scientists as persons and science as a discipline and how these perceptions are related to the personalities of girls and boys.

Sex Differences in Experiences

It is a pedagogical cliché that one 'should build on the experiences of the learner', and 'go from the concrete to the abstract'. These statements become more interesting and problematic when one realizes that children bring with them *different* sorts of experiences. By taking some experiences for granted and as a starting-point for abstraction, one may unintentionally favour certain groups of pupils. Science teaching builds on experiences that strongly favour the boys. Let us illustrate the point with some concrete examples.

The Norwegian version of the IEA SISS-study (The Second International Science Study) (Sjøberg, 1986) included a survey of children's out-of-school experiences that might be of relevance for the learning of science in schools. The questionnaire was answered by some 3000 pupils at two different ages: 11 and 16. The same children also answered questions on home background, interests and attitudes, future plans, etc. in addition to a large number of multiple choice science items. The purpose of including the list of experiences in the investigation was manifold: the list was meant to give a background for analysis of existing curricula and for possible revisions. The results also make it possible to investigate possible connections between experience and score on knowledge items from the same 'area' — for instance electricity. Here we restrict ourselves to an overview of the 'raw' results.

For each activity, an 'activity index' (between 0.00 and 1.00) was calculated from responses to a three point scale: 'never', 'two or three times' and 'often'. Averages for different sub-groups have been compared. These sub-groups were defined by different criteria: by geographical region, by demographic criteria, by measures for home background, etc. All these

Table 1: Mean values of the activity indexes as a result of the out-of-school experiences of girls and boys

Activity	11 years		16 years	
	Girls	*Boys*	*Girls*	*Boys*
Used needle and thread	0.95	0.73	0.97	0.66
Used a sewing machine	0.83	0.59	0.95	0.58
Knitted	0.94	0.57	0.94	0.43
Played with Lego building set	0.68	0.82	0.64	0.67
Made a model airplane,-boat,-car	0.23	0.69	0.27	0.73
Used a saw	0.66	0.86	0.76	0.94
Used a screwdriver	0.66	0.87	0.80	0.95
Used a hammer and nail	0.88	0.93	0.92	0.97
Used a spanner (wrench)	0.45	0.82	0.67	0.96
Recorded with a tape recorder	0.74	0.74	0.92	0.88
Recorded on a video tape recorder	0.16	0.25	0.20	0.29
Played video games	0.04	0.20	0.27	0.50
Used a microscope	0.30	0.50	0.47	0.61
Used binoculars	0.83	0.87	0.88	0.91
Used a magnifying glass	0.44	0.61	0.59	0.70
Used a camera	0.68	0.65	0.90	0.82
Used a stop watch	0.67	0.85	0.76	0.89
Used a measuring tape	0.83	0.77	0.94	0.83
Read the scale of a thermometer	0.70	0.75	0.93	0.90
Used a kitchen scale	0.69	0.65	0.94	0.76
Made bread or pastry	0.79	0.62	0.95	0.65
Used an air gun	0.20	0.59	0.42	0.84
Used a rifle or a shotgun	0.15	0.37	0.25	0.67
Made jam from wild berries	0.52	0.43	0.55	0.32
Waxed a pair of skis	0.75	0.82	0.82	0.87
Studied the Milky Way	0.33	0.39	0.41	0.34
Studied the moon with binoculars	0.28	0.36	0.25	0.38
Studied fossils	0.19	0.23	0.19	0.23
Collected wild mushrooms	0.33	0.35	0.45	0.35
Collected edible wild plants	0.35	0.33	0.33	0.29
Planted and watched seeds grow	0.72	0.60	0.76	0.57
Studied the life in a pond	0.53	0.58	0.50	0.50
Cared for a horse	0.46	0.32	0.46	0.33
Collected stones	0.68	0.58	0.59	0.40
Changed electric bulbs at home	0.59	0.74	0.95	0.95
Changed a fuse at home	0.12	0.32	0.49	0.81
Attached electric lead to plug	0.08	0.35	0.18	0.73
Studied the inside of a radio	0.17	0.51	0.26	0.78
Changed wheels on a car	0.11	0.43	0.17	0.43
Charged a car battery	0.09	0.31	0.12	0.56

Source: Sjøberg (1986)

divisions give differences in some of the experiences, not surprising in a country that stretches from a rather pleasant climate in a relatively densely populated south up to the tough coastal climate in the area far north of the Arctic Circle.

One particular way of forming sub-populations results in far greater difference between the groups than any other type of division, and that is division by sex!

The list of activities in the questionnaire includes some 100 activities. Table 1 gives the 'activity index' for boys and girls for some of the activities. In table 2 the gender differences for a small extract of the activities in table 1 are presented, grouped by positive values for each sex. These tables show only a very limited range of the results and are meant only to indicate the following points that emerge from the list as a whole.

1   *The pattern of experience is strongly connected with gender. Girls* dominate in most activities connected with home and household. They also dominate in activities connected with biology, gardening, nature study, health, handling and caring for animals. Activities like 'collecting stones' and 'take photographs' are also 'girls' activities'. *Boys* dominate most strongly in activities connected with cars (except for 'washing a

Table 2:   Experiences: Differences between boys and girls

Activity	Girl-boy difference	
	11 years	*16 years*
Girl-dominated: (positive value:		
higher index for girls)		
Knitted	0.37	0.51
Used a sewing machine	0.24	0.37
Made jam from wild berries	0.09	0.23
Collected flowers for a herbarium	0.18	0.21
Planted seeds and watched them grow	0.13	0.20
Collected stones	0.10	0.19
Read about how the body functions	0.00	0.12
Boy-dominated (positive value:		
higher index for boys)		
Used a saw	0.20	0.18
Played with a chemistry set	0.19	0.25
Changed a fuse at home	0.20	0.32
Used a gun or a shot gun	0.22	0.42
Helped with repairing a car	0.24	0.46
Used a car jack	0.36	0.52
Attached an electric lead to a plug	0.26	0.55
Renew the plugs on a motor	0.21	0.59

Source: Sjøberg (1986)

car', where boys and girls are equal). The activities include 'charging the battery', 'using the jack', 'renewing the plugs', etc. Boys dominate in activities related to *electricity*, strongly in activities like 'attaching a lead to a plug', smaller differences on 'changing batteries' and 'changing bulbs'. Boys also have higher activity index on the use of a variety of *mechanical tools*.

2   *Most differences in experience are dramatically larger at age 16.* Although the study is not a longitudinal study of the same children, it is likely that this finding can be interpreted as an *increase* of differences with age. (It is unlikely that societal changes have occurred in all these areas simultaneously.) And the pattern is interesting: whereas girls systematically score higher on 'male' experiences the older they get, it is often the opposite with boys: their scores become lower the older they get. (We find it likely that pupils think back a rather short time span when they judge whether they have done a particular activity 'often' or not. Therefore a score may decrease with age.) Compared with 11-year-olds, boys at the age of 16 have *lower* index on most household activities and also on activities like watching an egg hatch, raising tadpoles or butterflies, planting seeds to see them grow, growing vegetables in a kitchen garden, study fossils, make jam from wild berries, and collect flowers for a herbarium. So, while girls in general gradually become familiar with male experiences, the boys move even further away from the 'world of girls'.

Most of the 100 activities listed in the questionnaire have some relevance to science. They constitute possible starting points for school science, or they can be used as concrete examples in the treatment of science topics. If we compare the list of experiences sorted by sex differences, we are immediately struck by the fact that school science builds on boys' experiences. (This is at least the case in the traditional Norwegian curriculum, where physics has a strong position.) This is a clear expression of our assertion that science reinforces the masculine image and is part of boys' culture.

Sex Differences in Interests in Subject Matter

Differences in experiences are of course strongly linked with differences in personality predispositions. Several investigations shed light on this (for an international survey see Lehrke *et al.*, 1985). Our Norwegian results agree with most of these results. Some examples (all published in Lie and Sjøberg, 1984) are:

Example 1

Students at the ages of 12 and 14 are presented lists of topics that may possibly be covered in science lessons. They are invited to tag the subject matter that appeals to them. The results are analyzed for differences between groups. The pattern that is consistently clearest is the difference between the sexes. Generalizing, the pattern is the following: boys are strongly interested in subject matter related to cars and motors, girls are interested in subject matter related to health, nutrition and the human body. But the differences show up also in the kind of *context* that is implied in the description of the subject matter. In general, girls are interested when the subject matter is placed in a context related to daily life or to society (key word: 'relevance'). Girls are also in the majority on subject matter that has aesthetical ('snow crystals', 'the rainbow') or ethical aspects ('consequences of ...').

Different key words for 'the same' subject matter give widely differing results: girls are interested when key words are 'colours', 'the eye', etc., while boys are in the majority on items when 'pure' physics concepts 'light' or 'optics' are given. Similarly for 'acoustics': girls are interested in 'music', 'instruments' and 'the ear', while boys react more positively to 'sound'.

Example 2

A representative group of university students covering different fields of study gave answers very consistent with the above results. They were invited to give their views on 'what should be given higher priority in the school physics curriculum in order to make it more interesting' by tagging topics from a long list. The topics that came out on top of the list were: 'how physics is used in society', 'the physics of daily life', 'the body and the senses'. It is interesting to note that although the female students came out much higher than male students on those topics, they were also on top of the list for male students! This shows that a science curriculum more suited to the interests of girls need not be to the disfavour of boys.

Example 3

More open approaches to the same problem area have also been undertaken. In one investigation, 14-year-old students were invited to write some lines, given the following guidelines: 'Scientists make new things or try to understand what happens in nature and with people. If *you* could decide, what would you ask scientists to do?'

The results were analyzed and classified. The following aspects came out on top of the list for the two sexes:

Girls' research priorities		**Boys' research priorities**	
Body, health	23%	Technology	24%
Anti–nuclear weapon	14%	Astronomy	14%
Animals	14%	Animals	11%
History	13%	Body, health	9%

We see that the general pattern is the same as in the investigations with closed alternatives: girls are oriented towards biology, health, the body and towards the consequences of technology.

Sex Differences in Self-Concept and Value Orientation

In a study carried out in the central area of Norway in 1986, a total of 1364 students aged 15 to 17 years responded to an inventory which included scales on self-concept, values, and career aspirations. The students come from randomly-sampled classes in the eight and ninth grades of comprehensive schools and the first high school grade, all curricular electives being included (Imsen, 1987).

The self-description scale was in essence built up along the lines of Bem's Sex Role Inventory (Bem, 1974). A Likert-type scale containing twenty-four self-description items was developed. No androgyny-scores were calculated. A factor analysis of the twenty-four items gave the following factor structure:

FACTOR 1: ORIENTATION TOWARDS OTHERS, a description of one-self as considerate, kind, thoughtful and responsible.

FACTOR 2: INDEPENDENCE, a description of self as determined, independent, willing to stand up for oneself, and assertive.

FACTOR 3: EMPATHY, a description of oneself as one who consoles others, displays own feelings readily, easily moved to feel for others, and open-minded.

FACTOR 4: COMPETITIVENESS, a description of oneself as one who displays leadership, knowledge, ability, competitiveness and who takes risks, often seizing the initiative.

Girls showed the highest values for factors 1 and 3. Factor 2 showed no differences for boys and girls. The boys had the highest scores for factor 4. (All differences significant at $p < 0.01$.) Differences between boys and girls were most pronounced in respect to the empathy factor.

This indicates that the results on students' interests as to science are not merely opinions at a surface level. They correspond fairly well to boys' and girls' deeper understanding of their own personal potential.

This correspondence is clearly demonstrated when looking at general value orientation. In the same investigation, students also completed a version of the Rokeach Value Survey (Rokeach, 1973). This was rescaled from a ranking to a Likert scale. The results confirm the girls' 'soft' value orientations. They score higher than boys do for values such as openness, concern and sympathy for others. Boys, on the other hand, score highest on values such as efficiency, skill, boldness, ambition, knowledge, and reasoning power.

Our results on personal priorities and self-descriptions add up to a pattern describing the main differences between male and female sub-cultures. We will now take a look at how these differences are connected to the choice of future jobs.

Sex Differences in Choice of Future Jobs

The career wishes of the pupils in the above-mentioned study (Imsen, 1987) were divided into groups in two different ways: first as to the occupation preferred being a female or a male-dominated occupation, as defined by official employment statistics; secondly as to the occupation in question being a caring or a technical occupation. Results are shown in table 3.

The results in table 4 show that although most girls still want to pursue 'traditional' women's occupations, there is a considerable minority who aspire to traditional male occupations (some of which may be technical). More than three times as many boys as girls want a technical occupation. Totally, only 13 per cent of the girls would like to enter a technical or scientific occupation. By contrast, 47 per cent of the boys wanted to work in the field of technology. We also note that very few boys want to enter female-dominated occupations, and very few boys want to join caring occupations.

The results indicate that there is some movement among the girls to enter

*Table 3: Career aspirations among boys and girls (*Sex dominance in occupation according to 1980 census)*

| | | Occupational Category | | | | | |
| | | *Sex Dominance | | | Quality of work | | |
	N	Female	Neutral	Male	Caring	Technical	Other
Girls	695	373	46	258	279	90	326
Boys	625	63	38	511	29	286	310
Total	1289	433	84	769	308	376	636

Source: Imsen (1987).

Table 4:   Scores for gender and self-concept sub-groups for two categories of occupational aspiration (number in each sub-group in parentheses)

	FACTOR 1 OTHER-ORIENTATION		FACTOR 2 INDEPENDENCE		FACTOR 3 EMPATHY		FACTOR 4 COMPETITIVENESS	
OCCUPATION	Girls	.Boys	Girls	Boys	Girls	Boys	Girls	Boys
CARING	0.20	0.20	−0.11	0.29	0.55	−0.12	−0.34	0.71
	(267)	(29)	(269)	(28)	(275)	(29)	(268)	(29)
TECHNICAL	0.10	−0.11	0.04	−0.10	0.36	−0.55	−0.04	0.20
	(87)	(271)	(88)	(279)	(88)	(273)	(88)	(271)

Source: Imsen (1987).

male-dominated and technically-oriented studies. For the boys, the situation is much more static; they seem to avoid female-dominated occupations and occupations oriented towards care. This observation supports our assertion that the culture of boys is more rigid and difficult to change than the girls' culture.

In this investigation, there was also a link between self-concept as described in the last section and occupational aspirations. For the four factors above of self-description, the mean z- scores of sub-groups defined by sex and two categories of occupational aspiration are given in table 4. The total number of students was 1244, but the number of boys preferring caring occupations is low so the results should be taken with care. Table 4 shows that there is a clear tendency for girls describing themselves as empathic to want to take up work involving caring for others. Those who want a technical occupation are less empathic and more competitive and individualistic than the 'caring occupation' group. Still, the girls choosing technology are much more empathic than the boys in the same category of choice! According to this analysis, girls choosing technically-oriented occupations are qualitatively different from boys selecting the same occupations.

The SISS study referred to earlier (Sjøberg, 1986) also sheds light on factors lying behind the choice of future jobs. The 6500 participating students at the ages 11, 16 and 19 were asked to rate a list of factors that could have importance for their choice of occupation. As for many of the other variables in SISS, the greatest differences occur when the data are divided by sex. Table 5 gives data for three different populations. The table shows *differences* in job priorities between girls and boys at three different ages. The two first groups are representative samples from the total population. The age 19 group,

Table 5: 'Of importance for future job'. Differences between girls and boys (absolute values are for total group at age 16)

Factors	Age 11 (All) Diff.	Age 16 (All) Diff.	Abs.	Age 19[*] Diff.
Work with people instead of things	0.00	0.17	(0.45)	0.31
Help other people	0.08	0.13	(0.64)	0.23
Use my talents or abilities	0.00	0.03	(0.88)	0.01
Get a safe and secure job	0.01	0.02	(0.92)	0.03
Have an exciting job	0.02	0.00	(0.73)	− 0.05
Have free time for family and friends	0.02	− 0.01	(0.81)	− 0.11
Make my own decision	− 0.08	− 0.01	(0.60)	− 0.06
Make and invent new things	− 0.01	− 0.02	(0.48)	− 0.05
Control other people	− 0.03	− 0.04	(0.12)	− 0.06
Become famous	− 0.04	− 0.05	(0.15)	− 0.04
Earn lots of money	− 0.05	− 0.05	(0.75)	− 0.13
Have spare time for my own interests	− 0.02	− 0.05	(0.65)	− 0.11

Source: Sjøberg, 1986.

marked *, represents the students that have specialized in the natural sciences in the 'academic' branch of the school system.

In table 5 we have concentrated on the *differences* between the sexes. On top of the list are the 'female factors', on the bottom the 'male factors'. Before commenting on this, it is fair to say that the general pattern is great similarity in priorities. A measure for this is the total average for the population, indicated in parentheses in the table, for the 16-year-olds only. The differences must be judged in the light of this number.

But in spite of this reservation, several interesting observations on the differences can be made. The pattern remains the same for all the populations: girls score higher on aspects oriented towards *care* and *other people*, boys score higher on aspects that are *ego-oriented* and related to their own *personal* benefit. We also note that the differences *increase with age*.

The last group in the table is particularly interesting, since it consists of 'science specialists', that is, students who have elected science options. A frequently heard argument is that girls who choose male-dominated fields of study have to develop the same set of values and priorities as their male competitors, maybe even more than the men do. The results for the last group show exactly the *opposite* of that assertion: the differences between girls and boys are larger for this group than for any other group of pupils! Since the future scientists and technologists are recruited from this group, it gives strong support to the claim that women in science would have different priorities in their daily decisions. This result is in agreement with Imsen's (1987) personality- oriented studies presented above.

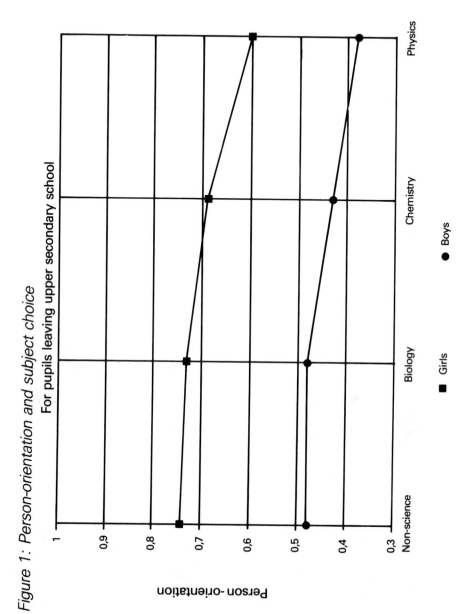

Figure 1: Person-orientation and subject choice

For pupils leaving upper secondary school

Person -orientation

Non-science   Biology   Chemistry   Physics

■ Girls   ● Boys

In the above presentation, we have pooled all 'scientists'. Let us now take a closer look at possible differences between the various 'kinds' of scientists in the population of 19-year-olds. A simple index of 'person-orientation' was calculated for each sub-population based on the addition of the score on the two questions: 'work with people instead of things' and 'help other people'. The sum was normalized to range from 0 to 1, the standard error for each sub-population was typically 0.02, and the differences between girls and boys are significant to <0.1 per cent. These indices are plotted in figure 1. The results are in line with what other researchers have found (Smithers and Collings, 1981): scientists are in general less person-oriented than non-scientists, physicists less than biologists. Within each group, girls are more person-oriented than boys. Our data also show that the *least person-oriented group of girls (physics girls) is more person-oriented than the most* person-oriented group of boys.

It is also interesting to note that biology students seem to be very similar to most other (non-science) students.

Let us now link this index of person-orientation to the future plans of the students. Figure 2 plots the index of person-orientation for groups of science students expressing different plans for their future. All differences between girls and boys are statistically significant to <0.1 per cent. We see here that medicine is an attractive field of study for students who are oriented towards other people. Students choosing science/technology have a very small index of person-orientation. In each group, girls are more person-oriented than the boys, although the difference between the different fields of study is greater than between the sexes.

Other Norwegian data give similar results: Elin Kvande has interviewed students who have recently completed their education as civil engineers (Kvande, 1984, a summary published in GASAT II, 1983). She has found that the female engineers are motivated to find jobs where their education could be used to the benefit of society and other people, while the male engineers are more oriented towards their own success: high salary, prestige and status. This study again shows that girls may go through a strongly male-dominated education with their feminine values and priorities intact.

Sex Differences in Educational Choices

The SISS project showed that 16 per cent of the total population of 17–18-year-olds chose to specialize in scientific school subjects in 1983–1984. Of these 43 per cent were girls, and this would seem to suggest that we have a high female percentage of science entrants in Norwegian upper secondary schools. But the picture changes if we look closer at their choice of subjects.

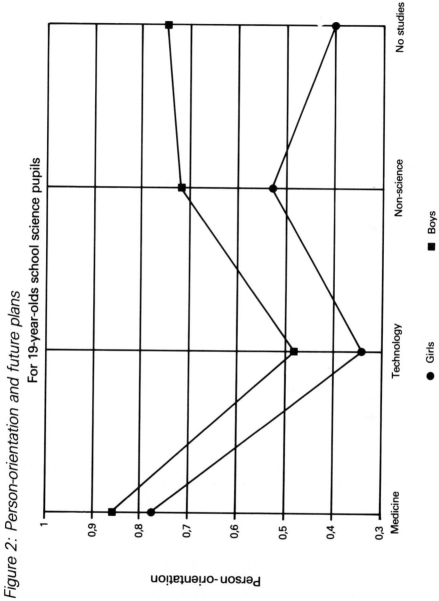

Figure 2: Person-orientation and future plans

Between two and three times as many boys as girls chose mathematics and physics. The girls would rather choose biology and chemistry. But, as indicated earlier, the combination physics and mathematics is the only one which qualifies for entrance to advanced technological studies (as well as to more biology-oriented studies like medicine, pharmacy, veterinary medicine and agricultural science). Many girls make choices that preclude entrance to such studies. Indeed, it has been suggested that curricular options merely amplify the disparity between boys and girls (Skog, 1983).

In a study conducted among 1884 students in the first year of upper secondary school in 1986, it was found that achievement level in science affects boys and girls differently in their subsequent choice of subjects. Among students achieving average marks, the probability that a boy will specialize in science is twice the probability that a girl will (Skog, 1986). This emphasizes our point that factors other than those of ability and achievement are crucial to understanding the process of educational choice.

At the Norwegian Institute of Technology, the proportion of female students is about 28 per cent. There was a steady increase in the female proportion during the 1970s and early 1980s. During the last few years, however, the increase seems to have peaked or even reversed. It should also be noticed that the percentage of women differs markedly as to kinds of course of study. The highest percentages of women are in chemistry and architecture; the lowest are in offshore and machine engineering and in computer science.

The Image of Science and the Scientist

A Range of Influences

Students learn about science from many different sources. During this process, they gradually develop an idea about what science is 'really' all about and how scientists are as persons. This image of science is probably more stable than the facts and laws students learn in their school lessons.

An image of science is projected in a mostly covert and implicit way, as a cumulative result of various influences at school: textbooks, teachers' behaviour and personalities (including the sex of the science teacher). Images of science are also developed through out-of-school influences: cartoons, fiction books, television series, mass media news coverage, etc. In many cases, the scientist is presented as an old, absent-minded professor (always male), sealed off from the rest of the world in his laboratory, where he invents strange chemicals or bombs that may blow the whole world to pieces. 'The crazy male scientist' is a nearly mythological figure, kept alive even in children's science programs on television.

The process of learning about science may be an example of the 'genderization of science'. The influences mentioned all carry the message that science is linked to the process of becoming masculine for boys but not to the process of becoming feminine for girls.

The (Lack of) Context of School Science

School science has a particular responsibility to convey a picture of the nature of science. This is done by selection of course material; certain topics are included, other topics are *not* included. The particular *context* in which science is presented is also important. (Lack of context is indeed also a particular context!) Ziman (1980) is hard in his criticism in his book, *Teaching and Learning about Science and Society*:

> There is one characteristic of science education above all others ...: it is carried out as if the historical, philosophical, sociological and economic aspects of life were quite non-existent, and unworthy of the slightest attention by a serious teacher. Their neglect conveys to the student images of science, images of the scientist, and images of the role of science in society which are damaging to science, to scientists and to society itself. (p. 30)

We would like to add to Ziman's list that this image is damaging also to the recruitment of girls to the sciences.

The image of science to be found in textbooks is still often based on an outdated philosophy of science, where science is presented as a pure and logical exercise, performed by disinterested, detached, neutral and objective observers who patiently put stone on stone to build an everlasting cathedral of permanent truth. The implicit purpose of science is to understand nature in order to control, manipulate and dominate, aspects that often are said to be masculine or patriarchal. Science is seen in isolation from political, religious, ideological and other human conflicts.

Such an image may have a strong appeal to orderly minds who do not want to get involved in issues of value, conflict and human involvement, and vice versa: this image of science scares away pupils with different personal priorities — mainly girls, but also many boys.

The somewhat caricatured image of science given above does not emerge from textbook analysis alone, there are many empirical studies to support it. Let us give two concrete examples from our own studies:

'The typical physicist'

University students from different faculties were presented with a list of different personal traits. They were asked to indicate on a scale whether 'the typical physicist or physics student' was more or less than average on these traits (Lie and Sjøberg, 1984, p. 59). The following 'personality profile' of the physicist emerged:

THE PHYSICIST

YES: More than average for the following traits:	NO: Less than average for the following traits:
Logical	Artistic
Intelligent	Interested in people
Determined	Politically engaged
Objective	Extrovert
	Imaginative
	Responsible

When we compare this image of the physicist with the self-concept of girls and with their important priorities for choice of occupation, we see that the image of the physicist is nearly the negation of what girls value.

The humane biologist and the inhuman physicist

In the Norwegian SISS study referred to earlier (Sjøberg, 1986), students are presented with several pairs of attribute words with opposite meaning on each side of a 5-point scale. The paired attributes used were: careless-accurate, stupid-intelligent, lazy-industrious, unimaginative-imaginative, selfish-caring, closed-open, boring-exciting, unartistic-artistic. The students were asked to use these scales to describe two different sorts of scientific researcher in the fields of 'physics or technology' and 'biology or medicine'.

The overall picture that emerged is that girls and boys differ very little in their perception of the typical scientist. Also worthy of note is the fact that the different populations of pupils in general have the same impression: rather young students in the obligatory school have the same conception of the scientist as the 19-year-old science specialist.

The average values (which may lie between $+1$ and -1 with 0 as neutral) for the image of these two sorts of scientists as perceived by the 19-year-old student are plotted in figure 3. The list of attributes was sorted using the values for the second scientist as criterion. Only the 'positive' word in the attribute scales is shown in the figure and a positive value corresponds to a 'positive' attribute. Figure 3 indicates that the two types of researchers are considered

Figure 3: The attributes of scientists as persons in the fields of 'physics/technology' and 'biology/medicine' as perceived by 19-year-old science students

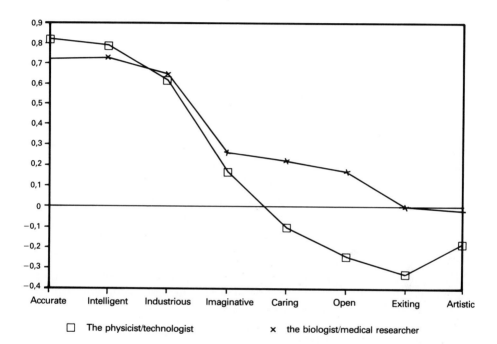

equal on some qualities, different on others. Both the biologist and the physicist are considered to be very accurate and intelligent, with the physicist a little in front. (This was particularly the case in the eyes of girls.) Both are also industrious. Both types are also rather imaginative, the biologist more than the physicist.

On the remaining qualities, the biologist came out more positive than the physicist: the biologist as caring, the physicist as selfish; the biologist as open, the physicist as closed; the physicist was also considered as boring and unartistic, while the biologist was considered to be 'neutral' on these traits.

Altogether, the image of the physicist is far from flattering. For most girls (and certainly also for many boys), it is expected that this image will be unattractive: on the one hand, the cool, rational intellect; on the other hand, the lack of warmth, care and human characteristics that we have seen are part of the girls' culture.

Faced with this empirically documented image of the physicist, two possibilities exist:

1   The impression is false, physicists are not like that!
2   The impression is correct, this is exactly how physicists are!

In the first case, science educators have a problem: how can false impressions like this be developed, even among 'science specialists' at school? And how can we change this stereotyped image?

In the second case, society at large has a problem: is it not frightening that people with these personalities shall hold positions with great influence and power, so central for the shaping of the future society?

We will not try to argue for a decision between those two possibilities but will indicate that we may have a vicious circle. That is, the image of science is likely to have a great influence on the recruitment of future scientists; and since girls are more person-oriented, it is likely that this image will have special significance for their choices. Persons who feel uncomfortable with the cold and intellectual image of physics are not likely to choose it as a career. Hence, we may recruit future scientists that correspond to this widespread stereotype; the hypothesis may be self-fulfilling.

Strategies for Change

Two Dimensions

It may be fruitful to have two different dimensions in mind when one considers strategies for change. One dimension concerns *the specificity* of the problem and goes from general measures to subject-specific measures as indicated earlier.

The other dimension concerns *the time scale* of the suggested strategies. This of course ranges from short to long periods of time. The two dimensions are indicated below.

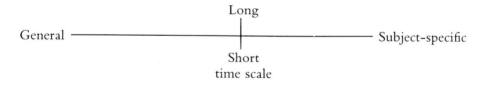

This representation is only meant to be an analytical tool, and both dimensions are continuous scales rather than dichotomies. As science educators, our main interest will, however, mostly be on the 'right side' of the diagram. This does not of course mean that the general measures are less important. It is also true that some of the general measures acquire special meanings when applied to specific fields. This is, for instance, the case with the idea of gender culture, which is a general concept that acquires more specific meaning when applied to science education.

In the following discussion of measures, we will have the above dimensions in mind.

Classroom Behaviour and Organization

Classroom behaviour and different ways of organizing the classroom are to a certain extent decided by the individual teachers. Things may change rather quickly without large changes in available material resources if the teacher decides to do so (but the process of changing teachers is certainly not a quick one).

Science teachers not only teach the content of science. As for other teachers, they communicate a hidden curriculum about the nature of their subject, they teach about social relationships, they function as role models, etc. It is very important that science teachers see themselves in such a wide perspective. In particular, they should be aware of the different gender cultures and the psychological factors that operate in a classroom. They should consider equality between the sexes also as *their problem* as science teachers.

It is usually not a part of the 'culture' of science teachers to look at their role from this perspective. In order to develop this perspective, it needs to be an integral part of science teacher education as well as of in-service courses.

In daily behaviour, it is important that the teachers give girls the same amount as well as quality of attention that they do boys and that they show that they hold similar expectations of girls and boys. Any kind of sexism, also in the form of 'jokes', should of course be avoided. Many case studies give good examples of how the 'non–sexist' classroom may function (Kahle, 1985).

Girls' possibilities in science–related careers should be given attention in all forms of *career advice* and other forms of counselling, whether this is done by ordinary teachers or specifically trained personnel. In any case, the science teacher is likely to have some influence in this area through the daily teaching practices. It is important to give support to girls who show interests and abilities in the sciences. A corollary to this is that teachers should be more sceptical with many of the boys who choose the sciences more out of male tradition than out of interest and aptitude. Maybe more boys thereby could find their way into important jobs related to care, areas that in most countries are totally dominated by women.

Different ways of organizing the science classroom may be effective in increasing the number of girls in science. The issues of 'single sex' versus mixed classrooms are discussed by many authors, for instance in the GASAT reports. It is, however, not possible to give universal advice on 'the best' way to do so from the empirical evidence that exists. Besides, schooling may have different aims that may conflict with each other. A separation of pupils by sex may be instrumental in increasing the number of girls who choose science, but may have other negative effects that may be considered more serious. In each particular context, the teacher should, however, be sensitive to possible unwanted effects of different organizational settings.

If scarce material resources are available for laboratory work, it is particularly important not to allow one group to make use of these to their own benefit. In situations of 'freedom', the result is too often that boys end up using the equipment while girls end up as 'secretaries', taking notes. In any case, teacher behaviour and classroom organization should encourage girls to take part in all activities, and counteract possible domination by boys. The ways to accomplish this will vary from one educational setting to another.

Curricular Changes

In some countries, curricular changes come about by government decisions. Although it may involve a long political struggle to change official policies, the changes come quickly when the central decisions have been made. Norway is a country with such a centralized school system. The considerations that will be mentioned in the following are to a large degree official policy in a curricular reform that is currently being introduced.

Science should be part of the curriculum from an early age. Young girls and boys have a natural curiosity that should be exploited and developed through science in schools. But more needs to be said about *what kind* of science that pupils should meet in schools, since research evidence shows that school science has a tendency to destroy the interest in science instead of nursing it. Empirical evidence, of the kind that we have given in previous sections, gives indications about what a 'girl-friendly' science might look like. It is important to stress that 'girl-friendly' science is probably a better science for all pupils and for Norway as well as for most other countries and also more in line with the officially stated aims of science education.

Let us briefly describe what such a science might look like. First of all, it is important that one removes all kinds of sexism from curricula and textbooks. This means that illustrations and examples must show both sexes in active situations and balanced with respect to frequency of presentation. When theoretical ideas are shown in practical use, it is important to look for examples that are based on girls' experiences and appeal to their interests.

But curricular changes must go deeper than just replacing boys with girls and trading one example with another. It is urgent to look at the *organizing principles* of the course material, and it is important to examine the *context* in which the material is presented. Let us refer to the discussion of this in our new curriculum.

The same content of science might be approached from different angles. The starting point as well as the end point are important for the pupils' motivation to work with the material. Our evidence shows that organization based on personal relevance is important, especially for girls; for example, the physical senses and the human body, the use of science to improve life for ourselves and other people.

Any curriculum operates in a context. Empirical evidence suggests that this is especially important to girls. Lack of a context also may be perceived as a particular context by pupils; that is, science will then be understood as something remote from real life both on the personal and the societal level. School science should be presented in the same context as 'real science' that is as an important tool for the shaping of destinies for people and nations and as potentially both good and evil, depending on how it is controlled. Therefore, examples of both positive and negative uses should be presented. Our new curriculum stresses that both science and technology are constructed by people with different interests and values. Science should be presented as any other kind of *human* activity, not merely as a pure and logical search for objective truth and eternal wisdom.

Finally, it would be an important achievement if school science could be what 'real science' often is: fun, full of aesthetics, enjoyment and intellectual stimulation.

The considerations above might be easier to fulfil in schools like those in Norway, where science is taught as an 'integrated' subject, since real examples seldom follow the boundaries of scientific knowledge. But this is not an absolute requirement, there are also good examples of separate sciences based on personal relevance and social applications, for instance the Dutch physics project, PLON (see chapter 14).

As mentioned, considerations like the ones above have been the foundation of recent curricular revisions in Norway. Equality between the sexes has even been put up as one of the main aims of science education. It is, however, a long way from an official curriculum to real classroom changes. But a good curriculum will, of course, help the process. A project that aims at converting the new curriculum into classroom practice has been initiated by the Norwegian Ministry of Education (Jorde and Lea, 1987).

Fewer Options — Later Choices

In many countries, the educational system requires specialization at an early age. Choices that later turn out to have important implications are made at a stage when pupils often are unaware of the consequences. Choices are frequently made at an age when the pupils are very sensitive to gender identity. These factors exert a pressure on both girls and boys to act according to traditions, according to the expectations held by the girls' and boys' culture. Hence, the notion of a 'free' choice is questionable under such pressures.

Even school systems that are labelled comprehensive and based on a common curriculum have 'options' at a rather early age. Empirical evidence above showed that these options reinforce the traditional gender-based divisions of society.

In many countries, an accepted and officially stated aim of the school is to *counteract* choices based on gender traditions found in society. If this is to be taken seriously, it may indicate a strategy of 'forced choices', where curricular options are deliberately used to *bridge the gap* in experiences between girls and boys.

Girls Need Science — Science Needs Girls!

This double assertion has been the basis of all that is said in this chapter. The first part of it is self-evident; girls and women have much to gain if they get access to careers in science and technology. They may gain both on a personal level (career opportunities, well paid and interesting jobs) and as a group (access to power and societal influence).

But the second part of the assertion is equally important: girls and women do have a significant contribution to make to the development and use of science and technology itself. We have used the concept of gender culture as an underlying theoretical concept. We have shown that the female culture involves a perspective of care and responsibility for other people. This perspective is likely to manifest itself in action if more women are involved in science. This may give the scientific communities a stronger orientation towards ethical responsibility and the use of technology for constructive purposes and to the benefit of underprivileged groups and generations to come. This is certainly a development that is needed in the world today.

Acknowledgements

We want to express our thanks to Dr Doris Jorde, for help and advice both on content and language. We would also like to thank Professor Jane Butler Kahle for encouragement and good advice given during her stay with us in Norway in May and June 1987.

References

BEM, S. (1974) 'The measurement of psychological androgyny', *Journal of Consulting and Clinical Psychology*, 42, pp. 155–62.

GASAT I (1981) RAAT, J. *et al.* (Eds) *Contributions, GASAT — Conference 1981*, Eindhoven, The Netherlands, Eindhoven University Press.

GASAT II (1983) SJØBERG, S. (Ed.) *Contributions to the Second GASAT Conference*, Oslo, University of Oslo, Centre for Science Education.

GASAT III (1986) HARDING, J. (Ed.) *Contributions to the Third GASAT Conference*, London, King's College.

GASAT IV (1987) DANIELS, J.Z. and KAHLE, J.B. (Eds) *Contributions to the Fourth GASAT Conference*, Ann Arbor, MI, University of Michigan.

GOULD, S.J. (1981) *The Mismeasure of Man*, London, W.W. Norton & Co.

HARDING, J. (1985) 'Science and Technology — A future for women?', paper prepared for the World Conference to Review and Appraise the Achievements of the United Nations Decade for Women, in Nairobi, UNESCO, Paris, July.

HARDING, J. (Ed.) (1986) *Perspectives on Gender and Science*, Lewes, Falmer Press.

HARDING, S. and HINTIKKA, M.B. (Eds) (1983) *Discovering Reality: Feminist Perspectives on Epistemology, Metaphysics, Methodology and Philosophy of Science*, Dordrecht, Reidel Publishing Company.

IMSEN, G. (1987) *Motivation Structure and Value Orientation in Women*, preliminary report (unpublished), Trondheim, University of Trondheim, Institute of Teacher Training.

JORDE, D. and LEA, A. (1987) 'Girls in school science', ongoing project at The Centre for Science Education, University of Oslo.

KAHLE, J.B. (1985) 'Retention of girls in science: Case study of secondary science teachers' in KAHLE, J.B. (Ed.) *Women in Science: A Report from the Field*, Lewes, Falmer Press.

KELLY, A., SMAIL, B. and WHYTE, J. (1984) *Initial GIST Survey: Results and Implications*, Manchester, Girls into Science and Technology.

KELLER, E.F. (1985) *Reflections on Gender and Science*, New Haven, CT, Yale University Press.

KESSLER, S.J. and MCKENNA, W. (1978) *Gender: An Ethnomethodological Approach*, New York, John Wiley & Sons.

KVANDE, E. (1984) *Kvinner og hogere teknisk utdanning. Delrapport 2: Integrert eller utdefinert?* (Transl: *Women and Higher Education in Technology. Report 2: Integrated or Out-defined?* Trondheim, Institute for Research on Industrial Environment, IFIM, SINTEF.

LAMBERT, H.A. (1978) 'Biology and equality: A perspective on sex differences', *Signs: Journal of Women in Culture and Society*, 4, pp. 97–117.

LEHRKE, M. *et al.* (Ed.) (1985) *Interests in Science and Technology Education*, Kiel, Institut für die Pädagogik der Naturwissenschaften.

LIE, S. and SJØBERG, S. (1984) *'Myk' jenter i 'harde' fag?* (Trans: *Soft girls in hard science?*) Oslo, Universitetsforlaget.

MATYAS, M.L. (1985) 'Factors affecting female achievement and interest in science and scientific careers' in KAHLE, J.B. (Ed.) *Women in Science: A Report from the Field*, Lewes, Falmer Press.

ROKEACH, M. (1983) *The Nature of Human Values*, London, Collier Macmillan Publishers.

SJØBERG, S. (1986) *Naturfag og norsk skole. Elever og loerere sier sin menign.* (Transl: *Science and Norwegian Schools. Pupils and Teachers Express Their Opinion*). Oslo, Universitetsforlaget.

SKOG, B. (1983) 'Curricular options — A barrier against women's participation in scientific and technological work?', in *GASAT II (1983)*.

SKOG, B. (1987) *Valgfrihet of Likhetsidealer.* (Transl: *Freedom of Choice and Ideas of Equity*). Project report, Trondheim, Institute of Sociology, University of Trondheim.

SMITHERS, A. and COLLINGS, J. (1981) 'Girls studying science in the sixth form', in KELLY, A. (Ed.) *The Missing Half*, Manchester, Manchester University Press, pp. 164–79.

ZIMAN, J. (1980) *Teaching and Learning about Science and Society*, Cambridge, Cambridge University Press.

12
Gender and Science Education II

Jane Butler Kahle

Introduction

For several years I have pondered a puzzle, well known to educators and scientists alike, which has some pieces clearly in place. Those pieces, labeled role models, ability, relevance, interest, anxiety and careers, only partially complete the puzzle. They only partially answer the questions: Why do so few girls enrol in optional science courses and elect scientific and technological careers? Why do women, compared with men, in scientific and technological jobs have lower rates of success and promotion? Recently, I have begun to collect other pieces of the puzzle which may allow us to complete it. The new pieces, gathered from international projects, research, and perspectives, are labeled: skills, image, experience, stereotypes, and instructional style. Along with others, I began to focus on the popular image of science, to analyze it, and to examine its effect on girls in school and on women in science.

The Image of Science

Science and Scientists Are Masculine

The words of our students portray vividly and clearly the popular, and accepted, image of science. Consider the following examples.

> A 15-year-old girl in America says: 'Men are scientists. It is a masculine job career, women don't go into it because being a scientist will make them look bad.' (Kahle, 1983)

> A composite picture of a scientist, developed from student drawings in Britain, suggests that a scientist is ... '[a] man in white coat with a bald

head and glasses, writing on a clipboard, standing in front of a bench covered with apparatus.' (Weinreich-Haste, 1981)

A female preservice science teacher in Western Australia remarks: 'A typical scientist ... actually could [be] the everyday average man. But their [sic] ways of thinking would appear to me to [be] a lot more broader. Broader in the sense of a question is being asked about everything. There is this continual attempt to find a new way, something more interesting, more innovative. He does appear to me in some way crazy.' (Rennie, 1986)

A 15-year-old Australian girl paints a vivid picture, when she says: 'A scientist is totally involved in work. Therefore, they don't care about appearance. [They] wear white coats, have beards — 'cause they're men. They just seem to care only about their science work. ... They don't care about meals. Somedays they starve themselves. They walk around with their science brain all day, and they've got their laboratories'. (Kahle, 1986)

These verbal images are dramatically reinforced by the visual ones which students and teacher trainees sketch when asked to 'Draw-a-scientist'. For example, a collection of over 170 drawings by Australian school children clearly portray scientists as white males (92 per cent), dressed in laboratory coats (63 per cent), and wearing glasses (86 per cent). Similarly, American 15-year-olds studying biology most frequently draw male scientists. Mason (1986) and Gardner (1986) collected drawings from over 450 American biology students as part of two projects, designed to encourage girls to take optional science courses. Approximately 88 per cent of the students in the control classes drew male scientists, while only 73 per cent of the students, involved in one of the three interventions, drew men. Similar results have been obtained in New Zealand and Norway. Eighty-seven per cent of the drawings by early adolescents (ages 12 and 13) in New Zealand are of men, while 80 per cent of the drawings of 10-year-old Norwegian children portray a male scientist. Internationally, at least in a range of countries, a scientist is visualized as a white, near-sighted male who has little regard for his personal appearance.

Not only students but also teachers hold stereotypic images of scientists. Rennie's (1986) analysis of seventy-nine drawings of scientists by Australian teacher trainees in their last year of preparation yielded the following picture: a white male (82 per cent) with 'unruly' hair (58 per cent) who wears a lab coat (57 per cent) and holds test tubes (56 per cent). When Rennie tried to describe the nature of the scientists drawn, she classified 51 per cent as looking 'somewhat unusual,' 21 per cent as appearing 'definitely crazy', 16 per cent as looking 'puzzled' and only 12 per cent as seeming 'ordinary'.

The images of scientists drawn by both children and teachers are not unusual, and they match the results found thirty years ago by Mead and Metreaux (1957), Chambers (1983) and Schibeci (1986). Furthermore, the image of a scientist, revealed by the words and drawings of our students, is not only male (i.e., a man scientist), but also it embodies traits associated with masculinity such as being cold, hard, unemotional, tenacious, logical and analytical.

Today, in the minds of our students and in the perceptions of their teachers, science is masculine. Indeed, the scientist has replaced the cowboy in the adolescent's imagination as the hero, or anti-hero, who is fearless, strong and lone. It is futile to argue that because that image might be largely derived from the media — television, movies, and advertisements — we are helpless to change it. There is a wealth of evidence to support the contention that, regardless of how, when, and where the masculine image of science evolved, schools and universities, teachers and professors, sustain it. In fact, gender is recontextualized within schools so that 'the notion of appropriate behaviour for each sex [is] converted into appropriate academic disciplines' (MacDonald, 1980). Once a subject has acquired a gender status, in this case, masculine, participation in it is seen to reinforce a boy's masculinity and to diminish a girl's femininity. The reverse is obviously true for subjects stereotyped as feminine such as French or typing.

Within the sciences, we find a shading of images; for example, students rate physics as more masculine than chemistry, which is followed by biology. Lesley Parker (1985) has said that 'most academic disciplines tend to be defined in terms of what males are good at. Science is no exception. To many people, *real science* means so-called *hard science*' (p. 16). This distinction permeates the thinking of many, including some science teachers, one of whom replied to a query about differential enrolment patterns in science for Western Australian students by saying: 'Real students take physics and chemistry' (Kahle, 1986). Garratt (1986) explains the dichotomy in the following way:

> Biology is perhaps perceived as being relevant to girls of all abilities, but only appropriate for boys of average ability. Conversely, physics may be seen as suitable for a broad ability band of boys, but only for girls of high ability. (p. 68)

The perception that physical science is tough, hard and analytical leads to its more masculine image, an image that is reflected in teacher and student participation patterns.

What, then, is the relationship of the established and evident image of science with gender and science education? Image is related to imagination; therefore, the image of science or of scientists may be inaccurate and fanciful. Furthermore, the image of science as masculine has developed with respect to the practice of science, not science education (Kelly, 1985). Gender, according to Evelyn Fox Keller (1986), is '... what a culture makes of sex — it is the cultural transformation of male and female infants into adult men and women' (p. 122). A consideration of gender and science education, therefore, provides an opportunity to re-examine the acculturation of both boys and girls within the context of learning science in schools. It is to be hoped that, as teachers and scientists, we may find ways to infuse science education with an accurate and neutral image.

Perpetuating the Masculine Image

What is the effect of the masculine image of science on science education? Alison Kelly maintains that 'the masculinity of science is often ... the prime reason that girls tend to avoid the subject at school.' Furthermore, she suggests that 'schools could play a transformative, rather than a reproductive role, in the formation of gender identities' (Kelly, 1985, p. 133). Science education, therefore, could affect the roles and opportunities which are culturally assigned to boys and girls.

According to Kelly (*ibid.*), there are at least four distinct senses in which science is masculine.

1 In terms of *numbers*; that is, who studies science at school, who teaches precollege and college science, and who are recognized as scientists (national academies, Nobel Laureates, fellowships and research grants, etc.).
2 In terms of *packaging*; that is, the way science is presented, the curricula and instructional techniques, the applications and examples as well as the texts and other published materials.
3 In terms of *practice*; that is, classroom behaviors and interactions including teacher expectancies, sex role stereotyping, student-teacher interactions and student-student interactions.
4 In terms of *biological differences*; that is, genetic or hormonal factors.

Since biological differences are largely hypothetical, have been analyzed elsewhere (Kahle, in press), and cannot be directly affected by schools, let us examine the first three points. That is, how do the *numbers, packaging* and *practice* of science education today reinforce both science's masculine image and enhance gender differences? And, how can science education tomorrow contribute to a neutral image and reduce gender differences?

Who does science?

The number of boys and girls who study science and of men and women who practise science contributes to its masculine image. In one sense, the media's image of a white male scientist accurately reflects the situation; there are more men scientists and they have higher status.

In primary education where the great majority of teachers are usually women, the real issue lies behind the overt numbers of students and teachers and in the covert ways in which boys and girls experience science. We have found that boys and girls bring different science experiences to school and that in school they receive very different science educations. From England (Smail, 1985), the US (Kahle and Lakes, 1983) and Australia (Parker and Rennie, 1986), there is clear documentation that fewer girls than boys handle science equipment, perform science experiments, or participate in science-related activities. The different experiences and interests in science that boys and girls bring to primary school science are perpetuated by the schools. The 'numbers game' in primary school is a subtle one. Equal numbers of girls and boys sit through science lessons, but they participate in them in unequal ways.

The image of science and science courses becomes more masculine in secondary school where the numbers of boys taking science and of men teaching science increase. In the US only 24 per cent of secondary school science teachers are women and it can be safely said that most of them teach biology. In the UK women comprise only 16 per cent of the teachers of chemistry and physics but 50 per cent of secondary biology teachers. In Western Australia women fill 75 per cent of the biology (including human biology) teaching positions, 54 per cent of general science ones, but only 8.6 per cent of chemistry, physics and physical science positions combined.

The ratio of male to female teachers is also clearly reflected in the ratio of students enrolled in various courses. In England boys constitute 70–80 per cent of all examination entries in physics, 60 per cent of all candidates in chemistry, but only 30–40 per cent of the biology examinees (Kelly, 1985). In the US the pattern is similar. Although virtually all high school students take biology, which functions as a required, introductory science course, only 30 per cent of high school girls, compared to 39 per cent of boys, take chemistry; physics, taken by 26 per cent of all high school boys, is studied by only 14 per cent of American girls. Enrolment data in Western Australia reveal a similar pattern. The percentage of girls taking the Tertiary Entrance Examination (TEE) in science reflects their enrollments. In Western Australia girls constitute 72 per cent of all students taking the TEE in human biology, 58 per cent in biology, 38 per cent in chemistry and 28 per cent in physics. Hildebrand (1987) reports that although the proportion of girls who complete year 12 in

Victoria has risen to 57 per cent, girls composed only 25 per cent of the physics and 40 per cent of the chemistry candidates. The numbers, whether of students or of teachers, suggest that science, particularly physical science, is masculine.

In terms of numbers, 30 per cent of college-bound high school senior women, compared to 50 per cent of high school senior men, intend to study science and engineering in college in the United States (NSF, 1986). In the UK the following male to female ratios were found for university examination entries in 1983: mathematics 3 : 1, chemistry 2 : 1 and physics 4 : 1. National data in Australia also suggest that, while women are entering tertiary courses related to biology, few are found in ones requiring physics. The percentages of women enrolled nationally by specific science faculties are: 33 per cent in science, 40 per cent in medicine, 30 per cent in dentistry, but only 7.5 per cent in engineering.

Among tertiary staff, the proportion of women to men decreases as academic rank increases. In the US, for example, women are twice as likely as men to be hired in non-tenure track positions (Hornig, 1987). Differences in promotion rates for men and women scientists in academia endure even when they are matched by type of institution, age and degree. A fascinating study of British radio astronomers has concluded that there is no evidence that the divergent career paths of women and men are the result of differences in scientific ability, yet differences in favor of the men existed for each matched pair (Irvine and Martin, 1986). As the authors say, 'early promise gives way to the frustration of unfulfilling jobs and any initial brilliance fades into obscurity much in the manner of a shooting star' (p. 98).

In industry as well as academia the numbers who do science and who are recognized as scientists favor males. Although Rossiter (1982) describes opportunities the government historically provided for the employment of US women scientists, Vetter (1987) portrays a different situation today. Although the numbers of women scientists and engineers have remained stable, their average civil-service grade and, therefore, salary are below those of men in the same fields.[1]

Both Vetter (*ibid.*) and Zuckerman (1987) have examined the numbers of women in relation to awards and recognition in science. Zuckerman postulates that there are no great differences in rewards for men and women scientists, saying that '... most have received few or none' (p. 142). She explains that women only constitute 2–3 per cent of the major academies and 2 per cent of Nobel Laureates because they are sparsely represented among full professors in major research universities.[2] However, Zuckerman ignores the differences in numbers of men and women who receive early recognition by fellowships received or by proposals funded. Such early rewards clearly affect future career opportunities (Long, 1987). Matyas (1985) and Vandervoort (1985), respectively, address two other types of awards — doctoral or postdoctoral fellowships, and role and status in professional associations. During doctoral studies, US women, compared with men, hold fewer National Science Foundation or other federal fellowships. In comparison with men, women students are more likely to support themselves (45 per cent female: 30 per cent male) and are less likely to hold university research assistantships (12 per cent female: 22 per cent male). Comparable numbers of men and women doctoral students hold teaching assistantships (approximately 20 per cent). Vandervoort reports that few US women hold offices in professional associations. However, the numbers and activities of women in various scientific societies vary considerably.

There are clear indications that science education has not reversed the *numbers game*. For example, researchers in Norway complain that female enrolment in tertiary engineering courses is effectively capped by the number of secondary girls (33 per cent) who elect physics at school. In the US Vetter (1987) reports that female enrolments in science and engineering majors peaked in 1984 and are slowly eroding.[3] A national study of US high school students, *High School and Beyond*, indicates that only 14 per cent of girls, compared with 40 per cent of boys, chose science majors in college. The effect of the numbers who do science cannot be underestimated. A study of 627 men and women science and engineering students at Stanford University concludes that '... When women were present in the largest number (medicine and biological sciences), the women surveyed demonstrated the least amount of self doubt and reticence to assert themselves' (AAC, 1986). Clearly, the actual numbers of men who do science, who teach science and who are recognized as scientists contribute to its masculine image today.

How is science packaged?

Texts, published materials, posters, library books, examples and exemplars all portray more male scientists and incorporate more of their work. Due to publisher guidelines, US textbooks now have 50 per cent of all illustrations and diagrams showing females and 17 per cent depicting blacks. However, those cosmetic changes mask the lack of substantive ones. For example, in the 1985 editions of two popular high school biology texts, between 75 per cent and 98 per cent of the cited scientific work described the contributions of men, while women's work was cited between 2 per cent and 4 per cent. Kerrie Mullins-Gunst's (1985) thorough analysis of thirty-nine chemistry books in Australia shows that only eighteen of the 140 (12.9 per cent) identifiable images in the six most commonly-used books are female. Furthermore, she explains that only five of the eighteen women are pictured without men present and that none of the six books contained an illustration of a female chemist from history. She relates that female images are 'depicted walking around, calling, showering, watching a waterfall, collecting aluminium cans, filling a car with petrol, wearing mascara or as nurses' (pp. 218–19). Perhaps the worst indictment from this study is that, in the more recent editions, pictures of women have been replaced by pictures of machinery.

Overall, science texts contribute to science's masculine image. As a physics lecturer at Macquarie University, New South Wales, explains, 'The masculine image of physics has been created in part by school and university textbooks in which only men appear in illustrations and words such as *her, hers,* and *she* don't get a mention' (Friedlander, 1986). The relationship of packaging and practice is discussed by Whyte (1986), who says:

> Bias in textbooks, and the lack of a motivating social context are thus two of the criticisms of the way the *content* of science ignores or bypasses girls' interests. The *process* of science teaching and learning is also discouraging to girls. (p. 91).

How is classroom science practised?

It is when we examine the practice of classroom science that we realize that schools are reproductive, not transforming agents, of gender differences and of the masculine image of science. Furthermore, it is in the practice of science in schools and classrooms that science education can have an effect. The practice of science involves interaction patterns between students and teachers, expectations of students by teachers, and sex-role stereotyping by students and teachers as well as the style and manner of teaching. Recently, a great deal has been written about classroom interaction patterns. The masculine identity of science is reinforced by participation patterns in the classroom where boys dominate discussions, equipment and teacher attention. Indeed, the physical space of the science laboratory is often pre-empted by boys. As Alison Kelly (1985) has said:

> The ordinary, everyday, taken-for-granted ways that boys behave form a link between masculinity and dominance in science. These behaviors are commonplace — so commonplace that they are virtually invisible. (p. 141)

The toughness, a key component of adolescent masculinity which is demonstrated by physical roughness on the playing field and verbal bravado in the classroom, is clearly evident in science classrooms. In fact, Whyte (1986) maintains that 'The *masculization* of science is forcefully underlined in the ways boys succeed in turning every aspect of the learning process into a *macho* endeavour' (p. 32). She cites example after example of boys 'dominating discussions' and 'hogging resources', while girls are left to 'fetch and carry' in the classrooms studied by GIST.[4]

In the US, elementary (primary) as well as secondary teachers on the average interact more with male than with female students in mathematics and science lessons (Eccles, 1985; Sadker and Sadker, 1985; Webb, 1984). According to Leinhardt *et al.* (1979), elementary-aged boys, compared to girls, receive six more hours of one-on-one mathematics instruction during one year. The cumulative effect of thirty-six additional hours of individual instruction during elementary school may help to account for the fact that boys' achievement levels in mathematics surpass those of girls' by the end of those years. Similarly, study after study documents that girls and boys enter primary school with equal interest in science but with unequal experiences in science (Kelly, 1985; Kahle and Lakes, 1983, Iliams, 1985). By the time girls graduate from high school, they lag far behind boys (on average) in science and mathematics achievement.

Girls' lack of science experiences is exacerbated by differential teacher behavior toward boys and girls. Ethnographic studies by Tobin and others document that boys and girls do not receive the same science and mathematics education. Boys are asked more higher order cognitive questions than are girls (Tobin and Garnett, 1986; Tobin and Gallagher, 1987) and boys are urged to 'try harder' when they do not succeed (Sadker and Sadker, 1985). Although teachers give boys specific instructions for completing a problem, they may show girls how to finish a task or do it for them. The subtle message for students is that boys have the ability to succeed in science and mathematics but that girls do not. A recent study suggests that this non-verbal message may account for a large portion of the gender differences observed in science achievement; for it causes girls to lose self-confidence in their scientific ability. Linn and her co-workers have examined the use of the 'I don't know' response by students on content items of the 1976–77 National Assessment of Educational Progress' science survey. They have found that 13- and 17-year-old girls are far more likely than boys to use the 'I don't know' response, especially on physical science items or items with masculine references. In fact, the study does not support traditional explanations such as better spatial ability or more positive science attitudes for boys' superior performance on the science items. Instead, they report that gender-related differences in responses are due to lack of confidence and to differences in prior instruction (Linn *et al.*, 1987).

Hildebrand (1987) cites studies which demonstrate that girls have fewer verbal exchanges with teachers, and Hyde (1986) reports that although one of her purposes was to interest girls in physics, recorded student-teacher interaction patterns in her classes show that she spent 82 per cent of her time with boys.

When teachers are asked to identify scientifically talented or gifted students, a cross-cultural pattern emerges. Both Australian and American teachers identify more boys. When observers record both the number and duration of teachers' interactions with the identified creative girls and boys, they find that teachers interact twice as often with the boys and for longer durations. In England, Margaret Spear (1984) has analyzed the marking of science papers attributed to 12-year-old boys and girls and has found that more male and female science teachers give higher marks when the work is attributed to a boy.

More subtle and, therefore, more dangerous, is the possibility that as teachers learn to monitor their verbal behavior patterns, they may continue non-verbally to communicate differential expectations. For example, studies document that teachers use the following strategies to indicate anticipation of a superior performance: leaning forward, looking into eyes, nodding and smiling. The critical problem with differential expectations is that they are group-based; that is, achievement expectations become a function of one's sex and/or race. Since students cannot change their sex and/or race, they accept the achievement expectation as something they cannot change. For example, Rowell (1971) reports that teachers who expected girls to have problems learning physics had girls who achieved less well than boys did. However, no achievement differences were found between girls and boys who were enrolled in physics classes taught by teachers who did not hold such views.

Sex-role stereotyping has become a new piece in the puzzle because our focus on who holds sex-role stereotypes has changed. Prior to the GIST study, it was assumed that stereotypic views of feminine appropriate roles influenced girls to avoid the physical sciences. The four-year British project, however, documented consistently that boys, from ages 11–14, held much stronger and more stereotypic views of appropriate careers for women than girls did. Indeed, casual expressions of disbelief or of disapproval from their male peers may be the most consistent and effective message girls receive concerning appropriate behavior and interest. Boys' responses to an occupational stereo-type inventory of thirty jobs indicated strong disapproval of 'masculine' activities for girls. Furthermore when boys and girls were asked to rate themselves on masculine/feminine scales, the boys consistently described themselves as higher on the masculine scale and lower on the feminine one. Girls' self-ratings, on the other hand, were more moderate. Whyte (1986) describes one effect of sex-role stereotyping when she reports, 'The chief barrier to girls opting for traditional "boys" crafts seems to be the fear of being uncomfortably visible in a male dominated group' (p. 146). That fear is omnipotent as girls make their subject choices, as they think about future careers, and as they separate out real from actual options.

What is the effect of the masculine image of science on students? Kelly *et al.* (1984) concluded that adolescent girls who perceive science as masculine performed less well in science. Smithers and Collings (in Johnston, 1986) suggested that secondary school girls who continue in physical science were generally less concerned with emphasizing their femininity and were less influenced by their peers. Gardner's (1986) study of women university students following three courses, all of which required high aptitudes and interests in science but each of which varied in its gender image, revealed differences among the three groups of students. She asked women students in engineering, biology and nursing to complete a Personal Attributes Questionnaire on which they rated themselves according to masculine and feminine characteristics. She found that only 18.5 per cent of the women engineers and 23 per cent of women biologists, compared with 42 per cent of the nursing students, rated themselves as typically feminine. The majority of the engineering and biology female students (62 per cent and 64 per cent, respectively) selected characteristics which classified them as either masculine or androgynous. Those classifications required high self-ratings on characteristics such as self-confidence and tenacity. However, Newton (1986) found that young women enrolled in engineering courses in Britain stressed the feminine aspects of their personalities, perhaps, in order to appear to be less different or unusual than women in other courses. The overwhelmingly masculine image of science might affect a girl's personal image as well as her attitudes towards other women in science. As Evelyn Fox Keller said, 'I am even more ashamed to admit that out of my desire to be taken seriously as a physicist I was eager to avoid identification with other female students who I felt could not be taken seriously' (AAC, 1982, p. 4).

Changing the Image of Science

Affecting Practice and Package

Can the image of science be changed? Alterations in both the practising and packaging of sciences in schools can and will affect both its numbers and image. For example, in primary schools do teachers:

> praise the loudest 'pops' when children are making hydrogen or the most beautiful soap bubbles? These seemingly insignificant choices set the tone of the lessons and influence the image of science presented to the class as harmful or caring. (Smail, 1985, p. 30)

At all levels, do they enhance equitable opportunities in science education? That is, are children allowed to call out answers? Are laboratory groups structured so that all have opportunities to 'do science?' Are basic skills reinforced? Do lessons incorporate tasks which develop spatial abilities? Studies of teachers who are successful in encouraging girls suggest that the way teachers *practise* science education makes a difference (Whyte, 1986; Rennie *et al.*, 1985; Kahle, 1985). In addition, positive practices may affect career, or option, choices. The influence of successful US high school biology teachers on the subsequent choice of college major by their students was assessed by Kahle (1983). When biology majors were asked to rank on a 1 to 5 scale (1 = very important to 5 = not applicable) various people who had influenced their decision to study biology in universities, the following average ratings were obtained: high school biology teacher (1.74), father (1.95), mother (2.32) and high school counselor (3.58). Clearly, the practice of science can affect who continues to study science.

In 1981 Galton identified three teaching styles in science: *problem solvers*, which involves a high frequency of teacher questions and a low frequency of pupil-initiated interactions; *informers*, which uses teacher delivery of facts and an infrequent use of questions except to recall facts; and *enquirers*, which uses pupil-initiated and maintained experiments as well as inferring, formulating, and testing hypotheses. Three major studies (Kahle, 1985; Whyte, 1986; and Johnson and Murphy, 1986) support Galton's conclusion that girls prefer the third style of teaching; that is, the enquirers. Interestingly, it is the style most often used in biology classes (often selected by girls), while the problem solver style is more frequently used in physics (which few girls elect to study).

Kelly (1985) asserts that the two main mechanisms by which the masculinity of science is constructed are boy-oriented curriculum packages and male-dominated classroom interactions. Both the practice and packaging recontextualize the gender appropriateness of science education for boys. Transforming society's gender identifications must involve both teachers and schools. Judith Whyte explains the effect of school science, as practised today, on girls' attitudes, interests, and achievement levels.

> The day-to-day experience of school science, its contents and teaching methods, must have contributed to the negative attitudes so generally displayed, but were beyond the power of GIST to change. Sex typing in subject choice is the outcome of complex processes in which girls' motivations and aspirations are powerfully affected by the expectations of those around them. (Whyte, 1986, p. 246)

Affecting Gender and Image

One solution to the lack of girls in science, which has attracted attention and some popularity in both England and Australia, is to foster single sex schools or, at least, single sex classes in mathematics and science in coeducational schools. I do not think that this piece completes the puzzle. Science is not truly masculine; that is, it is not cold, aloof, calculating, and isolated. Rather, it is a social, cooperative endeavor. Science is practised by both men and women, but effective collaboration may be impossible if the more sex-role stereotyped boys do not constantly and continually see girls in a science context, learn to share equally and cooperatively with girls in science classes, and accept as ordinary girls' achievement and enjoyment of mathematics and science. For example, Kelly (1985), indeed, has postulated that maintaining gender differentiation is not primarily due to teacher interactions in schools, but rather it is due to the behavior of children themselves. Separate, but supposedly equal, science classes will perpetuate, rather than transform the stereotypic roles society places on children. Whyte (1986) and others address the immediate value of single sex classes. 'Single-sex grouping (classes) in mixed schools seems to have a positive influence on girls' attitudes in science' (p. 236). However, she reports that '... the largest shift [in attitudes] was at Edgehill, a school where no single-sex grouping took place' (pp. 236–7). As a result, Whyte concludes that a feminist spirit, i.e., a belief in the ability and aptitudes of girls, imbued into mixed schools would solve the puzzle.

There is no doubt that society is responsible for both the masculine image of science and the gender identification of girls and boys. However, schools are responsible for reproducing and reinforcing both stereotypes. As Delamont (1983) states, '... schools have been more conservative about sex roles than either homes or wider society' (p. 242). Barriers to equitable science education include conflicting priorities in the schools, structure of the economy, and sex-role concept (Whyte, 1986). They also include the general ethos of schools, the attitudes of teachers, particularly those in elementary schools, the rigid sex-role stereotypes of boys and the prevalence of teaching patterns in secondary schools which reinforce male behaviors.

We know that the puzzle can be solved by individual teachers practising certain behaviors and instructional strategies and rigidly demanding non-sexist texts and instructional materials. Researchers, who have sought to identify factors leading to excellent and equitable science education and who have analyzed curricula, teacher behaviors and classroom climates, concur that an ideal science classroom or curriculum equally benefits all students (both boys and girls). A researcher in Colorado, after a six-month case study of a science teacher, noted for her success in motivating girls to continue to study science, summarized that premise in the following way:

> I think that rather than identifying a teacher who consciously encour-
> ages females in science, we have simply identified a very good teacher,
> whose talent, commitment, and rapport with her students combine to

make the study of science an interesting and enjoyable endeavour. (Kahle, 1983, p. 26)

Schools and teachers may play a transforming role, one which will allow all students to view both science and scientists in a different way.

Notes

1 According to Vetter (1987), women comprise 20.3 per cent of all federal chemists yet their average salaries equal only 79.2 per cent of male federal chemists' salaries. Likewise, women microbiologists, working for the government (37.2 per cent of the total), receive average salaries which are 78.7 per cent of men's salaries. In civil engineering, where women (4.4 per cent of the total) are younger than their male colleagues, their salaries average 73.9 per cent of men's salaries.

2 The percentage of women in various academies of science are: Deutsche Akademie der Naturforscher Leopoldina (1982) — 2.1 per cent; National Academy of Sciences (1986) — 3.4 per cent; Academie des Sciences (1982) — 2.3 per cent; Royal Society of London (1982) — 3.2 per cent (Zuckerman, 1987, p. 143).

3 Vetter (1987) notes that in the US bachelor degrees awarded to women have leveled off, and that recent surveys of incoming fresher women indicate a continuation of that trend. She projects that in computer science and mathematics alone women graduates could drop from a high of 22,400 in 1986 to about 9600 in 1989.

4 GIST (Girls in Science and Technology) was a four-year project in a large manufacturing area in the UK. Alison Kelly and Judith Whyte, project directors, carried out an intervention program in ten comprehensive schools, involving approximately 2000 children.

References

AMERICAN ASSOCIATION OF COLLEGES (AAC) (1982) 'The classroom climate: A chilly one for women?' *Project on the Status and Education of Women*. Washington, DC, AAC, pp. 1–22.

AMERICAN ASSOCIATION OF COLLEGES (AAC) (1986) *Project on the Status and Education of Women*, Washington, DC, AAC, 14, 4, 8.

CHAMBERS, D.W. (1983) 'Stereotypic images of the scientist: The draw-a-scientist test', *Science Education*, 67, pp. 255–65.

DELAMONT, S. (1983) 'The conservative school? Sex roles at home, at work and at school' in WALKER, S. and BARTON, L. (Eds) *Gender, Class and Education*, Lewes, Falmer Press.

ECCLES, J.S. (1985) 'Sex differences in achievement patterns' in SONDEREGGER, T. (Ed) *Nebraska Symposium of Motivation*, Vol. 2, Lincoln, University of Nebraska Press.

FRIEDLANDER, N. (1986) 'Why physics fails to woo the female', *The Australian*, 10 November, p. 15.

GARDNER, A.L. (1986) 'Effectiveness of strategies to encourage participation and retention of precollege and college women in science', unpublished doctoral dissertation, West Lafayette, IN, Purdue University.

GARRATT, L. (1986) 'Gender differences in relation to science choice at A-level, *Educational Review*, 38, 1, pp. 67–76.

HILDEBRAND, G.M. (1987) 'Girls and the career relevance of science: A case study', unpublished Master's thesis, Melbourne, Monash University.

HORNIG, L.S. (1987) 'Women graduate students: A literature review and synthesis' in DIX, L.S. (Ed) *Women: Their Underrepresentation and Career Differentials in Science and Engineering* Washington, DC, National Academy Press, pp. 103–26.

HYDE, S. (1986) 'Girls and science — strategies for change', *Pivot*, 3, pp. 28–30.

ILIAMS, C. (1985) 'Early school experience may limit participation of women in science', *Contributions to the Third GASAT Conference*, London, Chelsea College.

IRVINE, J. and MARTIN, B. (1986) 'Women in radio astronomy — shooting the stars?' in HARDING, J. (Ed.) *Perspectives on Gender and Science*, London, Falmer Press, pp. 80–102.

JOHNSON, S. and MURPHY, P. (1986) 'Girls and physics: Reflections on APU Findings', *APU Occasional Paper No. 4*, London, University of Leeds and Kings College.

JOHNSTON, S. (1984). 'Girls need a science education too', *Australian Science Teachers Journal*, 30, 2, pp. 18–23.

KAHLE, J.B. (1983) 'Factors affecting the retention of girls in science courses and careers: Case studies of selected secondary schools', *Final Report* (NSF 83-SP-0798), Washington, DC, National Science Foundation.

KAHLE, J.B. (1985) 'Retention of girls in science: Case studies of secondary teachers' in KAHLE, J.B. (Ed) *Women in Science: A Report from the Field*, Lewes, Falmer Press, pp. 193–229.

KAHLE, J.B. (1986) 'Equitable science education: A discrepancy model', Haydn Williams public lecture, Perth, Western Australian Institute of Technology, 17 October.

KAHLE, J.B. (in press) 'SCORES: A project for change', *International Journal of Science Education*.

KAHLE, J.B. and LAKES, M.K. (1983) 'The myth of equality in science classrooms', *Journal of Research in Science Teaching*, 20, pp. 131–40.

KELLER, E.F. (1986) 'How gender matters: Or, why it's so hard for us to count past two' in HARDING, J. (Ed.) *Perspectives on Gender and Science*, Lewes, Falmer Press, pp. 168–83.

KELLY, A. (1985) 'The construction of masculine science', *British Journal of Sociology of Education*, 6, 2, pp. 133–53.

KELLY, A., WHYTE, J. and SMAIL, B. (1984) *Final Report of the GIST Project*. Manchester, University of Manchester, Department of Sociology.

LEINHARDT, G., SEEWALD, A.M. and ENGEL, M. (1979) 'Learning what's taught: Sex differences in instruction', *Journal of Educational Psychology*, 71, pp. 432–9.

LINN, M.C., DE BENEDICTIS, T., DELUCCHI, K., HARRIS, A. and STAGE, E. (1987) 'Gender differences in national assessment of education progress science items: What does "I don't know" really mean?', *Journal of Research in Science Teaching*, 24, 3, pp. 267–78.

LONG, J.S. (1987) 'Discussion: Problems and prospects for research on sex differences in the scientific career' in DIX, L.S. (Ed) *Women: Their Underrepresentation and Career Differentials in Science and Engineering*, Washington, DC, National Academy Press, pp. 163–70.

MACDONALD, M. (1980) 'Schooling and the reproduction of class and gender relations' in BARTON, L., MEIGHAN, R. and WALKER, S. (Eds) *Schooling, Ideology and the Curriculum*, Lewes, Falmer Press.

MASON, C.L. (1986) 'Student attitudes toward science & science-related careers: An investigation of the efficacy of a high school biology teachers' intervention program', unpublished doctoral dissertation, West Lafayette, IN, Purdue University.

MATYAS, M.L. (1985) 'Obstacles and constraints on women in science', in KAHLE, J.B. (Ed) *Women in Science: A Report from the Field*, Lewes, Falmer Press, pp. 77–101.

MEAD, M. and METREAUX, R. (1957) 'The image of the scientist among high school children', *Science*, 126, pp. 384–9.

MULLINS-GUNST, K. (1985) 'An analysis of Australian chemistry textbooks', *Contributions to the Third GASAT Conference*, London, Chelsea College, University of London.

NATIONAL SCIENCE FOUNDATION (NSF) (1986) *Women and Minorities in Science and Engineering* (NSF 86-301), Washington, DC, National Science Foundation.

NEWTON, P. (1986) 'Female engineers: Femininity redefined?' in HARDING, J. (Ed.) *Perspectives on Gender and Science*, Lewes, Falmer Press, pp. 40–61.

PARKER, L.J. (1985) 'Non-sexist science education: An issue of primary concern', paper presented at the Science Teachers Association of Victoria Conference, Monash University, Melbourne, Australia, December.

PARKER, L.H. and RENNIE, L.J. (1986) 'Sex-stereotyped attitudes about science: Can they be changed?', *European Journal of Science Education*, 8, 2, 173–83.

RENNIE, L.J. (1986). 'The image of a scientist: Perceptions of preservice teachers', unpublished paper, University of Western Australia.

RENNIE, L.J., PARKER, L.H. and HUTCHINSON, P.E. (1985) 'The effect of inservice training on teacher attitudes and primary school science classroom climates', *Research Report Number 12*, University of Western Australia.

ROSSITER, M.W. (1982) *Women Scientists in America: Struggles and Strategies to 1940*, Baltimore, MD, Johns Hopkins University Press.

ROWELL, J.A. (1971) 'Sex differences in achievement in science and the expectations of teachers', *The Australian Journal of Education*, 15, 1, pp. 16–29.

SADKER, D., and SADKER, M. (1985) 'Is the OK classroom, OK?', *Phi Delta Kappan*, 55, pp. 358–61.

SCHIBECI, R.A. (1986) 'Images of science and scientists and science education', *Science Education*, 70, pp. 139–49.

SMAIL, B. (1985) 'An attempt to move mountains: The "girls into science and technology" (GIST) project', *Journal of Curriculum Studies*, 17, pp. 351–4.

SPEAR, M.G. (1984) 'Sex bias in science teachers' ratings of work and pupil characteristics', *European Journal of Science Education*, 6, pp. 369–77.

TOBIN, K. and GALLAGHER, J.J. (1987) 'The role of target students in the science classroom', *Journal of Research in Science Teaching*, 24, pp. 61–75.

TOBIN, K. and GARNETT, P. (1986) 'Gender differences in science activities', unpublished paper', Bentley, Western Australian Institute of Technology.

VANDERVOORT, F.S. (1985) 'Women's role in professional scientific organizations: Participation and recognition' in KAHLE, J.B. (Ed.) *Women in Science: A Report from the Field*, Lewes, Falmer Press.

VETTER, B.M. (1987) 'Women's progress', *Mosaic 18*, 1, pp. 2–9.

WEBB, N.M. (1984) 'Sex differences in interaction and achievement in cooperative small groups', *Journal of Educational Psychology*, 76, pp. 33–44.

WEINREICH-HASTE, H. (1981) 'The image of science' in KELLY, A. (Ed.) *The Missing Half*, Manchester, Manchester University Press.

WHYTE, J. (1986) *Girls into Science and Technology*, London, Routledge & Kegan Paul.

ZUCKERMAN, H. (1987) 'Persistence and change in the careers of men and women scientists and engineers: A review of current research' in DIX, L.S. (Ed.) *Women: Their Underrepresentation and Career Differentials in Science and Engineering*, Washington, DC, National Academy Press, pp. 127–62.

13
The Dilemma of Science, Technology and Society Education

Joan Solomon

Development and Dilemma

The growth of STS in the school curriculum was no tidy and well planned affair. It arose from a variety of causes, most of which were unimpeachable in purpose. And yet the subject is often contentious both in its nature and its method. It also highlights contradictions within science education itself. To some extent all educational theory is bound to entertain controversy: indeed it may well be healthy for it to do so. For STS the controversy — political as well as educational — is particularly sharp. Even for the student who participates in STS lessons there are tensions which attend other aspects of science to a much slighter degree.

The first part of this chapter will trace some of the main influences for the introduction of STS courses in our schools. In his book *Teaching and Learning about Science and Society* (1980) Ziman identified seven different possible approaches to the teaching of an STS course at tertiary level. All of these he managed to justify as valid and acceptable in some important sense. Looking back over recent history of STS at school level we find not just rationales proposed by innovating teachers but also the external pressures of politics and educational theory influencing curriculum. These forces contributed, from the start, to some inner conflicts and dilemmas of purpose.

The second part of the chapter will concern the students' reception of this knowledge. This will include classroom strategies, gender preferences, motivation and combination of the cognitive with the evaluative. These are no easy matters to explore, nor is there any great volume of research to draw upon. But in as far as STS courses deliberately set out to engage and develop the interests of the students in areas of great public concern, it has importance far beyond the classroom or the examination system.

The name *STS* for the whole genre of courses may be attributable to the influential collection of papers published under the name *Science Technology and Society* by Spiegel-Rosing and Price in 1977. By this date there was a small but vigorous international scholarly movement in *Science Studies* which examined the economic and political aspects of current science-based issues, as well as the history, sociology and philosophy of science itself. In Europe as EASST, and in North America as 4S such associations continue their work but, with few exceptions, there is precious little contact between them and the various educational groups which have sought to promote similar studies within school. This schism has been much to the detriment of the latter. The majority of school curriculum materials have been designed either by enthusiastic and self-taught teachers, or by professional industrialists and scientists without this science studies dimension to their thinking. On too many occasions this has produced courses with an intellectually flat, but content and evaluation rich, approach.

The Cultural Approach

The claim of science to be an integral and important part of the general culture is often traced back to C.P. Snow's influential lecture on *The Two Cultures*. This gave visibility to a claim which had been growing slowly since the beginning of the century and accelerating sharply since the Second World War. It was to have two different effects on education. In Britain the claim was gradually taken over by the science education community and used to argue that all children should have some science in their school curriculum, at least up to the age of 16.

But the kind of science education on offer was also to be changed. In the discussion paper of the Association for Science Education *Alternatives for Science Education* (1979) and their later *Education through Science* (1981) the emphasis was moved away from the kind of science education designed to prepare the most able for a university degree in science, towards a science for the citizen. The earlier paper proposed a whole year, at grade 8, entirely devoted to *science and society*. In the USA the report to the National Science Foundation by Hufstedler and Langenberg in 1982 shows a similar emphasis on developing a curriculum which would be more relevant to the community. It was a period when American education had been suffering from the *Back to Basics* movement and this report heralded a backlash which warned that science was diminished by being taught in this way, and urged the inclusion of scientific information related to personal, societal and vocational problems. The phrase 'scientific literacy' began to be heard and it was clear that some measure of real concern about the public understanding of science was being expressed. The National Science Foundation responded with recommendations for instruction on such themes as energy and the environment which would range 'from drill and practice to the simulation of complex problem situations'.

This comparatively modest movement towards relevance in science education was just one historical reaction to the growing importance of science in the curriculum. Another was more academic and cultural; it advocated a 'liberal studies in science' approach to secondary or tertiary level science education. Of the 'science greats' course at Manchester University, Jevons (1965) wrote,

> The precise core is provided by physical science, and it is supplemented by the more open-ended treatment of science considered from the economic, social, historical and philosophical points of view.

The emphasis on the history and philosophy of science claims a kind of continuity of thought with such venerable studies which had previously been embedded in other disciplines. Of course the history of science had never been totally excluded from the school science courses. Many textbooks were in the habit of including references to the 'Great Men' of science. Even the British school Nuffield courses which flourished in the 1960s drew attention to the historical development of a few scientific ideas, mostly in cosmology. The American PSSC and BCSC courses, dating from the same period, contain similar historical references. The objective, however, seemed to be more of a glorification of scientific progress than of an understanding of the problematic interactions between science and society.

The social history of technology is a more likely starting point for STS courses, and some classic school books did mention the industrial revolution in connection with energy and engines, or the production of explosives and fertilisers in connection with the chemistry of nitrates. Holmyard's widely used textbook of school chemistry (first published in 1925 and virtually unchanged up to 1960) is a particularly good example of an approach which might include both science and technology but had absolutely no ambition to foster interest in contemporary or controversial social issues.

Two of the earliest courses in school STS did, in their own ways, use philosophical or historical approaches. In 1972 Aikenhead and Fleming (1975) began work on a new tenth grade course for Canadian students — *Science a Way of Knowing* — which would allow them to make sense of their rapidly changing society. But Aikenhead wrote that the students made no progress without some instruction on different kinds of knowing.

> In our experience grade 10 students can seldom deal with the complex and sophisticated issues related to the interaction of science and society without having first achieved ... a way of recognising and handling the different types of knowledge involved. (Aikenhead, 1979)

At approximately the same time the Schools Council Integrated Science Project (SCISP) was developing a course in Britain which was similarly self-conscious about making explicit the thinking processes which might be used. Their textbooks spoke about searching for 'patterns' as the root activity of all science. In contrast to the previous example they included under this procedural banner the economic and social factors involved in the application of science, for example, *Science and Decision-making* (Hall, 1973).

The STS course which makes the most conscious use of historical preamble for teaching about topical issues is the later British course for grade 11 students, *SISCON-in-Schools* (Solomon, 1983). In each one of the eight different booklets recent history is used to show either how similar problems have been dealt with in the past, or how the quandaries of the present situation arose. The reason for this strategy is

> ... to stand back from the present and to see how technology and science (have) serve(d) a community ... (Addinell and Solomon, 1983)

This historical dimension is then used to establish a new perspective in matters which may be almost too controversial for useful immediate discussion.

Political Education for Action

The next influence for STS also came from outside the domain of school science. This was a movement which could be called 'Science for the People' and traced a heritage both from the left-wing scientists of the 1920s and 1930s (Haldane, Hogben, etc.) and also from those educationalists of the post–Second World War period who, like Skilbeck, wrote of education for 'social reconstruction'. The first SISCON *(Science In a Social CONtext)* movement for the teaching of STS within the tertiary sector shared many members with the British Society for Social Responsibility in Science. This in turn had been influenced by the international Pugwash movement and was permeated by many of the same ideals. For these activists it followed that the new science education should focus upon those issues about which citizens need to be educated for appropriate political action. Indeed the action itself was sometimes an explicit aim of the course.

In America environmental education was in many ways the precursor of STS education. It identified three kinds of skills to be developed in their students — cognitive skills which would enable them to understand issues, evaluative skills in which their affective reactions would be modified, and changes in behavioural action.

> ... responsible action denotes those behaviours engaged in for the purpose of achieving and/or maintaining a dynamic equilibrium

between quality of life and quality of the environment. Developing an
environmentally literate citizenry who are both willing and able to
engage in environmental action, is considered to be the ultimate goal
of environmental education. (Hines and Hungerford, 1984)

Since most of this environmental education was subsumed under social studies,
rather than science, its influence on later STS courses in Europe has been
regrettably small although more apparent in the growing movement for STS in
the States.

In countries such as Holland and Canada this more political theme
became apparent in the movement for STS within schools at much the same
time as public pressure groups became a common phenomenon, and laws to
allow freer public access to scientific knowledge were formulated and debated.
Acid rain pollution of the Great Lakes, the introduction of nuclear power in
Holland, Austria, and Sweden, mining for uranium in Australia and Canada —
all of these were local issues of problematique which merit an STS category
of their own later in this chapter. They are placed in the present context
because the issues were politically contentious and the courses based upon
them were strongly influenced by a public education objective to enable
citizens to partake in decision making action.

It is necessary, in STS courses, to recognise (social) forces, otherwise
you could be reduced to a puppet... to exert any real influence, which
is necessary to realize your social responsibility, is to transform
(insight from these courses) into action. (quoted in Rip, 1978)

Interdisciplinary Education and the Problematique Approach

All STS courses should be interdisciplinary and embrace elements from any of
the traditional science areas, as necessary. The justification for this assertion
becomes clear enough if we examine narrow efforts to show the application of
knowledge from one science discipline which touch on an STS theme. The
laudable idea of showing the relevance of school physics may, for example, lead
to a discussion of the electrostatic precipitation of solid particles in a factory
chimney flue. However, if the physics orientation prevents the discussion from
spreading into a consideration of acid rain, the desulphurization processes and
the subsequent disposal of sulphur, the effort is revealed as a very weak version
of real STS.

In most countries science education in the secondary school has developed
along disciplinary lines. Layton (1982) has outlined the long and checkered
history of integrated science in British education, but it is clear that modern

British schooling has called for, and is very slowly acquiring, a new kind of science teaching which does not measure its effectiveness by the demands of the most able. This permits its content to spread out beyond the usual subject limits. In other countries school science has always been multidisciplinary up to grades 8 or 9. This leads readily to an issue-based approach to STS teaching. But STS knows no frontiers and readily spills over into social studies, geography, religious studies and history, as well as the natural sciences. Many teachers have welcomed this as in keeping with a more holistic approach to education itself.

Interdisciplinarity can be a powerful enabler of STS and is also linked with it in more deeply theoretical ways. Ziman (1980) has pointed out how borrowing from different subject areas can dislodge 'the myth of scientism that there is a "science" (actual or potential) for dealing with every problem' (p. 117). In the school arena the ethical, cultural, and political aspects of any issue which cries out for STS treatment go further than debunking myths, they resurrect the vision of the great educators of every age.

But basing school STS education on the consideration of a series of issues has drawbacks as well as advantages. The issues are chosen because of their topicality, local, national or international, but the very heat engendered by such contentious issues, which may raise the students' motivation to learn, also all too often drives out any general lessons which may be drawn about the nature of science, technology or social decision making. The danger is all the stronger if the issues are taken in small packages, such as the British *Science and Technology in Society* (Holman, 1987). Here there is no definable course at all, just series of detachable leaflets each of which represents one lesson which is to be fitted into the 'interstices' of the normal school science curriculum in an order to be decided by the teacher.

The most attractive feature of the problematique approach to STS education is its extension to local topics which touch the students' community closely. Most of these materials have been produced by school teachers for their own pupils and are usually only printed by school reprographic centres. On a slightly larger scale we may find, for example, units from Israel on the development of fertilizers from the Dead Sea and the construction of a Mediterrean-Dead Sea canal. Sometimes a particular theme from health education may seem to be treated in the style of an STS issue, for example, fluoridation of water, or drugs and smoking (Zoller, 1985). But here we have topics which are not only important and close to the students' own experience, but which also carry a strongly didactic message from the teacher. It may be claimed that informed decision making is the objective of such a course; yet the existence of a predetermined goal in terms of the students' final frame of mind, reveal such units as different in spirit from those STS courses which aim to show that social decision making has no obvious *right answer*.

Vocational or Technocratic

The fourth and final strand comes out of an instrumental view of science and technology as the engine of industry which is itself the essential wealth-producer of society. In this kind of STS course the structure of industry is often studied for its own sake, e.g., *Science and Society* (Lewis, 1980) and not as that of a factional interest in the community's concerns. For the consideration of energy generation, environmental control, and the monitoring of new technology — all topics which figure largely in STS courses — the role of industry is too intimately identified with one line of argument for it to come credibly into the educational marketplace as a purveyor of STS courses. Many industries — Shell, BP and ICI to name but a few — have spent considerable sums on educational materials, but teachers of STS courses need to exercise care in their use if the students are to learn about all points of view of the topic.

In vocational courses it is essential for the students or apprentices to learn to see their work through the eyes of clients who will be using it. This means that courses for older school students such as those based on the British CPVE (Certificate of Pre-Vocational Education) may be required to study 'the impact of science and technology on our society' (*17+ A New Qualification, 1984*). Materials for this course have not been specified but they too seem likely to be strongly linked with the sponsoring concern.

In a wider context it has always been possible to view all education as a national investment. While the old belief in the 'trained mind' prevailed, no particular course of study needed to be specified so long as it was sufficiently taxing to stretch and train the mind. Science and technology were always too challenging and content-laden to fit comfortably into this scheme, and education adopted what Jevons (1967) has called the 'all or nothing' attitude towards science in the curriculum. Now that an education in science and technology is more highly valued for its contribution to industry, the attitude to their place in the general curriculum has changed in corresponding ways. It has been argued that some knowledge of the social and economic facets of science is essential for the mandarins of finance and the captains of industry. So some schools may believe that they face a challenge to begin the education of an elite who are destined to lead in the new science-based industries. This is STS for the technocrats — yet another dimension of vocational education.

Methods of Teaching STS

The special behavioural objectives of STS courses have led to some innovations in teaching method. It was clear that the aim to teach about the methods of decision making within society would be likely to involve classroom strategies which went some way towards mirroring them. Democratic debate in the political arena suggested classroom discussion. This, it was thought, would allow the students to make up their own minds while, at the same time, training them to be attentive to and tolerant of the views of others. So much was agreed by most teachers: the problem was how this should be achieved. Some teachers advocated free discussion right from the start of the course, others that important content should be taught as background to a later but more informed discussion. The stance of the teacher was also problematic. Much was written about the teacher as 'neutral chairman' of class discussion (see, for example, Stenhouse in *The Humanities Curriculum Project*, 1970); later it was suggested that the teacher's job was to present any side of the argument which had been omitted so that a 'balanced view' could be presented. Thirdly the argument that no teacher could, or should, hide their own views began to be heard. If the aim of an STS course was to encourage students to become responsible citizens who would participate in matters of public concern, was it sensible for teachers to pretend that they themselves had no opinion? Traditionalists have often accused STS teachers of indoctrinating the young and, unless teachers respond by representing all education as a kind of indoctrination, it is hard to see how they can defend themselves from the charge.

Gaming, simulations and role-play had only just begun to infiltrate the classroom, and were almost unknown in science lessons, before the advent of STS. The earliest appropriate games were often about the location of a power station, for example, Ellingham and Langton (1975). Since that time games and simulations have multiplied and diversified. There is now a great range from simple card games with large elements of fun and luck to more sophisticated and well documented packages where a number of outcomes are possible depending on the judgment of the individual players. With the growth of computer software for schools it was inevitable that some interactive materials on STS themes should have been produced. The best of these include considerable quantities of accessible data which enable the student to control various factors in a complicated environmental issue. In the larger sense, however, it does seem curious that a solitary activity in front of VDU should be used in place of interpersonal reactions for teaching the empathic listening to viewpoints of others which is so essential when difficult cultural and social issues are being considered.

Motivation and Gender Issues

The personal aspects of STS, and also how it is taught, have been claimed by several educationalists (for example, Harding, 1986) to be more comfortable to the way in which girls like to learn about science than is the traditional method.

The physical sciences have always had an impersonal image, and psychologists like Head (1980) have suggested that the adolescent boys who choose to study physics often do so because they feel more comfortable following an authoritarian line than having to recognize individual differences and to express personal opinions. Since these are some of the very characteristics which STS courses emphasize, and since factor analyses of girl and boy students often show that person-orientation is the most sharply differentiated characteristic of girls, it does seem likely that STS courses would help to redress the gender balance and attract girl students to the study of science.

But the problem of the motivation to study science goes beyond trying to produce what has been called 'girl-friendly' science. Studies in the United States and elsewhere have shown a steady decline in interest in science and in motivation for studying it during the years of secondary school education, and amongst boys as well as girls. Nor does it grow in popularity with the public at large. Several commentators have attributed this to a presumed uncaring attitude amongst scientists. The research of Fleming which will be described in the next section also supports this view. If this belief about science and scientists is widespread, then more STS education in schools might bring wider benefits than merely adding a liberal seasoning to the school syllabus. It might change the public view of science.

The nature of a subject is not uniquely determined by its subject matter: it is created by the community who practise it and is demonstrated in schools by those who teach it.

> Science is an institution in the world which is progressively presented to the child. The latter creates of science an object to which it then relates. The nature of this object and of the relationship to it will depend on the outcome of nurturing of the child, on the forms in which science is presented and how these interact. (Harding, 1986, p. 165)

The contradictions and dilemmas of this part of the analysis appear in that it is only those courses which aim to develop pupils' civic opinions and action which are attacked for being doctrinaire. And those features which might attract girls to science — openness and capacity for helping people — are at the opposite extreme to those for which adolescent boys so often choose to study it, and how the general public perceive it.

Thinking about Social Issues in Two Domains

STS courses have tended to make huge educational claims; with citizenship, decision making, and personal values at stake they have a great deal to aim for.

In her essay on *Teaching about Science, Technology and Society*, McConnell (1982) wrote

> Public decision making by citizens in a democracy requires an attitude of attentiveness; skills of gaining and using relevant knowledge; values of which one is aware and to which one is committed; and the ability to turn attitudes, skills and values into action. All these steps can be encouraged if a decision making perspective is incorporated into the educational process. (p. 13)

The time is ripe for some examination of these claims. In particular we shall want to know if STS courses do encourage the kind of citizen attentiveness that McConnell wants. This is the hub of the matter. We would be surprised if knowledge and the skills involved in gaining and using it were not teachable, at least to the more able students. That is the aim of most science courses. Likewise it is not particularly difficult to raise the affective side of problems in school classrooms and observe the values that students express. This is done frequently in religious and social studies. The more penetrating question is what happens when the value and the cognitive systems interact in the context of a science related issue. Do they produce attentiveness and a better decision making capability?

Many educationalists, like Mary Donaldson, have argued that children would learn better if the subject matter they were being taught was *embedded* in the thinking of the everyday world rather than being abstracted from it. It is an appealing idea and closely related to the argument about motivation for learning science which was mentioned in the previous section. Unfortunately, research results have not been entirely supportive of it. Henle (1962) showed how difficult it was for graduates to apply logical thinking to problems in which they were closely concerned. The same sort of result was obtained in the science classroom by Dreyfus and Jungwirth (1980) who compared how biology pupils applied logical reasoning in scientific and in everyday situations. It seemed that the affective and value laden attitudes provoked by the social context made the skills of applying knowledge or logical processes more difficult, especially for the less able pupils.

That evidence is not very surprising but it does highlight the difficulties that education in STS faces. When an issue has already been met and has raised affective judgments, the commonplace or life-world system of thinking, which uses value claims and typifications in place of logical argument and application of knowledge, may become paramount.

Several studies have shown that television may play a large part in informing viewers and raising their value judgments, but the evidence is less straightforward than is often assumed. Whilst it is true that many American studies of high school students (Weisenmayer *et al.*, 1984) have shown that they attribute the greater part of their knowledge of environmental issues to television, the same students are certainly not uniform in their value judgments. Studies on attitudes to television itself (for example, McQuail, 1983) have suggested that viewers interact with the information being presented almost as though it were a social occasion in which they were agreeing or disagreeing with a friend's opinion. Indeed he calls this process 'para-social interaction'. This implies that values will not be taken over wholesale from the media but negotiated through the channels of social or life-world thinking.

Investigations of the different methods of teaching recommended for STS have shown a mixture of results, partly at least because the researchers have looked for increases of enjoyment, of motivation for learning, for value development and for actual learning itself. This is too rich a range of outcomes for easy interpretation. A study of the use of simulation exercises, for example, found them to be not as good as more traditional methods for teaching concepts, but more enjoyable for the students, and more motivating. Teaching for problem solving skills may increase the students' powers of analyzing a situation for either its conceptual content, or its social values, but not necessarily for both. An empirical action research study by Maple (1986), for example, seemed to achieve significant success in teaching the control of experimental variables in school experiments, but could produce amoral travesties of experimental design when students applied their knowledge to societal situations.

These sorts of results, and others like them, have suggested that there are two quite contrasting domains of knowledge. In one the concepts are decontextualized and the mental processes involved are strictly logical. In the other (life-world) domain arguments are conducted about what would happen in a particular context, are expected to be opinionated and evaluative, are socially negotiable, and are not thought to extend to other contexts (Schutz and Luckmann, 1973). Movement from one domain to another is like a cognitive jolt, and is hard to achieve.

There is research on students' views on energy (Solomon, 1985), and also results from practical work conducted by the Assessment of Performance Unit Review Age 15 (1987) which tends to support this view. In the first study grade 8 students who had learnt a course on the physics of energy made richer evaluative judgments on the social uses of energy, when they were making no attempt to use their school learnt knowledge about the energy concept. The abler pupils who did use abstract scientific knowledge about energy seemed to find it harder to bring their evaluative judgments to bear upon the social issues at the same time. It was as though moving from one domain of knowledge to the other was too taxing. Closely related work seemed to show that students even store information acquired from the different domains of knowledge separately from each other (Solomon, 1983). The APU study of experimental work was designed to test for the same practical skills through two different sets of problems. In one the question seemed to be scientific since the context was the reaction times of chemicals. In the other the problem was about the time taken for sweets to dissolve in the mouth. Quite different results were obtained and the students were more, not less, successful when the context was scientific. Perhaps the scientific context contained less of the vague generalizations and affective reactions which might distract the students.

Recommendations for STS Education Based on Research

Aikenhead (1988) has used a careful multi-method study of Canadian students' views on science, technology and society to point out this divorce between the scientific and the social, and urge a change in science teaching. His grade 12 students claimed that they had gained most of their knowledge from television and closer questioning showed this to be more from cartoon characters than from more serious programmes. What they did think that they had learnt from school science classes, about the scientific method, was 'almost as inaccurate as the images conveyed by television'. Worst of all

> ... the students basically expressed the belief that science and technology have little to do with social problems.

Aikenhead believes that his study provides backing for the criticism that science instruction is wrong to ignore the social and technological context of authentic science.

Another study of Canadian students, Fleming (1986), used interviews to probe for personal reactions to science-based social issues. He offered the students information booklets to provide essential scientific background knowledge, but these were consistently rejected. Students seemed to have views on what scientists, as people, might think, and this relegated scientific knowledge to the status of personal opinion. We might interpret this as use of the socially acquired life-world attitude, with its empathic understanding, and reliance upon negotiated meanings, for thinking about scientific knowledge. Taking the scientific information in this spirit it is not surprising that the students felt no compulsion to use it in their evaluation of social issues. Like television viewers they treated the information provided as a para-social interaction (p. 18). At the same time they expressed the view that 'the real facts' would solve all the socioscientific problems. Perhaps we should deduce from this that the students did not recognize any difference between the skills of social evaluation and those of pure cognitive reasoning from unimpeachable premises.

If this were the case, then what pupils learn in conventional science lessons would be received in one of two fundamentally mistaken ways. Either it would be assumed to be no more than a cluster of new and negotiable life-world meanings, or it would be received as 'truth with a capital T' which would, the students claimed, obliterate any personal variations in the evaluation of its social application. In a trenchant criticism of school science Fleming concludes:

> It has often been argued by science educators that the analysis of socioscientific issues requires a background of information. It has, mistakenly, it appears, been assumed that this is scientific data. Instead adolescents require a thorough understanding of the processes of science which generate these data....
>
> The perceived obsession of science with the production of facts also allows one to deny any human side to science. Repeatedly, adolescents reported that scientists were interested in progress, and that progress was not concerned with human welfare.... Thus science curricula must present science as a product of human endeavour... the personal and emotional commitment to the creation of knowledge must be presented.

In the converse situation, when quality of evaluative, ethical, and moral reasoning is being assessed, researchers often report that the knowledge component is essential to the process. Just as Fleming argued for the human side to the learning of science, Iozzi (1979) has argued for a knowledge foundation to social decision making. He made a special study of the development of moral reasoning in environmental education and decided that it depended on background knowledge, as well as on interest and concern. He argued that both of these kinds of factors must be present in the learning process if decision making is to be achieved.

There is precious little research on the results of STS education within school. In Holland the PLON project for teaching physics with special emphasis on its social aspects has been in operation since 1980. Eijkelhof (1985) reported the results of a small pre- and post-test study of some Dutch students studying a PLON unit on ionizing radiation which emphasized the risk to health from nuclear and X-rays, and encouraged discussion of its acceptability. The unit engaged the students' interests well, but changed their attitudes to radiation very little. In particular the issue of radiation from nuclear waste was assessed almost exactly the same as it was before the course, and with the use of the same kinds of common-sense arguments. On the other hand a question about using radiation for the preservation of food elicited more favourable responses after the course, and many of the students showed some valuable use of knowledge derived from the course.

Eijelhof speculates that the students had already made up their minds about nuclear radiation from power stations before the course began since the subject has had high visibility in Holland for many years. How early adolescents begin to consider topical concerns in a personally committed sense is very hard to know. The review article of Weisenmayer *et al.* (1984) suggests that environmental attitudes are formed very early, often before the students reach grade 8 (12-years-old), and are then very resistant to change. Further inputs of information are welcomed, but tend to do no more than polarize existing views. The students seize upon facets of the ideas presented that support their own views and then tend to ignore the rest as irrelevant or biased. This is clearly not the outcome of STS education expected by McConnell.

It would be pleasant and satisfying if this chapter could end with recommendations for STS within the curriculum which were supported both by empirical research and by educational polemic. Unfortunately, the dilemmas which have dogged the implementation of STS also plague research into its school operation. It appears, as far as we now know, that students' attitudes are strongly influenced by out-of-school factors, and that they do not easily use the scientific knowledge which we teach them in conjunction with personal evaluation for social decision making. Holistic educational theory would insist that knowledge and evaluation are complementary and essential characteristics of human development, but offers no advice on how they should be taught.

But some of the research data can be used to bring the argument full circle. If, as Aikenhead and Fleming insist, the students do not perceive the difference between socially acquired negotiable knowledge, and abstract overarching scientific knowledge, then it is the first approach to STS (through an understanding of science as a way of knowing) which offers the most promise. Perhaps a philosophical introduction — appropriate to the level of the students — is a prerequisite for freeing the reasoning and valuing faculties to work together in social decision making. Only more research can tell.

References

ADDINELL, S. and SOLOMON, J. (1983) *Science in a Social Context, Teachers Guide*, Hatfield, Association for Science Education.

AIKENHEAD, G. (1979) 'Science: A way of knowing', *The Science Teacher*, 46, 6.

AIKENHEAD, G. (1988) 'Student belief about science-technology-society: Four different modes of assessment, and sources of students' viewpoints', *Journal of Research Science Teaching*, in press.

AIKENHEAD, G. and FLEMING, R. (1975) *Science a Way of Knowing*, Saskatoon, University of Saskatchewan, Department of Curriculum Studies.

ASSESSMENT OF PERFORMANCE UNIT (1987) *Age 13 Review*, London, DES.

ASSOCIATION FOR SCIENCE EDUCATION (1979) *Alternatives for Science Education*, Discussion Paper, Hatfield, Association for Science Education.

ASSOCIATION FOR SCIENCE EDUCATION (1981) *Education through Science*, Policy Document, Hatfield, Association for Science Education.

BYBEE, R.W., HARMS, N., WARD, B. and YAGER, R. (1980) 'Science society and science education', *Science Education*, 64, 3, pp. 377–95.

DREYFUSS, A. and JUNGWIRTH, E. (1980) 'A comparison of the "prompting effect" of out-of-school with that of in-school contexts on certain aspects of critical thinking', *European Journal of Science Education*, 2, 3, pp. 301–10.

ELLINGHAM, H. and LANGTON, N. (1975) 'The power station game', *Physics Education*, 10, pp. 445–7.

EIJKELHOF, H. (1985) 'Dealing with acceptable risk in science education', paper presented to the conference 'Science Education and Future Human Needs', Bangalore.

FLEMING, R. (1986) 'Adolescent reasoning in socio-scientific issues, Part I', *Journal of Research Science Teaching*, 23, 8, pp. 677–88.

HALL, W. (1973) *Science and Decision-making*, London, Longman and Harmondsworth, Penguin.

HARDING, J. (1986) 'The making of a scientist?' in HARDING, J. (Ed.) *Perspectives of Gender and Science*, Lewes, Falmer Press.

HEAD, J. (1980) 'A model to link personality to a preference for science', *European Journal of Science Education*, 2, pp. 295–300.

HENLE, M. (1962) 'The relationship between logic and thinking', *Psychological Review*, 69, pp. 366–78.

HINES, J.M. and HUNGERFORD, H.R. (1984) 'Environmental educational research related to environmental action skills' in *Monographs in Environmental Education and Environmental Studies (1971–1982)* ERIC, Ohio State University, pp. 113–30.

HOLMAN, J. (1987) 'Resources or courses? Contrasting approaches to the introduction of industry and technology to the secondary curriculum', *School Science Review*, 68, 244, pp. 432–8.

HUFSTEDLER, S.M. and LANGENBERG, D.N. (1980) *Science Education for the 1980s and Beyond*, Washington, DC, National Science Foundation and the Department of Education.

IOZZI, L. (1979) 'Moral judgment, verbal ability, logical reasoning ability, and environmental issues', unpublished PhD thesis, Rutgers University, NJ.

JEVONS, F. (1967) 'A science greats', *Physics Education*, 2, p. 196.

LAYTON, D. (1982) *Science Education and Values Education — An Essential Tension* in proceedings of an international seminar, London, Chelsea College.

LEWIS, J. (1980) *Science in Society. Readers and Teachers' Guide*, Hatfield, Association for Science Education and London, Heinemann.

McCONNELL, M.C. (1982) 'Teaching about science, technology and society at the secondary school level in the United States', *Studies in Science Education*, 9, pp. 1–32.

McQUAIL, D. (1983) *Mass Communication Theory: An Introduction*, London, Sage Publications.

McQUAIL, D., BLUMER, J. and BROWN, J. (1972) 'The television audience: A revised perspective' in McQUAIL, P. (Ed.) *Sociology of Mass Communication*, Harmondsworth, Penguin, pp. 135–65.

MAPLE, J. (1986) 'An investigation of the transferability of practical skills', unpublished MSc thesis, Oxford, University of Oxford.

RIP, A. (1978) 'The social context of science, technology and society courses in the universities' in BOEKER, E. and GIBBONS, M. (Eds) *Science, Society and Education*, Amsterdam, Vrie Universiteit, pp. 135–52.

SCHUTZ, A. and LUCKMAN, T. (1973) *The Structure of Life World*, Evanston, ILL, Northwestern University Press.

SOLOMON, J. (1983) Eight titles in the *SISCON in Schools* series and a Teachers' Guide, Hatfield, Association for Science Education and Oxford, Basil Blackwell.

SOLOMON, J. (1985) 'Learning and evaluation: A study of school children's views on the social uses of energy', *Social Studies of Science*, pp. 343–71.

SPIEGEL-ROSING, I. and PRICE, D.DE S. (Eds) (1977) *Science, Technology and Society: A Cross-disciplinary Perspective*, Beverly Hills, CA, Sage.

WEISENMAYER, R.L., MURRIN, M.A. and TOMERA, A.N. (1984) 'Environmental educational research related to issue awareness' in *Monographs in Environmental Education and Environmental Studies (1971–1982)* ERIC, Ohio State University, pp. 61–94.

ZIMAN, J. (1980) *Teaching and Learning about Science and Society*, Cambridge, Cambridge University Press.

ZOLLER, U. (1985) 'Interdisciplinary decision-making in the science curriculum in the modern socio-economic context' in HARRISON, G. (Ed.) *World Trends in Science and Technology Education*, report on second international symposium, Nottingham, Trent Polytechnic.

14
Broadening the Aims of Physics Education

Harrie M.C. Eijkelhof and Koos Kortland

Introduction

In December 1970 the annual conference for Dutch physics teachers was devoted to Harvard Project Physics. A few draft copies had circulated in the Netherlands and the lucky ones who could get hold of the materials reported to the conference about its flavour. The audience was excited about this approach to physics education, especially about its cultural and historic context, the readers and the practicals. It was felt that we needed such materials for our students to make physics as attractive as it could be in our view as teachers.

Following this conference a proposal was sent to the government for funds to finance a project in which the good ideas from the new physics curriculum waves (PSSC, PP, Nuffield) could be made available to Dutch physics teachers through materials.

Funds became available for curriculum development with, however, the condition that work should start for junior general secondary education in which physics is a compulsory subject. The project started in 1972 and was named PLON (a Dutch acronym for Physics Curriculum Development Project). Its main task was to modernize and update the existing physics curricula. Its field was limited to physics as in the Netherlands the sciences were (and are) usually taught as separate subjects, both in junior and senior secondary schools. In the first years the PLON team consisted of three curriculum writers (physics teachers), one evaluator (psychologist), a technician and a secretary. In later years the team was more than doubled according to the same ratio.

Some more changes took place in the course of the project (1972-86). In the first years a lot of inspiration was found in American, British, Australian and German projects and work was limited to junior physics. In the second half of the project's lifetime the materials got their own distinct style and conceptualization and most attention went to senior physics materials. At first the materials were strongly related to the local environment of the pupils and to the technology surrounding them. Later, in both the junior and senior curricula more attention was paid to the interaction between physics, technology and society (STS).

A chapter is not appropriate to describe all of the curriculum materials, teachers' guides, evaluation results, implementation, classroom experiences, etc. We have decided to limit ourselves to *the broadening of the aims of physics education towards STS*, to those products which have a clear STS label, to some of the problems faced by the team to write and rewrite materials and to some of the evaluation results. Finally we will draw some conclusions about our experiences in the PLON project and indicate along which lines we expect to be able to increase the quality of the materials in future.

A Broadening of Aims

A Shift of Emphasis towards STS

In general, physics education for students aged 12–18 in the Netherlands (but not only there) emphasizes the development of some scientific skills and an adequate mastering of scientific concepts, in order to lay down a solid foundation on which students can rely when entering those forms of tertiary education in which physics knowledge and skills are considered essential. Teaching physics in secondary schools therefore is aimed at preparing students for further education at tertiary level.

As a consequence most physics courses — also for the lower ability levels within secondary education — can be characterized as having a rather *academic*, theoretical nature based on the structure of physics as an academic discipline; little or no attention is paid to technological applications and to social implications of science and technology, and possibilities for adapting (parts of) the course to the different needs of individual students are lacking.

However, only a few students are, in due course, going to become scientists themselves. For the majority of students physics is a difficult and alienated subject, having little or no practical use after they have left secondary school.

During the 1970s this type of physics education (but also other school subjects) started to be questioned, not only — or primarily — by teachers, but also by different pressure groups in society.

A growing number of teachers adopted the idea that *relating physics to everyday life phenomena* (be they technological or natural) would make physics teaching more interesting for their students, thus countering the decreasing motivation among students (related to a number of social changes, one of these being the increasing percentage of students entering some kind of general secondary education as opposed to vocational training). Another possibility for countering decreasing motivation was seen by teachers: providing more opportunities for *individualized learning of students*, for accommodating differences in interests and abilities among students. At about the same time different pressure groups in society started asking for attention to technology within the existing school curricula. Some groups argued for this change in order to make the students (more) aware of the *importance of science and technology for maintaining a sound economy*, thus countering the increasingly negative image of industry due to its detrimental impact on the environment. Other groups used this impact on our environment to argue for attention to be paid to *alternative technologies and an ecological lifestyle necessary for survival in the long run.*

The tension between economic and environmental considerations led to a growing intensity of public debate, at first focussing on our energy future but very soon extending to more general discussion of the impact of scientific and technological developments on society in fields like (nuclear) armament, information technology, genetic engineering, etc. At the beginning of the 1970s some optional STS education started to develop at university level: STS courses were developed and taught, research started to deal with questions put forward by trade unions, environmental pressure groups and the like. The increasing societal debate on (the impacts of) science and technology and the emergence of STS at university level led to a growing pressure, both from within and from outside the secondary educational system, to *prepare students for a better understanding of the public debate and to provide them with the ability to take part in it in an informed and balanced way.* Education had to broaden the students' vision and had to present a framework for structuring the muddle of unbalanced, biased and fragmentary topic-of-the-day information on these complex socioscientific issues, had to provide some tools to help to make decisions on a (preliminary) point of view or course of action.

Internal and external pressures on the content of science education have led to a debate whether science education should broaden its aims and no longer concentrate mainly on the few students who will study science at university level. This debate not only takes place in the Netherlands, as can be seen from policy documents[1] of the Association for Science Education in the UK and the National Science Teachers Association in the USA, reports of the Science Council of Canada and English Examination Boards as well as numerous proceedings of conferences during the last decade.[2] The PLON project has been influenced by this debate, and the aims of physics education as stated within the project team have evolved over a number of years into a balance between:

- *preparing students for coping with their (future) life roles as a consumer and as a citizen in a technologically developing, democratic society* (emphasizing the use of physics as one of the tools for decision making at a personal and at a societal level and contributing to (more) thoughtful decision making);
- *preparing students for further education and/or (future) employment* (emphasizing an adequate mastering of scientific concepts and skills and providing an orientation on the use of scientific knowledge in different societal sectors and types of further education).

Development of Teaching Materials

The broadening and balancing of aims in a number of cases has led to the development of STS courses, to be taken by students in parallel with (or instead of) academic science courses.[3] Although the PLON project recognized the importance of these separate STS courses, we felt they might not be sufficient to solve some of the problems students experienced with the academic courses. This feeling has led to the development of physics curricula in which a specific integration of physics, technology and society was striven for: curricula based on both the good features of an academic course in physics and of STS courses about the impact of science and technology on society.

The PLON project intended to construct teaching materials which:

- contain physics (basic concepts and skills) which is useful in everyday life regarding decision making situations on a personal and societal level, *and — at the same time —* which is essential for those who continue studying physics in tertiary education;
- present an authentic view of physics, by paying attention to the history, the nature and the methods of physics;
- recognize the differences among students in interests, abilities and plans for the future;
- stimulate students to be actively involved in experiments, literature investigations, data retrieval and analysis, etc.

So far, we do not claim to be very original: others have argued in rather similar terms. However, we have had the opportunity to put our ideas into practice on a scale which is rather unusual in the 1980s. Some forty teaching units were developed and used (and are still being used) in the classroom (see table 1). And in a number of these units physics is dealt with in a *personal, social and scientific context,* in order to make students aware of the relevance but also the limitations of physics as a scientific discipline, in order to make physics socially relevant.

Table 1:   *PLON teaching units for secondary education*

	All ability streams		
grade 8	A first exploration in physics Men and metals Working with water Living in air Ice, water, steam		
grade 9	Bridges Seeing movements Colour and light Electrical networks Reproducing sound Water for Tanzania Energy in our homes Energy in the future		
	Lower ability stream	Average ability stream	Pre-university stream
grade 10	Forces Traffic and safety Stop or keep moving Heating and insulating Switching and controlling Machines and energy Nuclear arms and/or security Review for final exam	Comparing Weather changes Music Traffic Electrical machines Energy and quality	The human body Music Traffic The weather Energy
grade 11		Matter Light sources Ionizing radiation Electronics Review for final exam	Sports Electric motors Work and energy[*] Physics around 1900 Automation Particles in fields[*] Ionizing radiation Satellites[**]
grade 12			[*] systematic units [**] remainder of units for grade 12 still in the course of development

All units consist of a student's book, a teacher's guide and a technician's manual. All course material is written in Dutch. So far only two units have been translated in English: **Bridges** and **Water for Tanzania**. At the moment more work is being done in this field: a grade 9 physics course based on a number of PLON units is being developed in the UK and the units **Light Sources** and **Ionizing Radiation** are being translated/adapted in Canada and Australia.

The examples in the following section will provide some idea of how we tried to translate the above mentioned broadening of aims into teaching units for classroom use.

Examples of Teaching Materials

It is not possible to present a detailed description of each of the units with an STS label. To illustrate the general format of these units we will describe one of them in more detail: the unit **Ionizing Radiation** (grade 11, average ability and pre-university streams). After that we will give a shorter description of several other units. (Other units have been described elsewhere.[4])

General Format of a Teaching Unit

The general format of a unit is pictured in figure 1. The central theme in the unit, **Ionizing Radiation**, is the acceptability of the risk of applications of ionizing radiation.

The unit starts off with an *orientation*, introducing a number of everyday life situations in which the use of ionizing radiation might be an issue, and giving an idea of the nature of the risk concept (a combination, but not a straightforward one of probability and effects).

The next part contains *basic information* and skills about the nature, effects and sources of X-rays and radioactivity. Concepts important in risk assessment are introduced, such as half life, activity, dose, somatic and genetic effects.

After dealing with the basic information, groups of students start to work independently on either one of the three *options*: nuclear energy, nuclear arms and the use of radiation for medical purposes. Background information on risk and safety aspects of each of these areas of application is given or collected by the students. In several subsequent lessons, students *report* their findings to other groups in class.

In the final part of the unit (*broadening and deepening*) procedures are dealt with to analyze and evaluate personal and societal risks, like being prescribed a brain scan or like the dumping of radioactive wastes into the ocean. A framework for evaluating risks is presented through a series of questions on advantages, on short and long-term risks with and without the specific application and on possibilities for risk reduction.

In addition to the general format as described above, the role of physics (concepts, laws, models, etc.) in a unit is identified. A *basic question* — taken from the society students live in, and regarded as relevant to them with respect to their (future) life-roles as a consumer and citizen in society — is stated in the

Figure 1: General formal of a teaching unit

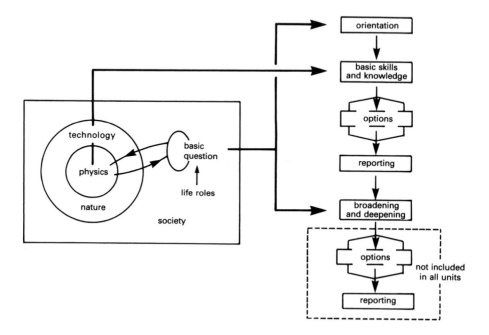

orientation of a unit (in the case of **Ionizing Radiation**: *How acceptable are applications of ionizing radiation to you?*). This basic question acts as an organizer for the series of physics lessons and determines the physics knowledge and skills to be taught in order to be able to find some (preliminary) answers to the basic question. (In this way the basic question also acts as a selection criterion for the physics content.) After that, the basic question turns up again in the last part of the unit, in which the physics concepts and skills are broadened and/or deepened by applying them to situations in which the basic question is prominent: does the physics taught help in finding answers, help in being able to cope with a technological device, a consumer decision, a socioscientific issue? This turning back to the basic question — to society — is essential because it reflects the relevance of our physics teaching.[5]

Some units have an optional part at the end, meant to acquire a certain skill (for example, using external sources of information, writing reports). Reporting on these learning experiences might be more informal.

Basic Questions and Concepts

Three units chosen to further illustrate the broadening of aims outlined in that section are dealing with basic questions related to:

- the (future) life-role of the student as a *consumer* (with the ability to cope with and make decisions about products of science and technology in everyday life on aspects like quality, safety, costs, health and environmental hazards, sensible use);
- the (future) life-role of the student as a *citizen* (with the ability to interpret public debates and to make (more) thoughtful judgments on controversial socioscientific issues);
- aspects of *further studies* or *(future) employment* (of a scientific, technological, or social nature), relevant for the specific group of students (mainly in senior secondary education).

Consumer physics

Focussing on the use of physics knowledge and skills in situations dealing with the (future) life-role of the student as a consumer, examples can be found in a number of units or parts of units. Most of these situations concentrate on making the best buy or using products in a sensible way.

- Which buy could be best: a filament bulb, a strip light or an (energy saving) SL-lamp? (*basic question* for part of the unit **Light Sources**, grade 11, average ability stream). Strip lights and SL-lamps cost more, but use less energy giving off the same amount of light. Which type of lamp is most economical in the long run? The relation between energy, power and time (physics concepts and laws) and the ability to draw and interpret diagrams (physics skills) are useful to arrive at an answer. Knowledge about the mechanisms of converting electrical energy into light (energy) in the different types of lamp provides a background for an understanding of the differences in light efficiency and colour of the light, and point at possible environmental implications (for example, mercury pollution).
- How might legal measures enforcing the use of seat belts and crash helmets improve traffic safety? (*basic question* for the unit **Traffic and Safety**, grade 10, lower ability stream). Concepts and laws from mechanics are useful for getting an idea of the magnitude of the force acting on a car driver during a collision (as compared to the force the human body can exert), of the way traffic safety devices like seat belts and crash helmets help to prevent injuries by diminishing the force on

the driver through lengthening the 'braking-distance', of the relation-ship between speed and braking distance (selecting a safe speed), etc.

Other units deal with topics like fuel economy in traffic (unit **Traffic**), choosing between different means of transport like bike or car, private or public transport (unit **Stop or Keep Moving**), influencing room acoustics in order to improve the quality of (reproduced) sound (unit **Music**) and checking electrical motors in order to be (more) able to carry out small repairs on household appliances (unit **Electrical Machines**).

From the teaching materials dealing with the basic questions related to the consumers' life-roles it follows that making fair comparisons is not easy at all. Even in what at first seem to be situations involving relatively simple decisions, the number of aspects requiring consideration turns out to be more than expected, for example, not only costs and safety aspects (prominent in most reports on consumer research), but also environmental implications. In clarify-ing these questions, the teaching materials aim to enable students to avoid naive and misleading choices.

Citizen physics

From the examples given above on consumer physics it might be clear that the distinction between consumer and citizen physics isn't too sharp. The knowl-edge about fuel economy can also be used to analyze and discuss the recent (Dutch) debate on increasing maximum speed on motorways (focussing on traffic safety aspects, whereas environmental considerations are not very prominent in the public debate); connected to the individual's choice of wearing seat belts is the question of enforcing the use of seat belts by law or promoting this use on a voluntary basis at a more societal level, etc. An important aspect of consumer physics is the possibility to translate a (more) informed, thoughtful judgment into direct personal action. (However, whether the student makes a choice, when he/she will do that and which way the choice turns out is his/her own responsibility.)

When dealing with citizen physics the aims are limited to making students aware of the public debate and to provide them with the means to interpret this debate in order to be able to reach a (more) informed, thoughtful point of view on the issue. The possibilities for personal action are more indirect: discussing the issue with others, voting behaviour.

In addition to the examples already mentioned under the heading of consumer physics a number of other examples can be found in the units that relate to citizen physics.

- Which type of waterpump is most suitable for pumping up drinking water in a Tanzanian village? (*basic question* in the unit **Water for**

Tanzania, grade 9, all ability streams). The basic question reflects the Dutch debate on the character of Third World aid programmes, in which alternative viewpoints come up: should ready-made industrial products be sent over or should Western countries provide the means for Third World countries to set up their own local industries. In the unit students assess different types of water pump, on criteria having to do with the operating principle (physics knowledge concerning the effects of pressure differences), different technologies (related to the construction and maintenance of the pumps) and social conditions in a typical Third World rural area.

- Can one survive a nuclear war? (*basic question* in the unit **Nuclear Arms and/or Security**, grade 10, lower ability stream). The unit concentrates on the effects of nuclear explosions in the short term (destruction by blast and heat) and in the long term (somatic and genetic effects of ionizing radiation due to fallout), and the (im)possibilities of protection against these effects. The knowledge base consists of the nature and properties of ionizing radiation and concepts like activity, half life, dose and their units of measurement.

Other units deal with lively debated issues like energy scenarios (units: **Energy in the Future** and **Energy and Quality**) and the pros and cons of the micro electronics revolution (unit: **Electronics**), but also with a debate which does not get too much attention: spending money on applied or fundamental scientific research (unit: **Matter**).

An authentic view on physics

Using physics as a tool to get a more firm grip on everyday life requires knowledge of the *limitations* of this tool. Physics (and science in general) does not give all the answers, not only because there are more factors besides physics influencing decisions (like economic, cultural, political factors), but also because of the nature of scientific knowledge[6].

The importance of modelling, but also the limitations of the models constructed, is most prominent in the unit **Matter**. However, the matter of the nature of scientific knowledge also turns up in other units: the controversy on the effects of low dose ionizing radiation on the human body (unit **Ionizing Radiation**), the uncertainties in the predicted rise of the sea level due to the greenhouse effect (unit **Weather Changes**). Models describing complex systems like the human body and the global carbon cycle are in no way adequate (yet). Uncertainties give way to different interpretations, also by experts.

The nature of scientific knowledge is explicitly dealt with in the unit

Matter (grade 11, average ability stream), *the basic question* for this unit being: what is the difference between applied and fundamental research, for example, into the structure of matter — and what about the bill? In order to get an idea of what fundamental research is and for what it might be useful, the unit **Matter** starts with the ideas of the ancient Greek on the structure of matter and going through the centuries finishes off with the quark model and the attempts at unifying the four fundamental forces. The unit gives an idea of the development of physics as a discipline (such as working with models and making order out of chaos), the part technology plays in the progress made in research (from vacuum pumps to super colliders) and of the way in which some physicists left their mark on the development of their discipline. To be able to assess the value of fundamental research into the nature of matter, an idea of what these huge-sums-of-money spending, high-energy-physicists are up to is necessary.

Presenting an authentic image of physics — physics as a developing product of human activity, in which objectivity and subjectivity are less separated domains than might be perceived by the general public — is a prerequisite for an adequate assessment of the role physics might play in dealing with consumer decisions and (debates on) socioscientific issues.

Teaching Methods

Next to the questions of 'why teach physics' and 'what physics to teach' comes the question of 'how to teach it'. What do we expect students to do during the lessons? Just reading long texts doesn't very much appeal to quite a lot of the students. In order to hold students' attention, a variety of student activities stimulating active involvement in physics lessons appears to be necessary. But not only for that reason. The (future) life-roles of students have a passive and an active component: not only knowledge is required, but also certain skills such as being able to read, watch and listen critically, to discuss, to work independently and to cooperate with fellow students, to communicate learning experiences, to perform experiments and set up investigations, to retrieve and structure relevant information and compare information from different sources critically.

Student activities have to be chosen carefully in order to give students a chance of acquiring these skills: skills necessary on the one hand for being able to do something with the acquired knowledge in practical situations in everyday life, and on the other hand for being able to tackle independently issues that couldn't be dealt with in the curriculum (time constraints) or issues that might come up in society in the time ahead.

So not only contents will have to change, also — and equally important —

the teaching methods: less 'talk-and-chalk' by the teacher and more classroom discussion, literature research, interviewing, practicals, etc. The role of the teacher in the classroom changes into stimulating and facilitating independent work of (groups of) students.

Some Problems and Solutions

It took us about thirteen years to develop some forty teaching units. Each of the units have been rewritten at least once or twice, and some three or even more times if that seemed to be necessary. One might say we have been working on a trial and error basis, and what was described in the section on teaching materials, to a large extent, reflects the final product of the last four years of curriculum development aimed at an integration between academic physics and STS.

In this section we will point out some — in our view most prominent — problems during this curriculum development work and some solutions we think we have found for these.

Contents: Contexts and Concepts

Choice of contexts

The choice of contexts to be incorporated in the curricula ideally would be influenced by the differences in interests, abilities and plans for the future among students, and by long-term developments in society.

At the level of the curriculum as a whole the different needs of students could be met by choosing a variety of general contexts of a more scientific, technological and social nature. In the first version curriculum the emphasis was a technological one, not too attractive for (mainly) girls. The revision of the curriculum therefore was aimed at diversifying the general contexts raised: units like **Weather Changes** (general context: nature) and **Music** (general context: culture) had to balance the more technological units like **Electrical Machines** and **Electronics**. But also minor changes in existing units appeared, like adding biographies of four physicists working at the end of the nineteenth and beginning of the twentieth century to the unit **Matter**, or — an approach the other way round — the disappearance of the operating principle of quite a number of different types of nuclear power reactor from the unit **Ionizing Radiation**.

So now the curriculum as a whole is more balanced with respect to the general contexts raised. If it is balanced enough remains an open question.

Linking physics to everyday life (at a personal and societal level) carries in itself the danger of the contents being initially timely, but not any more so a couple of years later. Therefore, we tried to choose the themes of our units, taking note of long-term developments in society derived from surveys of literature and discussions with a few experts. Within the boundary condition of developing a physics curriculum this has led to the choice of issues on energy, traffic, electronics, armament, space travel and Third World aid. Next to that a relevant overall concept for dealing with quite a number of issues seemed to be the concept of risk. And also the development of physics as a discipline had to be dealt with in order to present an authentic view of physics.

However, the choice of the contexts for the units was not a completely free one. First of all we had to consider the existing nationwide examination programmes. Although the project's task was to modernize and update physics curricula and to put forward proposals for changes in the examination programmes, one should not get too far away from what is customary within existing physics education. Being innovative in the field of curriculum development is a good thing, but adoption and implementation of the innovative materials by the teachers must remain feasible. Secondly we had to consider the desired variety of contexts in order to accommodate to differences in students' interests.

So, the choice of themes and basic questions for the units carries in itself the character of a compromise between desirability and (to a certain extent limited) feasibility.

Relationship between contexts and concepts

In the first years of curriculum development within the project the focus was on developing teaching materials stimulating independent work of students and students' learning from each other's experiences. With regard to the content of the units the aim was to relate physics to everyday life phenomena in the students' immediate surroundings: knowing about the physics behind natural and technological phenomena in the students' life-world instead of using physics as one of the tools for decision making at a personal and societal level. Once teaching materials have been developed, it is difficult to change them to fit into a new set of aims, not only for reasons of limited time, but also for reasons like not putting too much pressure on trial school teachers who have grown accustomed to working with the 'old' materials, who have put a lot of energy, time and (school)money into organizing practicals, etc.

Therefore the integration of academic physics and STS as outlined in the previous sections is not visible in all units, and the curricula as a whole have somewhat of a hybrid character. However, the question is whether this integration is desirable in all units. Relating physics teaching to less problematic everyday life phenomena might for instance be necessary for students to be able to tackle decision making at a personal and societal level.

Concerning the units in which the above mentioned integration was worked out to a satisfactory degree, we had some problems with the first version units: abundance of aspects in and weak coherence of the units.

Most themes encompass very complicated problems or large areas of knowledge, and boundaries with other disciplines are sometimes vague. Trying to aim at completeness will be very confusing for students and teachers, and there is a danger of non-physical and non-scientific aspects dominating a unit. One of the units with this problem was the first version of **Nuclear Arms and/or Security**, which had the character of a short introduction to polemology; physics was relegated to an appendix at the end of the unit. Teachers felt very uncomfortable with this unit, as they were not experienced in teaching polemology (which is not their fault!). Also the students, although a large majority of them thought that the topic of nuclear armament should be dealt with in school, felt the unit not very appropriate for physics lessons (about half of them). When revising the unit we tried to avoid this abundance of aspects by not aiming at completeness, by keeping in mind what the specific contribution of physics could be to develop an insight into the theme; other aspects should be dealt with in other school subjects (and the physics teacher might be able to encourage this to happen). So the second version of the unit dealt with the effects of nuclear explosions and the (im)possibilities of protecting oneself in such events. If students wanted to look into other aspects, the optional period at the end of the unit could be used for that.

Using the instrument of the *basic question* has been helpful in avoiding the abundance of aspects in the second version units, and has even been more helpful in strengthening the coherence of the units. When the various chapters of a unit are weakly connected to the basic question (if present at all in the first version units) and to each other, teachers easily neglect the innovative chapters and pay most attention to the traditional ones. Adapting to new content and teaching methods takes a lot of time and energy, and one has to be pushed a little bit to make the transition.

So the contextual knowledge (like the framework for thinking about the issue of risk evaluation mentioned on page 287) in the unit (**Ionizing Radiation**) has to be very closely connected to the physics content. But on the other hand the physics content must be associated with the contextual knowledge, that is, with the basic question. And here we come across the question: which physics concepts, laws, etc. should be taught and to what depth?

Concept development

As long as the basic questions for the units are not clearly defined (as in most first version units), the physics content tends to be close to what is traditionally being taught, except when dealing with new physics topics (like the quark model of matter, electronics). Or, in the case of traditional topics, teachers tend to stick to the traditional, well known content and tend to go into the same depth as they used to do.

One example comes from the units **Traffic and Safety** and **Traffic**. In mechanics the traditional approach to describing motion is the use of a set of equations like $\Delta s = v_0.\Delta t + \frac{1}{2}a(\Delta t)^2, \Delta v = a.\Delta t$ and $F = ma$. However, in order to be able to understand the way in which traffic safety devices like seat belts and crash helmets do their job, knowledge of the equations $F.\Delta s = \Delta(\frac{1}{2}m.v)^2$ and $F.\Delta t = \Delta(m.v)$ and an understanding of the concepts in these equations are perfectly suitable. Moreover, the equations represent in a very direct way the relationship between the relevant variables. For lower and average ability students there seems to be no need to burden them with the three distinct equations describing accelerated motion with the 'help' of an abstract concept like acceleration. And if students need any proof, the two 'laws of motion' stated above can be checked experimentally in both outside (real life) and laboratory conditions (which clearly shows that these equations — as well as others — are no more than approximations of reality). In this way, the physics content in the area of mechanics is reduced; but on the other hand, sometimes it had to be extended. In the same area of mechanics, motion traditionally deals with point-masses moving on frictionless planes. But in order to get a firmer grip on fuel economy in traffic, dealing with real objects, a quantitative treatment of frictional forces was necessary — a topic which was not traditionally taught.

As long as it isn't clear that a unit is dealing with *traffic safety* and *fuel economy*, in which mechanics is used as a tool to deal with practical situations in this area, the reduction and extension of physics content gets less attention from the teachers (and sometimes even from curriculum developers).

On the other hand one has to reckon with 'outside pressures', for example, from the school inspectorate, to keep standards high (that is, the standards of traditional teaching). Again, in many cases a compromise between the level of concept development necessary for dealing with practical situations in society and the standard level of concept development in the traditional curricula had to be reached.

One problem, however, could not be solved this way. Generally the degree of versatility students reach in applying the concepts, laws, etc. in different contexts is low: concepts developed within one specific context are not automatically used by students when solving problems in another — known or unknown — context. For lower and average ability streams this limited transfer can be accepted to a large extent, because key concepts from the fields of energy and mechanics, for example, appear in a number of units in different contexts. But this is not enough for students in pre-university streams. Their degree of versatility in manipulating concepts should be higher. A solution we found for this problem was the introduction of so-called *systematic units* in combination with the units dealt with up till this point in this chapter, to be characterized by the label of context-centred or *thematic units.*[7]

In a systematic unit concepts developed earlier in a number of thematic units act as a starting point. Concepts from different units are linked and defined more sharply in order to give students (in pre-university stream) insight into the systematic structure of physics as a discipline (mainly in the fields of motion, energy and work, and gravitational, electric and magnetic fields). Mathematical expressions of concepts and relationships between concepts are much more sophisticated and prominent (as compared to the thematic units) in order to widen their applicability in a variety of different contexts. The innovative curriculum for the pre-university stream therefore now consists of both thematic (in most cases the same units used in the average ability stream) and systematic units, thus reaching a balance of aims which seems necessary for preparation for university entrance as well as preparation for citizenship.

Student Activities and Differentiation

Stimulating active involvement of students in physics lessons and recognizing the differences among students in interests, abilities and plans for the future can be met by means of introducing a variety of student activities and differentiation within the units.

While developing the first versions of units, most effort went into defining the content of a unit. Of course student activities were present in the units, like (a lot of) practicals. But, apart from that, long texts and associated questions and exercises were used far too often. During revision more attention was paid to establishing a relationship between content and student activities and to the development of a greater variety of student activities: literature research using external sources of information, practical research projects, interviewing experts, excursions, videos and some simulation games.

Different needs of students can be met not only by a variety of student activities, but also during optional periods within a unit. In first version units differentiated parts tended to be either limited to non-essential sub-topics or to be so varied that a fruitful exchange of learning experiences wasn't feasible. And in some first version units the topics within the optional period were (far) too difficult to be studied independently, let alone to be explained by students to each other. Reporting sessions thus became problematic.

In the revised units the introduction of important concepts in the optional topics is avoided: they must be dealt with beforehand in the basic-knowledge-and-skills part of the unit. Also the topics of the differentiated chapters are chosen in such a way that they are supplementary to each other (for example, dealing with the second law of thermodynamics in either a theoretical, scientific or a practical, technological way in the unit, **Energy and Quality**, or dealing with the same concept (risk) in different sectors of society in the unit, **Ionizing Radiation**), thus facilitating the possibilities of students learning from each other. An extra incentive towards good quality performance of students during reporting sessions is the necessity to use the learning experiences of all groups of students during the broadening-and-deepening part of the unit.

Some Research Results about PLON

During the course of the PLON project the two research fellows had to work under high pressure from various sides. The curriculum writers wanted them to evaluate the units to get suggestions for improvement, policy people emphasized the need for research which could support their view that PLON 'is highly successful', 'doesn't work at all', colleagues from the educational research field would like to see if PLON experiences confirmed or refuted certain educational theories and, of course, both fellows had their own interest areas. So difficult choices had to be made and not all needs could be fulfilled.

Evaluation of First Versions

A great deal of work was done in evaluating first versions of units. It soon became clear that the aims of first version evaluation should not be set too high. The new units were so innovative in content and teaching methods that many 'infant diseases' could be detected. For instance management problems arose: equipment wasn't available in time and in sufficient quantities or didn't meet the expectations. Also students were often not sure of what was expected from them in the activities or in preparation of end-of-unit tests. And teachers felt insecure with the new materials: some topics were brand new for them as well, and some units required teaching methods they were not familiar with. Above all, teachers often didn't know what problems they would face with the new materials regarding difficulty, time and practicability.

So, we concluded that the success of a unit could not be measured by its first version. But these first evaluations appeared to be of great use to collect ideas for revision, for teacher guides and for teacher training. The results were seldom published, partly because we thought their use would be limited to those already involved, partly because we didn't like to provide tools to those who would love to abort PLON ideas before they were mature. Many of PLON's best ideas started rather immature and it often took several tries to get them in a proper form.

A variety of methods was used for first version evaluation. Very important were the meetings with the teachers of the trial schools. After each unit we met and discussed the experiences. Teachers appeared to be very creative in finding solutions for the problems caused by the curriculum writers; they also challenged the writers on new ideas so the latter were forced to explain clearly what they were aiming at behind the problems of introduction. A second source of information was the questionnaires we presented to the students. Questions dealt with the instructiveness, usefulness, clarity and difficulty of the unit, their interest in various topics and their ideas about student activities. Finally we visited schools and observed what was going on in the classroom. Visiting schools however is very time-consuming, especially if one would like to observe all lessons in one class about one unit. Therefore, this source of information was used to a lesser extent.

As an example we will describe results of an evaluation study on the use of the first version of **Water for Tanzania**. Six classes were involved. A teacher meeting was held after use of the unit, teachers and students (N = 106) filled in questionnaires and lessons were observed by PLON staff members and trainee teachers. In general this unit was highly appreciated by teachers and students, especially by the girls. Students enjoyed the lessons, in particular constructing and testing the various pumps.

However two problems were noted: one with the introduction of the unit and one with the simulation game.

The unit starts with an introduction about the country and life in a village. A considerable part of the students didn't like this part and had problems with getting acquainted with life in a Tanzanian village. As judgments of students differed strongly between classes this seemed mainly due to the way teachers introduced this section of the unit. One suggestion made was to back-up teacher activities in the teacher's guide. Another was to include student activities in which they would get more involved: that would make the introduction less dependent on the teacher's input.

The second problem noted had to do with the simulation game. Students had difficulties in setting proper requirements to the pumps. And in the decision-making stage of the simulation game they got so involved in 'their' pump that a thoughtful balancing of pros and cons did not take place. Students just acted as 'salesmen' of their pump. Constructing a pump led clearly to an identification with the pump which counteracted their roles as evaluators. This result led to the suggestion to set external requirements to the pumps and to ask students each to evaluate one pump on this set of requirements. In the second version of the unit **Water for Tanzania** this suggestion was followed.

Evaluation of Second Versions

Once the first versions were revised and the 'infant diseases' were cured a new round of evaluation started. A great deal of noise was now eliminated, so we tried to get a better insight into the impact of the units on students' learning and on their attitudes towards various topics. For this kind of research a distinction could be made between evaluation of units and curriculum evaluation. The former was aimed at studying learning of a particular physics topic in the context set by the unit. The latter kind of research paid attention to the effects of the curriculum as a whole. Results of this kind of research seemed to be of more interest to others so more of it has been published, however often in Dutch. Here we will describe some of the results of second version evaluation of both these levels.

At the unit level two differences from the first version evaluation results were remarkable. One is that some units which were highly criticized by students on the first version became rather popular in the second version. An example of such a unit is the senior unit **Traffic** in which mechanics is taught in the context of traffic. About two-thirds of the students seemed to dislike the first version; mainly because they did not know what was expected of them both in activities and in preparations for tests. Two years later the second version became one of the most popular units. On the main ideas of the unit no changes were made: the same concepts were taught in the context of traffic. But the instructions for the activities were better, the main concepts were properly introduced and a collection of test questions on traffic situations was included. A second difference with first version evaluation results was a less significant difference between classes. This might be explained with the argument that the confusing first versions demanded more from the teachers in terms of clarification of what was expected and/or that teachers felt more at ease with the unit after having taught the unit before. We haven't been able yet to find out which of these points is most important.

Evaluation of second versions of the units resulted in some more questions in need of clarification. Let us take, for example, the unit **Ionizing Radiation**. In first and second version evaluations it appeared to be a very popular unit, especially the medical parts of it with the girls. In the latter evaluation study pre- and post-unit measurement was done regarding the use of concepts in arguing about controversial statements regarding applications of ionizing radiation. It appeared that hardly any physics was used in arguing about the dumping of radioactive waste in the sea, a fiercely debated topic in the Netherlands. On the acceptability of food irradiation, a less publicly-known topic, we detected afterwards a better use of topics dealt with in the unit. But at the same time it became clear that students had misconceptions about radiation which did not change very much. For instance, students used the word 'radiation' where an expert would use 'radioactive substances'. So one of the questions which arose was what ideas students do have about radiation before instruction. It was decided to study this question in a new research programme (see next section).

In one of the studies at the curriculum level we asked students their opinion about the various units. In this study 191 students filled in a questionnaire at the end of a two-year PLON course in senior secondary education (average ability stream).

The results show that students prefer some units more than others. Popular units are those which relate to daily life or specific interest areas of students, for instance the units **Traffic, Music, Weather Changes** (boys) and **Ionizing Radiation** (girls). Students seemed to be less fond of units which are either theoretical or technological, such as **Matter, Energy and Quality, Electronics** and **Electrical Machines** (girls).

On the other hand students' responses showed more variety in answering the question: 'From which two units did you learn most?' Here their judgments are more spread over the units, especially those of the boys. It was also rather surprising that for some units answers were not in accordance with general preferences mentioned above. So 41 per cent of the boys found **Ionizing Radiation** very instructive; the same qualification was given by 23 per cent of the girls to **Electronics**.

In general, students appreciated the physics lessons with PLON materials. They were especially positive about the student activities and the applied character of the physics. According to them these characteristics should get even more attention and especially students' individual contribution to the lessons should be increased.

Some Current Research Programmes about PLON

After the formal end to the curriculum development work within PLON several research projects have been started to study more in depth the learning of particular physics concepts and curriculum effects. Regarding concepts the work has been concentrated on 'force', 'energy' and 'ionizing radiation'. In the research project on 'ionizing radiation', for example, two points are particularly interesting for those involved in STS education.

The first point is: what particular content should be chosen if the aim is that students should be able to use physics in daily life situations? Often STS materials suffer from an abundance of concepts, facts and processes and from a chaotic variety of situations in which science plays a smaller or larger role. But by what criteria are they chosen? How can decisions be made to include some applications and leave out others, and to deal with many concepts and processes superficially instead of with a few concepts at greater depth? The answers to these questions cannot come from teachers and curriculum writers alone as they could hardly be expected to be familiar with so many STS areas.

We have involved some fifty radiation experts in trying to find an answer using the experience of these experts in a variety of professional fields: health, power and other industrial companies, civil service, research establishments and environmental organizations. Currently a three-round Delphi study is being carried out. Of course, it is not the intention to let experts decide what is suitable for science education: they are not qualified to take all necessary aspects into consideration. But we do think that their experience should be made use of. STS education cannot mature in isolation from society.

The second point of interest for STS education has also to do with the de-isolation of science education. From many studies we know that students do have ideas about concepts and processes which have in science a particular meaning. In many areas of physics we have an idea of the kind of pre-concepts students have. But we do not know much about the source of these pre-concepts nor about the daily life situations in which these pre-concepts lead to unfounded conclusions with serious consequences. We could all give some examples of this but as far as we know a systematic study has not yet occurred. However, it is not unlikely that STS teaching would promote clashes between thinking in 'personal' and 'scientific domains'. Therefore in our **Ionizing Radiation** research programme we study the use of scientific concepts in the media: radio, TV, newspapers and magazines, and consult experts on the following kind of questions. Which meanings are given to words sounding familiar to scientists and the public? How do these meanings relate to each other? What are the most essential differences? Do these differences depend on the particular situations? What consequences does this have, for instance for an assessment of the risks of ionizing radiation? We hope to be able to use the results to rewrite the unit **Ionizing Radiation** in the future and to write a new teachers' guide.

Apart from this kind of research studies are also carried out at the curriculum level. In one project a longitudinal study is done to detect causes for the change of attitude of girls towards physics during the first two years of obligatory physics instruction. A comparison is made between the effects of using the PLON curriculum and an academic curriculum.

Another study concentrates on the impact of two important characteristics of PLON curricula: active involvement of students and physics learning in a daily life context. The effects of both learning environment characteristics on students' motivation and cognitive learning outcomes are being investigated.

In summary we could conclude that the experiences with the PLON curricula have resulted in a number of questions on which answers are required if we want to improve the quality of our curriculum materials in future. Finding these answers will use a great deal of our time and energy in the coming years.

Lessons to Be Drawn

It would be very premature to draw, in 1988, final conclusions about the impact of the PLON project on science education, particularly on the teaching of physics. Processes of change in education take a long time and are influenced by many factors from inside and outside education, such as teachers' salaries, class size, structure of education, job opportunities, teacher training, new examination programmes, etc. Innovators' feelings often drift between hope and fear.

At present only students at a limited number of schools (twenty-five) are allowed to take the experimental PLON examinations, which differ from the nationwide final examinations (as the obvious result of the project's task of modernizing and updating physics education). Administrators' fears of the number of schools opting for the PLON examinations (and the teaching materials) getting 'out-of-hand' have put some serious restraints on the dissemination of the teaching materials. However, there are some hopeful signs. PLON experiences have greatly influenced the discussion on new examination programmes for physics. Not all programmes have been finalized yet, but the new examination programme for the lower ability stream clearly incorporates many PLON ideas regarding content and contexts. Also in the drafts for the examination programmes for the average ability and pre-university streams much attention is paid to learning in personal, technological and social contexts. This will allow all schools in future to change physics education. Moreover, although the use of PLON materials in classrooms is limited, infusion of PLON ideas in recently published traditional physics textbooks is visible. Students graduating from the teacher training colleges are now familiar with PLON ideas and teaching materials.

However, how big the actual changes in many schools will be is yet unclear. Much will depend on textbook writers and on the enthusiasm of teachers. Recent increases of class size and number of teaching periods, and decreases in both salaries and number of students, are not favourable to changes in the classroom. Unfortunately, curriculum innovators are rather powerless regarding these trends.

Returning from politics to more familiar fields, we conclude that PLON has been able to draw a great deal of attention to alternative content and teaching methods for physics education. However, the project's area has been very wide: complete curricula have been developed for various streams in both junior and senior secondary education, a variety of aims was set and innovation regarded content, methods and differentiation. As might have been predicted, width cannot be combined with great depth. Now we know where more depth is required and so we concentrate our efforts on curricula for special groups (low ability students, high ability students) and special topics (environmental science). We have also learned how important concept development is in teaching physics in context. We hope with research in this field to lay the foundations for further improvement of science education in future.

Notes

1 These bodies have published policy statements as follows: (1981) *Education through Science*, Association for Science Education, Hatfield; (1982) *Science-Technology-Society: Science Education for the 1980s — An NSTA Position Statement*, National Science Teachers Association, Washington DC; (1984) *Science for Every Student: Educating Canadians for Tomorrow's World — Report 36*. Science Council of Canada, Ottawa; (1983) *Recommended Statement of 16 + National Criteria for Science*, GCE and CSE Boards Joint Council for 16 + National Criteria, Manchester.

2 For example: (a) (1978) *Integrated Science Education Worldwide*, ICASE Conference, Nijmegen (the Netherlands); (b) (1980) *World Trends in Science Education*, Atlantic Institute of Education, Halifax; (c) (1981) *UNESCO Congress on Science and Technology Education and National Development*, UNESCO, Paris; (d) (1982) *Second Conference on Science, Society and Education*, Leusden (the Netherlands); (e) (1982) *World Trends in Science and Technology Education*, Trent Polytechnic, Nottingham; (f) (1985) *World Trends in Science and Technology Education*, College of Advanced Education, Brisbane; (g) (1987) *Science and Technology Education and the Quality of Life*, Kiel, IPN.

3 Some current examples of these are: (a) LEWIS J. (Ed.) (1981), *Science in Society*, London, Heinemann Educational/The Association for Science Education; (b) SOLOMON J. (1983) *Science in a Social Context*, Oxford, Basil Blackwell/The Association for Science Education, Oxford; (c) EIJKELHOF, H.M.C., BOEKER, E., RAAT, J.H. and WIJNBEEK, N.J. (1981) *Physics in Society*, Amsterdam. VU Boekhandel.

4 Description of other units are: (a) LIJNSE, P.L. (1983) 'Energy and quality', paper presented at the Conference 'Entropy in the School', Balaton, Hungary; (b) EIJKELHOF, H.M.C., KORTLAND, J. and VAN DER LOO, F.A. (1984) 'Physics and nuclear weapons: A suitable topic for the classroom?', *Physics Education*, 19, pp. 11–15, (c) EIJKELHOF, H.M.C. (1985) 'Ethics in the classroom — Goals and

experiences' in GOSLING, D. and MUSSCHENGA, B. (Eds) *Science Education and Ethical Values*, Geneva, pp. 68–78, (d) EIJKELHOF, H.M.C. and VERHAGEN, P. (1985) 'A thematic approach to physics curriculum development for senior high schools', in LIJNSE, P.H. (Ed.) *The Many Faces of Teaching and Learning Mechanics*, GIREP, Utrecht, the Netherlands, pp. 411–21 (e) VAN GENDEREN, D. (1985) *Traffic — a thematic approach to mechanics in grade 10*; see 4d, pp. 384–9; and (f) KORTLAND, J. (1988) *Curriculum Emphases in the PLON Physics Curriculum*, proceedings of the Third International Symposium on World Trends in Science and Technology Education, Brisbane.

5 EIJKELHOF, H.M.C. and KORTLAND, J. (1986) 'The context of physics education', in HARRISON, G. B. (Ed.) *World Trends in Science and Technology Education*, Harrison, G.B. Nottingham, pp 79–81.

6 AIKENHEAD, G.S. 'Collective decision making in the social context of science', *Science Education*, 69, pp. 453–75.

7 DEKKER, J.A. and VAN DER VALK, A.E. (1986) 'Pre-university physics presented in a thematic and systematic way — Experiences with a Dutch physics curriculum development project', *European Journal of Science Education*, 8, 2 pp. 145–53.

Notes on Contributors

Peter J. Fensham is Professor of Science Education and Dean of the Faculty of Education at Monash University. He is involved in curriculum development, and policy and issues relating to science education in Victoria and Australia. He was the first President of the Australian Science Teachers Association and of the Australian Association for Environmental Education, and has been a participant and consultant in a number of UNESCO and ICSU–CTS projects and conferences.

John R. Baird lectures in Biology and Biology Education at Melbourne College of Advanced Education. He is currently at Monash University as Senior Research Fellow in the Faculty of Education. His research interests include the processes of teaching and learning, individual change, and classroom action research, particularly as they relate to learning strategies and metacognition. He has published research and review articles, and edited two books on these topics.

Rosalind Driver is Reader in Science Education at the University of Leeds, and is the Director of the Children's Learning in Science (CLIS) Project. Her research interests are children's conceptions of natural phenomena and the way these develop during schooling. Recently through the CLIS Project she has been investigating ways in which teaching can take account of students' conceptions and promote conceptual development in science.

Harrie M.C. Eijkelhof is a staff member of the Teacher Training and Educational Research Group, Physics Department, University of Utrecht. He has co-ordinated three curriculum development projects, and is author of *Physics in Society* and of PLON materials. His research interests are preconceptions, teaching and learning of ionizing radiation.

Richard F. Gunstone is Senior Lecturer in the Faculty of Education at Monash University. His research interests are the learning and teaching of science, and the use of research to improve the quality of learning and teaching in schools and in teacher education.

Avi Hofstein is Co-ordinating Inspector of high school chemistry in the Ministry of Education and Culture, Israel, and senior member of the Chemistry Group in the Department of Science Teaching, The Weizmann Institute of Science. He is involved in chemistry curriculum development, implementation and evaluation of chemistry curricula in the Israeli educational system.

Gunn Imsen is Associate Professor at the Institute of Teacher Training at the University of Trondheim. Her research interest is cognitive psychology, especially female motivation. She is author of a textbook in educational psychology.

Jane Butler Kahle is Professor of Biological Sciences and Education at Purdue University, Indiana. She is well known for her work on women in science. Her paper, 'The Disadvantaged Majority: Science Education of Women', won the 'implications' award of the Association for the Education of Teachers. She is Chairman of the Board of Directors of the Biological Sciences Curriculum Study. As leader of the Role and Status of Women in Biology Committee she edited *Women in Science,* another recent Falmer Press book. She was organizing chairperson of GASAT IV in 1987.

Sunee Klainin is a team leader in the Institute for the Promotion of Teaching Science and Technology (IPST). Before joining the staff of this curriculum development centre in Bangkok she taught chemistry in secondary schools. Postgraduate studies at the University of Keele and at Monash University led to master's and doctoral degrees. She has worked in the chemistry team at IPST, and now heads one of its development teams for science in vocational education.

Koos Kortland is curriculum developer at the Teacher Training and Educational Research Group, Physics Department, University of Utrecht. He co-ordinated the PLON project between 1981 and 1986. He is currently engaged in curriculum development for environmental education within the school subjects biology, chemistry, geography and physics at secondary level.

V.G. (Vinoo) Kulkarni is the Project Director of the Homi Bhabha Centre for Science Education. This centre is part of the Tata Institute for Fundamental Research in Bombay and enhances research and development in science education by its own original contributions. A central concern of its work is the identification of factors that hinder the universalization of education and devising methods to overcome them. Studies of language as such a factor in science learning, and specific programmes for enabling underprivileged groups of learners to enjoy what success in science offers, are current.

Douglas A. Roberts is Professor and Head of the Department of Curriculum and Instruction at the University of Calgary. His research interests are science curriculum policy and curriculum development, science teaching thinking (especially among pre-service teachers), and science teaching for students not academically inclined. He is editor of a series of teacher manuals on 'science and society' topics for non-academic students.

Bonnie L. Shapiro Assistant Professor in the Department of Curriculum and Instruction at the University of Calgary. Her recent research on children's ideas about the nature of phenomena emphasizes the implications of constructivist research approaches for classroom practice. Her research and writing interests also include language for learning in science, and technological and societal emphases in curriculum design.

Svein Sjøberg is Associate Professor and leader of the Centre for Science Education at the University of Oslo. Originally educated as a physicist, he also holds an MA in Education and a doctorate in science education. He is author of several science textbooks and research books in different aspects of science education.

Joan Solomon is Research Fellow and Tutor in the Department of Educational Studies at the University of Oxford. She has many years' teaching experience, is Project Co-ordinator for Science in a Social Context, and Research Fellow to the Science Teachers in Research Group at Kings College London. She is Science author of several books on science education.

Richard T. White came to Monash University, where he is now Professor of Educational Psychology, after a decade of teaching science in high school. His interests are learning theory, science education, and research methods. His chief concern is to develop principles and practices that will promote high quality of understanding, especially of science. His most recent work has been in association with an action research study, the Project for the Enhancement of Effective Learning.

Index

ACT tests, 199
action research, 69, 139–43
Alberta
  science curriculum policy in, 31–3,
    39–41
Alternatives for Science Education, 267
APU
  see Assessment of Performance Unit
'Are lab courses a waste of time?', 213
Aristotle, 30
Armstrong, H.E., 170
ASEP
  see Australian Science Education
    Project
Asimov, I.,96–7
assessment
  see also practical work, assessment of
  goal-based, 65
Assessment of Performance Unit (APU),
  184, 197, 276–7
Association for Science Education, 48,
  267, 284
Australia
  evaluation of science education in,
    4–5
  girls and science education in, 253–4
  science curriculum projects in, 13
  science education in, 1, 2, 4–5, 13,
    253–4, 255–6, 258
  science materials in, 2, 255–6
  students' images of scientists in, 250
  teachers and gender in science
    education in, 258
  university selection procedures in, 180
  use of US curriculum materials in, 2
  women as science teachers in, 253,
    254
Australian Science Education Project
  (ASEP), 13, 65, 196
Ausubel, D.P., 124

Back to Basics movement, 267
Baird, J.R., 125–7
BCSC courses, 268
behaviourist tradition, 84
Biology Laboratory Activity Checklist
  (BLAC), 203
Bloom, B.S., 122–3
boys' cultures, 224–5, 226–38
  see also gender
Britain
  Assessment of Performance Unit in,
    184, 197, 276–7
  Association for Science Education in,
    48, 267, 284
  CLIS projects in, 23
  continuous assessment in, 185, 208
  girls and science education in, 253,
    254
  Girls in Science and Technology
    project in, 219, 257, 258, 262n4
  integrated science education in, 269,
    270–1
  practical work in, 169, 171, 172
  primary science education in, 14
  Schools Council Integrated Science
    Project in, 269
  science curriculum development in, 2
  science curriculum projects in, 13
  science, technology and society
    courses in, 268, 269
  Secondary Science Curriculum
    Review in, 1
  sex-role stereotypes in, 258–9
  teachers and gender in science
    education in, 258
  university selection procedures in, 180
  women as science teachers in, 253
British Society for Social Responsibility
  in Science, 269
BSCS project, 65, 204, 207

309

25.00